LANGUAGE FOR DAILY USE

NEW HARBRACE EDITION

NEW HARBRACE EDITION

MILDRED A. DAWSON · ERIC W. JOHNSON

order for $4.44.
Very truly yo
James S.
James Silvi

NEW YORK – CHICAGO – SAN FRANCISCO – ATLANTA – DALLAS

LEVEL GOLD

LANGUAGE FOR DAILY USE

MARIAN ZOLLINGER · M. ARDELL ELWELL

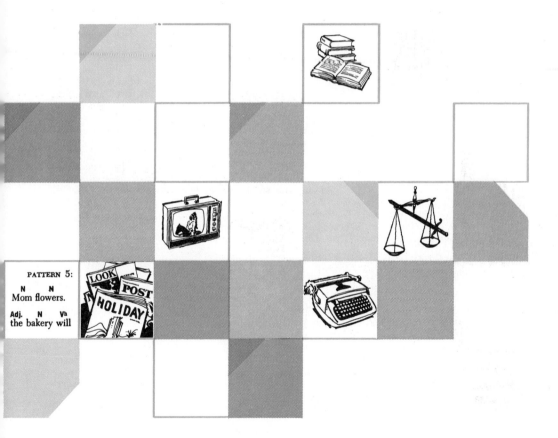

PATTERN 5:

N   N
Mom flowers.

Adj. N Vʰ
the bakery will

HARCOURT BRACE JOVANOVICH, INC.

PRINTED IN THE UNITED STATES OF AMERICA   ISBN 0-15-317288-6

ACKNOWLEDGMENTS: For permission to reprint copyrighted material, grateful acknowledgment is made to the following sources:

The Dial Press, Inc.: "Song of the Pop Bottles" from *A Bowl of Bishop* by Morris Bishop, copyright © 1954 by Morris Bishop.

Doubleday & Company, Inc.: From *Syrian Yankee* by Salom Rizk.

Esquire, Inc.: From "The Marvel of Hearing" by Peter Farb from *Coronet Magazine* of November 1959, © 1959 by Esquire, Inc.

Field Enterprises Educational Corporation: From "Death Valley" from *The World Book Encyclopedia,* copyright © 1964 by Field Enterprises Educational Corporation. International copyright © 1964. All rights reserved.

Harcourt Brace Jovanovich, Inc.: From *Abe Lincoln Grows Up* by Carl Sandburg. From "The Apprentice" from *Four-Square* by Dorothy Canfield. From *The Stars for Sam* by W. Maxwell Reed. From "Prayer" from *Yesterday and Today* by Louis Untermeyer.

Harper & Row, Publishers, Incorporated: From *The Prince and the Pauper* by Mark Twain. From *The Adventures of Tom Sawyer* by Mark Twain.

Highlights for Children, Inc.: "The Beautiful Planet of Mystery" by David Dietz from *Highlights for Children* of May 1961, copyright © 1961 by Highlights for Children, Inc., Columbus, Ohio.

Holt, Rinehart and Winston, Inc.: "Lodged" and "Stopping by Woods on a Snowy Evening" from *Complete Poems of Robert Frost,* copyright 1923, 1928 by Holt, Rinehart and Winston, Inc.; copyright renewed 1951, © 1956 by Robert Frost. From the Preface to *Winston Dictionary for Schools,* © 1958 by Holt, Rinehart and Winston, Inc.

J. B. Lippincott Company: From *My Friend Flicka* by Mary O'Hara. From "There Isn't Time" from *Poems for Children* by Eleanor Farjeon, copyright 1933 by Eleanor Farjeon; copyright renewed © 1961 by Eleanor Farjeon.

Little, Brown and Company: "I never saw a moor" by Emily Dickinson from *Poems by Emily Dickinson,* edited by Alfred Leete Hampson and Martha Dickinson Bianchi.

The Macmillan Company: "The Wilderness Is Tamed" from *Away Goes Sally* by Elizabeth Coatsworth, copyright 1934 by The Macmillan Company; copyright renewed © 1963 by Elizabeth Coatsworth. "The Hairy Dog" (page 341) from *Pillicock Hill* by H. Asquith, printed in Great Britain, imported in 1926 by The Macmillan Company.

Virgil Markham: "Preparedness" from *The Gates of Paradise and Other Poems* by Edwin Markham.

New Directions: "As the Cat" from *The Collected Earlier Poems of William Carlos Williams,* copyright 1938, 1951 by William Carlos Williams.

The New Yorker Magazine, Inc.: From "Don't Give Me One Dozen Roses, Give Me a Nosegay" by Noel Perrin from *The New Yorker* of April 4, 1959, © 1959 by The New Yorker Magazine, Inc.

New York Herald Tribune: "High Flight" by Pilot-Officer John Gillespie Magee, Jr., R.C.A.F., from *New York Herald Tribune* of February 8, 1942.

Oxford University Press, Inc.: From *Great Expectations* by Charles Dickens from *The New Oxford Illustrated Dickens.*

Rand McNally & Company: From *Aku-Aku* by Thor Heyerdahl, copyright 1958 by Thor Heyerdahl. Published in the U.S. by Rand McNally & Company.

The Reader's Digest: From "Titania of the Airways" by Archibald Rutledge from *The Reader's Digest* of May 1939.

Damon Runyon, Jr. and Mary Runyon McCann: From "Earthquake" from *Money from Home* by Damon Runyon.

Scott, Foresman and Company: Dictionary entries for "neighbor," "curfew," and "arrive" from *Thorndike-Barnhart High School Dictionary* by E. L. Thorndike and Clarence L. Barnhart, copyright © 1962 by Scott, Foresman and Company. Dictionary entry for "encyclopedia," pronunciation key, and page 594 from *Thorndike-Barnhart Advanced Junior Dictionary* by E. L. Thorndike and Clarence L. Barnhart, copyright © 1965 by Scott, Foresman and Company.

CONTENTS

4   Building Good Paragraphs   107

5   How Sentences Work   127

6   Enriching Your Vocabulary   157

7   Patterns of Sentences   181

8   Writing Stories and Reports   213

Your English Language

You are a human being, much more intelligent than any other type of creature on earth. Some creatures live as long as man; some are stronger; some are more agile; some are better fighters; some have a more acute sense of smell, sight, or hearing. Only man, however, can truly think, and it is this ability which has made it necessary and possible for him to develop complicated languages.

It is true, of course, that creatures other than man use very simple ways of communicating with each other. Dogs bark and howl; birds sing and chirp; monkeys chatter and squeal. Most animals have ways of giving simple commands to their young. Apparently, ants and bees can transmit to each other rather complicated directions about the location of food. But these "languages" are not like human language. They are not used for thinking. They are born into the creatures that use them, and their use is determined by instinct, not by learning. Each human being must *learn* his language; it is not born in him.

What Is Language?

No one knows just how language started. There are a number of theories about its origin, but none of them is completely satisfactory. All we know for sure is that wherever there are men, there is language.

Each of the approximately 2,800 human languages uses *symbols*. A given sound or combination of sounds is commonly accepted to refer to, or symbolize, a given meaning. Thus, if you hear or read *beatnik, wrestle, quickly, deep,* or *oak,* a picture or an idea comes to your mind. If words like these are put into proper order, very complicated ideas can be communicated. Words, then, are symbols that stand for commonly accepted meanings.

To discuss

1. Would a person be able to think without using words or language? Consider your own thinking. Do you think in words?

2. What are two main differences between the "languages" of animals and the languages of human beings?

3. What is a word? Check your answer in a dictionary.

4. What is *language*? Try to write a definition of the word. Then look up the definition given in several dictionaries.

5. How many languages are spoken or understood by members of your class or by their parents or relatives?

The Indo-European Family of Languages

The languages used by man are divided into nine language families, or groups. The names of these language families are listed at the top of the next page. Notice on the chart beneath the list that English belongs to the Indo-European family, which in turn is divided into nine big language groups. English itself is descended from the *Germanic* part of this family. Its direct ancestry is traced on the chart by a red line. However, English has absorbed over half of its vocabulary from the *Italic* (Latin) branch. This absorption took place when French-speaking peoples conquered German-speaking peoples and the languages of the two groups were mixed together. Today, the English vocabulary is a glorious mixture of words which came from Germanic words and French, Spanish, Italian, Portuguese, and Latin words.

To discuss

Examine the information given on page 3.

1. How many major language families are there?
2. Name ten languages which are not related to English.
3. What are the names of the nine big language groups represented by the Indo-European family?
4. To which language family does each of the following belong: *Russian, Chinese, Hebrew, Bantu, English, Hawaiian*?
5. Which of the following languages belong to the same language family as English: *Irish, Persian, French, Mongolian, Siamese, Swedish, Hindustani, Yiddish, Finnish, Polish*?

2

The Chief Language Families of the World *

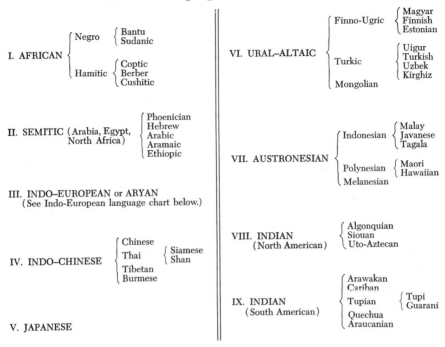

I. AFRICAN
- Negro
  - Bantu
  - Sudanic
- Hamitic
  - Coptic
  - Berber
  - Cushitic

II. SEMITIC (Arabia, Egypt, North Africa)
- Phoenician
- Hebrew
- Arabic
- Aramaic
- Ethiopic

III. INDO–EUROPEAN or ARYAN
(See Indo-European language chart below.)

IV. INDO–CHINESE
- Chinese
- Thai
  - Siamese
  - Shan
- Tibetan
- Burmese

V. JAPANESE

VI. URAL–ALTAIC
- Finno-Ugric
  - Magyar
  - Finnish
  - Estonian
- Turkic
  - Uigur
  - Turkish
  - Uzbek
  - Kirghiz
- Mongolian

VII. AUSTRONESIAN
- Indonesian
  - Malay
  - Javanese
  - Tagala
- Polynesian
  - Maori
  - Hawaiian
- Melanesian

VIII. INDIAN (North American)
- Algonquian
- Siouan
- Uto-Aztecan

IX. INDIAN (South American)
- Arawakan
- Cariban
- Tupian
  - Tupi
  - Guarani
- Quechua
- Araucanian

* Only the most important language names are given in this table.

The Indo-European Family of Languages (Simplified)

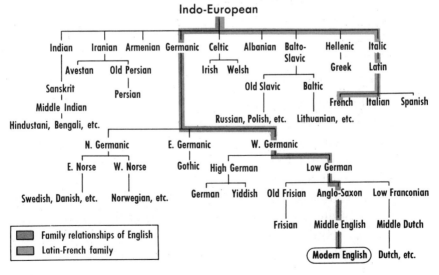

Indo-European

Indian — Iranian — Armenian — Germanic — Celtic — Albanian — Balto-Slavic — Hellenic — Italic

- Indian
  - Avestan
  - Sanskrit
  - Middle Indian
  - Hindustani, Bengali, etc.
- Iranian
  - Old Persian
  - Persian
- Celtic
  - Irish
  - Welsh
- Balto-Slavic
  - Old Slavic
    - Russian, Polish, etc.
  - Baltic
    - Lithuanian, etc.
- Hellenic
  - Greek
- Italic
  - Latin
    - French
    - Italian
    - Spanish

Germanic:
- N. Germanic
  - E. Norse
    - Swedish, Danish, etc.
  - W. Norse
    - Norwegian, etc.
- E. Germanic
  - Gothic
- W. Germanic
  - High German
    - German
    - Yiddish
  - Low German
    - Old Frisian
      - Frisian
    - Anglo-Saxon
      - Middle English
        - Modern English
    - Low Franconian
      - Middle Dutch
        - Dutch, etc.

Legend:
- Family relationships of English
- Latin-French family

3

Word Origins

The history of words, which is called **etymology**, tells how words are formed and how they change. Here are a few facts about the history of our language, illustrated by certain English words.

Anglo-Saxon

English originated when the German-speaking tribes of Angles and Saxons began in about A.D. 450 to invade the country that is now called England. They established their language in the territory. We call that language *Anglo-Saxon,* or *Old English.* Most of our plain, simple words such as *son, mother, cow,* and *day* are of Old English origin.

The word *neighbor* illustrates this. It comes from the Old English *nēah,* which meant "nigh (near)" and *gebūr,* which meant "countryman or dweller." Combine the two and you get "nearby countryman." You can see how the meaning of the word has evolved since then into its present broader meaning.

To discuss

Here is the entry for *neighbor* reproduced from the *Thorndike-Barnhart High School Dictionary:*

> **neigh bor** (nā′bər), *n.* **1.** one who lives near another. **2.** person or thing that is near another. **3.** a fellow human being. —*v.* **1.** live or be near (to). **2.** adjoin; border on. **3.** be friendly (*with*). —*adj.* living or situated near to another. [OE *nēahgebūr* < *nēah* nigh + *gebūr* dweller, countryman] —**neigh′bor less,** *adj.*

Copyright © 1962 by Scott, Foresman and Company, Chicago.

Study the section at the end in brackets [ ], which gives the etymology.

1. What do you think the symbols < and + mean?
2. What do you think *OE* means?
3. Have you heard of the word *boor*? Can you make an intelligent guess about how it got its present meaning?

French

In 1066 the French ruler William the Conqueror invaded England, bringing with him the French language. From that date on, English became a mixture of Germanic (Anglo-Saxon) words and French words. The French words used in English during this period are sometimes called *Anglo-French*. Most French words originated in turn from Latin. These facts are illustrated by the word *curfew*, which today means "a time in the evening after which certain persons must not be out in the streets."

In the Middle Ages peasants were required to put out their fires at a certain hour in the evening. This was announced by the ringing of a bell called the "cover-fire." The French word is *couvre-feu*. The following discussion exercise will enable you to figure out the etymology of *curfew*.

To discuss

Here is the entry for *curfew* from the *Thorndike-Barnhart High School Dictionary*:

> **cur few** (kèr′fū), *n.* **1.** a ringing of a bell at a fixed time every evening as a signal. In the Middle Ages, it was a signal to put out lights and cover fires. More recently it has been used as a signal for children to come in off the streets. **2.** bell ringing such a signal: *"The curfew tolls the knell of parting day."* **3.** time when it is rung. [< AF *coeverfu* < *covrir* cover (< L *cooperire*) + *feu* fire < L *focus* hearth]

Copyright © 1962 by Scott, Foresman and Company, Chicago.

Study the etymological part of the entry and answer these questions:

1. What does *AF* stand for? (See the text above.)
2. Explain how the word *curfew* came into English from Latin through French.

Latin

Many modern English words entered our language from Latin through French. The Latin spoken by the common people was called *Vulgar Latin,* and it is Vulgar Latin which is the main source of French. You already know how French came into English.

The word *arrive* is an example of an English word which entered our language from Latin through French. In olden times people frequently traveled in boats by river and canal. When they arrived somewhere, they literally came to the bank or shore and got off the boat. Knowing this much, discuss the etymology of *arrive.*

To discuss

Study and discuss the following entry from the *Thorndike-Barnhart High School Dictionary:*

> **ar rive** (ə rīv′), *v.,* –rived, –riv ing. **1. arrive at,** come to; reach: *You should arrive at school before nine o'clock. You must arrive at a decision soon.* **2.** reach the end of a journey; come to a place. **3.** come; occur: *The time has arrived for you to study.* **4.** be successful. [< OF *ar(r)iver* < VL < L *ad ripam* to the shore] —**Syn. 2.** See **come.** —**Ant. 2.** depart.

Copyright © 1962 by Scott, Foresman and Company, Chicago.

1. Why was the Latin which was spoken by the common people called "Vulgar Latin"? Look up *vulgar* in the dictionary and find the answer. What abbreviation for *Vulgar Latin* is used in the dictionary entry?
2. What do you think the abbreviation *OF* means?
3. What is the meaning of the word *etymology*?

By studying the etymologies in dictionaries, you can have a lot of fun and, at the same time, teach yourself much about your language and its vocabulary.

GOING AHEAD

In a college or unabridged dictionary, look up the etymologies of five of the following ten words. Be prepared to explain to the class how these words came into English.

1. artifact	6. childhood (look up *child* and *–hood*)
2. hand	7. succotash
3. etymology	8. astonish
4. pendulum	9. legislator
5. kindergarten	10. announce

The Vocabulary of English

English has a wonderfully rich vocabulary of about half a million words. It is a delightful language to use because there are usually several ways of saying almost, but not quite, the same thing. English is full of **synonyms**—words which have the same, or nearly the same, meaning. There is often an elaborate, long word in the language and a simple short-word equivalent of it. The elaborate words generally come from the Latin-French part of the vocabulary; the short, simple words from the Germanic (Anglo-Saxon) part. For example, here are two lists, one of elaborate words and one of simple words:

LATIN AND FRENCH ORIGIN	GERMANIC ORIGIN
disintegrate	break up
rejuvenate	make young again
extinguish	put out
surrender	yield
operate	make work
commence	begin
refrigerate	make cold

Exercise: Words with similar meanings

For each of the following words, substitute one or more shorter words which will express the same idea. Try not to use any words containing over six letters or more than two syllables. As far as you can, use one-syllable words. Use your dictionary to check the origin of the words you write.

EXAMPLE: 1. occupy
YOU WRITE: 1. *live in*

1. describe	5. congregate	9. consume
2. abominate	6. educate	10. originate
3. discover	7. strangle	11. fracture
4. release	8. conceal	12. continue

Basic English

English is a relatively easy language for foreigners to learn because a very small number of words—about 1,000—are enough to express almost any idea in a simple way. A non-English-speaking person, if he concentrates on these few words, can soon speak enough English to get along fairly easily. After these basic words are learned, picking up further vocabulary is quite simple. We can put together many small or common English words in order to get thousands of different meanings. For example, consider the verb *go*. In combination with other small words, here are a few of the meanings it can have:

go about	— travel, turn
go across	— cross
go after	— pursue, chase, follow
go against	— oppose, disobey
go among	— mingle with
go before	— precede, appear before

Exercise: Combining words

Combine the verb *put* with four of the short words listed below. Write synonyms for the meanings you get. Use the dictionary, if you wish. Then do the same for the verb *get*.

at	to	by	up
into	among	on	before
over	between	down	after
out	off	across	about

EXAMPLE: 1. put down

YOU WRITE: *1. put down – crush, defeat, lay down, write down, record*

▌GOING AHEAD▐

Examine the following list of short words and the phrases that are made up of short words. For each, see if you can think of or find a longer, more elaborate word. Check the origins of your words in the dictionary.

EXAMPLE: 1. throw out

YOU WRITE: *1. discard*

1. free (verb)	5. go with	9. light up
2. eat	6. come down	10. farming
3. think about	7. work with	11. go up
4. talk with	8. good for	12. fall back

Changes in the English Language

English, like all languages, is constantly changing. New words are added; other words are discarded. No person or group can stop the changing of a language.

Here are eight words which were taken either from the King James Version of the *Bible* (published in 1611) or from the book *Robinson Crusoe* by Daniel Defoe (published in 1719). All of these words would have been easily understood two or three hundred years ago in the sense given in parentheses.

1. passing (extremely)
2. confound (defeat)
3. ye (you)
4. yea (more than this)
5. sorely (in a sore manner)
6. except (unless)
7. unto (to)
8. nice (foolish)

Some of the words above are no longer commonly used by speakers of English; others are used, but in a sense quite different from that given after each word. These words illustrate the fact that some words die or certain of their meanings fall into disuse. This is a part of the changing of our language. In an unabridged dictionary, you would find these words labeled either *archaic*, which means "old-fashioned," or *obsolete*, which means "no longer used."

Now examine the words in the list below. You as a modern reader would understand them quite easily. They are all a part of our vocabulary, yet none of them would have been understood by the first readers of the King James *Bible* or of *Robinson Crusoe*.

1. to lobby
2. sideswipe
3. bulldozer
4. disk jockey
5. mortician
6. spoils system
7. carpetbagger
8. antibiotic
9. realtor
10. filibuster

To discuss

1. Study the list of archaic or obsolete words above. Which words are commonly used now, although with different meanings? Which words are no longer commonly used in any meaning?

2. Study the list of modern words above. Can you explain why each word would not be understood by readers of *Robinson Crusoe*? If you need to use your dictionary, do so.

Exercise: Archaic, obsolete, or modern words?

Some of the words listed below are archaic or obsolete, or have meanings that are. Write these words in a list headed *Archaic or Obsolete*. The rest are modern words that would not have been understood by English people living in the year 1700. Write these words in a list headed *Modern*. Check your answers in the dictionary.

1. erstwhile
2. bewray
3. television
4. Kodak
5. radio
6. bedight
7. carburetor
8. espial
9. penicillin
10. nylon
11. I.Q.
12. thy
13. ampere
14. eld
15. Thermos bottle
16. chain gang
17. hi-fi
18. prithee

New words in English

How do new words come into the language? One of the ways is through *borrowing* from other languages. It is through borrowing that we got such words as *bungalow* (from Hindustani), *bamboo* (from Malayan), *cherub* (from Hebrew), *smorgasbord* (from Swedish), and *horde* (from Turkish).

Another method of acquiring words is to make them out of materials already in the language. This process is going on right now through the methods of *compounding, shortening, blending,* and *coining.*

Compounding. This method is very common in English. It involves putting two words together to make one word. Here are some examples of compound words:

housetop	footsore	overflow
woodshed	overhead	busybody
airtight	downfall	offshoot

Many expressions are halfway between being two words and one word and are used with a hyphen between them, as *high-strung* and *double-quick.*

Exercise: Compounded words

See how many compound words you can list. Make your list without referring to a dictionary. When you have finished your first draft, check with the dictionary to see whether your words actually exist. Check your spelling, also.

Shortening. Shortening is also a common way to make new words in English. It involves dropping parts of a longer word to form a new one. For example, here is a list of words with their abbreviated forms. These shortened forms are now words in their own right.

ORIGINAL WORD	SHORTENED WORD
gymnasium	gym
airplane	plane
gasoline	gas
pianoforte	piano
mobile vulgus (Latin)	mob

If you look up the word *gas* in the dictionary, you may find that it is labeled *Informal* or *Colloq.*, which means "Colloquial." Colloquial speech is informal speech that would not be used in formal speaking or writing. However, as you yourself will recognize, the word *gas* is very much a part of our language today.

Exercise: Shortened words

Below are some words that are now a part of the common vocabulary of English. Each word is a shortening of an older, longer word. Copy the words on your paper. Then see if you can guess the longer word from which each was formed. Check your guess with a collegiate or an unabridged dictionary, if one is available. If the word is labeled *Colloq.* or *Informal*, put that label in parentheses beside the shortened word. (You will find that dictionaries do not always agree on what is colloquial or standard English usage.)

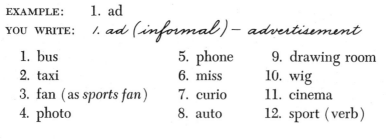

EXAMPLE: 1. ad
YOU WRITE: *1. ad (informal) — advertisement*

1. bus	5. phone	9. drawing room
2. taxi	6. miss	10. wig
3. fan (as *sports fan*)	7. curio	11. cinema
4. photo	8. auto	12. sport (verb)

Blending and *coining.* A less common but very interesting method of acquiring new words is the *blending* of two or more words, or parts of words, to get a new word.

WORDS BLENDED	BLEND
*mo*torists' ho*tel*	motel
*spl*ash and sp*atter*	splatter
*sm*oke and f*og*	smog
*motor*car and caval*cade*	motorcade

Another way that words are made is by pure invention, called *coining,* as a piece of money is *coined* from metal. Probably most words were originally coined—that is, someone, consciously or unconsciously, first said the sound, and it eventually became accepted into the language as a word, as a symbol for some meaning.

Read this verse of the poem "Jabberwocky," from Lewis Carroll's *Through the Looking-Glass:*

> "And hast thou slain the Jabberwock?
>   Come to my arms, my beamish boy!
> O frabjous day! Callooh! Callay!"
>   He chortled in his joy.

Can you find the coined words in the verse above, that is, words that Lewis Carroll made up? Only one of the coined words in the verse has been accepted into the English language as a part of our standard vocabulary. Read the verse again and see if you can guess which word it is.

At any given time there are a number of words knocking at the doors of the language, asking to be let in. There are other words dropping out of our language because of disuse. Some will enter (*chortle*—a blending of *chuckle* and *snort*); some will die (*erenow*). Radio, TV, comics, and advertising are the most frequent users of coined words.

Exercise: Blended or coined words

See how many words you can find in current magazines and newspapers that you believe were recently coined or blended from two or more words, or parts of words. Check with a recently published dictionary to see whether they have been accepted. Compare and discuss your lists of words in class.

Here are some examples of new words recently accepted into the language. Look up each of the words in a large and recently published dictionary. Write the origins for as many as you can find. Share your findings in class.

Here are some of the methods to consider: *shortening, blending, compounding, coining.*

1. automat	6. newscast	11. dry-clean
2. megaton	7. winterize	12. cheeseburger
3. dude	8. supermarket	13. wirephoto
4. blurb	9. radar	14. contact lens
5. astrojet	10. thruway	15. electronics

English in the World Today

According to our best estimates, English is spoken by about 250 million people throughout the world as a first language—by more people than any other language except Mandarin Chinese. However, perhaps even more important is the fact that English is understood by 600 million people, far more than any other language, nearly a quarter of the people on earth! Almost anywhere you go, you will find speakers of English: in airports, hotels, governmental bodies, schools and universities, and among scientists and other scholars. It is almost impossible for any nation to keep in touch with developments in science, business, politics, or any other major human activity unless it has in it a goodly number of speakers and readers of English.

The study of English is important in the schools of almost every nation. In fact, English is rapidly becoming the nearest thing to a universal language that the world has ever known.

To discuss

1. What advantages are there to being born in a country where English is spoken as the first language?

2. Can you think of any historical events and circumstances which help to explain the wide scattering of English over the globe?

3. What fact about our vocabulary helps to make English easy for non-English-speaking Germans and Frenchmen to learn?

PART I

Speaking and Writing
Your Language

CHAPTER 1

How Language Works: Nouns, Pronouns, and Verbs

One of the first things to learn in the study of grammar is *grammatical terms*, so that you can talk intelligently with others about your speaking and writing. For example, it is helpful to know that words in a language can be sorted into different classes, traditionally called the **eight parts of speech.** Here they are:

Noun	**Verb**	**Adverb**	**Conjunction**
Pronoun	**Adjective**	**Preposition**	**Interjection**

Learning the parts of speech and how they are used in sentences is an important part of your study of grammar.

The First Part of Speech: The Noun

Imagine that you are on an island with some intelligent people and that none of you knows any language. You would need a language to get along, of course. What would be the first words you would need to agree upon? Probably they would be the words to name the things around you: *tree, water, ocean, sand,* and *food.* List ten other things on the island you would need to name.

Probably all of the words you have listed are **nouns** which name things that can be seen or touched. The class of words called nouns does not name only things, however. Nouns also name people and places: *John Jones, Rock Island, sky, village, beach,* and *cove.*

As your language grew, you would then find the need to express feelings and ideas, things you cannot see or touch. For example:

QUALITIES: weakness, illness, health, pleasure, beauty, truth

AMOUNTS *or* MEASUREMENTS: pound, gallon, mile, inch, month

■ A **noun** is a word that names.

Exercises: The noun

1. On your paper, list the numerals from 1 to 5. Beside each numeral, write all the *nouns* you find in the sentence.

1. The old lady bought some peaches and bananas for her new monkey.
2. When the lightning struck, the children were on the back porch with Mrs. Crowley.
3. In his desk, John found an old shoe, two lollipops, and a battered book.
4. The mysterious stranger disappeared into the fog and was never seen in our village again.
5. Grandmother, a vigorous woman, mowed the grass and painted the house.

2. List twenty nouns which name things that are invisible. Then choose five of the nouns and use each of them in a sentence.

Common and proper nouns

In English, the class of words called nouns is commonly divided into two groups. Look at the italicized nouns in the following paragraph:

> While my *friend Paul* was shopping in *Chicago,* he met *Mr. James Cox* and *Mrs. Joseph Gurzow,* his two favorite *neighbors.* Then, after looking for the most inexpensive *store* in the *city,* he found *Artie's Bargain Bin,* where he was able to buy a miniature *truck,* a *Grant Flyer,* for his *brother Jack.*

Those nouns which are capitalized above name a special or particular person, place, or thing. They are called **proper nouns.** Notice that a proper noun can have more than one word: *Mr. James Cox, Mrs. Joseph Gurzow, Artie's Bargain Bin,* and *Grant Flyer.* Those nouns which are not capitalized name any person, place, or thing. They are called **common nouns.**

Can you find a proper noun in the sample paragraph above that can be matched with each common noun? For example, *friend* is the first common noun above; *Paul,* the proper noun, names a particular friend.

On pages 420–21 of the Review Handbook, you will find the rules for capitalizing the various kinds of proper nouns.

- A **proper noun** is the special name of a particular person, place, or thing. Proper nouns are always capitalized.

- A **common noun** is the name of any person, place, or thing. Common nouns are not capitalized.

Exercise: Common and proper nouns

Make two columns on your paper, one headed *Common Nouns* and the other headed *Proper Nouns.* Then list each noun in the sentences below under the correct heading.

1. The frantic search for gold began when James Marshall discovered a small nugget in a sawmill at Coloma, California.
2. He was building the sawmill for John Sutter on the bank of the American River.
3. They ended their lives as poor men, but a Mormon named Sam Brannan made a fortune.
4. He opened a store for the miners near the mill, and then dashed into San Francisco holding a container full of gold dust and shouting the news of the discovery.
5. Prospectors from all parts of the United States and from Europe and Mexico swarmed to the West in search of quick fortunes.

GOING AHEAD

Rewrite the following sentences, changing each proper noun to a common noun and each common noun to a proper noun.

EXAMPLE: 1. The boy hurt Bowser accidentally.
YOU WRITE: 1. George hurt the dog accidentally.

1. John was spanked by his mother.
2. His mother was reading *Peter Rabbit* to the baby.
3. Mike and Jeff are canoeing on Eaglesmere Lake.
4. At Smithfield Central High the coach was blamed for losing to another school.
5. Four boys were seen inside Rio's Body Shop during that month.
6. Vincent said, "That place sells gasoline and used cars."

Characteristics of Nouns

How can you be sure that a word is a noun? So far, you have read that *nouns name persons, places, things, or ideas.* Knowing this fact is helpful, but it is only a part of your study of nouns. There are other characteristics of nouns that are important. Learn them now, for they will help you to recognize a noun when you see one.

The plural of nouns

Examine the list of words below. Only five of the words can be used as nouns. Can you tell which five? If you are not certain, try to make each word plural and, on a separate sheet of paper, put it in the blank in this tryout sentence: "He saw two __?__." If you form a good sensible English sentence, that word is a noun in the sentence.

book	teach
replace	church
rotate	fountain pen
teacher	complete
enter	fox

Did you add *s* or *es* to the five nouns above to form their plurals? If you did, your list of nouns should be *books, teachers, churches, fountain pens,* and *foxes.*

Most of the nouns in our language can be changed from singular (one only) to plural (more than one) by adding *s* or *es.* *This statement is true only of nouns.* No other part of speech has this characteristic. Therefore, if you can put a word into the plural by adding *s* or *es,* you may be sure that the word can be used as a noun in a sentence.

NOTE: A few frequently used nouns form their plural in an irregular way—that is, by means other than adding *s* or *es;* for example: *man—men, child—children, mouse—mice, goose—geese, sheep—sheep.* The exceptions to the general rule, however, make up only a small group of the nouns in our language.

If you need help on spelling plural nouns, turn to pages 433–34.

■ Nouns that name only one person, place, or thing are in the **singular.** Nouns that name more than one are in the **plural.**

Exercise: Recognizing nouns

Test the following twenty words to see if they are nouns by determining whether or not they can be made plural by adding *s* or *es.* Use the tryout sentence, "He saw two __?__." Ten of the words can be used as nouns; ten cannot. List those that can.

1. cake	6. usual	11. beacon	16. develop
2. ordinary	7. toe	12. possess	17. bunch
3. read	8. discover	13. own	18. write
4. bush	9. ash	14. street	19. reasonable
5. face	10. feeble	15. desk	20. creature

The possessive of nouns

Examine the following sentences carefully. Notice that some of the nouns are italicized.

1. *John's* hat blew away.   3. Those *ladies'* faces please me.
2. Here is the *lady's* purse.   4. Two *boys'* papers are missing.

You notice that *John's, lady's, ladies',* and *boys'* are all nouns showing possession, or ownership. They are called **possessive nouns.** John owns the hat, the lady owns the purse, the ladies own the faces, and the boys own the papers.

Another characteristic of nouns is that most of them can show possession by adding an apostrophe and *s* (*'s*) or by adding an apostrophe alone. *No other part of speech can show possession in this way; only nouns.*

In earlier grades you learned how to punctuate possessives. If you need to review the rules for possessives, turn to page 424.

Exercise: Recognizing nouns

Below is a list of words, six of which can be used as nouns and six of which cannot. Test each word by seeing whether it can show possession by adding an apostrophe or an apostrophe and *s.* Use each possessive noun in a short sentence showing what is possessed.

1. book	5. furious	9. traveled
2. completely	6. visitors	10. impostor
3. clerk	7. plumbers	11. appears
4. factory	8. beautiful	12. perhaps

Determiners

Read the following paragraph and notice the italicized words in it:

> *The* log rolled off *their* truck and rumbled down *an* embankment. At *the* bottom stood *our* foreman, who bravely managed to leap out of *its* way. He had *a* narrow escape.

The articles *a, an,* and *the* are often called **adjectives.** The words *their, our,* and *its* are called **possessive pronouns.** Each one signals the approach of a noun in the paragraph above. Can you name the nouns?

Each time you see one of these noun signals, called **determiners,** in a sentence, you can be sure that a noun (or a word group used as a noun) will follow one or two or more words later.

Memorize these eight common determiners:

a	an	the	my	our	their	your	its

Of course, nouns often appear in sentences without determiners, as in "*Mr. Sikes* needed *courage.*" However, the presence of any one of the determiners above in a sentence often guarantees that a noun will soon follow.

Here, then, is another characteristic of nouns: *nouns are frequently preceded by determiners.*

Exercises: Determiners

1. Number your paper from 1 to 6. Beside each numeral, write the determiners in the following sentences and the nouns that follow them.

EXAMPLE: 1. Their cat ate a field mouse.
YOU WRITE: *1. their cat   a mouse*

1. A disaster struck our small community yesterday.
2. Mr. Parker, my good neighbor, is now an unhappy man.
3. A fire destroyed an orchard on their farm.
4. The fact is that your old goat started everything.
5. It had come across a neglected campfire in the woods nearby.
6. In search of its meal, the careless goat had scattered the smoldering ashes.

2. Use this very simple test to determine whether or not each word below can be used as a noun. If you can make a complete sentence, starting the sentence with "The ___?___" and using the word in place of the blank space, write the sentence on your paper. If you cannot, write "not a noun."

EXAMPLES: 1. drive
2. quietly

YOU WRITE: *1. The drive interested the tourist.*
2. not a noun

1. occupy
2. flake
3. happily
4. thoughtfulness
5. impostor

6. occupation
7. always
8. sleepiness
9. sloppily
10. dragon

11. glory
12. however
13. grunt
14. groans
15. onward

Summary

CHARACTERISTIC 1. Nouns name persons, animals, places, things, or ideas.

CHARACTERISTIC 2. Most nouns form the plural by adding *s* or *es*.

CHARACTERISTIC 3. Nouns often show possession by adding an apostrophe (') or an apostrophe and *s* ('*s*).

CHARACTERISTIC 4. Nouns are frequently preceded by determiners.

Exercises: Characteristics of nouns

1. On your paper, list in a column the nouns that appear in the sentences below. Be prepared to discuss the noun characteristics you have studied.

1. Those foxes quickly ate the apple and a fig.
2. A man's hand appeared above the picture.
3. Wandering sadly over the gloomy moor, I came upon their open cottage almost hidden in the heather.
4. A canary and a finch fought for the worm.
5. This coat is John's, and he paid a high price for it.

2. Explain the characteristics which each noun above demonstrates as it is used in the sentence.

The Pronoun

Most people do not enjoy awkward, purposeless repetition in writing; they like variety. Read the following two versions of a paragraph. Notice how monotonous—even ridiculous—the repetition is in one of them.

<table>
<tr><td>

Passage 1

But Flicka did not intend to be left. Flicka hurled Flicka against the poles which walled the corral. Flicka tried to jump the poles. The poles were seven feet high. Flicka caught Flicka's front feet over the top rung, clung, scrambled, while Kennie held Kennie's breath for fear the slender legs would be caught between the bars and snapped. Flicka's hold broke; Flicka fell over backward, rolled, screamed, tore around the corral.

</td><td>

Passage 2

But Flicka did not intend to be left. *She* hurled *herself* against the poles which walled the corral. *She* tried to jump *them*. *They* were seven feet high. *She* caught *her* front feet over the top rung, clung, scrambled, while Kennie held *his* breath for fear the slender legs would be caught between the bars and snapped. *Her* hold broke; *she* fell over backward, rolled, screamed, tore around the corral.

</td></tr>
</table>

Of course, you would never write a paragraph such as Passage 1 above. Passage 2 is the paragraph as originally written by the author Mary O'Hara in her book *My Friend Flicka*.

What is the difference between the first passage and the second one? Can you give a reason that explains the awkwardness and monotonous repetition in the first passage?

Pronouns and their antecedents

Passage 1 above begins: "But Flicka did not intend to be left. Flicka hurled . . ."

Passage 2 begins: "But Flicka did not intend to be left. *She* hurled . . ." *She* is a pronoun. It is used in place of the noun *Flicka*. A word that is used in place of a noun is called a **pronoun.** You know by reading the sentence that *she* refers to *Flicka*. The word that a pronoun refers to is called the **antecedent.** We can say, then, that the antecedent of the pronoun *she* is the noun *Flicka*.

Now, before you do an exercise on pronouns, look over the list on page 26 of the most commonly used pronouns in English.

I, me, my, mine, myself
you, your, yours, yourself, yourselves
he, him, his, himself
she, her, hers, herself
it, its, itself
we, us, our, ours, ourselves
they, them, their, theirs, themselves

■ A **pronoun** is a word used in place of a noun. The word to which a pronoun refers is called the **antecedent**.

Exercises: Identifying and using pronouns

1. List the pronouns which are italicized in Passage 2 on page 24. Next to each pronoun, write its antecedent.

2. On your paper, list the personal pronouns in the following passage in the order in which they appear. Beside each pronoun, write its antecedent in parentheses.

The lumberjacks in the Paul Bunyan story had a difficult time keeping warm. They grew long beards and covered themselves with blankets. When they began tripping over their beards all day, Paul declared a new camp rule, which he wanted them to follow. Here it is: A man with a beard over six feet long must keep it tucked inside his boots.

3. Write each of the following sentences, using a pronoun wherever you think it will make the sentence better:

1. George gave a toy to little Timmy, but the toy was broken.
2. After the politicians had voted, the politicians all went on vacation.
3. When Mr. and Mrs. Small came back from Florida, Mr. and Mrs. Small felt the cold severely.
4. When Mabel saw the new hat, Mabel wanted to buy the hat.
5. Frederick followed the animal until Frederick lost sight of the animal.

Possessive pronouns

You may have noticed in the exercises above that personal pronouns have a possessive form which shows ownership. Unlike nouns, they never use the apostrophe. They have special possessive forms.

Notice in column two below that the possessive pronouns modify nouns. (To modify a word means "to change or limit its meaning.")

PRONOUNS	POSSESSIVE PRONOUNS
I have a cat.	It is *my* cat.
You have a dog.	It is *your* dog.
He has a hamster.	It is *his* hamster.
She has a rabbit.	It is *her* rabbit.
It has a cold.	*Its* cold is contagious.
We have animals.	They are *our* animals.
They have no animals.	They are not *their* animals.

Other possessive pronouns are used as substitutes for nouns in sentences such as these:

> *Mine* is a cat. Is *yours* a dog? What is *hers*?
> All the animals are *ours*, not *theirs*.

The pronoun *his* can be used both ways: This is *his* pet skunk. The pet skunk is *his*.

PUNCTUATION NOTE: Remember that possessive pronouns never use apostrophes: *yours, his, ours, theirs, its*. *Its* causes special difficulty because it so often is confused with the contraction for *it is*: *it's*. Memorize this fact:

I T ' S always means *it is*.

EXAMPLES: *Its* claws are sharp. (possessive pronoun)
It's dangerous to get close. (contraction for *It is*)

Exercises: Using possessive pronouns

1. Substitute a possessive pronoun for each blank space below and write the complete sentences on your paper. Do not use the same pronoun more than twice in this exercise.

1. John said, "__?__ cat is more independent than __?__."
2. The boys packed __?__ knapsacks and put each piece of equipment in __?__ place.
3. These are __?__ books; __?__ are on the desk.
4. With __?__ brains and __?__ looks, you have an unbeatable combination.
5. __?__ are over there; __?__ are here.

2. Choose the possessive pronoun *its* or the contraction *it's* in place of each blank below. Copy the sentences on your paper.

1. __?__ a fine day for swimming.
2. Each book was on __?__ proper shelf.
3. I do not care whether __?__ blue or red.
4. __?__ appearance flabbergasted me.
5. I feel winter reaching out __?__ icy fingers, and __?__ a feeling I do not like.

Making the meaning clear

Can you explain what is wrong with the following sentences?

1. After you wash them, place the dishes on the shelves.
2. Laura and Janet decided to use her yard for the festival.

Did you see that the meaning in each sentence is not quite clear? In sentence 1, there is no clear antecedent of the pronoun *them*. The antecedent could be *dishes* or *shelves*. In sentence 2, you do not know whose yard will be used.

These sentences can be rewritten in several ways, depending on the meaning you want to convey. For example, you can say:

After you wash the dishes, place them on the shelves.
After you wash the shelves, place the dishes on them.

Sometimes you can clarify the meaning by repeating the noun, as:

Laura and Janet decided to use Janet's yard for the festival.

Remember: When you use a pronoun, make sure that its antecedent is clear.

Exercise: Writing clear antecedents

The meaning in each of the sentences below is not clear. Rewrite the sentences correctly.

1. Mr. Hollis and the janitor decided that his boiler needed repair.
2. Pamela and Leigh enjoyed listening to her new records over and over.
3. The doctor told George that he needed a vacation.
4. I put the letter in my jacket, but it has disappeared.
5. Put the vase on the table after you paint it.

Sentence Patterns

Word order in an English sentence is important. Your sense of the language tells you instantly that this grouping of words does not make sense:

His the rocket repaired Mike tips models of.

Here are the same words in the correct places for nouns and verbs in a sentence:

Mike tips his repaired models of the rocket.

Yet even this good English sentence may be inaccurate if the speaker intended to say:

Mike repaired the tips of his rocket models.

Thus you see that word order is important both for making sense and for expressing exact meaning.

● Rearrange the words in each group below to make a good English sentence. Some groups may be arranged in more than one acceptable order. Do not add or subtract any words.

1. We saw a huge iron before us oaken chest.
2. Four children in it hide-and-seek could have played.
3. A visitor welcome the traveler was at any home.
4. Corn was a common of food type in colonial days.
5. This valley a restful spot is surely.
6. Shelter and safety found we in an cave ancient.
7. Don't raincoat I have a or umbrella an.
8. Joe stories and writes cartoons draws the class for newspaper.

● Rearrange each numbered group of words below into good English sentences. Write two sentences for each group, using all of the words for each sentence.

1. Two, often, the, boys, venders, sold, to, fish, some
2. At, corner, the, lost, questioned, travelers, the, two, policemen, the
3. The, helped, old, his, hermit, fire, dog, Johnny, the, out, put, and

The Verb

At the beginning of this chapter you were asked to imagine you were on an island with some intelligent people, and that none of you knew any language. The first kind of word you invented was the *noun*. However, using only nouns and pronouns (substitutes for nouns) would leave you with a very weak language. All you would be able to do would be to name things. Before you could start making statements, you would need another class of words; you would need **verbs.**

■ A **verb** expresses action or being.

Action verbs

Most of the verbs in our language enable you to express action. They are words like *run, fall, stop, climb, drown, swim,* and *fight.*

If you were able to put nouns and verbs together, you would be able to say something on your island. You would use the nouns as subjects to name what you want to talk about, and the verbs to tell what the subjects do. These two parts form sentences:

Trees blossom.   Oceans drown men.

Men fight.   Bobo sees food.

The action expressed by a verb can be *physical,* as with verbs such as *ride, sew, speak,* and *close;* or the action can be *mental,* as with verbs such as *think, hate,* and *admire.*

Exercises: Action verbs

1. Name the action verb in each sentence below:

1. Those boys destroyed the snowman.
2. A contractor builds houses and factories.
3. She rode her bicycle through the flames.
4. The nervous little dog trembled miserably on the porch.
5. She hates puzzles and riddles.
6. I really think of you all the time.
7. The man jumped into the firemen's net.
8. The train rumbled on through the night.
9. Through the fog the boat's horn blew mournfully.
10. John, James, and Esther all saw the inside of the building.

2. Supply a different action verb for each blank below. Write the complete sentences on your paper.

1. The dog __?__ the cat.
2. My little brother __?__ his new trucks.
3. The old turkey __?__ his feathers.
4. On Sunday afternoons we __?__ tea to our friends.
5. We __?__ the former president of our service club.
6. Between the acts a large group of clowns __?__ onto the stage.
7. We __?__ the fence around the orchard.
8. The beavers __?__ the logs for their dam.

Linking verbs

There are thousands of action verbs in our language, but these alone will not enable you to state all the kinds of things you need to say in a language. You need to make statements which do not involve any action at all, mental or physical. Here are a number of such statements, with the verbs underlined twice:

1. John is intelligent.
2. Mr. Smathers was a millionaire.
3. That small mosquito looks hungry.
4. My best pal became a lawyer.

These verbs are called **linking verbs.** They link the subject of the sentence with a word that comes after the verb.

The words connected by linking verbs always refer to the same person or thing. In sentence 1 above, *John* and *intelligent* refer to the same person. (You could say *intelligent John.*) In sentence 2, *Mr. Smathers* and *millionaire* are the same person. Which words do the linking verbs in sentences 3 and 4 connect?

By far, the most common linking verb is the verb *be.* Its various forms do not look at all alike, and the only way to know them is to memorize them.

SIMPLE FORMS OF THE LINKING VERB BE

I *am* a student.   Jane *is* her father's favorite.
You *are* very beautiful.   The donkey *was* a bother.
Those people *were* rich five years ago.

Other common linking verbs are: *become, seem, look, remain, feel, taste, smell, sound,* and *appear.* Notice, however, that some of them can be used also as verbs of action.

AS LINKING VERB	AS ACTION VERB
1. That snake *appeared* harmless.	That snake *appeared* under the table.
2. Mary *feels* ill.	Mary *feels* the sharp blade.
3. The dog *smells* terrible.	The dog *smells* his dinner.
4. The trumpet *sounds* harsh.	The trumpet *sounds* a false note.
5. His dessert *tastes* good.	He *tastes* the dessert.

Exercises: Linking verbs

1. Find the verbs in the sentences listed below and write them on your paper. Next to each one, tell whether it is a *linking verb* or an *action verb*.

1. The world of the American Plains Indian was new to the first settlers.
2. These Indians roamed the West freely.
3. They followed the great herds of buffalo.
4. Buffalo meat and hides supplied them with food and clothing.
5. Hunters from the East became their enemies.
6. The extinction of the herds was disastrous.
7. Later, the plains people fought the farmers and ranchers with all their skill.
8. They were great horsemen and warriors.
9. The overwhelming number of white men defeated them.
10. In the end, their great civilization was lost.

2. Supply a different linking verb for each blank in the sentences below. Write the complete sentences on your paper.

1. The dog __?__ ferocious.
2. Gene Marsh __?__ quite sick.
3. In spite of his mistakes, Mr. Block __?__ president of the company.
4. No matter what happens, I __?__ pessimistic.
5. The boy __?__ an outstanding citizen.
6. This food __?__ fresh to me.

Characteristics of Verbs

One of the characteristics of verbs is that *they express time* (*tense*). They do this in three ways:

1. By changing form
2. By changing ending
3. By adding words to the verb

Observe how the verb *draw* changes tense:

PRESENT TENSE	PAST TENSE
I draw.	I drew.
I am drawing.	I was drawing.
He draws.	He drew.
He is drawing.	He was drawing.

How did *I draw* change to express past tense? How did *I am drawing* change to express past tense?

Suppose you wanted to put *I draw* into the future tense, what would you do?

The most common way for verbs to express the past tense is to add the ending *–d* or *–ed*; as, *like—liked, walk—walked, climb—climbed*. These verbs are called **regular verbs**.

Any word that can change tense by changing form, changing ending, or adding words is certainly a verb. No other part of speech can do these things. (In Chapter 9 you will study and practice using verbs correctly.)

Exercise: How verbs show tense

The verbs in the sentences below are italicized. On your paper, rewrite each sentence, following the instructions given in parentheses after the sentence. Compare your answers in class.

1. That house *is* a ruin. (Change to past tense by changing the form of the verb.)
2. The lion *devoured* the meat. (Change to future tense by adding a word and dropping the ending of the verb.)
3. Those books *will fall* off the shelf. (Change to present tense by changing a word and adding an ending to *fall*.)
4. The singer *is entertaining* the guests. (Change to past tense by dropping a word and changing the ending of the verb.)

Different shades of meaning

You have seen that a verb can express different tenses by adding certain words. A verb can also change its meaning somewhat by the same means. Look, for example, at the following sentences:

1. Jimmy Jones *will eat* his dinner.
2. Jimmy Jones *should eat* his dinner.
3. Jimmy Jones *can eat* his dinner.
4. Jimmy Jones *might eat* his dinner.
5. Jimmy Jones *did eat* his dinner.
6. Jimmy Jones *must eat* his dinner.

Each of these sentences has a different meaning. The verb *will eat* means something different from the verb *should eat; can eat, might eat, did eat,* and *must eat* are also different.

A verb composed of more than one word is called a **verb phrase.** The verb phrase is composed of the *main verb* and the **auxiliary verb** or verbs. Sometimes an auxiliary is called a **helping verb.**

Familiarize yourself with this list of the most common auxiliaries:

be (am, are, is, was, were, being, been)	will, would
do, did, does	shall, should
can	must
may, might	has, have, had

Verbs can change meaning by adding auxiliary verbs.

Exercises: Verb phrases

1. On your paper, copy the following verb phrases and underline the auxiliaries:

1. must dig
2. should blow
3. will be living
4. were being shot
5. is considered
6. had been seeing
7. might pop
8. must have been seized
9. did see
10. must go
11. must be going
12. should have been eating
13. had done
14. could be saving

2. Use ten of the verb phrases above in interesting sentences which you make up. Underline the verb phrases.

I Never Saw a Moor

I never saw a moor,
I never saw the sea;
Yet know I how the heather looks,
And what a wave must be.

I never spoke with God,
Nor visited in heaven;
Yet certain am I of the spot
As if the chart were given.

EMILY DICKINSON

Most of us "know" certain things without being able to prove them or requiring proof of them.

How does the author know how the heather looks if she has never seen it?

Discuss the different ways in which we "know" things—the scientific way, the way our senses give us knowledge, the way our emotions and our intuition tell us. Which method is the author of the poem talking about?

Words That Can Be Nouns or Verbs

Look at the words listed below:

1. smell
2. bear
3. catch
4. climb
5. increase
6. laugh

Can you tell which part of speech each word is? When the words stand alone, you cannot always tell. You must have some signal to guide you. One signal that would tell you that a word is a noun would be the article *the* coming before it. If you read *the smell*, *the bear*, or *the catch*, you know that the words are used as nouns, since *the* is a determiner (noun signal).

How could you know for certain that they were used as verbs? A simple way would be if they were preceded by an auxiliary. If you read *will smell*, *can bear*, or *did catch*, you know for sure that the words are used as verbs.

Exercises: Nouns or verbs?

1. Use each of the six words *smell*, *bear*, *catch*, *climb*, *increase*, and *laugh* in two sentences; first, as a noun and, second, as a verb. Use a determiner when you use the word as a noun. Use an auxiliary when you use the word as a verb. Follow the model shown in the example.

EXAMPLE: 1. smell

YOU WRITE: *1. The __smell__ annoyed me. (noun)*

They will smell the exhaust from the car. (verb)

2. Choose ten words that can be used as nouns or verbs. Write each word in two sentences, exactly as you did in the exercise above.

✓Check Test 1: Correct words

Take this test to see how much you remember about using pronouns and verbs correctly.

Write each sentence, choosing the correct word or words in parentheses.

1. (We, Us) members of the club are looking for volunteers.
2. This should be settled between you and (I, me).
3. The campaign was waged between Bud and (he, him).
4. I haven't any idea where she is (going, going to).
5. (We, Us) girls nominated Norma for class secretary.
6. Do you know where he (is, is at)?
7. The winner of the trophy was (he, him).
8. Chris visited Mickey and (he, him) last weekend.
9. Did you see (we, us) boys?
10. Give the dictionary to Priscilla and (I, me).

If you made any mistakes on this test, turn to the Review Handbook, pages 441, 452–53, and 456. There you will find review and more practice.

Sentence Patterns

You know a great deal about your language. For example, you speak and write mainly in units of sentences. You also have a sense of the order of words within a sentence. Read the following nonsense sentence and try to analyze some of the facts about English you already know by assigning each word to a part of speech:

My rulny moerts slaened the breulic very muppily.

There are only three English words in the nonsense sentence above, yet it sounds like a sentence because the order of words follows a pattern common to many English sentences. The endings of the words are also familiar, as, for example, the *-ly* ending in the adverb *muppily* and the *-ed* ending in the verb *slaened.*

My—*pronoun (determiner)*   the—*adjective (determiner)*
rulny—*adjective*   breulic—*noun*
moerts—*noun*   very—*adverb*
slaened—*verb*   muppily—*adverb*

Both the form of a word (its ending) and its position in a sentence are clues to its classification. Here are two recognizable English sentences with identical patterns—the same order of words as in the nonsense sentence above:

My husky brothers cleaned the attic very quickly.
My happy friends rowed the boat very lazily.

● Follow the instructions below and discuss your answers in class:

1. Name five adjectives which end in *-y.*
2. Name ten verbs that can have an *-ed* ending.
3. Name ten adverbs that end in *-ly.*
4. Name two clues which classify *moerts* as a noun in the nonsense sentence above.
5. Assign each of the words below to a part of speech:

   a. The freegliest toeries meelded too loppily.
   b. His bruedler cople foned our ling ferly.

The Singing Tree
by Kate Seredy
Illustrated by the author
The Viking Press

This beautiful and stirring story describes the life of Kate and Jancsi on the Hungarian plains during World War I. Before that war, their life had been gay and carefree, with folk festivals and weddings and all the activities on the Good Master Ranch, on which the family lived. But during the period covered by this story, the ranch becomes a haven for relatives, refugees, and prisoners.

You will enjoy this exciting and colorful book, made even more interesting by the author's illustrations.

About the author

Kate Seredy was born in Hungary. She spent two years as a war nurse, as she says, "sandwiching academic studies of anatomy between bouts of patching up anatomy in the raw in front-line hospitals."

In 1922 she came to America and liked it so much she stayed. She was a successful illustrator until the depression forced her into writing. While attempting to sell some of her work, she met an editor who said, "Go home and write a book about your childhood in Hungary." The author's well-known books for boys and girls are a result of this sound advice.

Test I

Under the headings *Common Nouns* and *Proper Nouns* on your paper, list the nouns in the sentences below:

1. Thomas Jefferson, the third President of the United States, was a man of many talents.
2. His ideas about government can be read in the Declaration of Independence.
3. He encouraged Lewis and Clark on their exploration of new territory.
4. His purchase of the Louisiana Territory from France helped to fulfill his dream of a country stretching across the continent.
5. As a statesman, inventor, violinist, and architect, he made great contributions to America.

Test II

1. List four characteristics of nouns.
2. Determine whether or not each of the words listed below can be used as a noun. Copy only the words that can be used as nouns.

1. car	6. foe	11. hat	16. portray
2. playful	7. usually	12. confuse	17. lunch
3. tell	8. reveal	13. female	18. write
4. bell	9. trash	14. avenue	19. relax
5. fact	10. really	15. lazy	20. fellow

Test III

1. List all the personal pronouns in the passage below:

Did you hear the good news? Diana, Bobby, and I were practicing a new song on our guitars yesterday afternoon at Diana's house. We didn't know it, but her brother was in the next room listening. His dance band is the most popular in town. Later, he asked us to appear in a spot performance at the school dance Saturday night. Imagine my surprise!

◄ *Jefferson invented many of the comforts of his own home, Monticello. The revolving chair in which he is sitting and the desk over the chaise are his own inventions.*

2. Copy each sentence below, choosing the correct word from each pair in parentheses:

1. (It's, Its) not her fault.
2. The couple saw the house and liked (it's, its) appearance.
3. (It's, Its) wings are covered with dust.
4. Are you sure (it's, its) locked?
5. Each letter reached (it's, its) destination.

Test IV

On your paper, list the numerals of the sentences in which there are antecedents that are not clear.

1. Jerry told his friend that he always entertained lavishly.
2. Gary read the instructions for the new games, but they confused him.
3. We filled the stalls with feed for the horses after we washed them.
4. The weary traveler met a knight on horseback and challenged him to a duel.
5. Alice gave a very short speech, but it inspired her audience.

Test V

Copy the verb in each of the sentences below. Next to each verb, write *action verb* or *linking verb*. Remember, some verbs contain more than one word.

1. A lifelike statue of a young Indian was the main attraction.
2. One after another, the tourists would touch it.
3. The young boys in the group were walking around it.
4. The guide had given some history about the Indian boy.
5. The story seemed almost unbelievable.

Test VI

Number your paper from 1 to 5. Write *noun* or *verb* for each italicized word below:

1. He is a *guard* at the museum.
2. They will *guard* the paintings closely.
3. Did they *ship* that car from Europe?
4. My *ship* will leave the harbor at noon.
5. A *walk* in the rain is refreshing.

Review and Practice

Exercise I

1. Review the lesson "The First Part of Speech: The Noun" on pages 16–19.

2. Copy each word group below, filling the blank with a noun to form a good English sentence:

1. The __?__ swam slowly into the __?__.
2. __?__ and __?__ are always fiercer than __?__.
3. Those __?__ bit my __?__ on the __?__.
4. __?__ bought __?__, __?__, and __?__.
5. These __?__ were cooked by my __?__.

3. Write the headings *Common Nouns* and *Proper Nouns* on your paper. List each of the nouns in the following sentences under the correct heading:

1. Four logs fell off the truck and injured old Mr. Thomas.
2. Elsa saw Mary and Melba shopping in Larson's Toy Shop on State Street.
3. Those pigs and sheep made so much noise in the morning that Jake, the old hermit, had to get out of bed and close the window.
4. George saw his father riding a horse on Devil's Hill.
5. The office and plant of the Deadsect Exterminator Corporation collapsed when termites ate away the beams under the floor.
6. Is that book as exciting as *Huckleberry Finn* by Mark Twain?

Exercise II

1. Review "Characteristics of Nouns" on pages 20–23.

2. Test each of these words to see if it can be used as a noun. Try to use a determiner in front of it or try to make it plural or possessive. Then use each noun you find in a sentence of your own.

1. heater	6. scholar	11. shoelace
2. kitten	7. within	12. ask
3. Oscar	8. either	13. sorrow
4. easily	9. schooner	14. freely
5. sit	10. dangerous	15. butcher

Exercise III

1. Review "The Pronoun" on pages 24–27.

2. On your paper, list all the personal pronouns in the passage below:

You should ask my brother Joe about alligators. He gave a talk in class about them. The research he did and his visit to an alligator farm made him an expert. He said that American alligators are huge. They can grow to twenty feet in length. In their natural habitat they can be dangerous to man. The baby alligator he brought home for Janet and me is so small and harmless that a tiny mouse would seem a ferocious beast next to it.

3. Use *its* and *it's* in two sentences each.

Exercise IV

1. Review page 28.

2. On your paper, rewrite the sentences which need correction in Test IV on page 42.

3. Write five sentences of your own, using pronouns and their antecedents. Draw an arrow from the pronoun to its antecedent.

EXAMPLE: 1. Mr. Stokes thinks that he has been insulted.

Exercise V

1. Review "The Verb" and "Characteristics of Verbs" on pages 30–32 and 34–35.

2. Supply a different action verb for each blank below. Write the complete sentence on your paper.

1. Mr. Jones __?__ sternly at the class.
2. Susan __?__ cowboy songs.
3. The river __?__ through this mountain range.
4. They __?__ his room yesterday.

3. Supply a different linking verb for each blank below. Write the complete sentences on your paper.

1. Chess __?__ my favorite game.
2. Flour and sugar __?__ the main ingredients.
3. The rooms __?__ cool and inviting.
4. The travelers __?__ thankful for the warm hospitality.

4. On your paper, list the verbs in these sentences. Be sure to include any auxiliary verbs. Next to each verb, write *action verb* or *linking verb*.

1. Her face looked yellow under the ugly light.
2. That lion appears friendly.
3. My brother smashed the expensive vase.
4. He shall remain a farmer until the end of his days.
5. That warm mince pie will taste good.
6. The kitten is tasting the cream.

Exercise VI

1. Review "Words That Can Be Nouns or Verbs" on pages 36–37.

2. Decide whether the italicized word in each sentence is a noun or a verb. Then write *noun* or *verb* beside the correct sentence numeral on your paper.

1. I will *tie* this knot securely.
2. I bought this red *tie* for Dad.
3. The *sun* is quite hot today.
4. You can *sun* yourself in the yard.
5. The bears *store* honey here.
6. That *store* sells HO trains.
7. My *plant* can grow indoors.
8. You must *plant* these bulbs early.
9. Bert put the *check* in the letter.
10. We always *check* our grocery bills.

CHAPTER 2

Speaking Effectively

"The first duty of a man is to speak; that is his chief business in this world," said Robert Louis Stevenson in his "Talk and Talkers." Perhaps Stevenson overstates the case, but anyone would agree that to speak well is important. To most people your voice is *you*; it is your main link with the world. With it you can inform, persuade, explain, amuse, and comfort. Any time you spend learning to use your voice better is time well spent.

Making Announcements

Think for a moment about the announcements you have heard at school. Probably some were poor because they did not get across the essential information: who? what? when? where? how much? Others may have failed because they were dull and did not interest the listeners; others, because the speaker could not be heard. Yet you can surely remember announcements which were clear, complete, interesting, and persuasive.

Below and on the next page are two announcements, typical of many that might be made to a school assembly:

Announcement 1

Do you like cake? Tomorrow, Wednesday, during recess and lunch periods, at the back of the lunchroom, there will be a sale of delicious cakes baked by the eighth-grade girls. Prices will range from 10¢ a slice to $1.00 a cake.

Why a cake sale? It's to earn money for our Foreign Student Fund. Without this fund, we never could have had Tomoko and Krishna with us this year.

Support the Foreign Student Fund! Satisfy your longing for the finest in cake! Tomorrow, Wednesday, at recess and lunch, bring your dimes and dollars to the back of the lunchroom and spend them for a good cause.

Announcement 2

Tomorrow there will be a big cake sale. You all know how much we have enjoyed having our two foreign students in school with us this year. The cake sale is for the purpose of raising money to pay the expenses of students from abroad. It will be in the lunch-room, at the back, so don't forget. Be sure that you bring your money with you.

To discuss

1. Explain in a class discussion which of the two announcements you have just read is better, and why.

2. See if you can list at least five standards for a good announce-ment. Show how these standards are met or not met by the two announcements about the cake sale.

Preparing the announcement

You may write out the text of an announcement in advance. Study it carefully to be sure you have included everything impor-tant. Then *memorize* the important items so that you can speak directly to the audience. If you prefer to read the announcement, practice reading it aloud several times so that you are very familiar with the words and thoughts. You can then read to the audience with only an occasional glance at your paper.

Speaking clearly

Since good announcements are usually quite brief, almost every word is important. You must speak very clearly, especially empha-sizing the key words. For instance, in Announcement 1 on page 47, the first key word is *cake*.

One way to make sure that a key word is understood by all is to pause briefly *before* you say the word, and then say it loudly and clearly:

"Do you like . . . (pause) . . . *cake?*"

To be heard by everyone in a large audience, *speak to the people in the back row.* If you look at them and throw your voice back to them, you will speak loudly enough to be heard by everyone in the room.

Guides for making announcements

Content

1. Give all essential information (who? what? when? where? how much?).
2. Repeat the most important facts.
3. Think of a clever way to attract attention at the start.
4. Be as brief as you can without sacrificing interest and completeness.

Delivery

1. Memorize the important items or practice reading orally.
2. Start speaking only when you have everyone's attention.
3. Speak to the back row.
4. Pay special attention to key words.

Exercise: Making announcements

Prepare and deliver an announcement to your class. Speak as if you were addressing a large group in the auditorium. Afterwards, ask the class to criticize your content and delivery.

You may choose any subject of your own, or you may use one of the following suggestions. Make up any specific details you need in order to make your announcement realistic and complete.

1. A play at school
2. A nature trip
3. A trip to a museum
4. A science contest
5. The formation of a club
6. A clothing collection for a community organization
7. The results of student elections
8. Tryouts for a play
9. A class picnic
10. An invitation to submit entries to a school magazine

GOING AHEAD

Find an opportunity to volunteer to make a real announcement to the student body. Possibly the school office or certain organizations would be glad to have you make announcements for them.

Giving Explanations and Directions

You will frequently need to explain to someone or to a group of people how to make something, how something works, how to do something, or how to go from one place to another.

Explanations

There are three essentials for making explanations:

1. *Know your subject.* If you are explaining how to pass a football or serve a tennis ball, you must think carefully about what is involved. Being able to do it yourself is not enough. It may help you to read what experts have written about it or to talk with an expert.

2. *Organize logically.* Your audience will understand an explanation best if the ideas are presented in good order. Put yourself in the position of a person who does not know the subject. Decide what he will need to know first. If you present each step in the order in which it occurs, your listener will be able to absorb the ideas most readily. A list of numbered steps will help you to make your explanation clear.

3. *Be interesting.* Too many speakers are satisfied merely to present the information they have in a straightforward way. If the subject is of great interest to the audience, that may be sufficient. However, with many subjects and many audiences it is necessary to *stimulate interest.* Especially important is an interesting beginning.

To discuss

Here are six beginnings of explanations. Which of them would succeed in arousing the interest of your class? Explain why each of them would succeed or fail to succeed.

1. With four pieces of tin can, a couple of flashlight batteries, some powdered pencil lead, some adhesive tape, and a spool of wire, you can make a telephone that will really work.

2. I shall now tell you six different ways to prevent forest fires.

3. Most of us, as you know, use the Dewey Decimal System. Let me explain this system.

4. I hold in my hand an instrument which has revolutionized writing and caused the inkwell to disappear. Yet most people do not know how it works.

5. It is quite complicated to explain to you how to bake a layer cake, but it is such an important thing to be able to do that I am sure you will all want to listen carefully.

6. Over 2,000 years ago King Hieron of Syracuse wanted to know if his crown was pure gold or whether he had been cheated by the craftsman who made it. He commanded Archimedes, a Greek inventor, to find out. One day Archimedes started thinking about the fact that when he got into his bath the level of the water rose. Suddenly he shouted "Eureka!" ("I have found it!") and ran out into the street. Thus the theory of specific gravity was discovered.

Once you have stimulated the interest of your listeners, you can *maintain* it by using pictures, models, diagrams, incidents, and specific examples. Be careful, though, not to get off the subject. *Remember*: Your principal task is to explain. If you do have something to show, be sure it is large enough to be seen by all. If you pass it around, it will distract attention from your talk.

One way to lose the attention of your listeners is to use special terms that they do not understand or cannot hear properly. Be sure to explain all special terms and to say them clearly. If you were telling how a helicopter works, you would need to explain such words as *rotor, cyclic pitch, torque,* and *autorotation.* It is helpful to write such words on the board as you use them.

Directions

Occasionally you will be asked by someone for the directions to a particular location. In your reply, be specific and brief. First, tell the person on what street or in what part of town he is presently located and the direction in which he will need to head. Then, in a step-by-step order, direct him by giving only the necessary street names, route numbers, or permanent landmarks he must use for guides. Always try to keep in mind where he might go wrong. Be accurate in your estimation of distances as well as directions involving left and right turns. As a courtesy, repeat the directions.

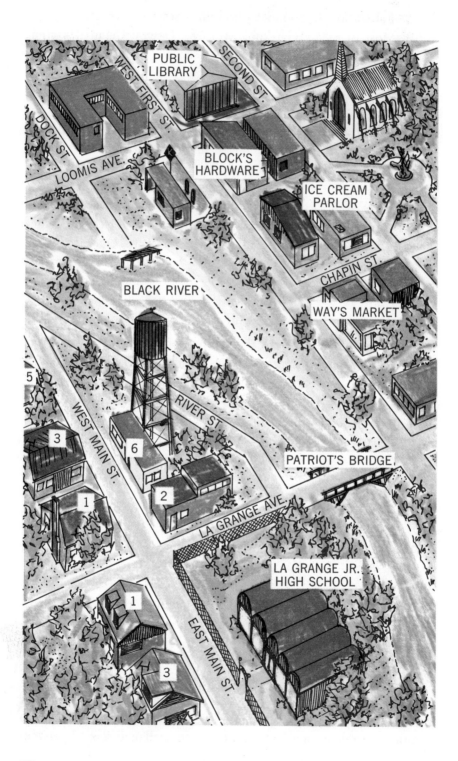

Exercises: Giving explanations and directions

1. Prepare a three-to-five-minute explanation of anything that interests you. You may explain how to perform some process or how something works. Here are some suggested topics:

1. How to Play a Game That the Class Does Not Know
2. How to Care for a __?__ (a pet)
3. How a Camera Works
4. How to Prepare a Favorite Recipe
5. How to Set Up a Tent Efficiently
6. What to Do if Lost in the Woods
7. How to Weave Baskets
8. How Hydroelectric Power Is Produced
9. How a Gasoline Engine Works
10. How to Ski or Water-ski

2. Give directions on how to go from your school to another building in your town or city, and then measure your accuracy by asking a classmate to name the building.

3. Study the map on the opposite page. Take turns in class giving directions on how to go from one place indicated on the map to another. (The numbers in the white blocks are house numbers.)

Conversation

The English clergyman Sydney Smith said about a friend: "He has occasional flashes of silence that make his conversation perfectly delightful." Good listening in silence is essential to good conversation; conversation is give-and-take.

You may have noticed that very young children seldom talk *together*; rather, they talk *at* each other. A sign of maturity is the ability to absorb and appreciate what one's friends are saying and to add to it interesting material of one's own. The best conversation is spontaneous and easy. The participants are guided by intelligence, humor, and courtesy. There is a place for challenge, but none for attack.

It is not difficult to start a conversation. Assume the other person is interested in what interests you, until you find he is not. The other person may be as shy as you may feel. Launch upon a subject to try to draw him out. Make a comment or ask a question about something you both know about: school, movies, radio, TV, sports, books, current events, social life. If you do not succeed on the first try, try again.

Here is a conversation typical of many that might occur in an eighth-grade home room during a recess period. Bob and Sue have just returned from a meeting of the student council. Read it aloud, with some of you taking the parts of Sue, Bob, Mike, Jane, and George.

BOB: But, Sue, it's obvious to me that everybody in our class would be better off if the school ran some dances or canteens for us. Why shouldn't it?

SUE: Well, you heard what Jim said at council. If the teachers and students spend a lot of time talking about dances and parties, there's not going to be enough time for school work. (*Mike, Jane, and George approach.*) Oh, hi! We're talking about the council meeting and whether we should have . . .

MIKE (*interrupting*): We know about it, Sue; we just heard from one of the ninth-graders. If you ask me . . .

BOB: Ninth-graders! That's the trouble around here. They try to run everything. Why, last year . . .

JANE: We all know how you feel about that, Bob, but let's hear what Sue thinks about the canteen idea.

SUE: Well, I think most of us have too much to do, anyhow. If the teachers are busy organizing canteens, when are we ever going to see them about our work, and when will they get papers marked?

GEORGE (*in a whisper to Mike*): Did you hear the story about the teacher who found a bunch of papers three years old in his desk drawer? He looked at them and said, "Never do today what . . ."

MIKE (*in a low voice*): Gosh, George, that's probably a good story, but wait till later to tell it, OK?

JANE: Listen! I agree with Sue. What are we in school for, anyway? It seems to me parties ought to be given in people's homes, not in school.

BOB ⎫ (*together*): ⎧But I think . . .
MIKE ⎭ ⎩That's right . . .

MIKE: Go ahead, Bob; I'm sorry.

BOB: Yeah. You're always interrupting. Well, anyway, I still think the best thing . . . (*Bell rings and the conversation stops.*)

To discuss

1. How does Sue show consideration for others when George, Jane, and Mike approach?

2. When Mike interrupts Sue, is he being impolite or helpful?

3. What do you think about Bob's remark concerning the ninth-graders?

4. Where in the conversation are there examples of a person dealing helpfully with someone who is troublesome? In each case, how is it done?

5. If George wanted to tell his story about the lost papers in the drawer, what should he have done?

6. How does Mike behave when he and Bob find they are both talking at once? How does Bob react?

7. Is it ever acceptable to interrupt a person in a conversation? Explain, using examples from this conversation or others you have heard.

8. Where in the conversation does someone politely bring the conversation back to the subject?

Guides for conversation

1. Be friendly, even if you do not like what is being said.
2. Be interesting. Have ideas and anecdotes to contribute.
3. Be easy and informal.
4. Listen carefully to what others are saying.
5. Keep the conversation going. Keep in mind ways to move the conversation into more lively topics if the need arises.
6. Bring out the best in others by asking for their opinions and their experiences.
7. If you disagree, do it pleasantly. Disagreement can be the basis of excellent conversation if no one assumes that he alone knows the truth.
8. Politely await your turn to talk. Interrupt only when you are sure it will improve the conversation and that the speaker will not mind.
9. Keep your sense of humor.
10. Address yourself to the group, not to the person next to you. If someone starts to talk to you privately, do your best to move the talk back into the entire group.

Exercises: Holding and judging conversations

1. Listen carefully to a number of conversations in the next day or two and write down examples of especially good behavior on the part of people you hear. Report the results to the class. Do not refer to people by name.

2. Divide your class into groups of four or five. Let each group choose one of the following opening remarks, and then hold a conversation before the class. Then judge how well each conversation meets the guides described on page 55. Try to make the conversations as natural as possible, even though they are carried on before an audience.

1. There have been an unusual number of absences from school this year.
2. My older brother is about to graduate from State College.
3. There's no better entertainment than a good book.
4. Oh, it's snowing again! I don't know if I can stand shoveling the walk once more.
5. I've never read a science-fiction book worth the time it took.
6. What shall we do this weekend?
7. Did you see __?__ on TV yesterday?
8. I'd rather be an only child than to have to compete with a lot of brothers and sisters.

TO MEMORIZE

FROM *Endymion*

A thing of beauty is a joy forever;
Its loveliness increases; it will never
Pass into nothingness; but still will keep
A bower quiet for us, and a sleep
Full of sweet dreams, and health, and quiet breathing.

JOHN KEATS

Do you agree with the idea the poet expresses? What things of beauty are you familiar with? Do you think their beauty, or similar things of beauty, will last forever? Notice the poet's choice of words that express happiness and quiet contentment.

Making and Acknowledging Introductions

In general, be friendly and natural when you are making introductions or are being introduced. This is the most important thing to remember. Look over the following rules and be prepared to make and acknowledge introductions in class:

1. Introduce a boy to a girl, mentioning the girl's name first: "Valerie, I'd like you to meet Otto Darnell. Otto, this is my best friend, Valerie James."

2. Introduce a younger person to an older person, mentioning the older person's name first: "Mr. Birch, I'd like to introduce Tim Napier from Chicago. Tim, this is Mr. Birch, our scoutmaster."

3. If no one else does it, introduce yourself: "My name is Alex Smart. I'm visiting the Smiths for a week."

4. Avoid the expressions: "Meet Bob Feldman," "Shake hands with Jim Sample," "Say hi to Johnny Webster."

5. When introduced to someone your own age, you may respond: "Hello, Mike," or "Hi, Mary." If the person is older, say, "How do you do, Dr. Medlar?" It is all right to add, "I'm very glad to meet you," but not "Pleased to meet you."

6. Boys always rise for introductions; girls do not rise except when they are introduced to an older person.

7. A boy should always shake hands when introduced to another boy or to a man; girls usually do not shake hands. However, it is always courteous to shake any hand that is offered to you.

8. Help get a conversation going between strangers by adding a conversational "icebreaker"; for example, "Joe raises champion pigeons at home"; or "Isabel knows a lot about kite-flying."

Exercise: Making and acknowledging introductions

Act out the following situations before the class. If you can add an icebreaker in each case, so much the better. The people introduced should then continue the conversation for a few moments.

1. Introduce a boy to a girl who is seated.
2. Introduce a friend of your own age to your father.
3. Introduce your mother to your teacher.
4. Introduce yourself to a group of three students.
5. Introduce four students to one other student.
6. Introduce a student to a teacher.

Group Discussion

Discussion means talking in a group so that everyone may consider different opinions about a subject. Discussion has a more definite purpose than conversation. A family may discuss whether to have a cookout or to eat inside; a class may discuss whether to elect a new chairman every month or to choose one to serve all year; a city council may discuss whether to raise taxes in order to build better schools; and legislators in the state or national government may discuss laws for highway safety or international trade. Discussion is an essential part of any democratic organization.

A good discussion is frank and friendly, and the opinions expressed and the suggestions made are constructive. The purpose is to give people a chance to express their views so that the group may decide what to do in a certain situation. Another purpose may be to pool their ideas in order to arrive at a balanced, well-informed opinion. Discussion is often the most efficient way to present all the information and opinions a group may need to settle a question.

To discuss

1. Discuss these questions in class:

    1. How do discussion and conversation differ?
    2. How do discussion and dispute differ?
    3. What are the qualities of a good discussion?

2. Below is a list of actions which might occur during a discussion. Some are helpful, some are harmful, and some may be either, depending on the situation and the way in which it is handled. Discuss each action in class, telling why you think it may be helpful or harmful to a discussion.

    1. Interrupting someone who is talking
    2. Considering the point of view of others
    3. Attempting to persuade others that your point of view is the right one
    4. Leaving all the talking to others
    5. Speaking only when asked a direct question
    6. Questioning the point of view of others
    7. Disagreeing with members of the group
    8. Being polite to members of the group

9. Keeping on the main subject of the discussion
10. Pointing out that the information given by someone else is inaccurate
11. Citing figures and statistics to support your views
12. Inventing experiences or facts to support your views
13. Telling someone that he is off the subject
14. Trying to do most of the talking yourself
15. Threatening those who disagree with you
16. Pointing out that a member of the group does not know what he is talking about
17. Changing the subject completely
18. Referring to the opinion of someone who is an authority on the subject under discussion
19. Allowing a person who is saying something wrong to finish his statement
20. Trying to suggest a solution or point of view with which everyone might agree

Most discussions in which you participate are probably *informal* and *unprepared*, as a discussion in your family or among a small group of friends. In class, discussions are usually more formal because the group is large and the teacher or chairman must preside and see that only one person speaks at a time.

It is sometimes helpful in a discussion to have members prepare themselves in advance. For example, if your class were to discuss intelligently the writings of Mark Twain, obviously you would have to read his books. If you were going to discuss the rules of your school, you should know what they are and do some thinking in advance about how they work. It is futile to discuss any topic if you do not know the facts about it.

Round-table discussion

One very useful type of discussion is the *round-table discussion*, used when a class or large group needs to gather opinions on a question quickly. The large group breaks into small groups, or round tables, each of which discusses the topic informally, perhaps appointing a temporary chairman to keep the discussion orderly and on the subject. Each round table may appoint one member to report its views to the class as a basis for general class discussion.

Panel discussion

Another type of discussion is the *formal panel discussion*. Here, three to six people may be chosen to prepare to discuss a subject. Each one investigates his subject and comes ready to present a point of view. The members of the panel then sit in front of the audience, and the chairman asks each member to present his point of view. Usually a strict time limit is set for each presentation.

In an *informal panel discussion*, the members come prepared to discuss the topic informally with each other before the audience. Later, the audience may be invited to join the discussion.

The chairman plays an important part in a panel discussion. He must present the topic, keep the discussion on the subject, allow each person to speak, one at a time, and keep the discussion moving.

Parliamentary discussion

The most formal kind of discussion is the *parliamentary discussion*. It is conducted according to the *rules of parliamentary procedure*. Its purpose is to bring a group, after orderly discussion, to a majority decision. Discussion must always center on a proposal, called a *motion*, and the discussion ends with a *vote*. Most of the formal business in any democratic organization is carried on according to parliamentary procedure. The book *Robert's Rules of Order* lists and explains the rules for parliamentary procedure.

Exercises: Holding discussions

1. Try out the round-table technique on one of the following subjects:

    1. A story or book which all members of the class have read
    2. A speech or program in assembly
    3. Evaluation of a unit of work just completed by the class
    4. The importance of space exploration

2. Conduct your class and school organization meetings according to the rules of parliamentary procedure. The best subject for such discussion is some business which requires a group decision: electing class officers, deciding on a class activity such as a picnic or canteen, deciding on a club program, discussing a committee report, deciding on a play to present in assembly.

3. Organize an informal panel discussion. The subject should be one where the panel members need to gather information or to prepare points of view carefully. Here are some suggestions:

1. The works of an author familiar to the class
2. A question of national or international politics (*Caution*: Do not be satisfied with a discussion where the panelists merely state opinions they have heard and are unable to support with facts.)
3. What to do about school problems such as behavior in the halls and school rules
4. What to do about a school recreation program
5. What to do about your community problems. Some of your problems may be similar to these:
   a. The need for parks
   b. Weekend social activity
   c. Traffic accidents
   d. Dirty streets

✓ Check Test 2: Forms of verbs

Take this test to find out whether you know how to use certain verbs correctly.

Write each sentence, using the correct form of the verb in parentheses.

(freeze)   1. The milk in the bottle on the porch has __?__.

(ride)   2. Several cowboys __?__ the bucking bronco in yesterday's contest.

(speak)   3. Have the committee members __?__ to the principal?

(speak)   4. Tom __?__ with enthusiasm after the applause died down.

(ride)   5. We have __?__ on the roller coaster three times.

(steal)   6. Mrs. Philpots has had her purse __?__!

(freeze)   7. When the pond __?__ early in November, we organized a skating club.

(steal)   8. They have __?__ five minutes of our time.

If you made any mistakes on this test, turn to the Review Handbook, pages 447–48. There you will find review and more practice.

You and Your Speech

You are a student in an oral world. Think for a moment of the hundreds of words used over TV and radio and words spoken by your family and friends that pound upon your ears daily. Think also of the great number of words that you use in communicating your thoughts and feelings to others. Of your total waking hours, probably 90 per cent of your time is spent in listening and in speaking. Too often you have heard pupils in school or adults at work who, with something worth saying, mumbled their words, spoke too softly, or in some other way failed to project their thoughts and feelings to others. You do not want this to happen to you.

Voice characteristics

Now is the time to learn some ways of improving voice and speech skills. The clearness with which you speak depends greatly upon how you say consonant sounds. The ease with which your listeners hear you depends upon your use of adequate volume. If your voice is pleasing to others, it has a warm quality and is free from disagreeable sounds.

You may not realize it, but your voice and speech habits add to or detract from what you say. Your voice and speech also tell others about you as a person. In order to improve your own voice and speech, you must first learn to listen critically. Since it is easier to listen to others than to oneself, let us start with a TV or radio assignment.

To discuss

1. Listen to several radio or TV announcers or performers of your choice. Keep a record of your reactions to their voices. Record your own comments by following this simple outline:

> Voice (pleasing or annoying)
> Speech (clear or unclear)
> Personality (likable or not likable)

Now try to explain in class why you wrote what you did. Is it difficult to give reasons? One purpose of this exercise is to show you that you *do* react strongly to speech, but you may not know exactly why you react or what you react to.

2. Now use the following check list for your own voice and speech. First, answer the questions as you think your voice and speech sound. Second, have one or more of your classmates answer the questions about your voice and speech. Then compare the two check lists. *Remember*: You may not hear yourself as others hear you. You must learn to listen to yourself.

Check list for voice and speech skills

Voice
1. Do I control volume?   (not too loud, too soft, or monotonous)
2. Do I have good pitch?   (not too high, too low, or monotonous)
3. Is the tone pleasing?   (not harsh, hoarse, or nasal)
4. Do I vary pitch, volume, and tone?

Speech
1. Do I have an acceptable rate?   (not too fast, too slow, or monotonous)
2. Do I say consonant sounds clearly and distinctly?   (no sloppy endings, omitted sounds, substituted sounds)
3. Do I have good rhythm?   (no hesitations or repetitions)

Words
1. Do I overuse some words and expressions?   (and, well, so, OK)
2. Do I say words correctly?
3. Do I use a variety of well-chosen words?

Communication
1. Do I look at my listeners when speaking?
2. Do I have any mannerisms that detract from my speaking?
3. Do I speak and read in a conversational manner?   (easy, fluent, good expression)

Articulation and Pronunciation

You may recognize sloppy, slovenly, indistinct, and incorrect speech as a problem of others in your class. General problems include sounds that are omitted, added, substituted, or distorted. Can you hear others who have these difficulties? Can you hear yourself? *Remember:* Clear and distinct speech depends greatly upon the manner in which consonant sounds are made. Good **articulation** means saying these sounds carefully and clearly. Vowels should be pronounced carefully, too. Practice listening to the sentence below as it is read aloud in class. Pay particular attention to the sounds for the italicized letters.

The *singing* is still *ringing* in my ear*s* (z).

Once you have located a consonant sound which you make poorly, try to improve it through practice. You must, however, produce it correctly first. Your lips, tongue, and teeth are the chief organs of articulation. These are your helpers. Use them correctly.

Examine the following diagram of the voice organs before you do the exercises on pages 66 and 67:

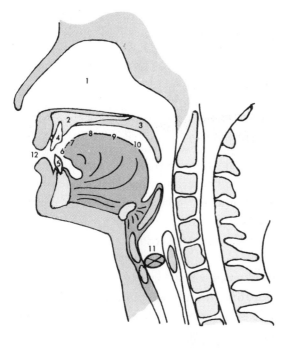

Organs of Speech

1. Nasal Cavity
2. Hard Palate
3. Soft Palate
4. Upper Teeth
5. Lower Teeth
6. Tip of Tongue
7. Blade of Tongue
8. Front of Tongue
9. Middle of Tongue
10. Back of Tongue
11. Vocal Cords (Larynx)
12. Lips

Exercises: Practicing voice control

1. To be heard, you must use *power* and *force*. Stand by your chair. Make believe you are lifting a heavy object. Say the following sentences as you pull up:

    1. Come, come—on the run.
    2. One, seven, nine, ten,
       Come on now and try again.

2. Those pupils with too loud voices need to control the power and force. Read the following word group easily and smoothly, speaking on a controlled outgoing breath. Train your ears to help you adjust to the correct volume for the room or space you are in.

        One, two, three, four,
        Five, six, seven, eight,
        Do you think we're going to be late?

3. Read a short paragraph from any textbook. Have your classmates answer the questions in the "Check list for voice and speech skills" on page 64 while you are reading.

4. Make a tape recording of a short talk or a short recording of your voice as you read a selection. Listen to the recording. Then try to make the corrections your teacher and your classmates say you need in order to improve your speaking and reading.

5. Make a final check of your voice and speech by answering each question on page 64 honestly. Practice on one or more problems each week. Make another recording near the end of the year to listen for improvements.

Saying common words correctly

Good **pronunciation** means knowing what sounds to say and what syllables receive stress. No one knows how to pronounce correctly all the words in the English language. There are too many of them, and English spelling is not always a reliable guide to pronunciation. Therefore, it is a sign of intelligence to ask how an unfamiliar word should be pronounced or to look it up in the dictionary.

There are certain common words, however, which no person who hopes to be called well educated will mispronounce. You may have studied many of them in earlier grades. Concentrate only on those words which cause you trouble.

66

Exercises: Practicing careful articulation and pronunciation

1. Here are thirty-two pronunciation demons. Say each word and check your pronunciation with a good dictionary. Pay attention to the syllables. Do you omit a syllable? Do you add a syllable? Do you place the stress on the correct syllable?

admirable	drowned	geometry	literature
athlete	elm	genuine	maybe
athletics	exquisite	governor	memorable
attacked	film	grown	mischievous
burglar	finally	history	poem
cement	formidable	hotel	police
champion	generally	influence	probably
chimney	geography	known	regular

2. Pronounce the italicized vowels carefully.

*A*merican	*sy*rup	*te*rrible	*w*restle
c*a*n	g*e*t	r*a*diator	*e*scalator
c*a*tch	col*u*mn	th*ea*ter	*e*ngine

3. Practice saying these articulation demons. Listen especially for the sounds of the italicized letters.

acros*s* (no *t*)	hun*d*red	*pr*onunciation
ap*r*on	in*tr*oduce	quan*t*ity
ar*ch*itect	len*gth* (ngkth)	re*c*ogni*z*e
becau*s*e (*z*)	stren*gth*	regu*l*ar
can*d*idate	coul*d*n't	representative
chil*d*ren	woul*d*n't	somewhe*r*e (no ending *s*)
circ*u*lation	li*b*rary	tol*d*
elec*tr*ic	on*c*e (no *t*)	nu*clear*
gove*rn*ment	*pe*rspiration	ra*tt*le
heigh*t*	*pr*oduce	ba*tt*le

4. Say each sentence and listen for the italicized sounds.

(*th*) *Th*is is *the th*eater *th*at *Th*elma chose.

(*t*) Wha*t* do you wan*t* in the bo*tt*le?

(*z*) He ha*s* picked the rose*s* on those two bushe*s*.

(*s*) My *s*ister has a *s*ample of the *s*ame cloth.

(*d*) Fre*d* tol*d* me I shoul*d*n't have wee*d*ed so many rows.

67

Making a Prepared Speech

A skilled speaker has a tremendous advantage over one who is not able to express himself effectively in public. A skilled speaker is likely to do better in his studies and in his chosen work. Also, he can serve his community better, both in school and in later life. How many situations can you think of where a person might need the ability to make a good speech?

There are many subjects about which you might make a prepared speech. You may wish to persuade people to vote for a candidate or to join you in an enterprise or to oppose some policy or activity. You may wish to entertain your hearers with a story or a personal experience.

Before you give a talk in class, study the guides on the next page. They summarize all the things you have learned in previous years about how to make a good speech.

Guides for making speeches

1. Choose a subject which is not too large or too small.
2. Know your subject.
3. Start and end with strong, interesting sentences.
4. Use illustrative materials if they can help make your talk clear and interesting.
5. Organize your ideas so that they are easy to follow.
6. Use notes written on 3″ x 5″ cards.
7. Speak clearly and carefully.
8. Avoid saying *er* and *uh*.
9. Make sure you can be heard easily by all.
10. Look at your audience.
11. Stand naturally, neither stiffly nor too informally.
12. Avoid useless gestures and body movements.

Exercise: Making a speech

Prepare and deliver a four-to-six-minute talk on any subject. Here are a few general suggestions:

1. Report on a good (or poor) television or radio program.
2. Report on a book you have enjoyed.
3. Report on an interesting person you have met or read about.
4. Report on a news event not known to most of the class.
5. Report on the activities of a group to which you belong.

To discuss

While the talks are being given, keep clearly in mind the "Guides for making speeches." Make brief notes about each speaker, and when each speech is over, or perhaps after every three or four speeches, have a class discussion of the strong and weak points of the talks you have heard. Perhaps the class will wish to agree on a marking system for rating the talks.

Remember that criticism includes courteous, thoughtful comments about both the virtues and defects of a speech, and that people often learn as much from praise as from correction.

Exercise: Making a speech

Write down the main points of criticism made about your speech. Then choose another subject and make a second speech, improving it on the basis of the evaluation.

Test I

On your paper next to the appropriate numeral, tell what important information is missing from each announcement below:

1. Here's a bulletin for all theater fans. This Friday evening Hawkins Junior High senior class will present the three-act comedy *The Rise and Fall of Danny Garth* in the school auditorium. Tickets are 50 cents and are on sale in Room 312 during lunch hour today and tomorrow.

2. They have done it again! The Handicrafts Club members have completed enough projects to hold an exhibition on Saturday afternoon, May 2, from 2 to 5 o'clock. No admission is needed. Some of the items exhibited will be on sale, with the proceeds going to charity.

Test II

Read each pair of statements below and decide which of the two is the better way to begin an explanation. On your paper, write *a* or *b* next to the appropriate numeral.

1. (*a*) This formula that I've written on the board represents one of the mysteries of the plant world. Why is it that it still baffles the scientists?
   (*b*) Here is an interesting formula. A lot of people have never seen it.

2. (*a*) Last year my brother was in a very serious accident and remained in the hospital for days. His recovery would have taken much longer if it had not been for one of the most unique devices I have ever seen. Here is how it works.
   (*b*) In hospitals I have seen lots and lots of machines. Last year I saw one in particular when my brother was in the hospital. Let me tell you about it right now.

3. (*a*) You all know that Alexander Graham Bell invented the telephone. Ever since then, the telephone has been used a great deal. However, very few people know how it works.
   (*b*) My number is 207–46–7726. No, it's not a Zip Code or my locker combination. It's a number that will set off the first electrical impulses of a very common household device: the telephone.

Test III

On your paper, list the numerals 1 to 5. Read each group of statements given below. If the statements are suitable for making or acknowledging introductions, write *Yes* next to the appropriate numeral. If they are not suitable, write *No* and explain *why*.

1. "George, I'd like you to meet Sarah Field. Sarah, this is my boating pal, George Granger."
2. "Hi, Reverend Baker. Pleased to meet you."
3. "Mrs. Burke, I'd like to introduce Tod Halstead. Tod, this is Mrs. Burke, our school nurse."
4. "Dad, this is Miss Quincy, my home-room teacher. Miss Quincy, I'd like to introduce my father."
5. "Lucy, this is my cousin, Tom Lucas. Tom, I'd like you to meet my sister's friend, Lucy Appleton."

Test IV

Read each statement below and, next to the appropriate numeral on your paper, tell whether the statement describes a *round-table, panel,* or *parliamentary* discussion:

1. This discussion, headed by a chairman, is one in which three to six people prepare beforehand to discuss a topic.
2. Discussion centers around a proposal called a motion.
3. A larger group divides into small groups for a quick, informal discussion on a question.
4. After a period of discussion in front of an audience by a few selected people, the audience is invited to join the discussion.
5. This is the most formal type of discussion used to bring a group to a majority decision.

Test V

1. Copy the following words on your paper as they are shown below. Then underline the syllable that receives the stress (the primary accent) in each word.

1. for-mi-da-ble   2. ce-ment   3. ho-tel   4. ad-mi-ra-ble

2. Count the syllables in each of these words: *governor, poem, finally, elm, film, athlete, mischievous, burglar, generally, drowned.* Copy each one on your paper, and next to it write *one, two, three,* or *four syllables.*

Exercise I

1. Review "Making Announcements" on pages 47–49.

2. List the five questions that should be answered by an announcement.

3. Write an imaginary announcement that would be appropriate for one of the following:

1. Weekend camping trip
2. Poster contest
3. Collection of annual class dues
4. Tryouts for the gymnastic exhibition
5. Campaign against littering
6. Tryouts for a class play

Exercise II

1. Review "Giving Explanations and Directions" on pages 50–51.
2. List the three essentials for making explanations. Subject Know
3. Write three beginnings of explanations that would arouse the interest of your class.

Exercise III

1. Review the lesson "Making and Acknowledging Introductions" on page 57.

2. On your paper, list the numerals from 1 to 5. Next to each numeral, write the word or words that would fit in each blank space below and complete the statement correctly:

1. Boys always __?__ for introductions.
2. Boys always __?__ when being introduced to another boy or man.
3. Introduce a boy to a girl by mentioning the __?__ name first.
4. Introduce a younger person to an older person by mentioning the __?__ name first.
5. Girls rise for an introduction only when being introduced to __?__ .

3. Write five conversational "icebreakers" that you might use to introduce five friends of yours to someone they do not know.

4. The expressions below are sometimes used in making or acknowledging introductions. On your paper, write the numerals from 1 to 6. Write *Yes* next to the correct numeral if the words are appropriate, and *No* if they are not.

1. I'd like you to meet . . .
2. Meet Karen O'Hanlon.
3. Pleased to meet you.
4. Shake hands with Bill Brewster.
5. I'm very glad to meet you.
6. How do you do, Mr. Meigs?

Exercise IV

1. Review "Group Discussion" on pages 58–60.

2. List two important characteristics of each of the following types of discussion:

1. Round-table
2. Panel
3. Parliamentary

Exercise V

1. Review "Articulation and Pronunciation" on pages 65–66.

2. Make a list of the words you need to practice saying correctly. Use them in sentences, and then practice saying aloud each of your sentences several times. Be careful to pronounce and articulate the words correctly.

CHAPTER 3

Using Modifiers

Let's go back to the island where you and your friends had to make up a language. You remember you first invented nouns to name things, and then verbs to make statements about the things you named. The use of only these two parts of speech gave you a very simple language. For example, with only nouns and verbs you could form sentences like these:

Animals wander.   Monkeys amuse children.

Of course, this is much simpler than the language you use every day to meet your needs. The words *animals, monkeys,* and *children* could mean any or all *animals, monkeys,* and *children.* In English, any number of words can be added to the nouns and verbs above to enlarge upon the idea expressed.

1. The wild <u>animals</u> in the jungle <u>wander</u> toward the water hole in the late afternoon.
2. Those chattering <u>monkeys</u> in the palm tree <u>amuse</u> the young <u>children</u> on the beach.

In the first sentence above, the words *The wild* and *in the jungle* have narrowed the meaning of the noun *animals.* They are called **modifiers.** The words *toward the water hole in the late afternoon* modify the verb *wander*; they tell *where* and *when.*

Look at the nouns *monkeys* and *children* and the verb *amuse* in sentence 2. How have they been modified?

Consider the word *stone.* Its meaning is quite general. Now we shall narrow its meaning by adding modifiers:

<table>
<tr><td>*the* **stone**</td><td>*the gray* **stone** *in my yard*</td></tr>
<tr><td>*the gray* **stone**</td><td>*the cracked gray* **stone** *in my yard*</td></tr>
</table>

Do you see? *To modify a word means to narrow or change its meaning.*

The Adjective

The most common modifier is the **adjective.** Here are two sentences in which the adjectives are underlined:

1. A little boy wants the stray cat.

2. Intelligent, elderly men were the leaders.

Which word does each underlined adjective modify? What part of speech are *boy, cat, men,* and *leaders?*

If you have answered the two questions above correctly, you will understand that *an adjective is a word used to modify a noun.* The articles *a, an,* and *the* are three of the most common adjectives.

In this sentence, possessive pronouns are used as adjectives:

3. My friendly old collie sleeps in his doghouse.

Adjectives can also modify pronouns, as in the sentence below:

4. He was intelligent.

Adjectives answer questions about nouns or pronouns. Some answer the question *Which one?* *that* train; *these* fish; *my* mother.

Others answer the question *How many?* *four* apples; *few* people; *several* houses.

Still other adjectives answer the question *What kind?* *bad* eggs; *small* potatoes; *slippery* roads.

Usually an adjective goes before the noun it modifies, as you have seen in most of the examples above. However, in certain types of sentences the adjective follows the noun or pronoun it modifies:

They seem noisy.   Readers are quiet.

■ An **adjective** is a word that modifies a noun or pronoun.

This kind and these kinds

This is singular, and as an adjective it must modify a singular word: *this kind.*

These is plural, and when it is used as an adjective, it must modify a plural word: *these kinds.*

The same is true for *those* and *that:* *those kinds; that kind.*

Exercises: The adjective

1. On your paper, copy in a list the nouns and pronouns italicized in the following passage. In parentheses after each one, write the word or words that modify it. Do not forget that articles and possessive pronouns such as *his* or *their* are used as adjectives.

EXAMPLE: 1. My big *brother* will not answer. *He* is angry.

YOU WRITE: *1. brother (My big)*

He (angry)

Across the broad *fields* galloped four noble *stallions*. As they snorted and arched their proud *necks*, *I* was curious. For behind them, under a small flowering *bush*, a young *boy*, wearing torn *shorts*, was sitting. *He* was calm and confident as he took a small silver *whistle* from his *pocket*. He puffed his brown *cheeks* and blew a shrill *blast*. Then, one by one, the *horses* lay down on the soft *turf* and allowed the *youngster* to walk up to them and clamber all over their *backs*.

2. Copy these nouns and modify each one with an adjective:

1. book	5. pencil	9. meal	13. log
2. typewriter	6. hog	10. bottle	14. picture
3. photograph	7. purse	11. peanuts	15. food
4. plumber	8. train	12. forest	16. gravy

3. Supply adjectives that will fill the blanks sensibly and interestingly. Copy the sentences on your paper.

1. On the girl's __?__ wrist I saw a __?__ bracelet.
2. My __?__ horse trotted down the __?__ __?__ road.
3. __?__ __?__ clouds threatened our picnic.
4. From under the __?__ water emerged thousands of __?__ things.
5. Give me a __?__ book and a __?__ afternoon, and I am really __?__.

4. Choose the correct word for each of these sentences:

1. I dislike (this, these) kind of movie.
2. (This, These) kinds of flowers fade easily.
3. It is (that, those) kinds of speeches that put people to sleep.
4. If I can choose, I'll choose (that, those) kind.

The Noun Adjective

You have learned that an adjective is a word used to modify a noun or pronoun. However, in English there are other words that modify nouns and yet do not have any other characteristics of adjectives. In these sentences such words are printed in italics:

1. The *newspaper* boy was my friend.
2. Our car bumped right into the *garage* door.
3. *Mr. Smith's* boy is helpful.

It is obvious, isn't it, that the italicized words modify the nouns that follow them? Now look closely at these words by themselves and tell what part of speech you think they are.

They seem to name things or persons, they can have plural forms, they can have possessive forms (*Mr. Smith* is already in the possessive form), and they can be signaled by *a*, *an*, or *the*, for example:

1. *A* newspaper is a thing. (signaled by *a*)
2. Those newspaper*s* are late. (plural form)
3. Our newspaper*'s* circulation is high. (possessive form)

The word *newspaper*, then, has all the characteristics of a noun. Can you show that *garage* and *Mr. Smith's* are nouns, also?

■ Nouns are words that can sometimes be used to modify nouns.

Exercise: Noun adjectives

Find the noun adjectives and tell which noun each modifies:

1. Hawaii's population growth began when people originally came to work on the sugar-cane plantations.
2. The island people immigrated from many lands.
3. The sugar and pineapple industries yield much income.
4. The islands are also known for one of the world's largest cattle ranches and for craft trades.
5. Surf sports are popular at the beach resorts and are often displayed on poster advertisements.

▶ *The plantations of Hawaii produce the finest crops of sugar cane in the world. The stalks resemble bamboo canes, but inside them is a juice from which sugar is made. On the opposite page, a cane harvesting machine is shown at work, and in the background is the sugar mill.*

Sentence Patterns

Study the following symbols, which represent the parts of speech you have studied in the previous grammar chapter:

N = Noun   LV = Linking verb
NP = Pronoun   Vh = Auxiliary (helping) verb
V = Action verb

These symbols, when arranged in the same order as words in an English sentence, can represent three typical sentence patterns:

SENTENCE PATTERN 1: N V   Fires burn.
SENTENCE PATTERN 2: N V N   Fires burn forests.
SENTENCE PATTERN 3: N LV N   Fires are a menace.

A pronoun is a word used in place of a noun and can be used in a sentence wherever a noun appears, for example:

NP V   They burn.

An auxiliary verb does not change the basic pattern of a sentence.

   N Vh V
1. Pat is writing.   (PATTERN 1: N V)

   N Vh V N
2. Pat has written poetry.   (PATTERN 2: N V N)

   N Vh LV N
3. Pat may become an expert. (PATTERN 3: N LV N)

● Write fifteen sentences that follow the three sentence patterns above—five for each pattern. You may add determiners (*a, an, the, my, our, your, their, its*) and modifying words, if you wish.

● Build sensible sentences, following the groups of symbols below. Determiners have been added to the symbols. Vary your sentence ideas.

1. *The* N V N
2. N LV *a* N
3. *The* N V
4. *The* N Vh V
5. *A* N Vh Vh V

6. NP Vh V *a* N
7. NP Vh V *the* N
8. N Vh Vh V NP
9. *The* N LV *a* N
10. *The* N Vh Vh LV *a* N

11. NP Vh V NP
12. *A* N Vh V *the* N
13. NP Vh Vh V *the* N
14. *The* N Vh LV NP
15. *The* N Vh Vh V *the* N

Proper Adjectives

You may remember that nouns were classified into two types: *common* and *proper*. Adjectives are similarly classified. Most adjectives are common adjectives, but *an adjective made from a proper noun is a* **proper adjective.**

PROPER NOUN	PROPER ADJECTIVE
America	an *American* artist
Europe	the *European* way of life
the Pacific	a *Pacific* salmon
China	*Chinese* cooking

> Always capitalize proper adjectives.

Exercise: Proper adjectives

Pick out and write in the order in which they appear the proper adjectives in the paragraph below, capitalizing each one correctly. In parentheses after each adjective, write the word it modifies.

swiss cheese and danish pastry are among the choicest european foods. However, french cooking is the type of cooking I like best. It contains spicier sauces than american cooking, but the taste is perfect. asian food is interesting, too, and the chinese people are the real experts on the asian continent. Actually, you don't have to go to Europe or Asia to enjoy exotic foods. A new york or san francisco resident can do just about as well right in his own home town.

SWISS CHEESE

FRENCH FRIES

DANISH PASTRY

APPLE PIE

The Adverb

Some verbs put action in a sentence but do not always describe an action as exactly and vividly as you would like. They often need words to modify them, just as nouns do. A modifier narrows their meaning and makes it clear. Study these sentences:

1. My brother eats *quickly*. (*How* does he eat?)
2. My brother eats *immediately*. (*When* does he eat?)
3. My brother eats *upstairs*. (*Where* does he eat?)
4. My brother eats *excessively*. (*How much* or *to what extent* does he eat?)

The modifiers italicized above are called **adverbs**. You see that in each case the adverb tells something about the verb.

Although the four adverbs above follow the verbs they modify, in many situations adverbs are quite movable and may come in any of several places in a sentence. For example, note in how many places the adverb *quietly* can be inserted in the same sentence.

Quietly my sister crept out of the house.

My sister *quietly* crept out of the house.

My sister crept *quietly* out of the house.

My sister crept out of the house *quietly*.

The word *not* is a special adverb; it makes a verb negative.

Many adverbs end in *–ly.* However, quite a few adverbs do not, and some words that end in *–ly* are not adverbs. For this reason, we cannot use the *–ly* ending as a definite characteristic that determines whether or not a word is an adverb. But it is useful to know that you can frequently add *–ly* to an adjective to form an adverb.

ADJECTIVES	ADVERBS
It is a *quiet* day.	They do it *quietly*.
Her *warm* gloves were lost.	I praised him *warmly*.
My *speedy* car stopped.	He drove *speedily*.
I admire his *bright* mind.	The light shone *brightly*.

■ Most **adverbs** are words that modify verbs.

Exercises: The adverb

1. In the sentences below, pick out each adverb and write it on your paper along with the verb it modifies. Underline the verb and draw an arrow from each adverb to the verb.

    1. The boy drove fast.
    2. That dog is barking loudly.
    3. Yesterday I saw my friend.
    4. Jim arrived home late.
    5. He always retires promptly at nine o'clock.
    6. My mother usually has breakfast early.

2. Here are five adjectives. Form an adverb from each by adding –*ly*, and use the adverb in a sentence.

1. brave   2. weak   3. thorough   4. ridiculous   5. rare

3. Use each of the following verbs in a short sentence in which it is modified by an adverb. Underline the verb. Draw an arrow from the adverb to the verb it modifies. In each sentence, use a different adverb from the list below:

VERBS		ADVERBS	
1. skipped	4. regretted	home	frequently
2. read	5. return	seldom	downstairs
3. travels	6. replied	not	completely
		always	carefully
		never	happily

Special adverbs: intensifiers

In the English language there are thousands of adverbs that modify verbs. These are the adverbs you have been studying so far. Now you come to a small but frequently used class of adverbs that are called **intensifiers**. These adverbs *modify adjectives and other adverbs*. Probably the most common of these is the adverb *very*. *Very*, although it is an adverb, cannot modify the simple form of a verb. You cannot say, "He walks very" or "The soprano very sang." But you can say:

    1. He walks very quickly.   2. The soprano sang very well.

Quickly is an adverb modifying the verb *walks*. *Very* is an adverb modifying the adverb *quickly*. It tells *how* quickly he *walks*. Which word does the adverb *very* modify in sentence 2 above?

Below is a list of some intensifiers that can modify adjectives and other adverbs. Try each of them in the blank of this tryout sentence:

That place was ___?___ peaceful.
                            ↑
                          (adj.)

INTENSIFIERS

fairly	less	quite	too
entirely	more	rather	utterly
extremely	most	somewhat	very
least	pretty	almost	

Do all of them fit?

■ Certain adverbs, called **intensifiers**, modify adjectives and other adverbs.

Exercises: Special adverbs

1. Name the adverbs in the sentences below. Tell whether the adverb modifies a verb, an adjective, or an adverb.

1. My very dear friend visited me.
2. John was quite angry with his friend.
3. That mouse was extremely timid.
4. The car traveled too fast.
5. The Washington Monument was very impressive.
6. Very gradually the boy found his way.
7. A somewhat unusual experiment was demonstrated.
8. An observant person would have discovered it more quickly.

2. Use each pair of words below in a sentence and show the modification by arrows.

EXAMPLE: 1. very slowly

YOU WRITE: *1. The color of the sky changed very slowly.*

1. rather rapidly	5. quite small
2. less expensive	6. more friendly
3. utterly quiet	7. very fast
4. somewhat noisily	8. least enthusiastically

Comparison of Adjectives and Adverbs

Often you will need to compare things when you speak or write. For example, you may say that you have a *rich* uncle. But if you have another uncle who has even more money, he is a *richer* uncle. And if you have many uncles with money, the one who has the most money is your *richest* uncle. (If all of your uncles are poor, you may have a *poor* uncle, a *poorer* uncle, and a *poorest* uncle.) These adjectives describe three degrees of richness or poverty.

Many adverbs can be compared, also. For example, here are three young children comparing the actions of their parents:

TOM: My mother cooks *well.*
JIM: Maybe. But my mother cooks *better* than yours.
MIKE: Well, listen. My mother cooks *best* of all.
TOM: All right, but my father can drive *fast.*
JIM: Mine drives *faster.*
MIKE: But mine drives *fastest.*

Any adjective or adverb that can be compared has *three degrees of comparison*: the **positive, comparative,** and **superlative degrees.** The comparative degree is used to compare two items, and the superlative, three or more items.

	POSITIVE DEGREE	COMPARATIVE DEGREE	SUPERLATIVE DEGREE
Adjectives	red	redder	reddest
	simple	simpler	simplest
	anxious	more anxious	most anxious
	thoughtful	less thoughtful	least thoughtful
	intelligent	more intelligent	most intelligent
Adverbs	soon	sooner	soonest
	fiercely	more fiercely	most fiercely
	frequently	less frequently	least frequently

You can see from the examples above that there are two ways of forming the comparative and superlative degrees. You can add the endings *–er* and *–est,* or you can add the words **more** and **most** or **less** and **least.**

How do you know when to use the endings *–er* and *–est* and when to use **more** and **most** or **less** and **least**? There is no simple rule to tell for certain. In general, one-syllable words add *–er* and *–est,* while words of three or more syllables use *more* and *most*. Two-syllable words may do it either way. Sometimes the dictionary will tell you how a word is compared.

If any spelling problems arise in connection with comparing adjectives, turn to pages 432–33 and study the spelling rules.

Irregular comparison

There are some very common adjectives and adverbs which change their forms when they are compared.

POSITIVE	COMPARATIVE	SUPERLATIVE
good well	better	best
many much	more	most
bad	worse	worst
little	less littler	least littlest

Two common errors

Can you explain what is wrong with these two sentences?

1. This apple is more tastier than that one.
2. The hounds arrived more sooner than the fox.

The mistake is called **double comparison.** In sentence 1 you have already expressed comparison in the ending *–er.* Therefore, you must not express it again by adding the word *more.* In other words, you may express comparison by adding *–er* or *–est* to an adjective or by preceding it with *more* or *most* (or *less* or *least*), but not by doing both. Sentences 1 and 2 should be written this way:

This apple is tastier than that one.
The hounds arrived sooner than the fox.

Another common error is to use the superlative degree when comparing only two persons or things:

WRONG: Who is the tallest, John or Bob?
RIGHT: Who is the *taller*, John or Bob?

WRONG: Which one traveled farthest, the plane or the train?
RIGHT: Which one traveled *farther*, the plane or the train?

Practice reading aloud the correct sentences above.

Exercises: Using adjectives and adverbs

1. Use each of the words below in a sentence. Use the word in the degree given in parentheses.

1. much   (comparative degree)   5. bad   (comparative degree)
2. little   (superlative degree)   6. well   (superlative degree)
3. good   (comparative degree)   7. best   (positive degree)
4. much   (superlative degree)   8. bad   (superlative degree)

2. Beside the appropriate numeral on your paper, write the correct form of the word given in parentheses.

(warm)   1. Which day was __?__, yesterday or Monday?
(soft)   2. Of the two girls, Lily has the __?__ voice.
(willingly)   3. Of the two athletes, George played __?__.
(slowly)   4. Which goes __?__, a turtle or a worm?
(fat)   5. That mosquito is __?__ than this one.
(late)   6. I slept __?__ than John.
(smooth)   7. Which is the __?__, Platt Road or Greene Street?
(warmly)   8. Does the sun shine __?__ in winter or in summer?
(repetitious)   9. Between the two speeches, Nancy's was __?__.
(well)   10. Of the four champions, he spells __?__.

TO MEMORIZE

FROM *Stanzas on Freedom*

They are slaves who fear to speak
For the fallen and the weak;
They are slaves who will not choose
Hatred, scoffing, and abuse,
Rather than in silence shrink
From the truth they needs must think;
They are slaves who dare not be
In the right with two or three.

JAMES RUSSELL LOWELL

One of the hardest things in life is to hold an unpopular opinion, whether it be in politics, religion, or such simple matters as clothing and dating.

How does the author of this poem use the word *slaves*? Why does he call them slaves? To what are they slaves?

Can you name some people from the past who *did* dare to be in the "right with two or three"? Do you know of, or know personally, any such people today?

Sentence Patterns

Add these two new symbols to your list:

Adj. = Adjective   **Adv.** = Adverb

Adjectives and adverbs are modifiers which add color and meaning to sentences, but like auxiliary verbs they do not change the basic sentence pattern. The one exception is the adjective that follows a linking verb, as in sentence pattern 4 below.

PATTERN 1: N V

  N   V   Adj.   N   V   Adv.
Poets write.   These poets write carefully.

PATTERN 2: N V N

  N   V   N   Adj.   N   V   Adj.   N
Poets write poetry.   Some poets write narrative poetry.

PATTERN 3: N LV N

  N   LV   N
Snakes are reptiles.

  Adj.   Adj.   N   LV   Adj.   N
The poisonous snakes are dangerous reptiles.

PATTERN 4: N LV Adj.

  N   LV   Adj.   Adj.   N   LV Adv.   Adj.
Snakes are dangerous.   Those snakes are not dangerous.

Remember: Possessive nouns (*Jane's, boys'*), possessive pronouns (*my, yours, his, her, its, our, their*), noun adjectives (*sugar* bowl), limiting adjectives (*this, that, these, those, some, several, many, each,* and others), and articles (*a, an, the*) are modifiers and are labeled **Adj.**

● Write sensible sentences according to the following combinations of symbols. After each sentence, indicate in parentheses whether it follows *Pattern 1, 2, 3,* or *4.*

1. N LV Adj.
2. Adj. N LV Adv. Adj.
3. Adj. Adj. N V Adj. Adj. N
4. Adj. Adj. N V Adv.
5. N^P LV Adv. Adj.
6. Adj. Adj. N V^h V^h V Adv.
7. Adj. Adj. N LV N^P
8. Adj. Adj. N V^h V Adj. Adj. N
9. Adj. Adj. N LV Adj. N
10. N^P V^h V^h LV Adv. Adj.
11. Adj. Adj. N V^h Adv. V N^P
12. Adj. Adj. Adj. N V^h Adv. LV Adj.

88

Take this test to find out whether you know how to use certain prepositions correctly.

Write each sentence, choosing the correct word in parentheses.

1. (Between, Among) the crowd of teenagers in the drugstore a feeling of suspicion had risen.
2. Everyone stood (at, to) one end of the soda fountain.
3. There had just been a bitter argument (between, among) John Alford and his girl friend Susie.
4. Right afterwards, John had retreated (in, into) the telephone booth.
5. His friend Zack had then spoken sarcastically (at, to) the rest of the girls.
6. All that was needed now to ruin everything for good was for somebody's parents to come (in, into) the store.

Adjective or Adverb?

A common error in English is to confuse adjectives and adverbs and to use one when you should use the other. To avoid this confusion, you should know whether the word you want modifies a noun or a verb. If it modifies a noun (or a pronoun), it should be an adjective. If it modifies a verb, it should be an adverb.

Complete these sentences with the correct word:

1. The chorus sang those songs (beautiful, beautifully).
2. Those songs were (beautiful, beautifully).

In sentence 1, will the word you choose modify the noun *songs* or the verb *sang*? Since the word will tell *how* the chorus sang the songs, you must use the adverb form *beautifully*.

In sentence 2, the word must tell *what kind* of songs and must be an adjective. Thus you use the adjective form *beautiful*.

Another way to know whether to use an adverb or an adjective is to notice what kind of verb the sentence has. If the verb is a linking verb such as *is, are, was, were, seem,* use an adjective after it, not an adverb.

For example:

She is pretty.
(linking   (adj.)
verb)

They are drowsy.
(linking   (adj.)
verb)

He seems lazy.
(linking   (adj.)
verb)

The verbs *look, taste,* and *feel* can be linking verbs or action verbs, depending on how they are used in a sentence.

The monster looked fierce.
(linking   (adj.)
verb)

The pie tasted sweet.
(linking   (adj.)
verb)

The monster looked fiercely at me.
(action   (adv.)
verb)

She tasted the pie reluctantly.
(action   (adv.)
verb)

> Use an adverb—not an adjective—to modify a verb.

Exercise: Adjective or adverb?

Choose the correct word from each pair in parentheses. Explain your choice in each case.

1. Those children play (noisy, noisily).
2. My uncle drives his car very (careful, carefully).
3. Jerry feels (sad, sadly) whenever he visits that place.
4. She sang (beautiful, beautifully) just before church.
5. Directions should be given (plain, plainly).
6. The pole vaulter cleared the bar (easy, easily).
7. The jump was (easy, easily) for the athlete.
8. The meal tasted (wonderful, wonderfully) to me.
9. The teacher spoke (serious, seriously) to the little boy.
10. Put your clothes away (neat, neatly).

Real and really

A common confusion of adjective and adverb occurs with the words *real* and *really*. *Real* is an adjective, never an adverb.

1. My fears were *real*.   2. *Real* heroes are often afraid.

What is wrong with the way the word *real* is used in the sentences at the left below? Compare the sentences with their correct versions on the right.

WRONG	RIGHT
1. Jay is a real friendly boy.	Jay is a *very* friendly boy.
2. I had a real good time.	I had a *really* good time.

Most and almost

Another pair of words that confuses many people is *most* and *almost*. *Most* is usually an adjective (*Most* people like pets.) and means "greatest in number" or "nearly all," or a noun (*Most* of them will refuse.). *Most* is rarely an adverb.

Almost is always an adverb and means "very nearly" or "not quite." Remember that it has two syllables and can be used only to modify a verb, adjective, or another adverb.

Compare these pairs of sentences:

WRONG	RIGHT
1. The car most exploded.	The car *almost* exploded.
2. Dinner is most finished.	Dinner is *almost* finished.

Good and well

The word *good* is always an adjective. Here it is used in several sentences:

1. The good eggs taste better than the bad ones.
2. The eggs are good.
3. The eggs taste good.
4. The eggs smell good.

Remember: After a linking verb, use an adjective, not an adverb.

Be sure to notice that in sentences 3 and 4, *good* is an adjective modifying *eggs*, not the verb *taste* or *smell*. It isn't the tasting or smelling that is good; it is the eggs.

Well is always used as an adverb, with only one common exception. As an adverb, *well* means "excellently" or "in a satisfactory manner."

1. John does his chores well.
2. I know my friend well.

EXCEPTION: When *well* is used to mean "in good health," it is an adjective.

1. The well baby cried less than the sick baby.
2. Call the doctor. The baby is not well.
3. I feel well after drinking the medicine.

> Always use **good** as an adjective; never use it as an adverb.

Bad and badly

The problem with *bad* and *badly* is similar to the one with *good* and *well*. All you need to remember is that *bad* is an adjective and *badly* is an adverb.

bad (adjective)	badly (adverb)
1. That is a bad boy.	1. That boy is sniffling badly.
2. That boy looks bad.	2. He plays tennis badly.
3. That boy feels bad.	

Notice in sentences 2 and 3 that the adjective *bad* modifies the noun *boy*. Why would it be wrong to say, "That boy looks *badly*"? You could say "The boy *plays* badly," because he does not know how to play very well, but you do not want to say he does not know *how* to look very well. Now, can you explain why "That boy feels bad" is correct?

Exercises: Adjective or adverb?

1. Choose the word *real* or *really* in place of each blank below. Be prepared to explain your choice in each case.

1. A __?__ thick rug covered the floor.
2. My grandmother was __?__ kind to me after the party.
3. A __?__ dense fog crept over the harbor.
4. Miss Spivens gave a __?__ hard test.
5. His house was a __?__ mansion.

2. Decide whether each blank below should be filled with *most* or *almost*. Explain your choice.

1. My trip __?__ wore me out.
2. __?__ girls like sad, romantic stories.
3. Several bad floods __?__ washed away the dam.
4. The school day was __?__ finished.
5. The car was __?__ completely destroyed.

3. Choose *good* or *well* in place of each blank below. Explain your choice.

1. Cool lemonade tastes __?__ on a hot day.
2. My aunt can't hear __?__ since the accident.
3. We were fed __?__ on the plane to Europe.
4. After the swim he felt __?__.
5. My cold is gone now and I feel __?__.
6. Mary is a __?__ girl when she behaves __?__.

4. Choose *bad* and *badly* in place of each blank below. Explain your choice.

1. The actors played their parts __?__.
2. Those overalls look __?__ on John.
3. That inexpensive meat tasted __?__ after two days.
4. The situation seems __?__ to me.

Prepositional Phrases as Modifiers

All of the modifiers you have studied so far have been single words—adjectives or adverbs. Now you come to a more complicated idea, but a very useful one—the idea that *groups of words can act as modifiers.* Here are some examples of groups of words modifying nouns or verbs:

1. The meat *on the plate* has been eaten.

2. Mrs. Tripple stumbled *up the dark stairs.*

3. He galloped *across the scrubby lawn.*

Notice the first word of each phrase in the sentences above. Each of these words—*on, up,* and *across*—is a **preposition,** and each of the phrases is called a **prepositional phrase.**

The preposition is another one of the eight parts of speech. It represents a limited class of words: there are only about sixty prepositions in the English language, but they are very frequently used.

A preposition shows a relationship between a noun or a pronoun that follows it and another word in the sentence. In the sentences above, the prepositions show a relationship between *meat* and *plate, stumbled* and *stairs,* and *galloped* and *lawn.*

The noun or pronoun which follows the preposition is called the **object of a preposition.** It may or may not have modifiers. What are the objects of the prepositions *on, up,* and *across* in the three sentences above? What are the modifiers of the objects?

Here is a list of the most common prepositions:

about	below	in	through
above	beneath	inside	to
across	beside	into	toward
after	besides	like	under
against	between	near	underneath
along	beyond	of	until
among	by	off	up
around	down	on	upon
at	during	onto	with
before	for	over	within
behind	from	since	without

NOTE: *Beside* means "at the side of." *Besides* means "in addition to."

Sit *beside* me. (at my side)
Who *besides* Clara has left? (in addition to)

■ A **prepositional phrase** is a group of words which begins with a preposition and ends with a noun or pronoun called the **object of the preposition.**

Exercises: The preposition

1. Make three columns on your paper, headed *Prepositions, Objects of Prepositions,* and *Modifiers of the Object.* Beside the appropriate numeral, write the words in each phrase below under the proper heading:

1. over the top
2. with him
3. in a nearby town
4. below the fifth floor
5. among our best friends
6. between us
7. at the boundary
8. along the straight line
9. by the old millstream
10. off the table and chairs

2. Use *beside* and *besides* in two sentences each.

Adjective phrases

Here are more examples of prepositional phrases:

1. The boy *on the bench* looked pale.
2. She ignored the dust under the old sofa and table.
3. The silence during the meeting at my house was quite embarrassing.

What part of speech does the phrase *on the bench* modify? This phrase is called an **adjective phrase.** Can you see why? The prepositional phrase does the same work that a single-word adjective does. What are the adjective phrases in sentences 2 and 3? Which words do they modify? Which prepositional phrase has two objects?

Since a phrase is a group of words that does the work of a single part of speech, the group of words must stay together and be considered as a unit. You can take the prepositional phrase as a unit out of a sentence and still have a meaningful statement. Try it with the sentences above.

Adverb phrases

Other prepositional phrases modify verbs. They are called **adverb phrases.** Here are some examples. Can you name the verb that each prepositional phrase modifies?

1. He hit his opponent on the jaw.
2. The plane landed before dawn.
3. The orator has spoken with great dignity.
4. Over the fence flew a fancy butterfly.

Adverb phrases answer the questions *Where? When?* or *How?* just as adverbs do.

In sentence 1, *on the jaw* tells where he hit his opponent. In sentence 2, *before dawn* tells when the plane landed. What questions do the adverb phrases in sentences 3 and 4 answer?

■ An **adjective phrase** modifies a noun or pronoun.

■ An **adverb phrase** usually modifies a verb.

Exercises: Prepositional phrases

1. On your paper, copy the prepositional phrases from the sentences listed below. In parentheses next to each phrase, write *adjective phrase* or *adverb phrase.*

1. Many legends have been told about phantom ships.
2. For various reasons these doomed vessels never reach port.
3. They usually sail against the wind forever and ever.
4. Some specter ships with ghostly crews even sail without wind.
5. Occasionally mysterious music comes from a ship without a crew.
6. The most famous phantom ship, the *Flying Dutchman,* is sometimes sighted near the southern tip of Africa.
7. Various stories center around the ship's captain and his crimes.
8. Captain Vanderbecken of one legend must battle the sea until the end of time.
9. A murder on the *Flying Dutchman* is described in another legend.
10. Many great works of literature have been based upon stories of phantom ships and their unlucky victims.

2. Copy the adverb phrases from the following sentences. Next to each one, write the question the phrase answers: *Where? When?* or *How?*

1. The criminal sped around the block and disappeared.
2. I read science fiction in the evenings.
3. Beside the white fence little pink roses were growing.
4. He will never make a million dollars with those methods.
5. The moving day was postponed until Saturday.
6. In his new car he drove around the block, over the bridge, and across the park.

3. Make up a prepositional phrase for each preposition below and use that phrase in a sentence. Underline the phrase and write whether it is an adverb or adjective phrase.

1. around
2. above
3. of
4. by
5. up
6. before

═══ **GOING AHEAD** ═══

Below are six prepositional phrases. Use each in two sentences, once as an adjective phrase and once as an adverb phrase. Label each sentence as in the example.

EXAMPLE: 1. before my birthday

YOU WRITE: *1. The weather before my birthday discouraged me. (adjective phrase modifies noun weather)*

The package arrived before my birthday. (adverb phrase modifies verb arrived)

1. in our house
2. behind the teacher's desk
3. at noon
4. during the storm
5. on the floor
6. by the park

98

Negative Adverbs and Double Negatives

A special and very common adverb is the word *not*. This word or its contraction form (*n't*) makes any verb *negative*:

1. He did *not* see the approaching beast.
2. The boat did*n't* sail today.

Some other negative words are: *no, never, nowhere, hardly, none, no one, nobody*. Never use any of them in close connection with the negative adverb *not* (or *n't*) or with each other. Study the following examples. Practice reading aloud the correct versions in the right-hand column.

	WRONG	RIGHT
1.	*Never* use *none* of them.	Never use any of them. Use none of them.
2.	Tom didn't ask *no one*.	Tom didn't ask anyone. Tom asked no one.
3.	He *never* went *nowhere*.	He never went anywhere. He went nowhere.
4.	Sue can't *hardly* walk after her fall.	Sue can hardly walk after her fall.

The adverbs *somewhere, anywhere,* and *nowhere* are sometimes misspelled or mispronounced. Do not add an *s* at the end of these words.

Exercise: Negative words

Rewrite each sentence below so that it reads correctly. If you can, rewrite the sentences in two ways.

1. I haven't got no eraser.
2. The dog never howls no more.
3. Mary didn't have nothing to give the dog.
4. As for money, she hasn't had none since Tuesday.
5. Please don't go nowhere without telling me.
6. Oscar said he hasn't seen no one behind the house.
7. That cat can't hardly stand up.
8. Bill never went nowhere without me.
9. Tom never had no place to set up his exhibit.
10. Don't build a fire nowhere near the house.

A Book to Read

Swallows and Amazons
by Arthur Ransome
J. B. Lippincott Co.

This is the story of the adventures of two brothers and their sisters in their sailboat, the *Swallow,* on the English lakes. If you like to read about sailing, camping, hidden treasure, and mysterious ships in the night, this is a book for you. Aided by Captain Flint, their Uncle Jim, the four Swallows compete in friendly rivalry with Nancy and Peggy Blackett, the owners of another boat, the *Amazon.* This book, which tells about life in the north of England, grows in excitement with each page.

About the author

After his school days at Rugby, England, Arthur Ransome, who wanted only to write books, worked in London and wrote "the most terrible rubbish" at night. Then he returned to the lake in the north where he had spent the long vacations of his youth and there began his successful career as a writer of books for young people.

Test I

On your paper, list the adjectives in the following sentences. Next to each one, write in parentheses the word it modifies. Include articles, possessive pronouns, and noun adjectives.

1. The anaconda is a tremendous South American snake, the largest serpent in our part of the world.
2. The front part of its head has shieldlike plates in the upper section.
3. This snake can close the tiny vertical nostrils in its broad snout while swimming under water.
4. On many Brazilian riverbanks the anaconda waits to capture iguanas and other small animals which contribute to its carnivorous diet.
5. These attractive shoes made from the snake's rough, scaly skin are beautiful but expensive.

Test II

On your paper, write these sentences correctly:

1. Ivanhoe was an english knight in the famous novel.
2. Barbarian tribes invaded the territory at the height of roman civilization.
3. Our canadian host showed slides of his european trip through swiss and austrian mountains.
4. Homer was a greek poet who described the battles of trojan heroes.
5. Both persian and turkish rugs hung on the walls.

Test III

On your paper, list the adverbs in these sentences. In parentheses, write the word each one modifies.

1. We jumped quickly into rather deep water in the lake.
2. The hikers finally found the somewhat muddy footpath.
3. Snow was falling gently on the lawn on that extremely cold day.
4. Quite suddenly we saw a ship on the horizon.
5. The very ugly building has stood too long.

Test IV

On your paper, list the numerals from 1 to 5. Write the correct form of the adjective or adverb in parentheses.

1. Who has the (ugly) beak, this parrot or that one?
2. Of the two boys, Joe did the (good) job.
3. Of all my friends, Walter works (carefully).
4. The snow melts (fast) at the foot of the mountain than on its summit.
5. Of the two, David spells (well).

Test V

On your paper, list the numerals from 1 to 10. Write the correct word from each pair in parentheses.

1. This egg smells (bad, badly).
2. The pioneers (almost, most) died of thirst.
3. This electric train runs (well, good).
4. I feel (bad, badly) after that insult.
5. That boat didn't sail (anywhere, nowhere).
6. Do it (good, well), or don't do it at all.
7. The high tide (almost, most) flooded the town.
8. A (real, really) sad thing happened.
9. We didn't call (nobody, anybody) (beside, besides) you.
10. (This, These) kind of advertising will make a (real, really) bad impression.

Test VI

List each prepositional phrase on your paper. Then write *adjective phrase* or *adverb phrase* next to it. In parentheses, write the word it modifies.

1. An elaborate celebration was planned by the town council.
2. For many months the town's centennial was discussed with great anticipation.
3. The descendants of the early settlers of the town dressed in pioneer costumes.
4. The parade started at the corner of Ely and Wood Streets.
5. The school band in colorful uniforms and two drum majorettes with twirling batons headed the parade along Main Street.

Review and Practice

Exercise I

1. Review "The Adjective" and "The Noun Adjective" on pages 76 and 78.

2. On your paper, list the adjectives in the following sentences. In parentheses, write the word each adjective modifies.

1. The intense, brilliant color in the sky is beautiful, and the fleecy white clouds add to its beauty.
2. In the early summer, when the gigantic icicles melted, we could hear sharp, repetitive noises as they fell upon the cold, hard ground.
3. A low brick wall and many clumps of tall, majestic trees separated the two farms.
4. The pale light of the late afternoon cast strange shadows across the green lawn.
5. The first prize for the most unusual and interesting poster goes to my best friend.

3. List only the noun adjectives on your paper. In parentheses, write the word each one modifies.

1. A painful sunburn can be a serious summer ailment.
2. Beef stew and tomato salad go well together.
3. She cut out beautiful paper dolls for the children's amusement.
4. The town hermit lived in a log cabin.
5. Heart disease is a major illness in this country.
6. Under the kitchen table lurked a strange alley cat.

Exercise II

1. Review "Proper Adjectives" on page 81.

2. Here are ten proper nouns. Change each to a proper adjective and use it in a sentence. If you are not sure how to form or spell the proper adjective, use a dictionary to look it up.

EXAMPLE: 1. Norway
YOU WRITE: *1. A Norwegian winter is dark.*

1. Mexico	3. Texas	5. Iceland	7. Rome	9. Belgium
2. Turkey	4. Canada	6. Spain	8. Athens	10. Mongolia

Exercise III

1. Review "The Adverb" on pages 82–84.

2. On your paper, list each adverb in these sentences. In parentheses, write the word it modifies.

1. The injured man limped quite slowly into the shed.
2. A rather large box had accidentally fallen off the truck.
3. That fierce dog always barks loudly.
4. The extremely weary travelers very soon wished they had not started.
5. They quickly discovered the cause of his utterly hopeless attitude.

Exercise IV

1. Review "Comparison of Adjectives and Adverbs" on pages 85–86.

2. On your paper, write the correct form of the adjective or adverb in parentheses.

(rapidly)   1. That boy ran __?__ of all.
(smart)   2. Of all the dresses on the rack, this one is __?__.
(noisy)   3. The __?__ of the two classes was kept after school.
(rough)   4. Is ice hockey or football the __?__ game?
(well)   5. Of the two champions, he debates __?__.

Exercise V

1. Review "Adjective or Adverb?" on pages 90–93 and "Negative Adverbs and Double Negatives" on page 99.

2. Choose the correct word from each pair in parentheses.

1. There wasn't (nowhere, anywhere) to go.
2. This is a (real, really) fine painting of the sea.
3. We couldn't see (good, well) enough to find the trail.
4. He is (most, almost) finished with the hammer.
5. Without refrigeration, the meat will smell (bad, badly).
6. You haven't seen (any, no) passenger pigeons in your lifetime.
7. They are (real, really) annoyed with her.
8. She feels (bad, badly) because she received low grades.
9. Who (beside, besides) Carlos can sing (good, well)?
10. (This, These) kind of sausage will taste (good, well).

Exercise VI

1. Review "Prepositional Phrases as Modifiers" on page 94–97.

2. Copy the prepositional phrases from the sentences listed below. Write the word each modifies. Tell whether the phrase is an *adjective phrase* or an *adverb phrase*.

1. The glove on the bureau was badly worn.
2. Can you see those pennies in the water?
3. I heard a burst of applause.
4. The old witch prepared a cup of magic tea and herbs.
5. My cousin from Annapolis was the life of last night's party.
6. Until midnight those wretched cats howled.
7. The penny in his mouth is the Scot's remedy for seasickness.
8. My group of friends will head for the beach on a hot day.
9. The girls in the class are rehearsing without enthusiasm.
10. Below the sign stood a mysterious man with a slouch hat on his head.

3. Use these prepositional phrases as adjective phrases in sentences of your own:

1. near the brook
2. with the groceries
3. in the museum
4. behind the tractor

4. Use these prepositional phrases as adverb phrases in sentences of your own:

1. in the evening.
2. with all our strength
3. toward the policeman
4. along the highway

CHAPTER 4

Building Good Paragraphs

You know how discouraging it can be to read a long, unbroken stretch of print on a page. When you write, you will help your readers enjoy and understand what you are saying if you group your ideas into paragraphs. You already know that a paragraph is indicated by an *indentation*. This indentation is an important writing technique.

What Is a Paragraph?

Read the following composition, noticing especially how the paragraphs are arranged. Be prepared to discuss it.

The Circus, the Elephants, and TV

1   Late Tuesday evening Mother, Dad, Jeffrey, Emily, and I decided to see the circus come into town. We had read in the *Evening Bulletin* that the silver circus train was due in the railroad yards at nine-thirty the next morning. According to the article, the elephants, horses, and llamas would be the first to get off, and they would parade down Market Street to Convention Hall.

2   Excitedly, we piled into our old car the next morning to see if we could find the right place on the railroad. Dad drove us down near the yards, but we didn't know just where the train was to pull in. Soon, however, we saw a crowd of people looking down from a bridge over the tracks. We parked our car and ran over to look, too. There, far below us, was the silver train, backing slowly toward the seldom-used platform where it was to unload.

3   "We're too high! We've got to get down there nearer the train!" yelled Jeff. We all agreed and piled back into the car. Dad drove around the block to a street on a lower level and parked. Soon we saw the circus train again, this time on our level. Immediately, we all ran toward the silver cars. No one wanted to be too late to see the elephants emerge.

4   As it turned out, we had a long wait while the train was switched back and forth on different sidings and broken up into small sections. Finally, just inside a partly open door, Emily saw a wrinkled trunk. She started to run toward the car, when a man shouted, "Keep back, little girl; we're going to unload."

5   The moment we had waited for was here. The door opened all the way, and some men jumped out to remove a ramp from beneath the car. They placed the ramp against the door and motioned to everyone to keep away. Gradually, a massive, gray, old-looking head appeared in the doorway.

6   Just then my attention was attracted to a man standing on a wheeled, shiny aluminum platform nearby. He was standing behind a camera and filming the scene. On his coat and in the front of the platform were labels reading "WRCV–TV." As the children crowded around the elephant, I realized that the chances were good that I would see some of us on the TV news that evening.

To discuss

1. How can you tell at a glance when a new paragraph starts in "The Circus, the Elephants, and TV"?

2. What is the main idea in the first paragraph? In which sentence is this main idea expressed? What point does each sentence add to *develop* the main idea?

3. Why did the writer choose to divide his story into paragraphs just where he did?

4. How did the writer vary the beginnings of his sentences in each paragraph? Did he vary the lengths of his sentences? What effects can this variety have on a paragraph?

5. Can you now explain what a paragraph is?

■ A **paragraph** is a series of sentences which develop one main topic or idea.

Exercise: The paragraph topic

All of the sentences in each paragraph in "The Circus, the Elephants, and TV" are related to a main idea, or topic. The topic in the first paragraph might be stated as below:

PARAGRAPH 1:   We decide to see the circus unload

In your own words, state the topic of each remaining paragraph.

Three Kinds of Paragraphs

Several kinds of paragraphs are commonly used by good writers. When a person tells a story or reports a series of events, he uses a **narrative paragraph;** it narrates, or tells, a story. The paragraphs in the passage about the circus are narrative paragraphs; that is, one follows another as the story unfolds.

Another kind is the **descriptive paragraph.** Here is an example:

7   My little sister's lively nature is impossible to repress. One evening she appeared in the living room doorway just as Mother and her guests were about to go to dinner. Beth's hair was soaking wet from her bath. She was wearing my pajamas, which were at least four sizes too big. The sleeves and legs flopped about over her hands and feet. Around her waist she had tied one of Father's best red neckties. Behind her she dragged a damp towel to which was pinned her old Raggedy Ann doll. Her face was still streaked with soapsuds, but her eyes sparkled. Her mischievous smile made it difficult to scold her.

A third type of paragraph is the **explanatory paragraph,** sometimes called an **expository paragraph.** Here is an example:

8   That the stars are all the same distance from us is also only a matter of appearance. Some are many thousands of times more distant than others. Occasionally three stars will appear to be close together and, perhaps, in a straight line. In reality, one star may be immensely farther off than the other two. They just happen to appear to us to be in a straight line and near together. As you might suppose, generally speaking, the fainter stars are farther away than the brighter ones. The bigger the telescope, the more of these faint, far-distant stars we can see.

from *The Stars for Sam,* by W. Maxwell Reed

To discuss

1. What is the main topic or idea around which each sample paragraph above is organized?

2. What does paragraph 7 describe? Which words show specific details and help to make the writer's description vivid? Which words appeal to one of your five senses?

3. What does paragraph 8 explain?

4. In what ways is the explanatory paragraph also descriptive? What is the chief difference between the two paragraphs?

◻ A **narrative paragraph** tells a story or recounts a series of events.

◻ A **descriptive paragraph** describes somebody, some place, or something.

◻ An **explanatory paragraph** explains something or sets forth a series of facts about some subject.

Exercise: Kinds of paragraphs

As you read each paragraph below, try to decide whether it is mainly *narrative*, *descriptive*, or *explanatory*. Remember, many paragraphs contain some elements of all three kinds.

9   The power of the teacher and his aids extended even into the homes; our homework was closely supervised. When the weather was pleasant, we gathered on the rooftops in the early evening and droned our lessons while two or three of the brightest pupils kept watch to be sure we weren't wasting our time or indulging in furtive tomfoolery. In winter, when we had to study inside, the watchers would steal up to the roof and listen down the chimneys for the telltale drone—or lack of it. To be caught not studying meant punishment the next day.

from *Syrian Yankee* by Salom Rizk

10   Not a soul was to be seen on shore, only a deserted, petrified world with motionless stone heads gazing at us from their distant ridge, while other equally motionless stone men lay prostrate in a row at the foot of a long terrace right in the foreground, on the lava blocks along the coast. It was as though we had anchored with a hovering spaceship off the shore of an extinct world, where once had lived beings of a kind other than those on our own earth.

from *Aku-Aku*, by Thor Heyerdahl

11   The hummingbird invariably lays two eggs, snow-white, and about as large as little peas; often more than one brood will be reared in a season. The young hatch in two weeks. When they are born, they are naked, helpless, blind; and they curiously resemble insects. The mother feeds them about every fifteen minutes with food that she has partly digested. In about three weeks the infants are ready to leave the nest, but first they try their wings. Each baby lifts its wings and beats them until they form a halo about him, but he does not at once rise. Many other young birds fall out of the nest and flop about helplessly, but not so the young hummer who, after he has tested his wings, takes sure flight.

from "Titania of the Airways," by Archibald Rutledge

From your reading in newspapers, magazines, or books, pick out three paragraphs—one *narrative,* one *descriptive,* and one *explanatory.* Bring the paragraphs to school and read them aloud so that your classmates may decide the type for each paragraph. Be prepared to explain your choices.

The Topic Sentence

The main characteristic of many good paragraphs is that all the sentences in the paragraph are related to a single topic. Very often that topic is stated in one sentence, usually at the beginning of the paragraph. This is called the **topic sentence.** Here is an example of a paragraph that begins with a topic sentence:

12   London was fifteen hundred years old, and was a great town—for that day. It had a hundred thousand inhabitants—some think double as many. The streets were very narrow, and crooked, and dirty, especially in the part where Tom Canty lived, which was not far from London Bridge. The houses were of wood, with the second story projecting over the first, and the third sticking its elbows out beyond the second. The higher the houses grew, the broader they grew. They were skeletons of strong crisscross beams, with solid material between, coated with plaster. The beams were painted red or blue or black, according to the owner's taste, and this gave the houses a very picturesque look.

from The Prince and the Pauper, by Mark Twain

The simplest and best way to learn to write a good paragraph is to start with a clear topic sentence and then develop it.

Exercises: The topic sentence

1. Study again sample paragraphs 1 to 12. Decide which of the paragraphs begin with a topic sentence, and on your paper after the paragraph numeral for each, copy the topic sentence. Then, in not more than two sentences, tell how the writer develops his topic. Put this information in parentheses. For example, after copying the first sentence in paragraph 1 as the topic sentence, the explanation of the writer's development may be stated as shown below:

(Writer develops topic by explaining how a newspaper article led to the decision.)

2. Below is a list of ten sentences. Five of them would make good topic sentences for a paragraph. Five of them would be more likely to take their places in a paragraph as a part of its development; that is, they do not tell you what the paragraph is mainly about. List the numerals 1 to 10 on your paper and, beside each numeral, write either T (for topic sentence) or D (for development).

1. I find autumn the most exciting season of the year.
2. After he crashed through the windshield and landed twenty feet away, he was only slightly scratched.
3. The mother wasp then flies away and dies.
4. The arrival of my baby brother changed my whole way of life.
5. Going steady in high school brings more misery than it does satisfaction.
6. Then the girl snarled, "No mail for *you!*"
7. Her thread snapped sharply as she stitched with monotonous rhythm.
8. As we reached the top, a magnificent view stretched before us.
9. This adventurous elf was about thirty feet from the clump of ferns.
10. Tremendous size can be a disadvantage to an animal.

3. Write five topic sentences of your own. See if you can make them interesting enough so that a person reading them would want to know more about the topic.

✓ Check Test 4: Capitalization

Take this test to see how well you remember the rules for capitalization.

Write the following sentences, using capital letters correctly:

1. On May 20, 1927, charles a. lindbergh left roosevelt field.
2. With his monoplane, *spirit of st. louis*, he was attempting to make a nonstop flight between new york and paris.
3. In thirty-three and a half hours he was greeted by the french people.
4. He returned to america on a cruiser called *memphis* and was welcomed by president coolidge in washington on june 11.
5. The demonstration he received in new york two days later still makes most celebrations of the fourth of july seem mild by comparison.

If you made any mistakes on this test, turn to the Review Handbook, pages 420–23. There you will find review and more practice.

Developing the Topic

Once you have written a topic sentence, your job is to develop it into a paragraph by adding details. If you have plenty to say on the subject about which you are writing, development will be easy for you. It is by no means always necessary to plan in advance just how you are going to put your ideas in order. You may find that they flow almost effortlessly.

For example, if you write the topic sentence, "I always feel __?__ (adjective) when I come into English class," several ideas will probably follow immediately. Another topic sentence might be, "Whenever I think of dogs (or cats), I think of __?__ (name)." For such a subject, development may be no problem. You let your ideas flow, being careful to remember that when you take up a new phase of the topic, you must start a new paragraph.

There are three types of details commonly used to develop paragraphs. These are: (1) *facts or examples*, (2) *incidents or anecdotes*, and (3) *reasons or explanations*. Most writers use a combination of these three. We shall, however, consider them separately here.

Development by facts or examples

Probably the most common means used to prove or illustrate the idea expressed in the topic sentence is to use facts or examples in developing a paragraph. Paragraph 8 on page 109 uses this method. It begins: "That the stars are all the same distance from us is also only a matter of appearance." Now read the entire paragraph again and see how clearly and interestingly W. Maxwell Reed uses facts to develop his point.

Another paragraph developed by facts is paragraph 11 on page 110, which begins, "The hummingbird invariably lays two eggs, snow-white, and about as large as little peas . . ." Then follows a series of facts about what happens to these eggs. Read it again to observe the development. How many facts does Archibald Rutledge use in his paragraph?

In paragraph 12 on page 111, Mark Twain develops the topic sentence, "London was fifteen hundred years old, and was a great town—for that day."

Exercises: Paragraph development by facts

1. Below are eight topic sentences. Choose five of them to copy on your paper. Then briefly list below each one several facts you might use to develop it.

1. Meat from several kinds of animals is a commonplace part of the diet of most Americans.
2. A person is likely to do better in life if he is a good reader.
3. Manners are principally a way of allowing life to run more smoothly.
4. Some people think of the most foolish ways to waste time.
5. It is a great advantage to a young person to receive a regular allowance.
6. Ever since Alice started doing her homework on a regular schedule, she has enjoyed life more.
7. Some eighth-graders exhibit a remarkable collection of bad habits.
8. Some people say that boys and girls are equal, but I don't think so.

2. Write a paragraph which develops one of the five topic sentences you chose for the exercise above.

Take the most interesting topic you outlined roughly for exercise 1 on page 114 and expand it into a theme two or three pages long. Perhaps two or three of the facts or examples you used could be expanded into paragraphs.

Development by incidents or anecdotes

You know from experience that nothing makes conversation or writing come alive more quickly than a real-life incident told from someone's experience. The use of such incidents is another way to develop a paragraph. Paragraph 7 on page 109 illustrates this. It begins: "My little sister's lively nature is impossible to repress." Now turn back and read the entire paragraph; it is both a narrative and descriptive paragraph.

Almost all of the paragraphs in "The Circus, the Elephants, and TV" use incidents to develop their topics. Read them again to study the technique.

Exercise: Paragraph development by incident

Of the eight topic sentences below, choose five to copy, and then list briefly below each of them one or more incidents or anecdotes which you might use to develop the topic. They need not be true; you may make them up. Then choose the two topic sentences you like best and write a full paragraph about each. You will probably do a better job if you write a first draft in pencil and then proofread and revise it carefully before copying your final draft.

1. Life in my family the first thing in the morning is rather ___?___ (choose an adjective).
2. I have some interesting characters among my friends.
3. Anger takes different forms with different people.
4. Experience had long since proved to Mary that honesty was the best policy.
5. Several times my plans have been radically changed by the weather.
6. Sometimes the first impression you make does not give a true impression of the person you really are.
7. An uncontrollable temper can get you into a great deal of trouble.
8. It usually pays to listen to good advice.

Development by reasons or explanations

Sometimes you will write a topic sentence which expresses an opinion that needs to be explained. For example, you may write, "The mountains are better than the seashore for a vacation spot." The reader will want to know why you think so, and you must develop your topic by giving reasons or explanations. Of course, you may also use facts, examples, incidents, and anecdotes (which are often in themselves reasons or explanations) to support your statement. Your main job, however, will be to give your reasons. Your paragraph might read as follows:

13 The mountains are better than the seashore for a vacation spot. In the first place, there is more to do there: climbing, camping, and swimming in mountain lakes, and the views are more beautiful and varied. Secondly, it is healthier in the mountains, where there is no danger of ear infections from salt-water swimming or danger of overdoses of sunburn. Moreover, the mountains are generally less crowded than the beaches. Who really enjoys being lost in a hodgepodge of sun worshipers? Finally, unless you are rich, the lower rental for mountain resorts will lure you from the sea, unless, that is, the mosquitoes have already driven you away.

To discuss

Look back over paragraphs 1 through 12, pages 107–11. Which of them do you think are examples of development by explanations and reasons? Do not be disturbed if you choose some of the same paragraphs which were cited as cases of development by facts or examples. After all, a well-chosen set of facts is certainly a good explanation.

Exercises: Paragraph development by explanation

1. Below and at the top of the next page are eight topic sentences which can be developed by reasons or explanations. Choose five of these topic sentences, copy each, and write below it several reasons or explanations to support the statement made in the sentence:

1. Parents would learn much if they would ask their children more questions.
2. What makes people interesting is that they are so different.

3. Robert didn't really want to go to the zoo with the rest of us that Saturday.
4. I often think how lucky I am to have been born in this age of modern medicine.
5. The best teachers are strict (or lenient) teachers.
6. It is quite simple to scramble eggs.
7. Every person should be required to learn to swim before he is allowed to graduate from high school.
8. Working too hard on your school lessons may make you miss some things that are even more important.

2. Choose the two topic sentences above that interest you most and develop each one into a well-constructed paragraph.

GOING AHEAD

Perhaps one or more of the paragraphs you worked on in the exercise above or in the exercise on page 115 are interesting enough for you to develop into a longer theme. In such a theme you will have space either to develop fully the single incident or opinion you have chosen, or to develop several incidents or opinions, each of which will contribute to the interest of your paper.

Organize your paragraphs well and check them for variety of sentence lengths and sentence beginnings.

TO MEMORIZE

FROM *The Arsenal at Springfield*

Were half the power that fills the world with terror,
Were half the wealth bestowed on camps and courts
Given to redeem the human mind from error,
There were no need of arsenals nor forts.

HENRY WADSWORTH LONGFELLOW

Longfellow wrote the poem from which the above stanza is taken many years before hydrogen bombs were conceived. The sentiment he expresses is even more potent today. How could the wealth used for purposes of destruction be used to "redeem the human mind from error"? What types of education does the world need? How could money be used to good advantage to improve your own community?

Staying on the Topic

Whether you are reading a book or listening to a speaker, it is both unpleasant and confusing to have your thoughts interrupted by an idea or statement that appears to be entirely unrelated to the subject. It is confusing, too, when a person starts off on one topic and wanders from that topic, ending up on another one. When you are writing paragraphs, be sure you have clearly in mind what your topic is, and then stick to it!

Here is a paragraph that contains a sentence that is unnecessary to the topic:

14   The first stages of learning to play the trumpet are torture to both the learner and the listener. The learner all too often cannot manage to make any noise at all, except a depressing sputter of air. Blowing air through a trumpet does, however, develop the lungs and improve the health. After a few sessions, most beginners are able to produce a few loud blasts, which are usually off key. Understandably, those who try to listen to young trumpeters often banish them to the attic or woodshed or some other hideaway well out of earshot.

To discuss

1. What is the topic sentence in the sample paragraph above?
2. Which sentence does not belong to the paragraph? Why not?
3. How are the other sentences in the paragraph directly related to the topic as stated in the topic sentence?

Exercise: Staying on the topic

Below and on page 120 are three paragraphs, each of which stays on its subject except for one sentence. Find each off-topic sentence and copy it on your paper beside its paragraph numeral. Be prepared to explain what the topic of each paragraph is.

15   What I like best about the weather is the time you get a taste of one season in the middle of another. For instance, what greater pleasure is there than a balmy, springlike day suddenly arriving in February? It's much more exciting than just another spring day in May. Or what a pleasing sense of adventure you get when a cold blast from the Pole quickly puts a bit of winter hail and sleet into the middle of summer! Last summer was one of the hottest we have had in many years.

16   My older brother has some strong opinions about girls' hairdos. He says that if hair were supposed to be curly, it would have been created that way. He states, too, that any female who will spend several hours, or several dollars, fluffing up her hair so that it is impossible to see around it in the movies, will never get asked on a date with him. It's too rude to the people behind. He likes nothing better than to take a nice girl on a movie date. Furthermore, he cannot stand girls whose hair is always changing color. "Maybe I'm a conservative," he laughs, "but I like to know what to expect when my girl friend comes downstairs to go out with me."

17   My strongest impression on my first night in Port-au-Prince, the capital of Haiti, was the variety and volume of dog utterances. No sooner had I settled into my hotel bed and pulled the mosquito netting around me, than there began a fearful, shrill yapping just under my window. This was answered by what must have been a larger dog, equally angry. He woofed in a deep bass for the next fifteen minutes. Between his woofs and the nearer yaps, my alert ears could catch a horrible howling across the street and a deep, menacing growl just beyond the howl. I could also hear in the distance the high, musical, rapid banging of the drums of a voodoo ceremony. It took me over a week to become enough accustomed to the canine night noises to get my first eight hours of sleep.

Here is a paragraph which starts on one topic but wanders to another. The sentence where the topic begins its shift is printed in italics.

18   There is nothing more peaceful and satisfying than fishing on a quiet lake. In the first place, the lakes around us have so few fish in them that you can be almost certain that no fish will disturb your line. Yet the line is there to provide a sense of purpose. You keep a hold on it, occasionally you look at the hook, and now and then you apply a fresh worm. But none of these movements are strenuous enough to disturb your peace of mind. *And it is certainly peace of mind that most of us seek.* Our lives are too rushed, too full, too jumpy. It is not good for our mental health to be constantly agitated. Every person, young or old, needs periods of quiet meditation if he is to lead a balanced, satisfied life.

To discuss

What was the topic when the paragraph started? What is the topic at the end? How might you revise the passage?

Exercise: Staying on the topic

Below are two paragraphs, each of which wanders from the topic with which it started. In your own words, write what the topic is at the beginning of each paragraph and what it is at the end of the paragraph. Then copy the sentence which leads the paragraph off the topic.

19   There is no pleasure greater than that of eating a boiled lobster. It is a demanding task, which drives all unpleasant thoughts from the mind. When you manage to crack open a claw and extract the sweet, tender meat, you feel you well deserve the taste treat in store for you. You dip the meat in melted butter and pop the tasty morsel into your mouth. You must be careful, however, not to eat too much lobster, for it is a rich food. I know two boys who were given a dozen lobsters by a Maine lobsterman. They bought a pound of butter, borrowed a large pot, and were soon deep in lobster meat. Although they finished all twelve lobsters, they got sick, and neither of them has been able to eat lobster since.

20   The qualities of a cat are more admirable than those of a dog. I admit that a dog is always friendly, always loyal, whereas a cat is often withdrawn and impersonal. Yet cats are so beautiful, so independent, so poised. Cats set a good example for us informal and hasty Americans. I have heard several foreign visitors say that, much as they admire our generosity and our sympathy for those in trouble, they find our busy, frantic ways quite exhausting. Therefore, when we meet sensitive foreigners, we Americans should try to curb our enthusiasm and be aware of what our foreign friends may expect.

Transitional Words and Phrases

Good writing does not contain awkward gaps between sentences or paragraphs. One sentence flows easily into the next. The reader's mind is carried from idea to idea. Similarly, in a longer theme, one paragraph flows easily into the next, and the progression of ideas is clear.

There are certain words or word groups called **transitional words** or **phrases** that help the reader to follow the flow of ideas more easily. These transitions are writing devices that help link a sentence (or paragraph) with the one that precedes or follows it.

Look again at paragraph 13, page 116, about the mountains and the seashore. Examine the transitions the writer uses:

line 2: In the first place
line 4: Secondly
line 6: Moreover
line 8: Finally
line 9: unless
line 10: that is

Read the paragraph aloud in class, emphasizing the transitional words so that you can sense how they work. Notice that the transitional words and phrases are set off from the rest of the sentence by a comma or commas.

As you write paragraphs, pay attention to transitional words. Read your work aloud to *hear* whether it flows smoothly. Refer to this list if you need a suggestion for linking your ideas:

COMMON TRANSITIONAL WORDS AND PHRASES

another	furthermore	nevertheless
at the same time	however	next
but, and, or	in addition	meantime
consequently	in fact	on the other hand
finally	in the same way	then
first, second, third, etc.	for example	therefore
	afterward	too, also

Remember, though, that all any transition can do is to make the logic easier for the reader to grasp. First, the writer's thinking must flow logically.

Exercises: Transitional words and phrases

1. Look through all the numbered paragraphs in this chapter and find at least ten transitions. Note on your paper the page in this book on which the transition appears. Also note the paragraph numeral. Then copy the sentence containing the transition and be prepared to explain which ideas are joined by the transition.

EXAMPLE: 1. page 107, paragraph 2, *however*
Soon, however, we saw a crowd of people looking down from a bridge over the tracks.

2. Rewrite the paragraph below. With transitions, change the choppy sentences into a smooth paragraph. Do not use the same transitional word or phrase more than once. Your transitional words need not always *begin* a sentence. They may appear *within* the sentence, if you like.

The Hittites lived in Asia Minor over four thousand years ago. They were barbarians. They were a remarkable people in many ways. They invented a system of writing. They had an intelligent code of laws. They were skillful in working with stone. Their chief contribution to the world was their knowledge of the practical uses of iron.

3. Write a paragraph explaining how to perform a process, giving special attention to transition. (Be careful not to overuse the word *then*. If too many sentences begin with *then*, your writing becomes monotonous.)

Use one of these suggested processes or any other you may prefer:

1. How to mount photographs for an album
2. How to choose clothes with color in mind
3. How to go from your house to school
4. How to make a set shot in basketball

Guides for building good paragraphs

1. Keep your topic clearly in mind.
2. State the topic in a topic sentence (usually, but not always, in the first sentence).
3. Be sure that each sentence relates to the topic and helps to develop it. Stay on the topic.
4. Remember that you may use facts or examples, incidents or anecdotes, reasons or explanations to develop your topic.
5. Be sure that the ideas in your sentences and paragraphs flow smoothly. Use transitional words and phrases where necessary.

Exercise: Writing paragraphs

Now that you have studied how to build good paragraphs, see how good a job you can do in writing some. Choose two or three different subjects and write a single paragraph on each. While you write, keep in mind the "Guides for building good paragraphs."

Test I

Tell what kind of paragraph would best develop each topic or idea listed below—*narrative*, *descriptive*, or *explanatory*. Write your answer next to the sentence numeral on your paper.

1. Our beach after a heavy storm at sea
2. A Halloween prank that backfired
3. How to throw a knuckle ball
4. The hectic dress rehearsal of our class play
5. The best way to prepare for a test

Test II

Copy the topic sentence in each of these paragraphs:

1. There were many reasons why Betsy should have awakened in a happy mood that morning. The sun was shining brightly through her window. She liked her new hairdo. This afternoon there would be a meeting of the decorating committee, the highlight of her week.
2. A hundred gay balloons waved gently from the ceiling. Leaves of crimson and gold festooned the windows. The newly waxed floor shone invitingly. Our somber old gym had been transformed for the first party of the year.

Test III

1. Copy from the following paragraph the one sentence that does not stick to the topic:

Many thoughtful persons believe our national political campaigns last too long. They are expensive and physically hard on the candidates. This year's campaign has been a very bitter one. It has been suggested that we could profitably cut the campaign period in half.

2. From the following paragraph, copy the sentence in which the paragraph starts to stray from the topic:

The famous book *Gulliver's Travels* is not a book of travel at all. The author, Jonathan Swift, intended it to be a biting criticism of the life of his times. Instead, it became a children's book because of the little folk and strange animals that are its characters. Swift made a large fortune. When he died, he left his fortune to the founding of an insane asylum in Dublin.

Review and Practice

Exercise I

1. Review "Three Kinds of Paragraphs" and "Developing the Topic" on pages 109–10 and 113–16.

2. With additional sentences, develop each of the topic sentences below into a brief paragraph. At the end of your paragraph, tell what kind it is and which type of details you used to develop it.

1. Our dog Frisky is very unpopular with my older sister.
2. At five o'clock in the morning, Main Street is a lonely place.
3. The first time I spoke at assembly, I got stage fright.
4. The route to our cottage is easy to follow.

Exercise II

1. Review "The Topic Sentence" on page 111.

2. Write a suitable topic sentence for a paragraph you might develop on these subjects:

1. Thomas Jefferson, the Musician	3. My Favorite Book
2. A Dull Party	4. A Local Landmark

Exercise III

1. Review "Staying on the Topic" on pages 118–20.

2. Read carefully the notes below which are taken from a paragraph. Decide which of the items stray from the topic "Lost on a Mountain." On your paper, copy only the notes which keep to the topic.

Lost on a Mountain

Group of hikers start up the trail
Bill stops to pick up rock specimens
Rock collecting is an interesting hobby
Bill takes the wrong path
Walks far and calls without success
Prepares to spend the night on the mountain
A book I have read about making camp
Bill builds a lean-to and starts a fire
Daniel Boone was often lost in the woods
Bill hears noises in the distance

CHAPTER 5

How Sentences Work

On the imaginary island referred to in Chapter 1, it was clear that to have a language, first of all you needed words to name things: nouns (or pronouns). But with nouns alone you could not say much. Once having named something, you needed to be able to say something about it, and for this purpose you used a verb. The lessons in this chapter will help you to understand how these two parts of speech form the foundation of English sentences.

The Sound of a Sentence

You have been speaking and writing good English sentences for many years without thinking very much about it. You do it easily because you have heard others producing sentences so often that you do the same mostly by imitation. *You know what an English sentence sounds like.*

One useful thing we can say about a sentence is that it *sounds complete.* Generally, the way a speaker shows the end of a sentence is to drop the pitch of his voice and to make a short pause.

To demonstrate this to yourself, close your books and listen to someone read the following paragraph aloud in a natural voice. See if you can count the number of sentences in the paragraph.

> The famous humorist Mark Twain had an old umbrella. Wanting to get rid of it, he threw it in the ash can. The next day the trashman returned it to him. Next, he hid it under a bush. A boy found it and returned it to him. He was getting weary of this, so he threw it down a deep well. Several days later a man who had been repairing the well returned it the third time. Then one rainy day he lent it to a friend. He never saw it again.

How many sentences are in the paragraph above? Did you hear the drop in pitch and the slight pause at the end of each sentence?

Exercises: The sound of a sentence

1. Below are ten groups of words. Read them aloud and be prepared to tell from the way they sound whether or not they are sentences.

1. Those fish over there.
2. Are swimming around slowly.
3. Those fish over there are swimming around slowly.
4. Up on the hill behind the barn.
5. My father spoke severely to the milkman.
6. The milkman retreated to his truck.
7. In the early spring our grass looks very green.
8. The green grass in the early spring.
9. Arithmetic, English, and science.
10. George likes arithmetic, English, and science.

2. Your teacher will read a paragraph to you. Listen to it, pencil in hand. Each time you note the pitch drop and pause which indicate the end of a sentence, make a little mark on a piece of scrap paper. When the paragraph is finished, see if you have counted the correct number of sentences in the paragraph.

The Two Main Parts of a Sentence

A typical sentence names something and then says something about it. The part that names is called the **complete subject**. The part that tells something about the subject is called the **complete predicate**. The word *predicate* comes from the Latin word *praedicare*, which means "to proclaim." You can think of the predicate, then, as proclaiming something about the subject.

Examine the sentences below. Notice that, in each case, the subject and predicate *together* make a statement. No part alone makes a statement or a sentence.

COMPLETE SUBJECTS	COMPLETE PREDICATES
1. Hawks	kill many field mice.
2. The old organ grinder	performed in the square.

The best method for finding the subject of a sentence is to ask yourself *who* or *what* did whatever was done, or *who* or *what* had something done to it. In sentence 1 above you ask, "What kills?"

"Hawks" is the answer, so *hawks* is the complete subject. The complete predicate is *kill many field mice*.

Who *performed* in sentence 2? "The old organ grinder" performed, so *The old organ grinder* is the complete subject.

What are the complete subjects and complete predicates in these sentences?

3. He ran away from my two-year-old brother.
4. An easy chair was placed beside the fireplace.
5. The electric car in the window pleased my brother.

Exercises: The complete subject and complete predicate

1. Name the complete subject and complete predicate in each sentence below:

1. Every child in the playground was crying.
2. Those yellow alley cats never bother him.
3. A large kettle of lobsters boiled on the stove.
4. I saw a large kettle of lobsters.
5. A brilliant idea flashed into my mind.
6. The cellar of our new house was flooded during the storm.
7. Several antique vases were displayed on the shelf.
8. That ancient rug on the wall was donated to the museum.
9. A true baseball fan never misses an important game.
10. John dashed over the fence and out through the fields.

2. Each word group below needs a subject or a predicate to make it a complete sentence. Copy the word groups on your paper and add whatever is needed. Try to make your subjects and predicates interesting and varied.

1. . . . roared into the station.
2. Every boy in the class . . .
3. . . . was filling the pitcher with lemonade.
4. . . . always picks a fight with my sister.
5. That young puppy of ours . . .
6. . . . saw the reason for not spending five dollars.
7. Signs of a hurricane . . .
8. . . . feebly struggled for air.
9. Jessica Lee . . .
10. The light on Fleet Street . . .

The simple subject and verb

The key word (or words) in the complete subject of a sentence is called the **simple subject.** Here are a few sentences with the complete subject italicized and the simple subject underlined:

1. *The unhappy <u>Nellie Burns</u>* composed sad songs.
2. *The <u>grass</u> in our yard* has grown two inches.
3. <u>*She*</u> fought hard and long.

What part of speech is the simple subject in sentences 1 and 2? What part of speech is the simple subject in sentence 3?

The key word (or words) in the complete predicate of a sentence is the verb (sometimes called the **simple predicate**). What is the verb in each model sentence above?

■ The **simple subject** of a sentence is usually a noun or pronoun.

■ The **simple predicate** is always a verb.

(If you would like to practice diagraming, turn to pages 380–404.)

Exercise: The simple subject and verb

In the following sentences, pick out only the simple subjects and verbs and write them on your paper. Underline the simple subject once and the verb twice.

1. Much early literature came from the minstrels and bards.
2. They chanted their tales to the simple melodies of the harp.
3. The bards were highly honored in a lord's castle.
4. Chieftains often took bards with them on battle campaigns.
5. The minstrels delighted their audience with songs about kings and heroes and battles.
6. For generations the profession of bard was handed down from father to son.
7. These storytellers often varied a few details of each story.
8. Yet the main ideas in many of the stories had historical truth.
9. The accounts of the ancient heroes were eventually recorded in written form.
10. These long, heroic stories are now called epics, or sagas.

▶ *During the Middle Ages, the period between the 400's and 1400's, the lord of a castle gave protection to the knights, ladies, and peasants of his area. A minstrel and his assistants always had a sympathetic audience in the occupants of the castle.*

130

Sentence Patterns

Prepositional phrases are modifying word groups; they modify words in the same manner as adjectives and adverbs. They add color and meaning to a sentence but do not change its basic pattern.

Prepositional phrases begin with prepositions and end with nouns or pronouns. The symbol **P** represents a preposition.

P Adj. N	in the kitchen
P N^P	for me
P Adj. Adj. N P N	near those peaceful lakes in Toronto

PATTERN 1: N V

  Adj.   N   V   **Adj.   N   P Adj.   N   V**
The cries stopped.   The cries of the baby stopped.

PATTERN 2: N V N

  N   V   N   **N   V   N P N^P**
Josie made soup.   Josie made soup for us.

PATTERN 3: N LV N

  Adj.   N   LV Adj.   N
The man was a salesman.

  Adj.   N P Adj.   N   LV Adj.   N   P   N
The man on the phone was a salesman from town.

PATTERN 4: N LV Adj.

  Adj.   N   LV   Adj.   **Adj.   N   P Adj.   N   LV Adv.   Adj.**
The stairs are steep.   The stairs to the cellar are too steep.

● Write interesting sentences, following the symbols below. After each sentence, write *Pattern 1, 2, 3,* or *4*.

    1. Adj. N P Adj. N LV Adj.
    2. N^P LV Adj. N P Adj. N
    3. Adj. Adj. N V P Adj. N
    4. N V Adj. N P Adj. Adj. N
    5. Adj. N P Adj. Adj. N V Adv.
    6. Adj. N P Adj. N V Adj. Adj. N P Adj. N
    7. N^P V Adj. N P Adj. N P Adj. N
    8. Adj. N P Adj. N P Adj. N LV Adv. Adj.
    9. Adj. Adj. N P Adj. N V^h Adv. V Adj. N P Adj. N
   10. Adj. N P Adj. N P N^P LV N

Transitive and Intransitive Verbs

You have seen that the verb in the predicate can express action or being. Action verbs can be divided into two groups, according to their use in sentences.

When the action of a verb is carried on to a receiver of the action, the verb is a *transitive verb*. When the action is completed in the verb itself, the verb is an *intransitive verb*.

Remember, however, you cannot usually tell whether a verb is transitive or intransitive unless it is used in a sentence.

TRANSITIVE: The wind *blows* the seeds away.
INTRANSITIVE: The wind *blows* from the ocean.

TRANSITIVE: I *am reading* that book.
INTRANSITIVE: I *am reading* rapidly.

Linking verbs, which do not express action, are also considered intransitive verbs.

INTRANSITIVE: He *is* my partner.

■ A **transitive verb** expresses action that is carried to a receiver of the action.

■ An **intransitive verb** does not have a receiver of the action.

Exercises: Transitive and intransitive verbs

1. Tell whether the verbs below are *transitive* or *intransitive*:

   1. Jim drives too fast for a beginner.
   2. He drives a tractor well.
   3. The cows are grazing contentedly.
   4. A collie is running up and down the field.
   5. He herds the sheep toward the farmer.
   6. We watched them for ten minutes.
   7. Jay sat on the white picket fence.
   8. That dog is an intelligent animal.
   9. The farmer also raises thoroughbred horses.
   10. In the stables, we saw a famous race horse.

2. Use these verbs in sentences: *destroy, read, study, break, write, ride.* Label each one as *transitive* or *intransitive*.

Active and passive voice

The **voice** of a verb tells whether the subject of the sentence performs or receives the action of the verb. Examine these sentences:

1. Phil *threw* the ball.

2. The ball *was thrown* by Phil.

In which sentence above is the subject the performer of the action expressed by the verb? In which sentence is the subject the receiver of the action?

In sentence 1, *threw* is in the **active voice.** In sentence 2, *was thrown* is in the **passive voice.** Passive voice verbs always have a form of *be* as an auxiliary, or helping, verb.

ACTIVE VOICE	PASSIVE VOICE
1. Sheila recites poetry.	Poetry was recited by Sheila.
2. I bought the ticket.	The ticket was bought by me.

■ A verb is in the **active voice** when its subject performs the action of the verb, and the action is carried to a word in the predicate.

■ A verb is in the **passive voice** when its subject receives the action expressed by the verb.

■ Only transitive verbs have voice.

Exercises: Active and passive voice

1. Tell whether each verb below is in the active or passive voice:

1. We held a meeting at Robert's house.
2. The meeting was held at Robert's house.
3. Your advice was ignored by Jerry.
4. Jerry ignored your advice.
5. The plans were presented by the committee.
6. The committee presented the plans.

2. Rewrite these sentences, changing the voice of each verb from *active* voice to *passive* or from *passive* voice to *active*:

1. The owner should be warned by someone.
2. Ronald carried two heavy boxes.
3. Mr. Stubbs has painted the hallway.
4. We were frightened by the sirens.
5. The safe can be opened by two people.

Four Types of Sentences

It is helpful to classify sentences according to their functions. What are some of the things you want to do with sentences? You want to make *statements,* you want to ask *questions,* you want to *get people to do things,* and you want to *express strong emotion.* Most English sentences can be classified as performing one of these functions.

Declarative sentences

A **declarative sentence** makes a statement. It ends with a period. For example:

1. Mary stood under the tree.
2. Two children were sitting beside my baby sister.
3. Two guests are here.

The usual order of the subject and predicate in a declarative sentence is: subject first, then predicate. However, sometimes to achieve sentence variety the order of subject and predicate can be reversed.

In the following sentences, notice that the subjects and predicates are in *inverted order*:

Under the tree stood Mary.
Beside my baby sister were sitting two children.
There are two guests here.

Exercises: Inverted order

1. Name the simple subject and verb in each sentence below:

   1. Beside Bill was an earnest-looking salesman.
   2. There was no time for action.
   3. Here comes the milkman.
   4. On the corner stood a policeman.
   5. Into the window crashed the ball.
   6. Over the wall jumped Ned.
   7. There trotted a young colt.
   8. There flashed across the sky a streak of lightning.
   9. Down the stream chugged a noisy motorboat.
   10. By the station there had been built a small house.

2. Some of the sentences below have subjects and predicates in usual order; others, in inverted order. Rewrite each sentence, reversing the order of subject and predicate.

1. Above the glaciers trotted agile goats.
2. Down the highway sped a large bus.
3. A lone man stood among the women.
4. Beyond the horizon glowed the light of a forest fire.
5. The planet Pluto is farthest in distance from the sun.
6. The thin boy slipped into the icy waters.

Interrogative sentences

An interrogative sentence asks a question. It ends with a question mark. For example:

Do boys shout?   Does my sister like olives?

Interrogative sentences are formed mainly by separating the auxiliary verb from the main verb and putting the subject between them or by beginning sentences with the word *how* and the **wh–** words *where, when, who, what,* and *why*:

DECLARATIVE	INTERROGATIVE
John ate the apple.	Did John eat the apple?
Canaries sing.	Do canaries sing?
George was going yesterday.	Was George going yesterday?
John drives to town.	Where does John drive?
That animal has wandered away.	Where has that animal wandered?

Imperative sentences

An imperative sentence makes a request or command. It ends with a period. Here are examples:

Leave the room immediately.   Please shut the door.
Kindly pass the butter.

Notice that these imperative sentences appear to have no subject. We explain this by saying that the subject *you* is *understood*, but not expressed.

(*You*) Leave the room immediately.
(*You*) Please shut the door.

Exclamatory sentences

An exclamatory sentence exclaims—that is, it expresses surprise, excitement, or other strong feeling. It is always followed by an exclamation point. Often an exclamatory sentence is simply a declarative, interrogative, or imperative sentence that expresses strong feeling.

Read each pair of sentences below aloud and show by your voice which kind of sentence it is:

DECLARATIVE: My doughnut sank.
EXCLAMATORY: My doughnut sank!

INTERROGATIVE: Where did you find my watch?
EXCLAMATORY: Where did you find my watch!

IMPERATIVE: Take off your shoes now.
EXCLAMATORY: Take off your shoes now!

There are two special sentence forms which are always exclamatory. These begin with *how* or *what*, but are not questions. Here are examples:

How beautiful she is!   What a brute he is!
How lovely your flowers are!

WRITING NOTE: Most young writers overuse exclamatory sentences. Use exclamation points only when you are sure you need them to express your idea. Never use more than one exclamation point after a word or sentence.

Exercises: The four kinds of sentences

1. For each sentence below, write *declarative* or *interrogative* beside the appropriate numeral on your paper. End punctuation has been omitted so that only the word order will give you your clue.

1. Rotary lawn mowers can be very dangerous
2. Does Richard always leave early
3. Have the canoes returned
4. What happened to Molly's elbow
5. The club members do serve the community well
6. When will you arrive at the station
7. You always leave too early
8. Why is Laura angry today

2. Rewrite each interrogative sentence below so that it will make a statement. Rewrite each declarative sentence so that it asks a question. Be sure to punctuate your sentences correctly.

1. Did the dogs stop chasing the rabbits?
2. The dictionary is his most useful book.
3. Young children love to climb trees. (Use *why*.)
4. Have you seen my little brother today?
5. He is building his house.
6. A rusty nail seriously infected his foot. (Use *what*.)

3. Copy the sentences below and insert end punctuation. Identify each one by writing *declarative, interrogative, imperative,* or *exclamatory* in parentheses. Underline the simple subject once and the verb twice, except in an imperative sentence, where you would underline only the verb.

EXAMPLE: 1. What an unusual collection you have

YOU WRITE: *1. What an unusual collection you have!*
              (exclamatory)

1. Please pass the papers forward
2. Do you ever dream about field mice
3. Did those dogs really climb the tree
4. How dull this movie is
5. What size do you wear
6. At the door stood three strangers
7. Go down the road about two miles
8. Where has the red candy gone
9. The whole building is collapsing on us
10. What a terrible disaster it is
11. Did he forget to enclose the money
12. In that house lives a clergyman
13. Thousands of seeds have blown away
14. How bright the sun is today
15. When did the postman deliver this letter

(You may want to study and practice diagraming the four types of sentences. If so, turn to Chapter 16, "Making Sentence Diagrams," pages 380–404.)

Sentence Patterns

The basic sentence elements in a sentence pattern do not change when the order of subject and predicate is inverted.

PATTERN 1: N V

              N   V   P Adj. N
(USUAL ORDER)   Mark jumped over the fence.

               P Adj. N   V   N
(INVERTED ORDER) Over the fence jumped Mark.

Interrogative sentences are really declarative sentences that have been transformed (changed). Their patterns can be seen easily if they are changed into declarative sentences.

PATTERN 1: N V

Adv. Vh N V
Where did Jay go?

N Vh V Adv.
Jay did go where.

PATTERN 2: N V N

Vh Np Adv. V N
Do you really like turnips?

Np Adv. Vh V N
You really do like turnips.

PATTERN 3: N LV N

LV Adj. N Adj. N
Is this apple a McIntosh?

Adj. N LV Adj. N
This apple is a McIntosh.

PATTERN 4: N LV Adj.

LV Adj. N Adv. Adj.
Is this apple too sour?

Adj. N LV Adv. Adj.
This apple is too sour.

● Write the numerals from 1 to 5 on your paper. Next to each one, write the letter of the group of symbols in Column 2 which matches a sentence from Column 1.

COLUMN 1	COLUMN 2
1. Beside Len stood a soldier.	a. Vh Adj. N LV Adj.
2. Did the boat really sink?	b. P Adj. N V N
3. Can Joe be a scout?	c. P N V Adj. N
4. Did you buy some grapes?	d. Vh Np V Adj. N
5. Do my clothes look neat?	e. Vh Adj. N Adv. V
	f. Vh N V Adj. N
	g. Vh N LV Adj. N
	h. LV Adj. N Adv. Adj.

● Identify each of the five sentences above as *Pattern 1, 2, 3,* or *4.*

● Write two sentences of your own for each group of symbols in Column 2 above.

Compound Subjects and Verbs

The word *compound* comes from the Latin *com–* (together) and *ponere* (to put), and means "put together." Compounding, or putting together, is a common process in any language. In English it is most commonly done by using the words *and*, *but*, and *or*. These three joining words are called **co-ordinating conjunctions.** Other co-ordinating conjunctions are *either . . . or, neither . . . nor, both . . . and.*

Study these example sentences. Each sentence has two or more subjects joined by a conjunction.

1. *John* <u>and</u> *Mary* sat together quietly.
2. My *mother* <u>or</u> my *father* will notice the mess in the kitchen.
3. *Stones, cement,* <u>and</u> hard *work* built this wall.

Verbs can be compounded, also. Examine these sentences:

4. Mike *sputtered* <u>and</u> *mumbled* for an hour after his defeat.
5. My mother *looks* severe <u>but</u> *acts* friendly.
6. George *bought* a basket, *filled* it with cookies, <u>and</u> *gave* it to me.

■ A **compound subject** consists of two or more subjects joined by a co-ordinating conjunction.

▢ A **compound verb** consists of two or more verbs joined by a co-ordinating conjunction.

(You may want to study and practice diagraming. If so, turn to Chapter 16, "Making Sentence Diagrams," pages 380–404.)

Exercises: Compound subjects and verbs

1. Find the compound subjects and compound verbs in the sentences listed below. Write them after the appropriate numeral on your paper. Do not include modifying words. Underline the conjunctions.

EXAMPLE: 1. That dog and this cat are friends.
YOU WRITE: *1. dog <u>and</u> cat*

1. Jack and Jill went up the hill.
2. Rivers, lakes, or seas may flood the land.

3. This reservoir traps and holds great amounts of water.
4. Meat and potatoes are the basis of a square meal.
5. The cyclone destroyed property, wiped out homes, and even damaged the rich topsoil.
6. John and James entered the school too early.
7. My friends and your friends started the squabble at the party.
8. The plums, pears, or peaches may soon be shipped to market.
9. These glasses hurt my nose and irritate my eyes.
10. John read the lesson but did not know the answer.
11. Neither Susan nor her brother will win any prizes.
12. Schools and colleges must raise funds or fail.
13. The raft floated downstream for a while and then turned toward the bank.
14. An albatross and a few gulls circled and soared around the schooner.

2. Write original sentences according to the following directions. Underline all subjects once and all verbs twice.

1. Use a compound subject.
2. Use a compound verb.
3. Use a compound subject and a compound verb.
4. Use a compound subject with the conjunction *either . . . or*.
5. Use a compound subject with the conjunction *both . . . and*.

Revising your writing

If you have written a passage with too many short sentences in it, you may want to revise it by combining some of them into longer sentences. There is nothing wrong with short sentences, of course, but it is not good writing to have too many of them strung one after the other. It is better to vary the length of sentences.

Two ways of rewriting short sentences are illustrated below:

1. FIRST DRAFT: The cows are fed at five o'clock. So are the horses.
   REVISED DRAFT: The cows and horses are fed at five o'clock.

2. FIRST DRAFT: John Mark crept into the kitchen. He saw two mice in the cookie jar.
   REVISED DRAFT: John Mark crept into the kitchen and saw two mice in the cookie jar.

Exercise: Revising sentences

Revise the following pairs of sentences into single sentences according to the directions in parentheses:

1. Herbert was about to go through the turnstile toward the waiting subway train. So was his little brother. (Use a compound subject.)
2. Joe thought he had put a token in the slot. He pushed against the stile. (Use a compound verb.)
3. Just then Joe heard the tinkle of a token on the floor. His brother heard it, too. (Use a compound subject.)
4. The stile stiffly resisted Joe's efforts. It wouldn't turn. (Use a compound verb.)
5. Joe's brother was shoving him from behind. He was also looking around in embarrassment as the angry people lined up behind him. (Use a compound verb.)

Making Subject and Verb Agree

The subject and verb in a sentence must fit together grammatically. That is, if you have a plural subject, you must use the plural form of the verb; if you have a singular subject, you must use the singular form of the verb. We call this **agreement in number.**

It is interesting to see how important the letter *s* is in agreement of subject and verb. What happens to the *s* in the sentences below?

SINGULAR	PLURAL
The boy fights.	The boys fight.
The horse stumbles.	The horses stumble.
A servant follows the king.	Servants of the court follow the king.

Do not let a prepositional phrase which comes between the subject and the verb confuse you. The verb must agree with the subject of the sentence. Which example above has a prepositional phrase between the subject and the verb?

Have, be, and do

The common verbs *have, be,* and *do* cause more than their share of trouble in the matter of subject and verb agreement, especially when used with compound subjects. Study the examples below:

SINGULAR	PLURAL
The horse or the mule is for sale.	The horses and the mules are for sale.
Either Walter or Jess has sent the note.	Walter and Jess have arrived.
Ed or Al does good work.	Ed and Al do good work.

When is the singular form of a verb used with a compound subject? When is the plural form used with a compound subject?

Now study the subject and verb agreement in these sentences:

Either the pig or the chickens are eating the food in the trough.
Either the chickens or the pig is eating the food in the trough.

A compound subject joined by the conjunctions *or, either . . . or, neither . . . nor* is singular when each of its parts is singular. When a compound subject contains a singular part and a plural part

143

which are joined by these conjunctions, the verb must agree with the part that is nearer the verb.

Collective nouns

You can tell if most nouns are singular or plural and choose your verb form accordingly. However, there are certain singular nouns that name a group, for example:

committee	jury	flock	club
group	class	family	herd

These nouns are called **collective nouns.** They can be used in a singular sense or in a plural sense.

SINGULAR: The jury has given its verdict.

PLURAL: The jury are arguing about the case.

SINGULAR: The committee has made its report.

PLURAL: A committee of five are discussing the program.

Notice that a singular verb is used when the collective noun acts as a unit. A plural verb is used when there is individual action.

Collective nouns have plural forms as well: *jury–juries, class–classes.* Their plural forms, of course, are always used with plural verb forms.

Exercises: Subject and verb agreement

1. Choose the correct form of the verbs in parentheses in the following sentences:

1. Our parents and grandparents (is, are) away.
2. Both Tom and his cousin (was, were) absent.
3. Either George or Joan (has, have) the instruction sheet.
4. (Hasn't, Haven't) those children and their friends come home yet?
5. Marian and her roommate (hasn't, haven't) seen a movie in over a year.
6. Neither the new buildings nor the store near them (has, have) a glass wall.
7. (Does, Do) the coach and his assistant sit on the bench?
8. (Has, Have) Bob and Barbara seen your work?
9. (Is, Are) Ellen and Jill planning a visit?
10. That boy or his friend from upstate (is, are) in trouble.

2. Write sentences of your own, using the following forms of *have*, *be*, and *do* with compound subjects:

has	was	don't
haven't	were	have
doesn't	hasn't	does

3. Choose the correct form of the verb from each pair in parentheses.

1. The group (has, have) elected a leader.
2. The herd (is, are) scattering in different directions.
3. The family (is, are) packing their suitcases.
4. (Has, Have) the jury disagreed?
5. Janet's family (is, are) the largest one of all.
6. Our club (needs, need) a meeting place.
7. The group of boys (has, have) been talking about their vacations.
8. A flock of birds (was, were) seen this morning.

4. Use these collective nouns in two sentences each, once in the *singular sense* and once in the *plural sense*:

committee	class	company
crowd	audience	team

TO MEMORIZE

Preparedness

For all your days prepare,
   And meet them ever alike:
When you are the anvil, bear—
   When you are the hammer, strike.
                    EDWIN MARKHAM

Edwin Markham lived in America at a time when there arose a widespread concern for the common worker and the burdens he had to bear. What is Markham's advice? Do you think the common worker could be inspired by Markham's suggestion?

The poet's most widely known poem was inspired by Jean François Millet's painting, *The Man with the Hoe*. Try to find a reproduction of Millet's painting and then read Markham's poem.

Avoiding Run-ons and Sentence Fragments

Inexperienced writers commonly make two kinds of sentence errors. They sometimes run sentences together, failing to separate each sentence from the next by a period, question mark, or exclamation point, or they often punctuate a part of a sentence as if it were a complete sentence. The first error is called a **run-on;** the second is called a **sentence fragment.**

Run-ons

For a moment, think over what you know about sentences. In this chapter you read that sentences *sound complete* and that the end of a sentence is commonly indicated by a pause and a drop in the pitch of the voice.

You also reviewed the fact that nearly all sentences have a *subject* and a *predicate*. If you apply this knowledge to your writing, you should be able to avoid run-on sentences. Study these examples:

1. The snow fell rapidly soon the ground was covered.
2. Why are you using that glove, it's mine.

In item 1 above there is no punctuation between two sentences. In item 2, the comma between two sentences is incorrect; end punctuation is needed.

1. The snow fell rapidly. Soon the ground was covered.
2. Why are you using that glove? It's mine.

A good way to detect and correct run-ons in your writing is to *read your paper aloud*, pencil in hand, and *hear* your sentences. As you hear the sentences, be sure you have punctuated them properly.

Exercise: Correcting run-ons

Decide whether or not each passage contains a run-on sentence. If it does, rewrite the sentence correctly. If it doesn't, write *correct* next to the appropriate numeral on your paper.

1. The water skier ran into rough seas and was soon swimming.
2. These snakes are dangerous however, most snakes are quite harmless.
3. Those reckless children climbed far up the tree and got stuck there.

4. In the Guatemalan jungles explorers found great abandoned cities, no one knows the reason for their evacuation by the ancient people.
5. Is Fido your dog he certainly is a handsome creature.
6. The thief slid down the rainspout then he sped away in a black car.

Sentence fragments

Although sentences should sound complete when they are read aloud, many writers do not "hear" what they write and therefore punctuate parts, or fragments, of sentences as though they were complete sentences. Read these examples aloud:

COMPLETE SENTENCE: Mary was in the music room practicing her two songs for the concert.

FRAGMENT: practicing her two songs for the concert

COMPLETE SENTENCE: The play-off game in the intercity basketball league was canceled because half of the players were sick in bed with the flu.

FRAGMENT: because half of the players were sick in bed with the flu

Can you explain why the fragments above are not sentences? Do they sound complete? Which fragment has a subject and predicate and yet does not sound complete?

Exercises: Run-ons and sentence fragments

1. Some items below are complete sentences and others are sentence fragments. Copy each fragment and its numeral on your paper and add words of your own to make complete sentences.

1. After she had enjoyed all the pleasures of the park.
2. Everyone speaks well of him.
3. Speeding straight down the expressway.
4. Because my books are too heavy.
5. If his dog attacks me again.
6. The storm howled outside my window.
7. Hidden just below the surface of the earth.
8. Looking straight down the canyon.
9. They fought everyone on the block.
10. Sewing is a useful skill.

2. Read the following passage carefully. Then, on your paper, copy the passage, correcting all the fragments and run-ons in it.

In England during the time of Shakespeare the practice of numbering houses or shops in the large towns had not begun. Instead, each house or shop displayed a sign. Which jutted out at a right angle. Over the crude roadway below. The sign was usually simple and had a recognizable picture. Such as a fox, a bell, a white stag, or maybe a green dragon a barber's shop was designated by a pole. With red and white spirals winding round it. These signs have a very interesting charm some signs today are still displayed over or beside a few of the inns in England.

✓ Check Test 5: Lay, lie and learn, teach

Take the following test to see whether you use the verbs *lay–lie* and *learn–teach* correctly.

Write each sentence, using the correct word in parentheses.

1. Circus equipment (lay, laid) all over the ground.
2. It did not (lie, lay) there long before the tents were up, and the show had begun.
3. Mike and I (lay, laid) our books on the ground near the show tent.
4. "If we (lie, lay) on our stomachs," Mike suggested, "maybe we could crawl under the tent without being seen."
5. We were almost inside when someone (lay, laid) his hands on our ankles and gave a yank.
6. Dirt flew from the shallow gutters where we had (lain, laid).
7. The hard leather toe of a man's boot (lay, laid) before our eyes.
8. We had (taught, learned) enough about policemen to know that the man was not in costume.
9. "That will (teach, learn) you!" he warned.
10. The embarrassment certainly has (taught, learned) us a good lesson.

If you made any mistakes on this test, turn to the Review Handbook, page 449. There you will find review and more practice.

Banner in the Sky
by James Ramsey Ullman
J. B. Lippincott Co.

"In the heart of the Swiss Alps, on the high frontier between earth and sky, stands one of the great mountains of the world. To men generally it is known as the Citadel, but the people of the valley beneath it seldom call it by that name. They call it Rudisberg— Rudi's Mountain. And that is because, in the long-ago year of 1865, there lived in that valley a boy called Rudi Matt. . . ."

For years Rudi had dreamed of challenging the Citadel, but he told no one of his dream. Then, in a fateful encounter on the Blue Glacier, Rudi met the Englishman, Captain Winter, who also believed that the Citadel could be conquered. When you read of Rudi's joining the party to make the great assault on the mountain, you will follow them, foot by foot, by rope, ax, and handhold, upward over rock, ice, and snow to a magnificent and terrifying climax.

About the Author

James Ramsey Ullman is a world traveler and mountaineer. His two sons, Jim, Jr., and Bill, share his love for high places. He was a member of the first American expedition to Mount Everest in 1963. Another book of his you would enjoy is *Down the Colorado with Major Powell*. His most famous adult book is *The White Tower*.

Mastery Tests

Test I

Pick out only the simple subject and the verb from each of these sentences and write them on your paper. Underline the simple subject once and the verb twice.

1. Two small shacks stood near the old spinning mill.
2. That strange noise in the attic lasted three days.
3. He has been working since last Thursday.
4. Thousands of termites are crawling under the roof.
5. Those gray birds in the barnyard have eaten all the feed.

Test II

1. Head two columns across your paper: *Transitive, Intransitive.* List the numerals 1 to 4 down the left of the first column. Find the verbs in the sentences below. Decide whether each verb is *transitive* or *intransitive,* and write the verb in its proper column.

1. Peter painted the garage last Saturday.
2. The smoke rose from the chimney in a black spiral.
3. That man is an astronaut.
4. A new star was discovered by the astronomer.

2. For each verb below, tell whether the verb is in the *active* or *passive* voice by writing *A* or *P* next to the sentence numeral on your paper:

1. Mary and I study algebra together very well.
2. The game was won by the visiting team.
3. The berries were eaten by insects.
4. They sent a reply this morning.

Test III

Copy the following sentences on your paper and insert the correct end punctuation. In parentheses, write *declarative, interrogative, imperative,* or *exclamatory.* Underline each simple subject once and each verb twice.

1. Into the sunset rode our hero on his horse
2. Did the two children behave well for the baby sitter
3. What a resonant voice he has
4. Please march in a single file
5. Where has the messenger gone

Test IV

Find the compound subjects and compound verbs in the sentences below. Write them after the appropriate numerals on your paper. Do not include modifying words. Underline each coordinating conjunction.

1. Yesterday Mike and I worked out on the trampoline in the gym.
2. I try very hard but seldom succeed.
3. First, bake the cake in a moderate oven and then serve it hot with ice cream.
4. The old Sioux and his scout cornered and captured ten of the Cherokees.
5. Wind or rain struck furiously against the fuselage but rocked the air liner just slightly.

Test V

Choose the correct verb from each pair in parentheses. Write it on your paper next to the sentence numeral.

1. His friend and his foe (agree, agrees) on this matter.
2. Neither Washington nor Lincoln (was, were) the author of that speech.
3. A large squad (was, were) out for football.
4. Either the abler students or the teacher (has, have) charge of the planning.
5. (Does, Do) the oak and the maple tree shade the house?

Test VI

On your paper, copy the two passages below correctly. There are fragments and run-ons.

1. The shortstop calmly raised his glove six inches, the line drive neatly smacked into the pocket. Then he turned and looked toward second, with a flick of his arm, he snapped the ball to Jones, and a neat double play was completed.
2. The seventh-graders produced a comedy for the morning assembly it was a phenomenal success. With all the fan mail coming in. The actors were quite proud of themselves, they immediately discussed plans. For a second comedy for next month.

Review and Practice

Exercise I

1. Review "The Two Main Parts of a Sentence" on pages 128–30.

2. Find the simple subject and verb in each of these sentences and write them on your paper. Underline the simple subject once and the verb twice.

1. My friend grew three inches during the summer vacation.
2. A severe blizzard damaged several large trees.
3. The graceful sailboat glided into open ocean.
4. The Indians on the plains menaced the pioneers in the valleys.
5. The chief of the tribe was the strongest Indian on the reservation.

Exercise II

1. Review "Transitive and Intransitive Verbs" on pages 133–34.

2. Write four sentences with four different verbs. Make the verbs in the first two sentences *transitive*, and in the last two sentences, *intransitive*.

3. Write two sentences with verbs in the *active voice* and two with verbs in the *passive voice*. Draw an arrow from the verb to the word which receives the action.

Exercise III

1. Review "Four Types of Sentences" on pages 135–37.

2. Copy the following sentences on your paper and insert the correct end punctuation. In parentheses, write *declarative, interrogative, imperative,* or *exclamatory*. Underline each simple subject once and each verb twice.

1. Down the long corridor walked the ghost of the castle
2. When will the lecture begin
3. Leave a note for the milkman
4. On the burned scrap of paper was scribbled a message
5. How dark the sky has become

Exercise IV

1. Review "Compound Subjects and Verbs" on pages 140–41.

2. In the sentences below, find and name the compound subjects and verbs:

1. Suddenly the doe spied us and dashed into the woodlands nearby.
2. The quarterback dashed along the outside but fumbled the ball on the ten-yard line.
3. The conductor turned around, stepped from the podium, and took a bow.
4. Every year my old aunt and her friend plow the garden and plant all sorts of vegetables.
5. Our mayor and several councilmen held an emergency meeting last week and discussed sites for the new school.

Exercise V

1. Review "Making Subject and Verb Agree" on pages 143–44.

2. Choose the correct verb from each pair in parentheses.

1. Neither Margaret nor Florence (have, has) any energy left.
2. (Was, Were) Grace and Alice shopping together?
3. Neither the bears nor the trainer (likes, like) a silent audience after an act.
4. (Doesn't, Don't) Donald and Max want a vegetable garden this year?
5. Our family (is, are) always at home for Thanksgiving.

Exercise VI

1. Review "The Sound of a Sentence" on page 127 and "Avoiding Run-ons and Sentence Fragments" on pages 146–47.

2. Decide which word groups below are sentences, and list their numerals on your paper:

1. Operating his electric train in the damp cellar.
2. A book about prehistoric creatures.
3. Oscar won't believe his cousin's story.
4. Drinking apple juice and eating pretzels.
5. This dog of mine does not like people.
6. There beside the grazing cow.

7. One useful classroom tool is the textbook.
8. Between the two performers stood the announcer.
9. A letter from his friend in Pittsburgh.
10. He just plowed the field.
11. That fierce-looking dog behind the fence.
12. Over the river and through the trees in the forest.
13. A low growl of a mother lion was heard.
14. A sizzling hamburger makes an excellent snack after school.
15. The boys feel that way, too.

3. Copy the passages below correctly:

1. The sky is brilliantly blue today tomorrow it will probably be filled with smog.
2. Has the bell rung yet, we must be in class promptly.
3. The absent-minded professor left his car on the ferry for the night, he discovered his loss the next morning.
4. There was John. Sitting on the porch. He had never sat still so long before. His mother was a little worried. Because he was always rushing about. And making noise.
5. There will be a concert tonight. In the large auditorium. A hundred musicians will participate, a few singing groups will also appear. Do you know where we can buy tickets, there are two of us. Who want to attend.

CHAPTER 6

Enriching Your Vocabulary

Some people learn and use unusual words for the pure pleasure of it. Such a one is Noel Perrin, who began an article in *The New Yorker* in this way:

It is well known that when three or four beasts (or birds) of the same kind are gathered together, a special name applies to the group. A flock of geese in a barnyard is a gaggle, and a flight of wild geese in the sky is a skein. Everyone knows that. Even old ladies like my Great-aunt Alexandra know this sort of thing, as I once discovered to my cost.

"That's a fine clowder of cats you have, Aunt Alex," I told the old dowager one day when I was bringing her some peanut brittle from my mother.

She gazed fondly down at the five sleek tabbies with whom, at that time, she shared her apartment. "Ah," she said musingly. "It seems only yesterday that they were a kindle of kittens."

"If you let them get any fatter," I retorted, nettled, "they'll look like a pride of lions."

"You'll be calling them a pod of whales next," she snapped.

I could think of no better answer than retreat. As quietly as if I were in training to join a sloth of bears, I crept out the door and went on home. . . .

You will probably never have any practical use for the words *gaggle* or *clowder*, unless you want to try them out on somebody for the fun of it. However, there are practical reasons for developing a rich vocabulary. It enables you to communicate better with the world, both in speaking and writing, to understand the ideas and feelings of others, and to convey your feelings and ideas to them.

Learning New Words from Experiences

There is no quick road to a rich vocabulary. Chances are you cannot remember where, when, or how you learned most of the words you know. Can you tell, for example, how you first learned the words *tree, giggle,* and *brave?* Perhaps, when you were two and a half, someone pointed to a tree and said, "Tree!" and you learned it. Perhaps you and a friend were laughing in a silly way and your mother said, "Stop that giggling!" and thus you learned *giggle.* Perhaps you did something courageous and your father said, "You are a brave child!" You never looked up any of these words in the dictionary, yet you know what they mean.

You can see that, no matter what you do, your vocabulary will increase gradually, simply by the experience of living. You can help to speed its growth, however, by having experiences that expose you to words. For instance, a visit to a ship may expose you to—and, if you are alert, may teach you—such words as *binnacle, bridge, forecastle, hawser,* and *starboard.* If you watch soccer games, you may learn *goalkeeper, center forward, penalty kick, fullback,* and *dribble.*

To discuss

Discuss experiences you have had which have exposed you to special vocabularies, and give examples of words from each.

If you cannot think of such an experience, think of something at which you are an expert, a hobby or sport, for example, and give five to ten words from its special vocabulary. Remember that a word may be very familiar to you (as *touchdown* is familiar to a person who knows football) and be quite new to a person who does not know the subject about which you are talking.

Exercise: Special vocabularies

Think back over any unusual experiences you have had in the past year during which you were exposed to new words. Name the experience and list from five to ten new words you learned from it, with the definition of each. Include new meanings of familiar words, as, for example, the word *hold,* in relation to the *hold* of a ship. Use a dictionary to check or improve your definitions. Before you do the exercise, study the example at the top of page 159.

bridle: leather headgear, used to guide the horse

stirrup: metal or wooden ring with a flat base attached to saddle in order to hold the rider's foot

bit: part of the bridle which is put in horse's mouth and used for controlling the horse

mane: long hair growing out of the top of a horse's neck

fetlock: tuft of hair above hoof on back of horse's leg

halter: strap for leading a horse

GOING AHEAD

Join a committee to choose the most interesting vocabulary papers written for the exercise above. Make sure the definitions are clear and correct. Then arrange them in a bulletin-board exhibit.

Learning New Words from Context

Reading widely and being alert to new words is an excellent way to increase your vocabulary. This method is called **getting the meaning from context**. The context of a word is the part of a sentence or passage which precedes or follows it closely enough to give the reader a clue to its meaning. For example, in Mark Twain's *Tom Sawyer*, you read:

1. She [Aunt Polly] began to try all manner of remedies on him. She was one of those people who are *infatuated* with patent medicines and all new-fangled methods of producing health or mending it.

2. So he [Tom] thought over various plans for relief and finally hit upon that of *professing* to be fond of Pain-Killer. He asked for it so often that he became a nuisance. . . .

3. Peter [the cat] sprang a couple of yards in the air, and then delivered a war whoop and set off round and round the room, banging against furniture, upsetting flowerpots, and making general *havoc*.

To discuss

Study the passages from *Tom Sawyer* above. What are the meanings of *infatuate, profess,* and *havoc*? How did the context help you to guess the meaning of each word?

Reading and hearing words in context is the way you have learned most of your vocabulary, even though you may never have been conscious of it. If you become conscious of how to get meaning through context, you can *accelerate* your rate of learning new words. Can you guess the meaning of the word *accelerate* from the context of the previous statement?

Exercises: Getting word meanings from context

1. Guess the meaning of each italicized word below from its context. On your paper, write each word and its meaning. Be prepared to explain orally how the context enabled you to determine the meanings. Discuss your results in class. In case of doubt or disagreement, use a dictionary to check.

1. Dr. Cripps was as *versatile* as a one-man orchestra.
2. The stray cur chewed on the old leather boot in vain; he found it *inedible.*
3. The interest charged by that finance company was so high that the judge said it was a perfect example of *usury.*
4. This ingenious *contraption* used by some fishermen is supposed to help them locate fish in the ocean.
5. The thief *skulked* in a shadowy alley, waiting until dusk to make his escape.
6. The dresser drawer was so *warped* that we couldn't slide it open to see what was in it.
7. It took three hours for the clean-up committee to collect the *debris* that was scattered all over the picnic ground.
8. The Van Dusen–Porter *nuptials* were more splendid than any other marriage in town since my grandmother's.
9. After agreeing to pay me thirty-five cents a week, he suddenly *repudiated* the agreement and paid nothing.
10. The threatening black clouds and the sudden gusts of wind that *buffeted* their canoe made the boys realize that their situation was *ominous.*

2. For the next three or four days, keep a list of words and definitions which you have learned through context in your reading for school and for pleasure. Before you hand in your paper, check each of your definitions with a dictionary to see whether your guess from context is correct. Tell where you first saw the word.

Using the Dictionary

The American statesman Benjamin Franklin was an ambitious and practical man, full of good advice. In 1760 he suggested to Mary Stevenson, a young girl who was studying French, that she read books (he sent her some with his letter) with "a good dictionary at hand, to consult immediately when you meet a word you do not comprehend the precise meaning of."

Perhaps you will find it too "troublesome and interrupting," as Franklin admitted Mary would find it at first, "to be constantly leaving the book and going to the dictionary, but this is a method that will quickly teach you many words."

Certainly a good dictionary is the single most important tool you have for building your vocabulary. Develop the habit of using it when you come across a word that you do not know and cannot possibly guess from context.

Exercise: Using the dictionary

Each of the italicized words in the following sentences has one or more common meanings which you know. However, the context of each word reveals that the common meaning does not fit. In the dictionary, find the meaning of the word that does fit, and write it on your paper.

EXAMPLE: 1. When my sister *snubbed* her horse, she fell forward.

YOU WRITE: *1. snubbed: checked or stopped suddenly*

1. Before the wave *combed,* the surf rider saw the floating log.
2. The child was able to *command* three tricycles and two express wagons for the fair.
3. That old lady was *committed* to the hospital yesterday.
4. George *improved* his evenings by reading good books.
5. The sky *lowered,* and we ran for shelter.
6. That was my *maiden* trip into those hills I came to know so well.
7. My *persuasion* is not the same as yours, although I attend the same church.
8. Although the man's face was familiar, I could not *place* him.

161

Vocabulary notebook

You should be aware of new words wherever you come across them. In newspapers, magazines, and books you will find many. You will also hear new words on the radio, on television, in classes, and in meetings you attend. If you list these new words in an alphabetized vocabulary notebook, reviewing and using them frequently, they will become a part of your vocabulary. Study this sample page of a vocabulary notebook:

> *riven*: torn or split apart (I read
> it in *The Daily Courier*.)
> The local Democrats are riven
> by financial disputes.
> *renege*: fail to keep a promise (I heard
> a speaker say that some
> countries had reneged when it
> came to paying war debts.)
> My brother promised to help me
> mow the lawn, but he reneged
> at the last moment.

Exercise: Starting your vocabulary notebook

Transfer the words you listed for the exercise on page 161 into your vocabulary notebook. Continue adding to this list. Note new words or new meanings for familiar words that you come across in your listening and reading. After each word, write its definition and tell where you found it. Then use the word in a sentence of your own.

Guides for remembering words

1. When you come across a new word, look it up in the dictionary.
2. Enter the word in an alphabetized vocabulary notebook. Follow the word with a definition.
3. Use the word in the next day or two.
4. Once a month, review the words and definitions in your vocabulary notebook.

Studying Prefixes, Roots, and Suffixes

You have read that many words came into English through French, and that French is derived from Latin. Latin, in turn, was derived from Greek. When you look up words in the dictionary, you will often find that parts of these words come almost unchanged from Greek or Latin. It is especially useful, as a method of vocabulary enrichment, to learn the meanings of some of the most common word parts.

Prefixes

Do you remember what the term *prefix* means? It derives from the Latin *prae-*, meaning "before," and *figere*, meaning "to fix." Here are some common prefixes from Latin and Greek which will give you the keys to the meanings of many English words:

PREFIX	MEANING	EXAMPLE
ab–	*away*	*ab*duct
ad–	*to, toward*	*ad*vance
anti–	*against, not*	*anti*trust, *anti*social
bi–	*two, twice*	*bi*cycle, *bi*yearly
co–, com–	*with, together*	*co*exist, *com*press
dis–	*undoing of or reverse of*	*dis*connect, *dis*content
ex–	*out of, formerly*	*ex*port, *ex*urbanite
fore–	*before*	*fore*ground
im–, in–	*into, not*	*im*press, *im*perfect, *in*active, *in*sight
inter–	*together, between*	*inter*mingle, *inter*fere
intra–	*within*	*intra*mural
mis–	*bad, wrong*	*mis*fortune, *mis*count
non–	*not*	*non*resident
post–	*after*	*post*script
pre– } pro– }	*before*	{ *pre*view { *pro*logue
re–	*back, again*	*re*cede, *re*adjust
semi–	*half*	*semi*circle
sub–	*under, below*	*sub*way
super–	*above*	*super*structure
trans–	*across*	*trans*oceanic
un–	*not*	*un*happy

To discuss

1. In class discussion, see how many words you can write on the board that can be made with the prefixes listed on page 163. Be sure you know the meaning of each word. Have two or three expert dictionary users look up each word that is listed.

2. For each prefix, turn to your dictionary and find one or two words that were not thought of in class.

Word roots

A **word root** is a word or part of a word from which a number of other words grew. Such a root is *fin*, which is part of the Latin words *finis* ("end" or "limit") and *finere* ("finish"). Out of this root grew English words such as:

finite	definite	indefinite	confine
infinite	finish	define	final

Here are a few quite common roots from parts of Latin and Greek words. A knowledge of these roots will help you to make intelligent guesses about the meanings of many words.

WORD ROOT	MEANING	EXAMPLE
act	*act*	re**act**ion
auto	*self*	**auto**biography
cide	*killer, killing*	insecti**cide**
cise	*cut*	con**cise**
geo	*earth*	**geo**centric
graph	*write*	tele**graph**
logy	*study, science*	zoo**logy**
man	*hand*	**man**ipulate
meter	*measure*	speedo**meter**
ped	*foot*	**ped**al
phobia	*fear*	claustro**phobia**
phone	*sound*	tele**phone**
port	*carry*	trans**port**
script	*write*	in**script**ion
spec	*look*	**spec**tator
thermo	*heat*	**thermo**stat
vis	*face, see*	**vis**age, **vis**ual
voc	*voice, call*	**voc**alist, **voc**ation

To discuss

In class discussion, see how many words you can list which use the roots listed on page 164. Check with a collegiate or unabridged dictionary to be sure your guesses are correct. Give the meaning of the root and of each word listed.

Exercise: Building words

See how many combinations of the roots and prefixes listed in the text on pages 163–64 you can make which will result in good English words.

SPELLING NOTE: When a prefix is added to a word root, the spelling of the beginning of the word root does not change.

EXAMPLES:

1. *in*   + *spec* = inspect
2. *trans* + *act*   = transact
3. *ex*   + *port* = export

Suffixes

A suffix is similar to a prefix except that it belongs at the end of a word or word root instead of at the beginning. It derives from the Latin *sub*, which means "underneath"—that is, *below* or *after* the root.

Suffixes are joined to the end of a word to change its meaning. Here are some common suffixes and their meanings:

SUFFIX	MEANING	EXAMPLE
–ant		serv*ant*
–ent		presid*ent*
–er	*one who*	join*er*
–ist		humor*ist*
–or		act*or*
–eer	*one who deals in or is concerned with*	auction*eer*, election*eer*
–ful	*full of, characterized by*	cup*ful*, spite*ful*
–ize	*to cause to become; to make into; to subject to the action of*	standard*ize*, American*ize*, critic*ize*
–less	*without*	hope*less*
–ward	*toward*	back*ward*

SUFFIX	MEANING	EXAMPLE
–ance		annoy*ance*
–ence		insist*ence*
–hood		child*hood*
–ism	*state of being, condi-*	skeptic*ism*
–ness	*tion of*	rude*ness*
–sion		ten*sion*
–tion		prepara*tion*, connec*tion*
–tude		quie*tude*
–ic	*having the nature or*	com*ic*
–ish	*quality of*	baby*ish*
–like		child*like*

To discuss

In class discussion, see how many words you can list on the board that end with the suffixes listed above and on page 165.

Exercise: Using suffixes

Choose ten of the words listed on the board and use each one in a sentence. Underline the suffix in each word you use.

TO MEMORIZE

FROM *Prayer*

From compromise and things half done
Keep me with stern and stubborn pride;
And when at last the fight is won,
God, keep me still unsatisfied.

LOUIS UNTERMEYER

Besides editing and collecting poems for anthologies, Louis Untermeyer has written many poems himself. Above is an excerpt that casts a little light on the philosophy of this American poet. In this passage he prays that his "stern and stubborn pride" will keep him from compromising or finishing things only halfway. Furthermore, when he has been victorious, he prays that he will not relax in victory but continue to accomplish even more out of a feeling of dissatisfaction with previous success. Do you agree or disagree with the poet's philosophy? Why? Do you think that his philosophy is typical of most Americans?

Words Convey Feelings

The meaning of a word can change greatly, depending on the circumstances in which it is used. For example, the word *plump* is favorable when applied to a roasting chicken and not so favorable when applied to a girl on a diet for reducing. If you call Fido a dog, no one will mind, but if you call your brother a dog, he will probably object strongly. The riches of your vocabulary can be better used if you are aware of the feelings that some words can suggest in certain circumstances. The feeling of a word must be considered a part of its meaning.

Exercises: Words convey feelings

1. Here are ten sentences, each containing an italicized word. Beside the appropriate numeral on your paper, write *favorable* or *unfavorable*, depending upon which feeling you think each word conveys as it is used in the sentence.

1. "Stop being a *baby*," said Mrs. Nix to her thirteen-year-old son.
2. A lovely *baby* was born to the Larsons yesterday.
3. That's no home; it's just a *house*.
4. Their *house* was the center of much pleasant activity.
5. That *speech* made a fine impression on us all.
6. Must you make a *speech* every time you open your mouth?
7. She's too *intelligent* and acts as if she knows it all.
8. The *intelligent* collie went right to the spot where the ball was hidden.
9. The chairman *read* his speech instead of speaking it.
10. Our counselor *read* to us from a Sherlock Holmes mystery.

2. Choose five of the words listed below. Use each word in two sentences. In the first sentence, use the word so that it will have a pleasant meaning. In the second sentence, let the word convey an unpleasant meaning. Compare and discuss some of your sentences in class.

1. big	4. status	7. funny
2. horse	5. clever	8. warm
3. argument	6. steep	9. smooth

Most young people today are interested in slang, as young people probably have been since language began. Slang is a part of the vocabulary of English, but slang words usually stay in the language temporarily. They are never used in standard, formal English. Of course, there are hundreds of words that have both a slang meaning and a standard meaning. The word *pad* is an example. Its slang meaning is "the place in which one lives."

● Can you write one standard definition and one slang definition for each of these words?

> 1. cool   2. cream   3. joint   4. panic   5. creep

● How many other words can you think of that have both slang and standard meanings? Write some of them down, giving both definitions, labeling them *slang* or *standard*, and using each word in two sentences, one for each meaning.

Check Test 6: Punctuation

Take this test to see how well you remember the rules for punctuation.

Write the following sentences, using correct punctuation marks where they are needed:

1. My brother was rather disappointed with the old jalopys appearance but he was determined to make it a showpiece.
2. He remembered some hints he had read in a story called The Tin Lizzie Gleams Again.
3. Rick Oslow Mike Stammer and Ned Lincoln pitched in and helped him.
4. This jalopy is going to look like new Rick said.
5. For twenty one days they hammered dents out of the fenders painted the car and added chrome gadgets.
6. Today at 4 30 P M they finally finished.
7. Wow exclaimed Mike as they drove down the street Everybodys looking at us.
8. A newspaper photographer took a picture and put it on the front page of the Village Times.

If you made any mistakes, turn to the Review Handbook, pages 424–30. There you will find punctuation rules and practice.

Choosing the Right Word

One of the advantages of having a rich vocabulary is that you will be able to choose from a large store of words or meanings to convey your ideas appropriately. However, you must learn to use good judgment in your choice of words.

Plain or fancy words?

Some pupils mistakenly think that using long, fancy words at all times is the sign of a good speaker or writer. Generally, however, plain words are preferable to long, fancy ones. For example, in class or on the public platform, there is no virtue in using long words just for the sake of using them. It would certainly be better to ask your teacher, "Please, may I speak now?" than to ask, "Will you kindly permit me to engage in oral communication at this time?" Unless you are trying to be funny, a speaker is better introduced by saying, "I am glad to present Dr. Humphreys, who is well known to all of us for his work on teen-age problems," than, "It affords me inestimable gratification to make a presentation of Dr. Humphreys, of whose celebrated reputation for investigations into the sphere of ephebic preoccupations we are all appreciatively cognizant."

It is poor taste to use your vocabulary in such a long-winded and tiresome fashion. Of course, these examples are greatly exaggerated. But the point is: in general, say things plainly. Use longer words only when they suit the occasion and sound natural.

Exercise: Rewriting sentences

Read the following exaggerated examples of wordy statements. Rewrite them in plain but suitable English. Get rid of the wordiness and the foolishly fancy vocabulary.

1. *From a note to a school principal:*
   We should be gratified if you would bestow upon us permission to depart from this educational institution thirty minutes in advance of the customary hour of dismissal.
2. *From a school report on a film:*
   The motion picture I was privileged to witness continued for too lengthy a duration, but the terpsichorean activities were admirable.

3. *From a theme on "What I Want to Be":*

I cherish the ambition of becoming a nurse because of the following considerations: As a nurse I would have unparalleled opportunities to assist in the art of healing; as a nurse I would receive ample pecuniary rewards; and as a nurse I might have the opportunity to establish a nuptial tie with a practitioner of medicine.

The precise word

While you do not want to use fancy language for its own sake, you do want to choose words that will convey precisely and economically the idea you have in mind. For example, the plainest, clearest way to say, "He kept putting off until a later time what he should have done at once," is to write, "He procrastinated." *Procrastinate* is a long word, but here it says precisely what is meant, and it takes the place of fourteen words.

If you want to say that a person held first one opinion and then another and had great difficulty in making up his mind, you could do it neatly in two words by writing, "He vacillated."

Exercise: Rewriting sentences

Here are ten rather wordy statements. Replace all of the italicized words in each sentence with the one verb from the list below which expresses the meaning precisely and concisely. In most cases you will need to change the tense of the verb. You may use the dictionary to check the meaning of any unfamiliar word.

EXAMPLE: 1. The policeman *pulled* the club from the thief *by violent twisting.*

YOU WRITE: *1. The policeman wrested the club from the thief.*

wrest	bewilder	buttress
warble	diminish	yearn
puncture	saturate	deflate
articulate	exasperate	dissect

1. At nightfall the shouting in the park *grew less and less.*
2. Betty and Jean's constant bickering *caused* us *much irritation and annoyance.*

3. The cowboy *had a strong, restless longing* for another chance to prove his riding skill.
4. In the science laboratory two older students carefully *cut open and examined* the dogfish.
5. I *let the air out of* my tire and then repaired the leak.
6. The workmen used boulders to *build a support to hold up* the wall.
7. With a hose they *completely filled* the sod *with water*.
8. The complicated arguments of the lawyer *put* the jury *into a state of confusion*.
9. He *said* each word *carefully and distinctly* so that those in the back of the hall could hear.
10. The little wrens *sing* all day *with little trills and small melodies*.

Synonyms

Synonyms are words that have similar meanings, as the words *noise* and *din*, for example. However, there is usually a shade of difference in meaning. For instance, *din* suggests that the sound was long-lasting, confused, and probably unpleasant. *Noise* is a more general word.

A rich vocabulary will enable you to choose from a number of synonyms the right word to express your exact thought. For example, here are three sentences, each containing a blank which requires a word meaning "old":

1. The ___?___ furniture in the modern, chrome-plated bar seemed out of place.
2. In school it is our ___?___ custom to sing Christmas carols in the last assembly before the holidays.
3. The archeologist showed the class some ___?___ pieces of pottery he had found in a Pharaoh's tomb.

To discuss

Discuss in class which of these three synonyms best fits each blank in the sentences above: *time-honored, antique, ancient*. Can you explain why? You may need to refer to the dictionary. Do you see how each of the three words expresses a somewhat different idea?

Exercise: Choosing the right word

Read each sentence listed below. Choose from the words in parentheses the one which you think is most suitable. Assume that in every case you are writing seriously, not humorously. In some cases there may be more than one suitable choice, and your answer will be a matter of taste. Be prepared to explain your choices to your classmates.

1. I have known Dr. Wise since my childhood and have always considered him my (pal, acquaintance, chum, friend).
2. Mrs. Wessel, it is late, and I feel I must (hit the hay, sack out, go to bed, seek repose).
3. The (basis, base, bottom, foundation) of the house was crumbling.
4. The air in the decaying old cellar was (wet, damp, aquatic, saturated).
5. My (spouse, husband, man, mate) is taking care of the (children, brats, kids, moppets).
6. A party guest should always (devour, eat, consume, nibble) his meal politely.
7. He quickly (peeked at, pored over, surveyed, glared at) the contents of the library.
8. Admiral Byrd organized a(an) (trip, visit, expedition, tour) to the South Pole.
9. The lad's (puerile, juvenile, boyish, childish) manner pleased the old man.
10. The football captain was the undisputed (boss, leader, director, conductor) of the team.

Words with specific meanings

You can often make your writing and speaking more interesting by using a word with a specific rather than a general meaning. Instead of saying, "Mother served meat for dinner," say, "Mother served corned beef for dinner." It is more interesting to read, "A policeman and a ballet dancer approached me" than, "Two people approached me."

Wherever possible, sharpen your speech and writing by using specific words rather than general ones.

To discuss

In class, practice finding the specific word to describe an action performed by a classmate. For example, let five pupils act out the verb *look*, each in a different way, while someone at the board writes your suggestions of a verb that describes precisely the action performed. (See the picture on the facing page.) NOTE: Suggest only verbs. Do not add adverbs.

Now have five students act out these three verbs, each in five different ways: 1. *walk*   2. *say*   3. *touch*

Exercise: Using words with specific meanings

The italicized words in the following sentences are general words. Rewrite the sentences, making these words more specific.

EXAMPLE: 1. The *man walked* into the *building*.
YOU WRITE: *1. Mr. Stokes dashed into the police station.*

1. *A car went* down *the street*.
2. *Two kinds of dessert* were served after the *meal*.
3. *The women* bought some *clothes* in the *store*.
4. *The boy looked* at *another boy* in anger.
5. *The boys* carrying their instruments *walked* around the *field* once before they began playing the music.
6. *The football player got* the ball and *went a number of yards, making* the winning touchdown.

GOING AHEAD

There are many interesting differences between the English spoken by Americans and that spoken by the British. If you should visit England, you would need to exercise some care in choosing the correct word so as not to be misunderstood. See if you can translate the italicized words in these British sentences into American English:

1. You'd be *daft* to put *petrol* in a *pram*.
2. He opened a *tin* of *biscuits*, pulled down his *braces*, and watched a good *cinema* on the *telly*.
3. The *lift* taking us from the *tube* was smeared with *marge*.
4. I heard on the *wireless* that a *lorry* full of frozen *sweets* had upset while *overtaking* another *lorry*.

Test I

Determine the meaning of each italicized word below by examining the context of the sentence in which it is used. Write the meaning next to the appropriate numeral on your paper.

1. The duchess was so magnificently *arrayed* that even the fashion designers turned their heads to look at her pearl-embroidered gown and ermine coat.
2. The helicopter did not move up or down, back or forth; it just seemed to *hover* over the injured man.
3. Instead of relieving the rash, the drug seemed rather to *aggravate* it.
4. The new student in our science class is so *timorous* she blushes if anyone even says her name.

Test II

1. Number your paper from 1 to 10. Use your knowledge of prefixes to get the meaning of each word below. Write the meaning next to the appropriate numeral.

1. reconstruct	6. compress
2. subnormal	7. postgraduate
3. predetermine	8. interstate
4. bimonthly	9. foretell
5. transatlantic	10. intrastate

2. Copy the following word parts. Add a word root to each one to make the word that has the definition given in parentheses. (The italicized word in each definition gives the meaning of the word root needed to complete the word.)

EXAMPLE: 1. in__?__ (*cut* into)
YOU WRITE: *1. incise*

1. hydro__?__ (*fear* of water)
2. neuro__?__ (*study* of the nervous system)
3. in__?__ible (not able to be *seen*)
4. pesti__?__ (a *killer* of pests)
5. __?__physics (the physics of the *earth*)

3. Copy the suffix in each of the following words. Next to it, write its meaning. Then write the meaning of the entire word.

EXAMPLE: 1. visitor
YOU WRITE: *1. or = one who;*
                 one who visits

1. planner
2. madness
3. penniless
4. earthward
5. tragic

Test III

1. Number your paper from 1 to 5. Next to each numeral, write the letter of the word (*a, b,* or *c*) which best expresses in one word what all the italicized words say.

1. Mahia had developed an *unreasoning and foolish passion* for the orphan. (a) illusion, (b) infatuation, (c) indifference
2. "I never *fail to fulfill a promise!*" he shouted. (a) revert, (b) lie, (c) renege
3. After feeding the white stallion, the stableboy carefully brushed the *tufts of hair that grow above the hoof at the back of the legs.* (a) mane, (b) fetlocks, (c) haunches
4. Science now tells us that the universe may be *limited, measurable, and have a beginning and an end.* (a) infinite, (b) infallible, (c) finite
5. Dr. Clark specializes in *the science that treats of animals with reference to their structure, functions, evolution, and classification.* (a) zoology, (b) archeology, (c) physiology

2. After each italicized word below are six other words. *Two* of the six are synonyms for the italicized word. Copy the italicized word and then write its two synonyms next to it.

1. *procrastinate:* favor, lie, ring, postpone, produce, defer
2. *din:* meal, drill, noise, shade, uproar, darkness
3. *saturate:* mystify, await, soak, fulfill, drench, relax
4. *ominous:* foreboding, friendly, jealous, hungry, sinister, favorable
5. *exasperate:* anger, dissect, soothe, dig, irritate, depart

Review and Practice

Exercise I

1. Review "Learning New Words from Context" on pages 159–60.
2. Write the meaning of the italicized word in each of the following sentences. Guess the meaning from the context of the sentence.

1. With the waves mounting higher, and our boat rapidly filling, we knew we were in a *perilous* situation.
2. The criminal showed no *remorse* for his evil deed, but seemed almost proud of it.
3. Because of her great love for the outdoors, my grandmother is a *fervent* supporter of all laws designed to preserve our national parks.
4. When, after three days, the exploring party had not yet returned, the men back at the base began to feel *apprehensive* about it.

Exercise II

1. Review "Studying Prefixes, Roots, and Suffixes" on pages 163–66.
2. Add a prefix to each of these words. Then write the new word and its meaning.

1. annual
2. scholastic
3. color
4. pilot
5. date
6. national
7. respectful
8. see
9. continental
10. direct

3. Copy the italicized word root in each word below and give its meaning. Then write another word which contains the same root.

EXAMPLE: 1. *port*able

YOU WRITE: *1. port = carry; porter*

1. *voc*abulary
2. *spect*acular
3. in*cise*
4. auto*graph*
5. *manu*ally
6. de*scrip*tion
7. homi*cide*
8. psycho*logy*
9. *meter*ed
10. *vis*ion

4. Write three words which end in a suffix meaning *one who.*

5. Write two words which end in a suffix meaning *one who deals in.*

6. Write four words which end in a suffix meaning *state of being.*

7. Write two words which end in a suffix meaning *having the nature of.*

Exercise III

1. Review "Words Convey Feelings" and "Choosing the Right Word" on pages 167 and 170–73.

2. Number your paper from 1 to 5. Decide whether the italicized word in each sentence below conveys a favorable or an unfavorable feeling. Then write *favorable* or *unfavorable* next to the appropriate numeral.

1. "The *old* customs have all disappeared," Mrs. Jensen lamented.
2. "This is a really *old* table," the antique dealer declared.
3. Oh, that's an *old* joke we've heard many times.
4. This kind of *fragile* party decoration can only be used once.
5. She handled her *fragile* china carefully.

3. Use each of the words listed below in two sentences. In the first sentence, let the word convey a *favorable* feeling. In the second sentence, let the word convey an *unfavorable* feeling.

1. thin   2. child   3. discussion   4. stubborn   5. funny

4. Write two synonyms for each of the following words. Then use each synonym you have written in a sentence that shows the different shade of meaning it has.

1. loud   2. large   3. friend   4. trip

CHAPTER 7

Patterns of Sentences

A pattern is a way of arranging things so as to make a design or to make something orderly. In the picture at the left, the artist has shown some patterns in nature. How many can you see? Can you think of other patterns in nature?

You already know that there are patterns in language, and you have worked with some of them. The idea of patterns is so important that in this chapter you will find a further explanation of the earlier patterns and then go on to one new pattern. There are millions, perhaps billions, of different English sentences. Yet if you examine these sentences carefully, you will discover that they can be grouped into a few different sentence patterns.

Sentence Pattern 1

The sentence patterns below are the patterns of **simple sentences**, which have one subject and one predicate. Either the subject or the predicate (or both) of a simple sentence may be compound. All of the sentences you have studied so far have been simple sentences.

Here are the basic parts of *Sentence Pattern 1*:

Sentence Pattern 1

SUBJECT + VERB
Dogs   bark.
Pupils   study.

The sentences above are skeleton sentences, consisting only of the two basic parts: a simple subject and verb. Although you do not use such sentences very often, they illustrate clearly the first sentence pattern.

The following sentences are similar to the types of sentences you use every day:

The <u>dogs</u> in our alley <u>bark</u> loudly all night.
Some <u>pupils</u> at Central Junior High <u>study</u> for weeks before the final test of the year.

The words added to "dogs bark," and "pupils study" are all modifying words or phrases which enlarge the picture of the subject and verb but do not change the basic sentence pattern. The sentences are still *Pattern 1* sentences. In each sentence, notice that the subject does something.

■ *Sentence Pattern 1* contains a subject and a verb.

Exercises: Sentence Pattern 1

1. Find the simple subject and verb in the sentences below. On your paper, write the skeleton sentences.

EXAMPLE: 1. Those cows in the middle of the road will not move.
YOU WRITE: *1. Cows will move*

1. The team arrived in time for spring training.
2. The new stars on that TV show perform excellently.
3. A new safety light shone brightly on the corner of Shippen Street and Lee Road.
4. Many famous and busy men paint in their spare time.
5. Two large bears were creeping around the rickety shack.
6. The red trucks in the parking lot rolled slowly out to the street.

2. Use the subjects and verbs below to write five *Pattern 1* sentences. Add only modifiers to the subject and verb—adjectives, adverbs, or prepositional phrases.

SUBJECTS	VERBS
1. boys	run
2. jet	soars
3. Indians	live
4. pictures	hang
5. baby	cries

Sentence Pattern 2

Some ideas cannot be expressed with only a subject and verb plus any modifiers as in *Sentence Pattern 1.*

Direct objects

Examine the subjects and verbs below:

1. Bobby found . . .
2. Mark hit . . .

As you read the subjects and verbs above, you probably asked, "Bobby found *whom* or *what*? Mark hit *whom* or *what*?" Another sentence element is needed to complete the idea.

Sentence Pattern 2

SUBJECT	+	ACTION VERB	+	DIRECT OBJECT
Bobby		found		me.
Mark		hit		the baseball.

The action performed by each subject above is carried over to an object. When a word appears after an action verb and receives the action expressed by the verb, as the pronoun *me* and the noun *baseball* do above, it is called a **direct object.**

Notice that the subject performs an action toward something or somebody in a *Pattern 2* sentence. *Remember*: Modifiers do not change the basic pattern of a sentence.

Bobby quickly found me behind the shed in the playground.

Direct objects can be compounded. Since compounded sentence parts do not change the sentence pattern, the following sentence is a *Pattern 2* sentence:

My best friend built a rowboat and a sailboat last summer.

(You may want to study and practice diagraming. If so, turn to Chapter 16, "Making Sentence Diagrams," pages 380–404.)

- A **direct object** is a noun or pronoun that receives the action performed by the subject of a sentence.

- *Sentence Pattern 2* contains a subject, an action verb, and a direct object.

Exercises: Sentence Pattern 2

1. On your paper, write the headings *Subjects*, *Action Verbs*, and *Direct Objects*. Find the skeleton words in each sentence below and write them under the correct headings.

EXAMPLE: 1. The ants in this colony have been cutting leaves all day.

YOU WRITE: *Subjects*   *Action Verbs*   *Direct Objects*
1. *ants*   *have been cutting*   *leaves*

1. The mean goat butted our young friend.
2. The farmer steadily weeded his garden.
3. Our house attracted much attention after the fire.
4. The scouts cooked their hamburgers and frankfurters over a wood fire.
5. The rickety chair barely supported that gigantic man.
6. Those comical monkeys at the zoo ate a bunch of bananas.
7. Clean white snow covered the trees, lawns, and houses.
8. Our beloved Aunt Meg filled the sandbox for the toddlers.
9. Those bad-tempered cats sometimes scratch friendly visitors.
10. That spray killed the mosquitoes and flies instantly.

2. Examine each sentence below and tell whether it follows *Pattern 1* or *Pattern 2*. Name the skeleton words for each.

EXAMPLES: 1. My little sister sat on the terrace all day.
2. Every Saturday Joe mows the lawn.

YOU WRITE: 1. *Pattern 1.*   *sister sat*
2. *Pattern 2.*   *Joe mows lawn*

1. His tomatoes ripened quite fast.
2. That autumn the leaves fell too early.
3. Little Bess still bites her fingernails.
4. Poison ivy grows on all the fenceposts in our county.
5. The two boys are scooping water out of the boat.
6. The thrush sang his song beautifully.
7. A giant balloon sailed gracefully over our heads.
8. George read the lessons in his textbook carefully.
9. Our lawn is growing rapidly.
10. The elderly farmer blamed the weather for his small crop.

3. Write five *Pattern 2* sentences. You may add words which modify some of the skeleton words.

184

Sentence Patterns 3 and 4

The verbs you have just seen in *Pattern 2* sentences are all action verbs. The third and fourth common sentence patterns are always built around linking verbs.

Subject complement

Earlier, you studied the difference between an action verb such as *chased* and linking verbs such as *is, are, was, were, became, seem.*

1. The guard *chased* Glenn.
2. The guard *is* Glenn.
3. The guard *was* handsome.

In the first sentence *Glenn* and *guard* refer to different persons. The verb expresses action that is carried over to a direct object—*Glenn*. Sentence 1 is a *Pattern 2* sentence.

In the second sentence above, the linking verb connects a noun to the subject—a noun that means the same person as the subject.

Glenn in sentence 2 is a **subject complement,** or *predicate noun.*

When a linking verb connects the subject to an adjective that describes the subject, the adjective is also called a subject complement. Another term commonly used is *predicate adjective.*

Name the adjective that describes the subject in sentence 3 above.

Remember: When verbs are used as linking verbs, they do not express action.

Sentence Pattern 3

SUBJECT   +   LINKING VERB   +   SUBJECT COMPLEMENT
(NOUN OR PRONOUN)

Squirrels   were   a menace.

Sentence Pattern 4

SUBJECT   +   LINKING VERB   +   SUBJECT COMPLEMENT (ADJECTIVE)
Alligators   can be   dangerous.

In *Sentence Pattern 4,* notice that, for the first time, there is an adjective which is part of the basic sentence pattern. This is the only pattern you will study in which an adjective is part of the pattern, or skeleton, of the sentence. With this one exception, modifying words do not change the basic pattern.

In the *Pattern 3* and *Pattern 4* sentences on the next page, modifying words have been added to the skeleton words.

Those *squirrels* in the garden *were* really a *menace*.
Some Florida *alligators can be* quite *dangerous*.

(You may want to study and practice diagraming. If so, turn to Chapter 16, "Making Sentence Diagrams," pages 380–404.)

▪ A **subject complement** is a word that appears after a linking verb and refers to the subject or describes the subject.

▪ *Sentence Pattern 3* contains a subject, a linking verb, and a subject complement (noun or pronoun).

▪ *Sentence Pattern 4* contains a subject, a linking verb, and a subject complement (adjective).

Exercises: Sentence Patterns 3 and 4

1. Examine the following sentences. Next to the appropriate numeral on your paper, tell whether each sentence follows *Pattern 3* or *Pattern 4*. Beside each, write the skeleton of the sentence.

1. His brother is a big bully.
2. Janice always looks beautiful.
3. An English notebook is useful during class.
4. That amateur became an expert by the next summer.
5. This cheap perfume smells too sweet.
6. The monster in the show really looked mean.
7. During the rainy season our shoes became soggy.
8. The old witch in the forest was angry with the dwarfs.
9. His famous uncle became a United States senator.
10. This small car is a very common foreign automobile.

2. Write five *Pattern 3* sentences of your own and then five *Pattern 4* sentences. Underline the skeleton words.

3. Write *Pattern 1, 2, 3,* or *4* next to the appropriate sentence numeral on your paper.

1. Malcolm keeps white rats in his garage.
2. You are always complaining about something.
3. That announcement was a surprise.
4. She is ironing the laundry.
5. This lace tablecloth is quite beautiful.
6. He dashed into the hardware store.

FROM *Abraham Lincoln's Second Inaugural Address*

With malice toward none, with charity for all, with firmness in the right as God gives us to see the right, let us strive on to finish the work we are in . . . to do all which may achieve and cherish a just and lasting peace among ourselves and with all nations.

ABRAHAM LINCOLN

This address was delivered by President Lincoln shortly after the close of the War Between the States. He did not live to carry out his resolutions. Do you think they were commendable? From this statement, would you say he was a magnanimous victor?

Sentence Pattern 5

A fifth common sentence pattern is shown by the skeleton sentence: *John gave Susan gifts*. Like **Pattern 2**, it is composed of a subject, a verb, and a direct object, but it has an additional sentence element which distinguishes it from **Pattern 2.**

Indirect object

In a **Pattern 5** sentence, there is a noun (or pronoun) that tells *to whom, for whom, to what,* or *for what* the action of the verb was performed. This noun or pronoun is called an **indirect object.** It appears before the direct object in a sentence.

Here are several examples of **Pattern 5** sentences. The skeleton words are italicized.

Sentence Pattern 5

SUBJECT	+ VERB	+ INDIRECT OBJECT	+ DIRECT OBJECT
1. My *mother*	bought	me	some *apples.*
2. Those *cows*	give	the *farmer*	good *milk.*
3. *He*	sold	John	his old *car.*

It may help you to understand indirect objects to think of them as objects of the preposition *to* or *for*, but that the preposition is not stated in the sentence; it is "understood." Thus the first sentence above might be understood to read: "My mother bought (for) me some apples."

Read sentences 2 and 3 with the preposition *to* or *for* before each indirect object.

An indirect object never appears in a sentence that does not contain a direct object.

(You may want to study and practice diagraming. If so, turn to Chapter 16, "Making Sentence Diagrams," pages 380–404.)

■ An **indirect object** is a noun or pronoun that tells *to whom, for whom, to what,* or *for what* the action of the verb was performed.

■ *Sentence Pattern 5* contains a subject, an action verb, an indirect object, and a direct object.

Exercises: Sentence Pattern 5

1. In each of the five sentences below, write the skeleton sentence and underline the indirect object:

1. The old lady baked him a birthday cake.
2. Those soldiers sent Mary several old coins.
3. Blue skies bring picnickers great joy.
4. She brings Mr. Jones the evening paper.
5. My Model T Ford gives me adequate transportation.

2. Write five *Pattern 5* sentences of your own. In each, underline the skeleton sentence.

✓Check Test 7: Writing dialogue

Take this test to see how well you remember the rules for writing dialogue.

Rewrite the following dialogue, using correct punctuation and capitalization. Begin a new paragraph each time one is necessary.

I can't seem to figure out that problem Malcolm said hesitantly, I've tried and tried what is it anyway asked Sidney oh, during math class today Malcolm explained I was asked to describe the left side of some silly pecan pie Sidney interrupted well, what's so hard about that what's so hard Malcolm exclaimed why, I have considered every mathematical possibility and cannot arrive at a solution that satisfies my keen mathematical mind I have tried explaining it by fractions and even by angles it just cannot be done you've created your own problem, Sidney laughed anyone knows that the left side of a pie is the part that isn't eaten.

If you made any mistakes on this test, turn to the Review Handbook, pages 423, 426, and 430.

Review of Five Sentence Patterns

The following skeleton sentences illustrate the sentence patterns you have just studied:

Pattern 1: Boys play.
Pattern 2: Boys play baseball.
Pattern 3: Boys are players.
Pattern 4: Boys are playful.
Pattern 5: Boys sent us tickets.

What are the basic sentence parts in *Pattern 1*? Which pattern contains an adjective as part of the basic pattern? Which patterns have a direct object? Which pattern has a noun as a subject complement? Which pattern has an indirect object?

Which two sentence parts are included in all five patterns?

Exercise: Sentence patterns

Below are twenty sentences, four of each sentence pattern. Decide which pattern each sentence represents and write its numeral in parentheses after the appropriate sentence numeral on your paper. Then write the skeleton sentence.

1. The men over there are soldiers.
2. My alarm clock rang too early this morning.
3. Sharks can be dangerous to swimmers off tropical beaches.
4. The fast-moving car hit a small child on Penn Street.
5. The soda bottle exploded all over the kitchen floor.
6. The fiercest dog became leader of the pack.
7. My room is always a mess on Saturday morning.
8. Paula bought me a guitar.
9. Her new mattress is too hard for comfort.
10. He gobbled it up completely in less than five seconds.
11. Those fragile peacock feathers tickled my chin.
12. The floor became rougher with constant use.
13. They gave Mom a new apron.
14. Our relatives arrived two days after the end of school.
15. Grape juice tastes delicious on a hot day.
16. Dad will build me a larger kite.
17. We heard a wonderful story the other day.
18. Those cruel-looking men over there are actors.
19. That bright-eyed yellow monkey eats from my hand.
20. Edna told them the final score of the game.

Patterns of Interrogative Sentences

Most of the sentences you have studied can be transformed (changed) into interrogative sentences. For example:

Pattern 1: Dogs bark.   Do dogs bark?
Pattern 2: Joe delivers papers.   Does Joe deliver papers?

In order to see the pattern in interrogative sentences, change them to the declarative form.

Can you tell the patterns of the sentences below?

1. Are those birds sparrows?
2. Did that boy kick the fence?
3. Will you give me the book?
4. Is this mushroom poisonous?

Which sentence above illustrates a *Pattern* 2 sentence? Which one illustrates *Pattern* 3? *Pattern* 4? *Pattern* 5?

Exercises: Patterns of interrogative sentences

1. Identify the pattern of each sentence below:

1. Are those tadpoles very large?
2. Are crows large birds?
3. May we swim in the neighbor's pool?
4. Where did the old lady drop her suitcase?
5. Will Bill teach us that trick?
6. Is a silver dollar a large or small coin?
7. Are his long lectures very interesting?
8. Does corn grow rapidly during the dry season?
9. Did Tracy give you the answer?
10. Was the actress speaking her lines clearly?

2. Here are ten declarative sentences. On your paper, transform each of them into an interrogative sentence. Underline the skeleton sentence and indicate its sentence pattern in parentheses.

EXAMPLES: 1. Mary passed the test.
YOU WRITE: *1. Did Mary pass the test? (2)*

1. Typewriters are extremely useful machines.
2. The rug on our living-room floor is dirty.
3. That small moth ate a hole in my expensive suit.

4. In midsummer the crickets chirp all night long.
5. That foolish boy swam out into deep water.
6. My dog won the race.
7. The job was completely impossible for him.
8. This painting is the *Mona Lisa.*
9. Mother sewed me a costume.
10. Joe gave his brother a job.

Compound Sentences

So far, the sentences you have studied have been simple sentences. Although one or more of the elements in a sentence pattern may be compounded, the sentence remains a simple sentence, as:

The dog ate the steak.
The cat ate the steak.
Both the dog and the cat ate the steak.

All the sentences above are simple sentences that follow *Pattern 2*. However, when two or more complete sentence patterns are compounded, the result is a **compound sentence.**

The farmer plowed his fields. (simple sentence)
His wife worked in the garden. (simple sentence)

    Pattern 2   *Pattern 1*
The farmer plowed his fields, and his wife worked in the garden.
(compound sentence)

When a sentence pattern is part of a compound sentence, it is called an **independent clause.** Independent clauses are joined by co-ordinating conjunctions.

Name the clauses in the compound sentence above. What is the subject and verb in each clause? Which clause contains a direct object?

A compound sentence may contain more than two clauses.

A crash was heard, bells sounded, and Copper barked furiously.

Interrogative sentences can also be compounded:

Are you feeling better, or shall I call the doctor?

An independent clause can stand alone as a simple sentence. Read aloud each clause in the compound sentences above.

Remember: Some common co-ordinating conjunctions are *and, but, or, either . . . or, neither . . . nor, both . . . and*. They join words, phrases, and clauses of equal rank and importance.

(You may want to study and practice diagraming. If so, turn to Chapter 16, "Making Sentence Diagrams," pages 380–404.)

■ A **compound sentence** contains two or more sentence patterns joined by a co-ordinating conjunction.

Exercise: Compound sentences

For each of the sentences below, select the simple subject and verb in each independent clause and the conjunction that joins the clauses. Write them on your paper, as in the example.

EXAMPLE: 1. Sancho Panza warned his master, but the knight would not listen.

YOU WRITE: *1. Sancho Panza warned (but) knight would listen.*

1. Have you read the stories about Don Quixote, or have you ever heard about him?
2. Don Quixote was a hilarious Spanish knight, and Sancho Panza was his equally funny squire.
3. Many of the experiences of the misguided knight were riotous, but the funniest episode was Don Quixote's adventure with the windmills.
4. In Don Quixote's eyes the thirty or forty windmills were giants, their capture was necessary, and he was the man for the job.
5. Don Quixote galloped forward toward the whirling wing, and boldly he thrust his lance into it.
6. Sancho hurried upon his donkey to Don Quixote, but the squire did not understand his master's actions.
7. Either Sancho Panza had poor eyesight, or Don Quixote was just a little insane.
8. Don Quixote stuck to his original belief, but he accused a jealous magician of turning the giants into windmills.

GOING AHEAD

Make a list of the independent clauses in the exercise sentences above. Beside each one, identify its pattern—*Pattern 1, 2, 3, 4,* or *5.*

Punctuating Compound Sentences

Look back at the compound sentences in the exercise on page 192. Notice how they are punctuated: in each, a comma precedes the conjunction.

However, if the two parts of the compound sentence are very short, no comma is needed. Study the examples below:

NO COMMA NEEDED: 1. The water is cold but the air is hot.

COMMA NEEDED: 2. The water in the bay is cold, but the air from the marshes is hot.

NO COMMA NEEDED: 3. Ma was sewing and Pa was whittling.

COMMA NEEDED: 4. Ma was sewing on her old patchwork quilt, and Pa was just whittling idly in his chair.

It may be necessary to insert a comma in order to make the meaning clear, as in this example:

CONFUSING: I invited Paula and Larry objected.

CLEAR: I invited Paula, and Larry objected.

> Use a comma before the co-ordinating conjunction in a compound sentence, unless the sentence is a very short one.

Compound sentences or simple sentences?

The two sentences below are punctuated correctly. Can you explain why one sentence has a comma before the conjunction and the other does not?

1. Our basketball team won four straight games, and the coach was jubilant.
2. Our basketball team won four straight games and then lost the play-off game to a small school from upstate.

Did you see that sentence 1 is a compound sentence? If you remove the modifiers, you will easily see a complete sentence pattern on either side of the conjunction.

team   won   games   (and)   *coach   was   jubilant.*
(subj.) (verb) (dir. obj.)   (subj.) (verb) (subj. comp.)

Now read each independent clause in the example sentence without the conjunction. Each clause can stand alone as a complete sentence.

However, sentence 2 is a simple sentence with a compound verb. If you remove the conjunction from the sentence, you do not have two complete sentences.

team won games (and) *lost game*

Exercises: Punctuating correctly

1. Some of the sentences below are compound sentences and need a comma before the conjunction. Others are simple sentences with a compound verb and need no comma before the conjunction. Copy the compound sentences and punctuate each one correctly.

1. Brad clambered far up the ladder but his sister remained at the bottom.
2. This situation is impossible and we are quite unhappy about it.
3. My sister spends an hour each morning in front of her mirror but is never satisfied with the result.
4. The skies were cloudy but the fishermen left the harbor anyway.
5. The space capsule orbited easily and re-entered the atmosphere as planned.
6. I ride my bicycle every day but my older brother is interested only in cars.

2. In the paragraph below, there are simple sentences and compound sentences. Copy the paragraph correctly on your paper. Use end punctuation, capital letters, and commas where they are needed.

That afternoon my brothers and I spoke in whispers everyone in the house walked on tiptoe and even Brownie lay asleep by the kitchen stove Dad was working on the bills and Mother was sitting beside him at the table all of the bills were spread out in front of Dad but even so he was asking questions about each one suddenly Brownie barked and little Annie cried the silence had been shattered Dad frowned and with resignation pushed his chair away from the table Mother gathered the bills together and we then started a loud boisterous game of cowboys and Indians

3. Write five compound sentences of your own which need a comma before the conjunction.

Improving your writing

In writing a compound sentence, be sure that the clauses have a definite relationship. Compare these sentences:

INCORRECT: Jack won the gold medal, and we arrived before the contest.

CORRECT: Jack won the gold medal, and we celebrated with a party.

It is also necessary to choose the conjunction that will express the correct relationship between the clauses. The conjunction *and* adds one idea to another that is related to it. The conjunction *or* expresses a choice or difference between two ideas; *but* expresses a contrast.

POOR: The show was interesting, and it was too long.

GOOD: The show was interesting, *but* it was too long.

POOR: We must protect the young tree, and the wind will snap it in two.

GOOD: We must protect the young tree, *or* the wind will snap it in two.

Exercises: Improving your writing

1. Combine each pair of sentences to form a compound sentence:

    1. I am writing a story. It is not finished.
    2. He had called me twice. I did not hear him.
    3. We must protect our soil. The waters will wash it into the seas.
    4. That star is bright tonight. Last night it couldn't be seen.
    5. Johnny may drive us to the stadium. We may take a bus.

2. Add a co-ordinating conjunction and an independent clause of your own to each of these sentences to form a compound sentence:

    1. We came to the old swimming hole.
    2. Daniel was waiting for an hour at the corner.
    3. The shortstop caught the ball.
    4. Are you making the costumes?
    5. The stagecoach driver pulled the reins.

3. Bring to class examples of good compound sentences that you find in your reading.

Sentence Patterns in Compound Sentences

Review the symbols you have studied this year. Notice in the list below the addition of the symbol for a co-ordinating conjunction:

N = Noun
N^P = Pronoun
V = Action verb
LV = Linking verb
V^h = Auxiliary (helping) verb

Adj. = Adjective
Adv. = Adverb
P = Preposition
C^c = Co-ordinating conjunction (*and, or, but*)

Co-ordinating conjunctions simply compound various sentence elements; they do not change a sentence pattern. For example, these two sentences follow *Pattern 2*: N V N

N C^c N V N
Burt and Jon make speeches.   (Compound subject)

N V N C^c V Adj. N
Burt makes speeches and gets the votes.   (Compound verb)

In a compound sentence, a co-ordinating conjunction connects two separate sentence patterns:

PATTERN 2   PATTERN 2

N V N C^c N V Adj. N
Burt makes speeches but Jon gets the votes.

● Write the symbols for *Pattern 1, 2, 3,* and *4.*

● Write interesting sentences which follow these groups of symbols. Your sentences will have compound sentence elements.

1. N C^c N V
2. N V N C^c V N
3. N LV Adj. N C^c Adj. N
4. Adj. N LV Adj. C^c Adj.
5. Adj. Adj. N V N C^c N

6. N^P V P Adj. N C^c P Adj. N
7. N V N P Adj. N C^c N
8. Adj. N C^c Adj. N V Adj. N
9. N^P V Adv. C^c Adv.
10. Adj. N V Adj. Adj. C^c Adj. N

● Write compound sentences which follow these groups of symbols. *Remember*: There is a complete sentence pattern on either side of the co-ordinating conjunction.

1. Adj. N V Adj. N C^c N^P V
2. N^P V^h V Adj. N C^c N^P LV Adj.

3. N V^h V Adj. N C^c N V^h V N
4. Adj. N LV Adj. C^c N^P V Adv.

Complex Sentences

You have seen how ideas are expressed in simple sentences and compound sentences. There is yet another type of sentence—one that you use frequently in speech and writing. This is the **complex sentence.** Here are three examples:

1. The puppies were sleeping when the fire broke out.
2. They were not hurt although the flames came close to them.
3. Because the fire damaged our house, we stayed in a hotel for a few days.

Each of the complex sentences above is made up of two clauses. One of the clauses in the sentence is the **main clause** which expresses the main idea of the complex sentence; it is an *independent clause* which can stand alone as a sentence. The other clause is the **subordinate clause,** and this part of the sentence is *dependent* upon the main clause and cannot stand alone.

In the first sentence above, the main clause is: *The puppies were sleeping.* The subordinate clause is: *when the fire broke out.* Both clauses follow *Pattern 1.* Read aloud each main clause and subordinate clause in sentences 2 and 3. Can you name the sentence pattern of each clause?

■ A **complex sentence** has a main clause and one or more subordinate clauses.

Subordinating conjunctions

The word that begins subordinate clauses is a **subordinating conjunction.** If you place one in front of a clause, it can no longer stand alone. It makes the clause subordinate.

PUNCTUATION NOTE: When a subordinating conjunction and its clause introduce a sentence, the clause is separated from the rest of the sentence by a comma. Find an example in this lesson.

A few common subordinating conjunctions are listed below. Familiarize yourself with the list.

SUBORDINATING CONJUNCTIONS

after	if	when
although	since	whenever
as	that	where
as if	though	wherever
because	unless	whether
before	until	while

Subordinating conjunctions enable you to join ideas to each other. They help you to write a variety of sentences and to avoid too many short, choppy sentences. Examine the way in which these two short sentences have been combined by subordinating one sentence to the other:

1. The apple trees did not die.
2. There was a bad drought.

Although there was a bad drought, the apple trees did not die.
(subordinate clause)   (main clause)

Choose your subordinating conjunction carefully to express just the meaning you want. Notice how the meaning of this sentence differs with each change of conjunction:

MAIN CLAUSE   SUBORDINATE CLAUSE

Richard left the party { after / before / while / as / though } refreshments were served.

▪ A **clause** is a group of words containing a sentence pattern.

▪ A **main clause** is a clause that is independent and can stand alone.

▪ A **subordinate clause** is a clause that is dependent upon a main clause and cannot stand alone.

▪ A **subordinating conjunction** is a word used to introduce a subordinate clause.

Exercises: Complex sentences

1. List in the order in which they appear the eight subordinating conjunctions in the following passage. Then read aloud the subordinate clause introduced by each.

Because my little sister is afraid of worms, I never take her fishing. When we were younger, I used to take her often. I never do now, although I enjoy her company. One day she decided to go with me if I would put all the worms on the hook for her. However, whenever she saw a worm, she screamed as if it were crawling down her neck. I had to row right back to shore before we had caught a single fish. Until my sister overcomes her fear, she should not go fishing.

2. Combine each pair of sentences below into a complex sentence by subordinating one sentence to the other. Use a variety of subordinating conjunctions. *Remember*: The subordinate clause may be placed before or after the main clause.

1. The orchestra was playing furiously. We left.
2. I picked up the toys. Father wanted me to.
3. Bob saw the riders. They sped by the church.
4. The hayride ended. The snow had stopped.
5. They have not visited Mildred. She moved far away.
6. The sun comes out. We can go to the beach.
7. He examined the box. He had not seen its contents.
8. Please don't rustle your program. The actors are speaking.
9. We have not seen Grace. She moved to Atlanta.
10. His car rattled down the hill. John put on the brakes.

Adverb clauses

All of the subordinate clauses you have been studying are called **adverb clauses** because each one modifies the verb in the main clause. For example:

1. The baby screamed *as we drove away*.

The subordinate clause *as we drove away* modifies the verb *screamed*. Here are other examples:

2. *When I arrived*, John greeted me.

3. *While the dinner was being served*, my mouth watered.

4. George fled *because he was afraid*.

Do you see how the three subordinate clauses modify a verb just as adverbs do?

(You may want to study and practice diagraming. If so, turn to Chapter 16, "Making Sentence Diagrams," pages 380–404.)

■ A subordinate clause that begins with a subordinating conjunction and modifies a verb is an **adverb clause.**

Exercises: Adverb clauses

1. Copy the adverb clauses from the sentences below and underline the subordinating conjunction in each. In parentheses after each clause, write the verb it modifies.

EXAMPLE: 1. While we ate, the entertainer sang a song.
YOU WRITE: *1. While we ate (sang)*

1. I called you because I need your help.
2. Whenever they eat mushrooms, I worry.
3. He rode the horse as if he had been doing it all his life.
4. While my teacher was out of the room, I sat quietly.
5. Before you lose that money, give it to me, please.
6. The expedition turned back although better weather was predicted.
7. It rained steadily until we reached camp.
8. If you will not help me, I may lose my job.
9. After we had eaten a hearty lunch, Jay and the others went to a movie.
10. Because our train traveled so fast, we arrived hours ahead of schedule.

2. Write five sentences of your own with adverb clauses.

Adjective clauses

So far you have been learning about complex sentences that contain adverb clauses. Now study the following complex sentence:

1. The girl *who waved to you* is the skiing champion.

Here the subordinate clause is introduced by the word *who*. This word is a pronoun whose antecedent is the noun *girl*. It joins or *relates* the subordinate clause to the noun *girl*. Therefore, *who* is called a **relative pronoun.** The entire clause modifies the noun *girl* and is called an **adjective clause.**

The relative pronouns are *who* (*whose, whom*), *which*, and *that*. Now read the following complex sentences:

2. Frank drew the diagram *that you copied.*
3. The shack *which you see over there* is our clubhouse.
4. Bonnie is the girl *who dances so well.*
5. Near the pool is the lifeguard *whom we hired.*
6. The man *whose voice you hear* is my old uncle.

In each complex sentence listed above, (1) read the main clause, (2) read the adjective clause, (3) name the relative pronoun, and (4) name the noun which is modified by the clause.

(You may want to study and practice diagraming. If so, turn to Chapter 16, "Making Sentence Diagrams," pages 380–404.)

(See also pages 244–45 for lessons on using relative pronouns.)

■ A **relative pronoun** relates a subordinate clause to a noun or pronoun in the main clause.

■ A subordinate clause that begins with a relative pronoun and modifies a noun or pronoun is an **adjective clause.**

Exercise: Adjective clauses

On your paper, write the adjective clause in each sentence below. Underline the relative pronoun and, in parentheses, write the noun or pronoun modified by the adjective clause.

EXAMPLE:　1. My brother, who tinkers with cars, will soon become an automobile mechanic.

YOU WRITE:　*1. who tinkers with cars (brother)*

1. My sister, who studies at the academy, composed a sonata.
2. There is the chair that I made.
3. Behind the truck I found the ball which I had lost earlier.
4. The peacock, whose tail is so beautiful, has a bad temper.
5. I am the one who has never been away from home.
6. My job, which I enjoy very much, pays very little.
7. The robbers who were arrested by the police had stolen a worthless rhinestone necklace.
8. The tires that I bought at the new store were not good ones.
9. Sam's younger brother, who is intelligent, flunked the test.
10. The artist whom you admire is now very old.

Improving your writing

You can sometimes use adjective clauses to improve a passage which sounds choppy because of too many short sentences. Look at this example:

> TWO SENTENCES: The World Series was won by the Yankees. They have won it more often than any other team.
>
> COMBINED: The World Series was won by the Yankees, who have won it more often than any other team.

You can use adjective clauses also to get rid of too many *and*'s. For example:

> COMPOUND SENTENCE WITH <u>AND</u>: I did my laundry, and it is now hanging on the line.
>
> COMPLEX SENTENCE WITH ADJECTIVE CLAUSE: I did my laundry, which is now hanging on the line.

Exercises: Improving your writing

1. Combine the following pairs of sentences into one complex sentence which has an adjective clause. In each you will need to use the relative pronoun *who, whose, whom, which,* or *that.*

1. James was obliged to punish his dog. It then bit him.
2. Up the path walked a giraffe. Its head disappeared above the trees. (Use *whose.*)
3. Our football captain is an excellent leader. He has played the game for five years.
4. I want to sell my guinea pigs. They don't interest me any longer.
5. The stream overflowed its banks. It was only ten feet from our house.

2. Revise the following compound sentences by removing the *and* and subordinating one of the sentences into an adjective clause:

1. Yesterday George cut his finger, and it then got infected.
2. There are two monkeys, and they have no mate.
3. My older sister has a warm personality, and it makes her popular with her friends.
4. That fellow is my friend, and he won the race.
5. Alice began a new hobby, and it takes all her time now.

Noun clauses

You have seen how subordinate clauses are used as modifiers. Now examine these sentences:

1. I know the *secret*.
   (subj.) (verb) (dir. obj.)

2. I know *that Jack can play the game*.
   (subj.) (verb) (dir. obj.)

In sentence 1, the noun *secret* is a direct object. In sentence 2, the entire clause is the direct object. It is called a *noun clause* for this reason. Noun clauses are used in sentences in the same way that nouns are used. Study these examples:

AS SUBJECT: *That Lisa did not call* surprises me.

AS DIRECT OBJECT: They did not believe *that Jay was busy*.

AS OBJECT OF PREPOSITION: We made lemonade for *whoever is thirsty*.

AS SUBJECT COMPLEMENT: The fact is *that he was not helpful*.

(You may want to study and practice diagraming. If so, turn to Chapter 16, "Making Sentence Diagrams," pages 380–404.)

■ A clause that does the work of a noun is a **noun clause**.

Exercises: Noun clauses

1. Find the noun clause in each sentence below. Tell whether the clause is used as subject, as direct object, as object of preposition, or as subject complement.

1. He can see that I am sorry.
2. I suppose that they will accept.
3. Whatever you decide is fine with me.
4. No one knows who is responsible.
5. What he has just revealed will change our plans.
6. That you are sincere is doubtful.
7. Give the plans to whoever wants them.
8. Your problem is how you will convince them.
9. Maude was concerned about what you said.
10. You may discover later that you have misjudged his actions.

2. Write four sentences to illustrate the uses of the noun clause. Refer to the examples above, if you need to.

Sentence Patterns in Complex Sentences

You know the symbol for a co-ordinating conjunction. Now examine the second symbol below, **C^s**, which stands for a subordinating conjunction.

C^c = Co-ordinating conjunction (*and*, *or*, *but*)
C^s = Subordinating conjunction (words such as *after*, *although*, *because*, *if*, *when*, *as*, and *until*)

There is a complete sentence pattern on either side of a co-ordinating conjunction and a subordinating conjunction. However, the subordinating conjunction makes the sentence pattern which it begins dependent in meaning upon the main sentence pattern.

PATTERN 1 PATTERN 2

Adj. N V C^c N V N^p

COMPLEX SENTENCE: The fellows waited until Hal called them.

● Identify the sentence patterns in the sentences below, as shown in the example. Write whether the sentence is a compound or a complex sentence.

PATTERN 1: N V   PATTERN 3: N LV N
PATTERN 2: N V N   PATTERN 4: N LV Adj.

EXAMPLE: 1. Father is upset when I raise my voice.
YOU WRITE: *1. (Pattern 4) C^s (Pattern 2) complex*

1. I shall write a letter if time permits.
2. Janet wrote the note but I was the delivery boy.
3. The dog is fine although he has had a fight.
4. Dick drives well because he has had good training.
5. I will light the candles, and you carry the cake.

● Write compound and complex sentences which follow these groups of symbols:

1. N V Adj. Adj. N C^c N^p V^h V Adj. N
2. N^p LV Adj. C^s N V N^p Adv.
3. Adj. N V^h V Adj. N C^s N V
4. Adj. N LV Adj. C^s N^p V Adj. Adj. N
5. Adj. N P Adj. N LV N C^c N^p V P N^p

A Book to Read

The Adventures of Tom Sawyer
by Mark Twain
Illustrated by Jo Polseno
Grosset & Dunlap, Inc.
© 1963

Tom Sawyer is probably best known for whitewashing a fence. However, this adventure is only one of many in this book that you will find highly amusing. Tom is usually either outwitting his ultra-conservative Aunt Polly, trying to understand his sweetheart, Becky Thatcher, or plotting some wild adventure with his disreputable cohort, Huck Finn. A book that contains a description of Tom and Huck at their own funeral is bound to have all of the ingredients of a good story. There are underground caves. There is hidden treasure. All is adventure in this exciting book that gives a true picture of life along the Mississippi River a century ago.

About the author

Mark Twain, whose real name was Samuel Langhorne Clemens, was born in Missouri in 1835. His pen name was taken from the call of the leadsmen on the river steamers, who would take a sounding and then call out "Mark twain!" meaning that there were two fathoms of water. Though he left school at twelve, when his father died, Twain's literary works were so admired that eventually he was awarded honorary degrees by Yale and Oxford. He was proud of his ability to record accurately the dialects used by different classes of people who lived along the Mississippi River.

Test I

1. Here are the sentence patterns you have studied:

Pattern 1: Subject—Verb
Pattern 2: Subject—Action Verb—Direct Object
Pattern 3: Subject—Linking Verb—Subject Complement (Noun or Pronoun)
Pattern 4: Subject—Linking Verb—Subject Complement (Adjective)
Pattern 5: Subject—Verb—Indirect Object—Direct Object

On your paper, list the numerals from 1 to 10. Next to each, write 1, 2, 3, 4, or 5 to identify the pattern of each sentence below:

1. The fog caused many accidents. P2
2. They found the river at sunset.
3. The scouts rode ahead of the others.
4. Most Indians in these parts are friendly.
5. Grandma Moses was a well-known painter.
6. Our rehearsal always begins late.
7. I made Bob an interesting sandwich.
8. Were some people envious of his record?
9. He is the tallest boy in class.
10. Mother bought me some modeling clay for my birthday.

2. Write the skeleton words from the sentences above, leaving space between them. Identify each word by writing one of these labels above it: *subj., verb, dir. obj., subj. comp.,* or *indir. obj.*

EXAMPLE: 1. I sent Nancy a letter in January.
YOU WRITE: *subj. verb indir. obj. dir. obj.*
                1. I sent Nancy letter

Test II

Copy these compound sentences. Underline the simple subject once and the verb twice in each clause.

1. Those books are too difficult, but these books are too easy.
2. The dinner was roast lamb and the dessert was mint ice cream.
3. The weather was quite hot, and we sat under the sprinkler.
4. Dad punished me severely, but Sue's father gave her praise.
5. Those woodsmen felled the trees, and the mills gobbled them up.

Test III

There are simple sentences and compound sentences listed below. On your paper, copy only the compound sentences and punctuate them correctly.

1. "Jack Spratt could eat no fat and his wife could eat no lean."
2. The water is too cold for a swim but we can lie on the beach.
3. Mother bought me a dress but would not buy me a hat.
4. The campers put up their tents and then unpacked the cooking equipment.
5. The meat was tender and tasty and the potatoes were superb.
6. The lions and tigers in the zoo roared angrily but they did not frighten the crowds.

Test IV

List the numerals from 1 to 5 on your paper. Identify each sentence as *simple, compound,* or *complex.*

1. Clouds and mists hung over the mountaintops in the early hours of the day.
2. Modern ships have every safety device, and fire drills are held regularly.
3. My uncle arrives early in the evening and stays until midnight.
4. The welcome signs at the station surprised us when we arrived.
5. I have the picture that you want.

Test V

List the numerals from 1 to 5 on your paper. Identify each italicized clause below as an *adjective clause, adverb clause,* or *noun clause*:

1. *When he was a young man,* Alfred Nobel experimented with nitroglycerin in his father's factory in Sweden.
2. He hoped *that he could make a dangerous substance into a safe and useful explosive.*
3. Finally, in 1865, he discovered a blasting gelatin, *which later was called dynamite.*
4. *After Alfred Nobel became one of the world's richest men,* he established a fund for the now famous Nobel prizes.
5. Two Americans *who have won Nobel prizes in literature* are Pearl Buck and Ernest Hemingway.

Exercise I

1. Review the lessons on sentence patterns, pages 181–90.

2. Identify each skeleton sentence below as *Sentence Pattern 1, 2, 3, 4,* or *5*:

1. Cows moo.	11. Snakes are reptiles.
2. Cows give us milk.	12. We like spinach.
3. Cows eat grass.	13. Did I send you a book?
4. Cows are lazy.	14. I sent a book.
5. Cats scratch people.	15. Colds are contagious.
6. Students attend games.	16. Do bears eat ants?
7. Students study.	17. Satellites orbit.
8. Flowers look pretty.	18. Dogs bark loudly.
9. Children enjoy toys.	19. Dogs bite strangers.
10. Children play happily.	20. Give the dog his dinner.

3. Tell whether each word (except modifiers) in the sentences above is used as *subject, verb, direct object, subject complement,* or *indirect object*.

Exercise II

1. Review "Compound Sentences" on pages 191–92.

2. Copy these compound sentences. Put parentheses around each independent clause. In each clause, underline the simple subject once and the verb twice.

1. John will give Clara money for a present, or he will send her a gift.
2. You must come to the party early, or you will miss the fun.
3. Calvin plays the piano, Lonnie sings, and I wave the baton.
4. Can those pupils learn fast, or do they need encouragement?
5. The author had written several books, but he never became famous.

3. Name all of the skeleton words for each sentence above.

Exercise III

1. Review "Punctuating Compound Sentences" on pages 194–95.

2. Some of these sentences are simple sentences, others are compound. Copy only the compound sentences on your paper, punctuating each one correctly.

1. Young Sam will mow the lawn now and then I will rake the leaves afterwards.
2. The clock had not yet struck five and everyone had left.
3. Our cat has strayed away but she may return before nightfall.
4. Today or tomorrow Carol will speak to Miss Elkins and explain the situation to her.
5. We reached the corner and Paul rushed forward with a smile and a handshake.
6. The soldiers in the barracks lounged on their cots and discussed their families and friends.

Exercise IV

1. Review pages 191–205.
2. Identify each of these sentences as *simple, compound,* or *complex*:

1. Williamsburg, which was the capital of Virginia until 1799, is now a favorite place for tourists.
2. The tracks of a rabbit or some other wild animal led right into the cave.
3. Suddenly a squall struck the tiny sailboat, and we rushed to the rescue with our large motorboat.
4. Although the boys were not hungry, they gobbled the homemade pie.
5. They attached the hose to the faucet, and soon the fire was extinguished.

Exercise V

1. Review "Complex Sentences" on pages 198–205.
2. Find and list the clauses in these sentences. Next to each one, write *adjective clause, adverb clause,* or *noun clause* in parentheses.

1. The fire started because someone had been careless.
2. When the library opens tomorrow, I'll be at the door.
3. That dog, which had never bitten anyone before, rushed at the delivery boy.
4. Whatever he said was meant in jest.
5. You can tell that he is ill.
6. We know the boy who found the fossil.

CHAPTER 8

Writing Stories and Reports

In Chapter 4 you learned that a good paragraph has unity; that is, it stays on its subject and develops it interestingly. You saw how the ideas flowed smoothly from one sentence to the next. This type of development must also apply to a longer paper composed of several paragraphs. Such a paper must keep to and develop its subject. Each paragraph must be related to the paragraph before it and to the one that follows it, whether the paragraphs tell a story (narration) or give information (exposition).

Planning a Story

The English poet William Cowper wrote:

> A tale should be judicious, clear, succinct;
> The language plain, and incidents well link'd;
> Tell not as new what everybody knows;
> And, new or old, still hasten to a close.

Most people enjoy reading stories, especially stories about the adventures and experiences of their friends, exciting events in history, or almost anything that tells of people facing the problems and incidents of life.

Choosing your subject

The first step in writing a story is to choose your subject. You will probably write best from your own experience, because you know more about that than anybody else. You can delve into your memory and bring forth specific details about sights, sounds, smells, tastes, and physical feelings. You can recall your emotions: your joy, your sorrow, your excitement, your anger. You can reproduce just what people said to each other. Once you have aroused the interest of your reader, it is the development of specific, real details that holds his interest and increases his enjoyment of the story.

If you do not want to write directly about something that happened to you, you may still use your own experience. Your story may be set in a place you know well and can describe convincingly, even though you give it another name. A character may be a person you know, or he may have a combination of the qualities of several people you know. The events you describe may have been experienced or seen by you. Most good authors, even when writing fiction, write from their own experience and knowledge of life.

To discuss

Study the list of story titles below. Which ones are subjects about which you could write from your own experience? Which ones are foreign to your experience?

1. The Bank Robbery
2. A Secret That Wasn't Kept
3. How I Saved a Life
4. The Lost Argument
5. Frostbitten on Everest
6. The Day __?__ Got Angry
7. The Crop That Failed
8. Her First Day as a TV Star
9. Breaking a Crime Ring
10. Ruined by a Million Dollars
11. Earning My First Dollar
12. The Fight
13. The Marines Attack
14. A Crisis in My Room
15. A Stunt That Didn't Work
16. Bat Boy for the Braves
17. Lost in a Tropical Jungle
18. A Trip I Never Should Have Taken
19. A Conversation on a Bus
20. The Accident

Exercises: Planning stories

1. From the list above, select and list five or more titles about which you would be able to write from your own experience. Prepare to tell informally and rather briefly to the class a story that would go with one of the titles you chose. You may write the story and read it, or you may tell it orally. For this exercise, your writing need not be a finished product, since the purpose is only to get as many story ideas as possible before the class.

2. Probably the stories told by your friends in class suggested new ideas to you for stories you might write from your own experience. Make a list in class of all the ideas that occur to you. From time to time, go over your list of ideas and add to it. Write them neatly in your English notebook. You will soon develop for yourself a list of story ideas which you may use for future writing assignments.

Writing a Story

The story you told or wrote for the exercise on page 214 was done quickly and was not a polished narration. Now it is time to look more closely into how a typical story is put together. The plan of a story is called the **plot.** The plot is the pattern of events or situations; it is *what happens.* Usually the plot is developed through four main parts of a story, which are explained as follows:

Parts of a story

Opening. The opening sets the stage for the story, probably introduces the main character, and arouses the interest of the reader.

Development. Once the interest of the reader is aroused, the development presents a chain of events and actions. Atmosphere is created through description and realistic detail. All of these help to carry the story forward.

Climax. The climax is the high point of suspense in the story, the "big moment."

Closing. The closing tells how the story comes out. If there is a problem, it gives the solution. It usually leaves the reader feeling satisfied.

Here is a personal-experience story that was written by a boy in junior high school. He tells about a childhood experience as though it were happening to a young boy named George. Read the story and be prepared to discuss it.

Birthday Surprise

A few days before his birthday, little George Crane started snooping through the house for his birthday presents. He knew that packages had been brought into the house, and he was curious beyond control. Upstairs and downstairs he looked but couldn't find a thing. He hunted in the cellar and even in the garage, but not a sign of a present could he discover.

George heard his mother getting dinner in the kitchen. He went in and said to her, half smiling, "Why did you hide my presents so well this year?"

Mrs. Crane stopped work and looked at him in surprise. "Why, George," she exclaimed, "we always hide your presents so you'll have a surprise to enjoy!"

"But, Mom," George started to whine, "I remember last year I found my skates behind the TV. And the year before that I found my HO trains and played with them when you weren't home."

"You didn't!" cried his mother.

"Yes, I did," the boy replied. "And each time I would put the presents back and you never knew it."

At this, Mrs. Crane laughed. "Well, this year I thought of a wonderful place for hiding presents, and you will never find it!"

George went away for a short time but soon returned and pestered and coaxed his mother to reveal the hiding place. She said, somewhat louder and more impatiently, "You don't really want to know where your presents are because then you would have no surprise on your birthday."

George coaxed some more. "Please, Mom, don't be mean. Tell me, Mom, please. Go on, Mom, tell me; I want to know."

Mrs. Crane became so annoyed she stopped her work and shouted, "All right! Do you really want to know? You may have your presents right now—all of them! Just say the word."

George was astonished. He never expected such an easy victory.

There was a long silence. George just stared at his scuffed shoes. Then his mother insisted again, "Do you want your presents? Say yes or no!"

Slowly George started to laugh. Gradually, both he and his mother were laughing heartily because they both knew that he didn't really want his birthday surprise given away.

In a few minutes George left the kitchen and went outside to ride his bicycle. He felt happy, even though he knew he had lost the argument. When his birthday arrived, he ran down the stairs even more eagerly than usual. "Nothing is better," he thought, "than being really surprised on your birthday."

To discuss

1. Tell briefly the plot of "Birthday Surprise."

2. Which part of the story constitutes the opening, which the development, which the climax, and which the closing?

3. How does the writer arouse your interest? What is the earliest point at which you really want to know how the story ends?

4. From this point until the climax, how many lines are there? What percentage of the story is devoted to the development?

5. What lines show how the problem is going to be resolved?

6. Is the closing brief? Do you find the ending satisfying?

Selection and development

One of the most important skills of a good story writer is that of selecting from all that he might tell about a subject the part that is most likely to interest the reader, and then to develop that part. *Select* and *develop* are key words. Too many young writers feel that they must try to tell *all* the events that happened. Notice how the author of "Birthday Surprise" begins with the interesting part of the story: "A few days before his birthday, little George Crane started snooping through the house for his birthday presents." He did not tell what time George got up that morning or what he ate for breakfast and lunch. None of these things was needed. He *selected* the most important part: the contest between George and his mother in the kitchen. That part he *developed* fully and realistically, and then hastened to a close.

Exercises: Selection and development

1. Below and on page 218 are three story titles. Following each is a list of items you as author might include in a 500-word story on the subject. Select only the items which you think need to be included in the story and which should be developed fully. Write the numeral of each of these items on your paper under the appropriate title. Be prepared to defend your choices in class discussion. Be sure that each item you select keeps to the subject announced by the title.

I. "Lost on the Subway"

1. What time I got up
2. What I had for breakfast
3. How my little sister pestered me before my trip
4. Why I was going into the center of the city
5. The trouble I had buying my subway token
6. The people I saw on the car
7. My failure to remember the name of my stop
8. The man who asked me whether I needed help
9. A friendly conductor who telephoned home for me and put me on the right train
10. My destination reached
11. Errand in town completed
12. My trip back home on the subway

II. "The Big Catch"

1. I sit on the bank of the stream, nearly asleep
2. I feel something heavy on my line
3. I wonder if a tremendous bass is on my hook
4. I can almost see the smiles of admiration as I walk home with my catch
5. With great effort I finally land my catch—a rubber boot
6. I throw the boot back
7. My mother calls me for supper
8. My father asks me what sort of luck I had
9. I tell him about the boot
10. We decide to drive to a lake the next Saturday to see if we can catch some bass
11. I watch a good TV program
12. Mother makes me go to bed

III. "The Dog Fight"

1. How much I love dogs
2. A pet poodle called Butch we once had years ago
3. I earn the money for dog food and license by selling papers
4. What kinds of food we feed our dogs
5. How we got our present dog Goldy
6. Goldy's bad temper when other dogs come into our yard
7. Goldy fights with Fido, our neighbor's dog
8. Fido's injuries
9. My father makes us get rid of Goldy
10. How I feel going to school the next morning
11. Coming home and finding no dog to play with
12. Why I hope to be a veterinarian

2. Write, in one brief paragraph each, the plots of the three stories. Remember, the plot is only the sequence of main events. It is not the full story.

3. Choose one of the three story suggestions above and write a 500-word story based on it, using only those items you selected for the exercise. The story will be fiction, but use your own experience, memory, and imagination to develop interestingly the key ideas.

On the next page, read how one young author began his story.

The Dog Fight

Goldy is our lovable, intelligent, evil-tempered mutt. Since she never gets mad at me, I guess I like her better than anyone else in the family does. In general she's a pretty reasonable dog, but the one thing she can't stand is another dog coming into our yard.

Late one Saturday afternoon when I was in the house reading, I heard a rapid series of sharp yips . . .

Using Dialogue in Stories

Almost everyone likes to read a story with conversation in it. Conversation makes writing come alive; it makes the characters seem more real. Suppose you were assigned to write a story set in your school home room. You might write:

> As I came into Room 22, our teacher, Miss Fellows, was talking earnestly to Mary Burtt, asking her to get her violin as quickly as possible. Mary said that she didn't understand why she should get it. Just as Miss Fellows was about to explain, Mr. Fowler, the principal, appeared at the door and asked to speak to her. She told Mary to wait a moment and hurried out of the room. At that, a classmate explained that Sue was absent and that they needed someone to play in assembly that morning. This distressed Mary, who felt sure that she could not play without any practice.

Or you might write:

> As I came into Room 22, our teacher, Miss Fellows, was saying earnestly to Mary Burtt, "Please get your violin as quickly as possible."
>
> "But why?" asked Mary. "You know I haven't—"
>
> "Oh, Miss Fellows," called a vigorous voice from the hall, "may I speak to you a moment?"
>
> "Yes, Mr. Fowler, I'll be right there," replied Miss Fellows, seeing that it was the principal. "Kindly wait just a moment, Mary." Our teacher hurried from the room.
>
> "Listen, Mary," explained a classmate, "unfortunately Sue is absent, and they need someone to play in assembly this morning."
>
> "Oh, that's impossible!" cried Mary. "How can I play without any practice?"

The two versions above are about equal in length, and they say just about the same thing. Which one do you find the more lively and interesting? Why?

The second passage on page 219 is written in dialogue, or conversation. It is a series of *direct quotations* of words people actually used. The first passage is *indirect quotations;* it tells *about* what people said but does not directly quote them. Generally, but not always, your stories will be more readable if you use dialogue in them.

To discuss

Test your knowledge of the rules for punctuating dialogue by trying to answer the following questions based on the second passage on page 219. If you cannot remember or figure out the rule, refer to the "Guides for punctuating dialogue" below.

1. Why are there six paragraphs?
2. Why are there quotation marks around only part of the first sentence?
3. Why does the word *may* in the third paragraph begin with a small letter?
4. How many sentences does Mary use the second time she speaks? Why is the word *kindly* in line 8 capitalized?
5. Why is the word *please* in line 2 capitalized?
6. Is there always a punctuation mark to separate a quotation from the rest of the sentence? Answer with examples from the six paragraphs.
7. Which comes first—the quotation mark or the comma, question mark, or exclamation point? Point out examples.

Guides for punctuating dialogue

1. Begin a new paragraph each time there is a change of speaker.
2. Enclose all quoted words with quotation marks.
3. If a quoted sentence is divided by words that tell who is speaking, do not begin the second part of the quoted sentence with a capital letter (unless it is a proper noun).
4. Begin the first word in each quoted sentence with a capital letter.
5. Use a comma, question mark, or exclamation point to separate quoted words from the rest of the sentence.
6. The quotation mark usually follows other punctuation.

Exercises: Writing conversation correctly

1. Copy the conversation below, punctuating it correctly. Do not forget to begin a new paragraph for each speaker.

Billy's mother saw him coming home from school with a cut lip and black eye Billy, you're a bad boy she said you've been fighting again I was just keeping a little boy from being beaten up replied Billy well said his mother that was brave of you, dear who is the little boy I am, Mommy said Billy

2. Below are five examples of indirect quotations. Rewrite each one and make it a direct quotation.

EXAMPLE: 1. John said that he was lost.
YOU WRITE: *1. "I'm lost," said John.*

1. Mary replied that it was too cold to go outside.
2. The boy said that he didn't like hot dogs and added that anybody who served them to him was no longer his friend.
3. Douglas whispered that he knew exactly where the money was hidden.
4. Madame Dupuis shouted that she had had enough insults for one day and that she wanted some peace.
5. Our teacher replied that Jay should never have gone in the first place, and that he was lucky to have reached home with only a few bruises.

3. Write a conversation among three people. Try to use at least two divided quotations. When you have finished, be sure to check your punctuation against the guides on the facing page.

━━━━━ **GOING AHEAD** ━━━━━

Write a story on any subject you wish. It may be a true experience or fiction. Choose a subject you know something about. Plan your story carefully: the opening, the development, the climax, and the closing. Remember what you have learned about selection and development. If it is appropriate for your story, use dialogue to increase interest.

Before handing in your story, follow carefully the suggestions on page 230 of this chapter, which tell you how to proofread and correct your papers. Then write your final copy.

Planning a Report

Your purpose in writing a story is mainly to entertain the reader or to express some truth about life. Your purpose in writing a report is to give information on a subject and to give it clearly and interestingly. This kind of writing is called **exposition.**

Selecting a topic

Probably most of the reports you will write in school will be on subjects assigned to you in connection with a course you are taking. Often you will be given a choice among a number of related topics. If possible, choose a topic which *interests* you and about which you are reasonably sure you can find adequate information.

Do not choose too broad a topic. For example, a report on "Industry in the United States" would be far beyond the scope of a school report, but a report on a single industry in your community, or on a single company, might be manageable. The topic "Fish" would be too broad; one on "Quick-Freezing Fish for Market" would be more manageable.

Exercise: Selecting a topic

Below are ten titles for a report of 300 to 500 words. Most of them are too broad for a school report; a few are probably suitable. Write down the titles of the unsuitable topics and after each, write a title which would be on the same subject but a limited part of it.

EXAMPLE: 1. The Rivers of America
YOU WRITE: *1. The Rivers of America*
              Steamboats on the Mississippi

1. How Silkworms Make Silk
2. ___?___ as a Hobby
3. Famous Battles in American History
4. Training Rules in Our School
5. Space Exploration
6. Alaska
7. How Edison Invented the Electric Light
8. Tropical Islands
9. The Advantages of Compact Cars
10. Volcanoes, Earthquakes, and Hurricanes

Preliminary outline

The first step in organizing your report—a step you should take even before looking for information—is to think carefully about the subject you have selected and to jot down a rough outline or list of the main topics you think you will want to cover. This outline need not be in perfect form. Its purpose is to give you a framework within which to fit the information you will find. The preliminary outline should be done in pencil, so that you can easily make additions and changes.

A preliminary outline on the topic "American vs. English Bicycles" might look something like this:

American vs. English Bicycles
I. The most common American cycles
 General appearance
 Features
 Cost
II. The most common English cycles
 General appearance
 Features
 Cost
III. Advantages
 American cycles
  Lower cost
  Availability of parts and services
  Variety of models and equipment
 English cycles
  Lightness
  Durability
  Gear system
  Ease of riding
IV. Opinions of users
 John Almy
 Manager of Hill Cycle Shop
 Uncle Jack
 Myself
V. Conclusion

Remember: This preliminary outline is made before you have done any research. It is an important rough guide to help you in gathering facts. It will doubtless be changed as you go more deeply into the subject.

Exercise: Making a rough outline

Choose one of the topics listed below and make a preliminary outline. Do it in pencil, roughly following the model on page 223. The material for this outline should come entirely from your own knowledge and experience. Your search for information will come later. If you prefer, choose any topic of your own that interests you. Keep your rough outline; you will need it again.

1. The Most Important Types of Bridges
2. How to Be a Good Baby Sitter
3. Early Steam Locomotives
4. The Uses of Balloons
5. Bamboo
6. Pirates in American History
7. The Position of __?__ in Baseball (or Hockey)
8. How to Shoot in Basketball
9. The Grizzly Bear and His Habits (or any other wild animal)
10. How Breakfast Cereals Are Made
11. Seeing Eye Dogs
12. Motorboats vs. Sailboats
13. Bobsledding
14. Bookbinding
15. How Bottles Are Made

Getting the facts

Many reports do not succeed as well as they should because the reader did not use his intelligence in trying to find information. Think for a moment about where you would find information on the subject "American vs. English Bicycles." You would look in encyclopedias at school and in the public libraries; you would look in the *Readers' Guide* for recent articles on the subject of bicycles; you would examine the card catalog of your school library to see if there were any books about bicycles. But this should not be all. You would talk to the people you know who own bicycles and ask them about their experiences and opinions. Who in your community would be likely to know more about the subject than any other person? Probably it would be someone in the local bicycle repair shop. An interview with him may prove profitable. Of course, you should not forget your own experience.

Never be satisfied with only one source of information in doing a report. Explore all sources, and when you have gathered your facts, compare them carefully. If you write your facts on 3″ x 5″ cards, it will be easier to compare and organize them.

A good report is well organized; that is, the writer establishes the subject definitely in the first paragraph; he stays on the subject and divides it intelligently into its main parts, treating one part at a time. In order to organize your report well, you will need to know how to use an outline.

If you need review on how to use the various sources of information, turn to Chapter 12, "Study Skills," and read pages 310–12.

Exercise: Gathering information

You have made a preliminary outline for the exercise on page 224. Proceed in the next few days to gather information on the subject from all available sources. Use your preliminary outline to guide you, revising it as you find you need to. You may find that you have omitted topics which are necessary. Add them. On the other hand, you may find no information on a topic you had included. Omit such a topic. Keep your outline; you will need it later on.

The final outline

Your final outline should be prepared with great care, since it is the one you will follow as you write your report. It should be in correct form. The first step is to sort out your notes and arrange them into categories or topics if you have not already done so.

You will probably find that your final outline is quite different from your preliminary one. On the next page, look at the beginning of the final outline for the report on bicycles. The original topic "American vs. English Bicycles" proved too large to manage in a small paper.

Choosing the Bike to Suit You

I. Type of bicycle
  A. Need
    1. Lightweight for recreation or racing
      a. High-pressure tires
      b. Light wheels and gears
    2. Middleweight for job (deliveries) or use on rough terrain
      a. Heavy wheels
      b. Wide, soft-type tires
  B. Comfort
    1. Frame
      a. Curved, for low riding position
      b. Triangular, for high riding position
    2. Adjustable handlebars and seat
    3. Gear shift for easier pedaling and speed
      a. Permits adjustment to road conditions
      b. Decreases fatigue
II. Safety factors
  A. Brakes
    1. Regular foot brake
    2. Optional hand brakes
  B. Excellent lights and bell
III. Cost factors

(This is only part of an outline.)

To discuss

1. Compare the final outline for the report on bicycles on page 226 with the preliminary outline on page 223. Discuss how these two outlines differ.

2. What are the main headings in the final outline? How are they numbered?

3. How many main heading and subheading categories are there? Explain their arrangement.

4. Give a capitalization rule for writing outlines.

5. Give a punctuation rule for writing outlines.

6. If you had to finish the outline, what are other possible main headings you could add to it?

Exercise: Writing a final outline

Write the final outline for a 300- to 500-word report, using the rough outline you wrote for the exercise on page 224. This outline should be handed in for approval by the teacher before you proceed with the actual writing of your report.

TO MEMORIZE

FROM *Othello*, Act III, scene iii

IAGO: Who steals my purse steals trash; 'tis something, nothing;
'Twas mine, 'tis his, and has been slave to thousands.
But he that filches from me my good name
Robs me of that which not enriches him
And makes me poor indeed.

WILLIAM SHAKESPEARE

Do you agree with the character in Shakespeare's play who speaks these lines? Which would you rather lose—a large sum of money or your good name? Can loss of one's "good name" mean loss of friends, job, love?

Just how important *is* a "good name"? In school? in a job? in government? in business?

In your own words, explain the meaning of the last three lines above.

Writing a Report

You are now ready to write your report. You will probably follow your final outline closely. Even at this stage, however, if your outline does not fit your needs, change it. There is no virtue in sticking to the outline just for the sake of sticking to it. Be sure, though, that you do not allow yourself to get off the subject or to omit or repeat important items.

Give special attention to paragraphing. Probably you will begin a new paragraph each time you start a new topic on your outline. Some of your topics may need more than one paragraph. Remember what you learned in Chapter 4 about topic sentences. Also look again at the section on transitions on pages 121–22. Be sure that the mind of the reader is carried easily from paragraph to paragraph in your report.

Making a bibliography

When you have finished your paper, you should list your published sources of information. Below is an accepted form for listing the books and magazines from which you get your information:

Books
>Benét, Laura, *Famous American Humorists,* Dodd, Mead & Co.,
>1959, pp. 14–64.
>Latham, Julie, *World Book of Dogs,* World Publishing Co.,
>1953, pp. 37–42.

Magazines
>Hano, Arnold, "The Star Nobody Knows," *Coronet,* January,
>1960, pp. 156–61.
>Langewiesche, Wolfgang, "The Thing from Outer Space,"
>*Reader's Digest,* April, 1963, pp. 81–85.

Exercise: Writing a report

Write the first draft of your final 300- to 500-word report. Do it in pencil so that you can revise it easily before you do your final draft.

Before handing in your report, follow carefully the suggestions in the lesson on page 230, which tells you how to proofread and revise your papers.

Proofreading and Revising Your Paper

It is a rare person who can write a perfect paper on the first draft. Almost all writers, including the most expert and experienced ones, proofread and revise their writing before they are satisfied with it.

After you have finished the first draft of your paper, put it aside for a day or more. When you come back to the paper, you will see it with fresh eyes, and your mistakes will be more obvious to you.

When you reread your paper, do it *aloud*—really aloud! Then you will hear some of the errors in your paper. Read it as though you were a stranger to it. Be as critical as you can.

Read with a pencil in hand and a dictionary at your side. If you do not like what you have written, or if you find yourself stumbling over a clumsy sentence or paragraph, *change it*.

STEP ONE: Revise the first draft of your paper, checking and correcting each of these items:

1. *Punctuation*—Look up the rules if you need to.
2. *Capitalization*—Have you forgotten anything?
3. *Paragraphing*—Is your paper divided into topics?
4. *Sentence structure*—Have you any run-ons or fragments? any awkward sentences?
5. *Spelling*—Look up any words about which you have doubt.

STEP TWO: Check your final draft by answering these questions:

1. Is my paper arranged according to class standards for written work?
2. Is it properly dated and headed?
3. Is it neat and legible?

STEP THREE: When you get your paper back, follow these suggestions:

1. Note carefully all the teacher's comments and markings.
2. Correct the paper, taking into account all the comments of your teacher, even those which may require you to rewrite parts or all of your paper.
3. Share the paper by reading it to a person or group and getting their reactions.
4. After every correction or comment has been understood and dealt with, file your paper for future reference.

Test I

1. List on your paper three chief purposes of a story opening.

2. Tell which part of the story carries it forward with a chain of events, actions, and appropriate detail.

3. What is the high point of the story called?

4. Which part tells how the story finally came out?

Test II

Copy the following conversation. Insert capital letters and punctuation marks in the proper places.

Just one small piece of chocolate cake won't make you fat coaxed Mother

That's right Grandmother agreed you will lose your good health if you deny yourself food

If you feel well, you shouldn't worry about being fat chimed in our neighbor, who weighed about two hundred pounds herself

Only Laura's brother gave her moral support he said stick to your diet, Sis don't let the family wear you down

Test III

1. List three good possible sources of information for class reports.

2. Arrange the list of headings below in correct outline *order* and *form*. First decide on the main headings. Then group the subheadings under them.

the whooping crane

wing spread six to eight feet
its size
four to five feet high
slaughtered by pioneers
small number hatched each year
shooting prohibited by law
efforts to save it
sanctuary protected
threatened extinction

Exercise I

1. Review "Writing a Story" on pages 215–17.

2. On your paper, list the four main parts of a story: *Opening, Development, Climax,* and *Closing.* Read the four short paragraphs below. Decide from what part of the story each paragraph was taken. Write its numeral beside that part.

1. Along the final lap shot Princess, her mane flying, her legs moving in even rhythm. Easily, gracefully, but with steady purpose, she crossed the finish line.
2. Before Princess was a year old, we knew she would be a very special horse. For one thing, she loved to run, which she did with power and grace around the pasture.
3. I first saw the new black colt one early morning in May. She was standing by her mother in the pasture behind our barn.
4. For four years, Princess reigned unchallenged as the fastest horse in our county.

Exercise II

1. Review "Using Dialogue in Stories" on pages 219–20.

2. Read the selection below and decide where each paragraph begins and ends. Then write the selection on your paper. Use capital letters and punctuation marks correctly.

I think we should have taken the right turn at that small lake Anne said that wasn't a lake Jack grumbled just a pond but that man at the service station called something a lake, so where is it Anne retorted well, we're lost anyway mother remarked cheerfully maybe we had better turn back Anne then became really annoyed and said I was due at Fran's farm thirty minutes ago I would think a grown man could tell the difference between a lake and a pond

Exercise III

1. Review "Planning a Report" and "Writing a Report" on pages 222–28 and 229.

2. Based on the standards for selection given in the text, list five topics that would be suitable for you to report on to your class.

3. Write a rough preliminary outline for one of the topics you just listed for part 2 of this exercise. Then list three possible sources of information that may help you develop the topic you chose.

4. Copy the following outline of a report on ways to select a possible vocation. The main headings and subheadings are listed in the correct order. Only the form needs to be corrected.

ways to select a vocation

    I   consider personal interests
         favorite school subjects
         hobbies
         things I like to do
   II   talk with adult workers
         professional people
         mechanical workers
         artists in various fields
 III   consider requirements for preparation
         type of mind
         money for training and education
         time

5. Write a report of three paragraphs based on the outline you corrected in part 4 of this exercise.

CHAPTER 9

Pronoun and Verb Usage

More mistakes are made with pronouns and verbs than with any other parts of speech. When you studied the characteristics of these two large groups of words, you saw how they change their forms with different uses. This fact contributes to many of the problems which arise.

This chapter is designed to help you correct some of the pronoun and verb errors you may make. In studying the lessons, keep in mind that memorizing and practicing saying correct forms aloud are the best ways to master usage problems.

Personal Pronouns

Personal pronouns have **subject forms** and **object forms.** Here is a list of the two forms of the personal pronouns. Notice that the pronouns *you* and *it* have identical forms for subject and object. These two will cause you no trouble.

SUBJECT PRONOUNS	OBJECT PRONOUNS
I	me
you	you
he	him
she	her
it	it
we	us
they	them

Subject pronouns are used in sentences as *subjects* and *subject complements.* Object pronouns are used as *direct objects, indirect objects,* and *objects of prepositions.*

For the most part, you use pronouns correctly in sentences in which only one subject or one object is needed. For example, your ear tells you to use *I* and *me* correctly in sentences like these:

SUBJECT: *I* told the truth.
INDIRECT OBJECT: Tell *me* the truth.

The problem arises when the pronoun is part of a compound subject, object, or complement; that is, when the pronoun is connected to one of these sentence elements by means of the conjunctions *and*, *or*, and *but* in sentences like these:

COMPOUND SUBJECT: John and *I* told the truth.
COMPOUND INDIRECT OBJECT: Tell John and *me* the truth.

Whenever there is any doubt about which pronoun to use, the subject or object pronoun, remove part of the compound subject and use the pronoun alone. Do the same with other compound sentence elements to which a pronoun is connected. Try this method with the following sentences:

COMPOUND OBJECT OF PREPOSITION:
The boy fought against my friend and (I, me).
COMPOUND DIRECT OBJECT:
Mary chose the others and (I, me).

Your ear would never let you say "The boy fought against I" or "Mary chose I." You would naturally say *me* for both sentences.

With pronouns that are used as subject complements, your ear may not help you. That is because you have frequently heard the object pronouns used in informal speech in sentences such as "It is me." However, formal speech and writing require the subject pronoun in the subject complement position.

COMPOUND SUBJECT COMPLEMENT:
The owners are John and *he*.

Always use the forms **I, he, she, we,** and **they** in the subject position—as subject or subject complement.
Always use the forms **me, him, her, us,** and **them** in the object position—as direct object, indirect object, or object of a preposition.

Exercises: Using personal pronouns

1. Decide how each italicized pronoun below is used in the sentence, as *subject, subject complement, direct object,* or *object of a preposition:*

1. Mrs. Ray chose *him* first.
2. Gladys told the story to *them*.
3. Dad gave *me* a present.
4. The troublesome person in that situation was *I*.
5. *She* finished the task quickly.

2. Choose the correct form of the pronoun from each pair in parentheses. Check your answers in class, and then practice saying the sentences aloud correctly.

1. His son and (he, him) went over to look at the wreck.
2. That salesman asked for my mother or (I, me).
3. Give all entries to the chairman or (she, her).
4. The children and (we, us) enjoyed ourselves very much.
5. She came over and sat down between Mary and (I, me).
6. Please give Margo and (I, me) one more chance.
7. Please send the package to Mrs. Ritz or (they, them).
8. Mr. Frankel sent Charles and (I, me) for the posters.
9. Around George and (he, him) I saw a great crowd of people.
10. Two of the slowest workers are Ned and (she, her).
11. Those pebbles struck Paula and (we, us).
12. The ticket sellers are David and (I, me).
13. The snowball hit Jon and (he, him).
14. We saw you and (they, them) at the record shop.
15. Hand Stella and (I, me) the packages.

Pronoun agreement

Personal pronouns refer to nouns which are called **antecedents.** You have already worked with antecedents of pronouns. Study these sentences:

1. The student finished *his* work.
2. The students finished *their* work.

The noun *student* is the antecedent of *his*. *Students* is the antecedent of *their*. Notice that the pronoun agrees with its antecedent in number. (If you need to refresh your memory on the singular

236

and plural forms of pronouns, review page 415.) A singular pronoun must have as its antecedent a singular noun. A plural pronoun must have a plural antecedent.

Now look at these sentences:

3. *Sam* received *his* pay.   4. *Clara* received *her* pay.

What other fact about pronouns and antecedents do the sentences above illustrate?

The pronouns *he, his, him* are in masculine gender and must refer to nouns of the same gender. The pronouns *she, hers,* and *her* are in the feminine gender, and they, too, must agree with their antecedents. Lifeless things, such as *desk* and *book,* of course, are in the neuter gender. The neuter pronouns are *it* and *its.*

When the antecedent may refer to either a boy or a girl, the masculine pronoun is used; for example:

5. Each *volunteer* brought *his* equipment.
6. The *pupil* found *his* notes.

To say "Each volunteer brought his or her equipment" is not incorrect; but it is unnecessary. The pronoun *his* is all that is needed.

To say "Each volunteer brought their equipment" is incorrect. The subject is singular; therefore, the pronoun that refers to it must be singular, also.

> A **pronoun** must agree with its antecedent in number and gender.

Exercise: Pronouns and antecedents

Use the pronouns *his, her,* or *their* in place of each blank below:

1. One student will give __?__ opinion of the play.
2. Not a boy contributed __?__ time to the project.
3. Neither girl could make up __?__ mind.
4. Neither boy has made __?__ speech.
5. How many actors had forgotten __?__ lines?
6. Both girls tried __?__ best.
7. Some pupil has lost __?__ notebook.
8. Which child has not eaten __?__ dinner?
9. Some girl has left __?__ knitting on the chair.
10. No member is ready to give __?__ report.

Compound Personal Pronouns

When –*self* is added to some personal pronouns, **compound personal pronouns** are formed.

	SINGULAR	PLURAL
FIRST PERSON:	myself	ourselves
SECOND PERSON:	yourself	yourselves
THIRD PERSON:	himself herself itself	themselves

When these pronouns are used to intensify, or strengthen, a noun or pronoun, as in these sentences, they are called **intensive pronouns**:

    1. I *myself* will do it.
    2. They *themselves* caused the fire.

Compound personal pronouns are also used as *direct objects, indirect objects*, or *objects of a preposition*. In these sentences they are called **reflexive pronouns** because they refer back to the subject:

    3. I hurt *myself* with those words. (direct object)
    4. He gave *himself* a pep talk. (indirect object)
    5. She often talks to *herself*. (object of a preposition)

Be sure to pronounce and spell these pronoun forms correctly. Notice especially the spelling of these two: *himself, themselves*.

Exercise: Compound personal pronouns

Use the correct compound personal pronoun in place of each blank below. Write the sentences on your paper.

    1. I gave __?__ the last choice.
    2. We __?__ must prepare for the ordeal.
    3. They truly surpassed __?__.
    4. He hurt __?__ in the gym.
    5. She is usually honest about __?__.
    6. If the boys try, they can help __?__.
    7. He __?__ is responsible for the action.
    8. He always blames __?__ first.
    9. They __?__ declared a holiday.
    10. The fish tired __?__ by jumping.

Indefinite Pronouns

In addition to noun antecedents, there are certain pronouns which can be antecedents, also. They are called **indefinite pronouns** because they do not name particular persons or objects. Read these sentences, which have indefinite pronouns as subjects:

1. Each of us does his work well.
2. Few of them have ever seen snow.
3. Many are working on their homework.
4. Everyone in the room is very nervous tonight.

Which pronouns are singular and which are plural? How can you tell? Now study the following list of indefinite pronouns:

Indefinite Pronouns

SINGULAR		PLURAL
another	neither	any
any	nobody	both
anybody	none	few
anyone	no one	many
each	one	none
either	some	several
everybody	somebody	some
everyone	someone	
everything		

When you use a singular indefinite pronoun as subject, use the singular form of the verb. When you use a plural indefinite pronoun, use the plural form of the verb:

One of us is wrong.

Many of them were lost at sea.

Note that *none, any,* and *some* may be singular or plural, depending on the meaning in the sentence they are in:

SINGULAR	PLURAL
Some of the cheese was eaten.	Some of the oranges were eaten.
Is any of that stew left?	Are any of the boys late?
None of his energy is gone.	None of the tickets were sold.

Remember: A pronoun must agree with its antecedent in number and gender.

> *Each* of the members gave *his* opinion.
> *One* of the girls will change *her* mind.
> *Many* of the passengers lost *their* belongings.

Exercises: Indefinite pronouns

1. For each sentence below, choose the correct verb form to agree with the subject:

1. Everyone at the meeting (is, are) confused.
2. One of the books (was, were) damaged.
3. Both of those people (annoy, annoys) me.
4. Neither of my teachers (was, were) angry after class.
5. One of the logs (is, are) damp.
6. Most of the apples (have, has) been eaten.
7. None of your beauty (have, has) faded.
8. (Is, Are) everybody ready to answer the question?
9. Some of us (is, are) too tired to go further.
10. Each of the pots (have, has) a dent.

2. Choose the correct pronoun in place of each blank below:

1. Everyone in the cast had __?__ chance to take a bow.
2. Nobody in the group was able to finish __?__ homework.
3. Each of the voters wrote __?__ choice on a slip of paper.
4. Everybody in the class may bring __?__ parents to the show.
5. Many of my friends left __?__ money at home.
6. Each of you has __?__ instructions.

Sentence Patterns

Review the symbols and the sentence patterns you have studied.

N = Noun	**Adv.** = Adverb
N^P = Pronoun	**P** = Preposition
V = Action verb	**C**^c = Co-ordinating
LV = Linking verb	conjunction
V^h = Auxiliary (helping	**C**^s = Subordinating
verb)	conjunction
Adj. = Adjective	

PATTERN 1: N V Subject–Verb
PATTERN 2: N V N Subject–Action Verb–Direct Object
PATTERN 3: N LV N Subject–Linking Verb–Subject Complement (Noun or Pronoun)
PATTERN 4: N LV Adj. Subject–Linking Verb–Subject Complement (Adjective)

Here is a new pattern, *Pattern 5.* It contains a subject, an action verb, an indirect object, and a direct object.

PATTERN 5: N V N N

N   V   N   N
Larry bought Mom flowers.

Vʰ   N   V   N   N
Did Larry buy Mom flowers?

Adj. N P Adj. N   Vʰ   V Nᵖ Adj.   N
That clerk in the bakery will give us some cookies.

A *Pattern 5* sentence *always* contains a direct object as well as an indirect object. An indirect object normally appears before the direct object in a sentence. Like other sentence elements, the indirect object can also be compounded.

Nᵖ V   N   Cᶜ Nᵖ Adj.   N
I gave Jane and her the message.

◦ Write two sentences for each group of symbols below:

1. N V N Adj. N
2. N V Nᵖ Adj. Adj. N
3. Vʰ N V Nᵖ Adj. N
4. Adj. N P Adj. N V Nᵖ Adj. Adj. N
5. Vʰ Adj. Adj. N P Adj. N V Adj. N Adj. N

6. Adj. N Cᶜ Adj. N V Nᵖ Adj. Adj. N
7. Adj. N P Adj. Adj. N V N Cᶜ Nᵖ Adj. Adj. N
8. Vʰ Adj. N P Adj. N V N Cᶜ Nᵖ Adj. N

◦ Make up compound and complex sentences that illustrate the patterns indicated in parentheses.

EXAMPLE: (Pattern 2) **Cᶜ** (Pattern 1)
YOU WRITE: *Mother had offered help,*
but we foolishly refused.

1. (Pattern 1) Cᶜ (Pattern 2)
2. (Pattern 1) Cˢ (Pattern 1)
3. (Pattern 3) Cᶜ (Pattern 3)
4. (Pattern 4) Cᶜ (Pattern 1)
5. (Pattern 5) Cˢ (Pattern 2)
6. (Pattern 2) Cᶜ (Pattern 2)

Demonstrative Pronouns

The pronouns *this, that, these,* and *those* demonstrate or point out the persons, places, or things referred to. You may remember that these words can be used as adjectives in sentences like these:

This meal is tasty.   *Those* problems are easy.

However, when they are used alone, they are **demonstrative pronouns.**

The pronouns *this* and *these* point out persons, places, or things that are near. *That* and *those* point out persons, places, or things farther away.

This is my magazine.   *These* are my gloves.
That is your magazine on   *Those* in the window are
   the porch.   expensive gloves.

> Never use **here** and **there** after a demonstrative pronoun.

Exercises: Demonstrative pronouns

1. Choose the correct words to complete these sentences:

1. (This, That) is my broken finger.
2. (These, These here) are the ones you want.
3. (These, Those) I saw on my vacation last year were the first Indians I had ever seen.
4. My sweater is (that, that there) on the chair.
5. Do (these, those) in the neighboring state have the same law?

2. Use *this, that, these,* and *those* as demonstrative pronouns in sentences of your own.

Interrogative Pronouns

The interrogative pronouns *who* (*whose, whom*), *which,* and *what* are used to introduce questions.

1. *Who* called?   4. To *whom* are you speaking?
2. *Whose* house is this?   5. *Which* is your car?
3. *Whom* do you want?   6. *What* have you seen?

The pronoun *who* changes form according to its use. *Who* should be used when it is the subject of the sentence. *Whom* should be used when it is the direct object or the object of a preposition. *Whose* is the possessive form. *Which* and *what* do not change their forms.

How is each interrogative pronoun used in the example sentences on page 242?

> Use **who** as the subject of a sentence. Use **whom** as direct object or object of a preposition.

Whose—who's

The pronoun *who* is part of the contraction *who's*, which means *who is*. Do not confuse this contraction with the possessive pronoun *whose*.

Whose turn is it? (possessive pronoun)
Who's next? (contraction)

Exercises: Interrogative pronouns

1. Choose the correct word from each pair in parentheses. Check your answers in class and then practice saying the sentences aloud correctly.

1. By (who, whom) was this written?
2. (Who, Whom) did Viola choose?
3. (Who, Whom) said that?
4. (Whose, Who's) going to the show?
5. To (who, whom) did you say that?
6. (Whose, Who's) fault is it?
7. (Who, Whom) should I invite?
8. (Who, Whom) chose me?
9. (Whose, Who's) the hero?
10. To (who, whom) did you write?
11. (Who, Whom) saw this one?
12. For (who, whom) did you vote?
13. With (who, whom) did you go?
14. In (whose, who's) room are you?
15. (Whose, Who's) waiting outside?

2. Write four sentences, two using *whose* and two using *who's*.

Relative Pronouns

When *who* (*whom, whose*), *which*, and *that* are used to begin adjective clauses, they are called **relative pronouns.**

1. The girl <u>who</u> *asked the most questions* is an honor student.
2. He is a performer <u>whom</u> *I admire.*
3. Pat is a boy <u>whose</u> *questions are usually intelligent.*

Relative pronouns have two important functions in sentences. First, they connect the adjective clause to an antecedent in the main clause. Second, they are an important part of the clauses they introduce.

In sentence 1 above, *girl* is the antecedent of the relative pronoun *who.* *Who* also acts as the subject of the adjective clause:

<u>who</u> <u>asked</u> the most questions

In sentence 2, *whom* is the direct object of the verb *admire* in the adjective clause:

whom <u>I</u> <u>admire</u>

In sentence 3, *whose* is a possessive pronoun and modifies the noun *questions*:

whose questions are usually intelligent

What are the antecedents of *whom* and *whose* in the sentences above?

Who, whose, and *whom* are used to refer to antecedents that name persons. *Who* is the subject form; *whom* is the object form; *whose* is the possessive form.

Which is used when the antecedent names a thing.

That is used when the antecedent names a person, animal, or thing.

1. The book *that* I read was written by Charles Dickens.
2. The hammer, *which* was here yesterday, is not in the tool box now.
3. She is the teacher to *whom* the pupils tell their problems.

Can you name the relative pronoun above that is used as the subject of its clause? Which relative pronoun is used as the direct object? Which one is used as the object of a preposition?

Exercises: Relative pronouns

1. In place of each blank below, tell which form is the correct one to use: *who, whose,* or *whom:*

1. Show me the girl __?__ is the most helpful.
2. I met the boys __?__ attended the meeting.
3. The girls __?__ you invited are my friends.
4. His brother, __?__ has gone on an errand, is my assistant.
5. Is this the person to __?__ you told your story?
6. No one __?__ I knew caused any trouble.
7. The boy __?__ Father and I invited is new in town.
8. Terry is the one __?__ dog follows him to school.
9. We do not know the stranger __?__ walked into the yard.
10. Is she the one in __?__ you confided?

2. Supply the correct relative pronoun for each sentence.

1. I know a dog __?__ is friendly to cats.
2. The senator __?__ helped to build the new playground is Mr. Carlstadt.
3. The one to __?__ we owe our lives is Jack.
4. The social worker __?__ we like is visiting our house tonight.
5. A TV program __?__ I always watch is on now.

Restrictive and nonrestrictive clauses

Study these two sentences:

1. The book which tells about the sea is *Kon-Tiki.*
2. This book, which was written by Thor Heyerdahl, is a good adventure story.

In sentence 1, the adjective clause is called a **restrictive clause** because it is necessary to the meaning of the sentence. It restricts, or limits, the meaning. A restrictive clause is not set off with commas.

In sentence 2, the adjective clause is set off with commas. The clause adds information to the sentence, but it can be removed without disturbing the basic meaning of the sentence. It is called a **nonrestrictive clause.**

You can remove the clause in sentence 2 and have the same meaning, but you cannot in sentence 1. Try it.

Use commas to set off nonrestrictive clauses.

Exercise: Punctuating correctly

There are four sentences below which need commas to set off nonrestrictive clauses. Copy each one and punctuate it correctly.

1. The President who was forced into a war with pirates was Thomas Jefferson.
2. These pirates to whom the United States had been paying ransom demanded more money.
3. The rulers of the Barbary States whom the pirates acknowledged as chiefs encouraged the capture of American ships.
4. The pirates who made the most trouble were from Tripoli.
5. The *Constitution* which helped to sink pirate ships is a famous frigate.
6. "Old Ironsides" which is another name for the *Constitution* played an important role in our history.

Tenses of Verbs

Earlier you saw that the main characteristic of verbs is that they can express time by changing their forms or endings and by sometimes adding auxiliaries (helping verbs). The time which a verb expresses is called its **tense.**

The simple tenses

Action which takes place right now—in the present—can be expressed by using the verb in the **present tense.** Its form is the same as the name of the verb.

Yes, I *see* you.   I *hear* it now.

Action that was completed in the past can be expressed by using the verb in the **past tense.** Notice that the past tense changes form, as with the verb *see,* or adds an ending, as with the verb *hear.*

Yes, I *saw* you.   I *heard* it yesterday.

Action that will take place in the future can be expressed by using the **future tense** form of a verb. The future tense uses the auxiliary *shall* or *will* with the present form.

I *shall see* you.   You *will hear* it tomorrow.

◄ *The frigate* Constitution *was used to fight the pirates of the four Barbary States, Morocco, Algiers, Tunis, and Tripoli. In what famous song do the words "the shores of Tripoli" appear?*

247

The simple tenses, then, are these: PRESENT TENSE: time, *now* PAST TENSE: time, *before* FUTURE TENSE: time, *later*.

The perfect tenses

Action which was just completed in the past but extends up to the time of speaking can be expressed by using the **present perfect tense.** With this tense, the auxiliary *have* or *has* is used.

I *have seen* you.   He *has heard* you.

Action which took place and was completed before another past action can be expressed by using the **past perfect tense.**

I *had seen* him once before the party.
He *had* never *heard* the song until she sang it.

For action which will be completed before some definite future time, the **future perfect tense** can be used.

I *shall have seen* the play by next summer.
He *will have heard* the story by then.

Notice that the three perfect tenses are all used to show *completed action.*

Now examine all six tenses of the verb *eat.*

SIMPLE TENSES

Present Tense

	SINGULAR	PLURAL
FIRST PERSON:	I *eat.*	We *eat.*
SECOND PERSON:	You *eat.*	You *eat.*
THIRD PERSON:	He (she *or* it) *eats.*	They *eat.*

Past Tense

FIRST PERSON:	I *ate.*	We *ate.*
SECOND PERSON:	You *ate.*	You *ate.*
THIRD PERSON:	He *ate.*	They *ate.*

Future Tense

FIRST PERSON:	I *shall eat.*	We *shall eat.*
SECOND PERSON:	You *will eat.*	You *will eat.*
THIRD PERSON:	He *will eat.*	They *will eat.*

PERFECT TENSES

Present Perfect Tense

FIRST PERSON: I *have eaten.* We *have eaten.*

SECOND PERSON: You *have eaten.* You *have eaten.*

THIRD PERSON: He *has eaten.* They *have eaten.*

Past Perfect Tense

FIRST PERSON: I *had eaten.* We *had eaten.*

SECOND PERSON: You *had eaten.* You *had eaten.*

THIRD PERSON: He *had eaten.* They *had eaten.*

Future Perfect Tense

FIRST PERSON: I *shall have eaten.* We *shall have eaten.*

SECOND PERSON: You *will have eaten.* You *will have eaten.*

THIRD PERSON: He *will have eaten.* They *will have eaten.*

Exercises: Verb tenses

1. Name the tense of each italicized verb below. Compare your answers in class.

1. The settlers *migrated* to the lands west of the Mississippi River.
2. Many trails *stretch* through and beyond the Appalachians.
3. *Remember* the hardships of the settlers and Indians.
4. Before the War of 1812, the Indians *had controlled* the region near the Ohio River.
5. The big land rush *began.*
6. The Indians *retreated* before overwhelming odds.
7. The country *will* never *see* such migration again.
8. In the following years, pioneers *will have settled* in all parts of the country.
9. I *have* recently *read* a book about those historical events.
10. Our librarian *has recommended* it.

2. Use these verbs in sentences of your own. Use each one in the tense shown in parentheses.

1. write   (past tense)
2. see   (present tense)
3. eat   (past perfect tense)
4. hear   (present perfect tense)
5. know   (future tense)
6. travel   (future perfect tense)

Tenses of passive verbs

The six tenses may also be used with verbs that are in the passive voice. Here are the six passive tense forms of the verb *promote*. Notice that some form of the verb *be* is used as an auxiliary. In the perfect tenses and in the future tense, you see one or more additional auxiliaries.

PRESENT:	He *is promoted.*
PRESENT PERFECT:	He *has been promoted.*
PAST:	He *was promoted.*
PAST PERFECT:	He *had been promoted.*
FUTURE:	He *will be promoted.*
FUTURE PERFECT:	He *will have been promoted.*

Exercises: Passive verbs

1. List on your paper the six passive tense forms of the verbs *eat* and *see.* Compare your answers in class.

2. Write sentences of your own, using the verb *write* in the six passive tense forms.

Progressive forms of verbs

There are times when we want to express action that keeps going on. We then use the *–ing* form of a verb, which is called the **progressive form.** The progressive form always uses some form of the verb *be* as an auxiliary. Examine these six tenses of the progressive form of the verb *read*:

PRESENT:	He *is reading.*
PRESENT PERFECT:	He *has been reading.*
PAST:	He *was reading.*
PAST PERFECT:	He *had been reading.*
FUTURE:	He *will be reading.*
FUTURE PERFECT:	He *will have been reading.*

Exercises: Progressive forms

1. Write the tenses of the progressive forms of the verbs *write* and *think.*

2. Write sentences of your own, using these verbs in progressive forms: *wait, sit, think, wonder, start.*

The Principal Parts of Verbs

All verbs have three basic forms called **principal parts.** They are the *present tense, past tense,* and *past participle.*

The different tenses of a verb are based on these three main forms.

Regular verbs will cause you no trouble. They form their tenses according to a regular system. Here are a few regular verbs arranged by principal parts. Examine them and see if you can then explain the system.

PRESENT	PAST	PAST PARTICIPLE
hope	hoped	(have, has, had) hoped
play	played	(have, has, had) played
raise	raised	(have, has, had) raised
dive	dived	(have, has, had) dived

Some verbs have changes in spelling when the ending *–d* or *–ed* is added.

carry	carried	(have, has, had) carried
fit	fitted	(have, has, had) fitted
drag	dragged	(have, has, had) dragged

With the verbs *drown* and *attack*, do not add extra letters or syllables. Their correct past forms are *drowned* and *attacked.*

If you need to refresh your memory of the spelling rules, turn to the Review Handbook, pages 432–33.

Irregular verbs

Most of the verbs in our language form their principal parts in the regular way—that is, by adding *–d* or *–ed* to the present tense. Unfortunately, the verbs that are not regular often cause difficulty.

If you hear these irregular verbs used correctly often enough, you will probably imitate the correct forms easily. Otherwise, you must make a conscious effort to master the principal parts of any verbs that give you trouble.

Keep in mind, as you study these irregular verbs, that the past participle form should always be used with an auxiliary verb (helping verb).

The principal parts of some common irregular verbs are listed on the next page.

PRESENT	PAST	PAST PARTICIPLE
arise	arose	(have, has, had) arisen
beat	beat	(have, has, had) beaten (*or* beat)
become	became	(have, has, had) become
buy	bought	(have, has, had) bought
catch	caught	(have, has, had) caught
drive	drove	(have, has, had) driven
fall	fell	(have, has, had) fallen
find	found	(have, has, had) found
forget	forgot	(have, has, had) forgotten (*or* forgot)
forgive	forgave	(have, has, had) forgiven
get	got	(have, has, had) got (*or* gotten)
hang	hung	(have, has, had) hung
hide	hid	(have, has, had) hidden
shake	shook	(have, has, had) shaken
shrink	shrank	(have, has, had) shrunk
sink	sank	(have, has, had) sunk
spring	sprang	(have, has, had) sprung
strive	strove	(have, has, had) striven
swear	swore	(have, has, had) sworn
swim	swam	(have, has, had) swum
swing	swung	(have, has, had) swung
tear	tore	(have, has, had) torn
tell	told	(have, has, had) told
wear	wore	(have, has, had) worn
wring	wrung	(have, has, had) wrung

Some verbs, such as *burst, hurt,* and *hit,* have only one form for all three principal parts.

Read over the principal parts of the irregular verbs listed above. Then cover the second and third columns with a sheet of paper and see if you can recite the principal parts of each verb quickly and correctly. Copy those you miss in your English notebook.

Now, over the next week, memorize the principal parts of the verbs which caused you trouble. If you have many to learn, take the verbs in groups of five and master one group at a time.

(If you wish, you may practice with a friend. Let your friend check you as you recite the principal parts.)

For review of the principal parts of all the irregular verbs you studied in earlier years, turn to the Review Handbook, page 447.

Exercises: Using verbs correctly

1. If you find you have memorized the principal parts on page 252 correctly but that you still misuse some of the verbs in your speaking and writing, learn the principal parts in a sequence of sentences such as the examples below:

Now I *become* angry.
Then I *became* angry.
Often I *have become* angry.

2. Choose the correct form of the verb in parentheses for each blank in the sentences below. *Do not use the present tense form of the verb.*

(buy)   1. I __?__ this coat in a discount store.

(drive)   2. This jalopy has been __?__ everywhere.

(fall)   3. The giant sequoia had __?__ a century ago.

(forget)   4. We __?__ that last week he had __?__ his lines, too.

(get)   5. We do not know how Ida __?__ two tickets for the play.

(hide)   6. Ella __?__ behind the sofa; she has __?__ there before.

(wear)   7. What I __?__ yesterday, I would not have __?__ last year.

(arise)   8. A wild goose __?__ from the marshes.

(sink)   9. His doughnut __?__ beneath the coffee.

(tell)   10. The troubadour __?__ us a very strange story.

(become)   11. Late that night I __?__ very ill. I had never __?__ so ill before.

(burst)   12. In that year the dam __?__ and flooded the farm.

(drag)   13. We have always __?__ these extra chairs to the dining room.

(drown)   14. Many of us almost __?__ in that ferry disaster.

(hang)   15. The old kite __?__ in the tree where it had __?__ last week.

(wring)   16. The young girl __?__ out the clothes as if she had never __?__ out anything before.

(shake)   17. My nerves were __?__ badly when the earthquake __?__ the city.

(shrink)   18. That shirt __?__ so badly that I think it has __?__ to half its original size.

(strive)   19. The police __?__ to recover the money.

(swear)   20. I had __?__ secrecy three times, but I __?__ again.

3. Use each of these verbs in a sentence of your own. Use the verbs in the past tense form.

    catch   swing   spring   swim   hurt

4. Use each of these verbs in a sentence. Use the past participle form.

    forgive   find   tear   beat   hit

Ought

The verb *ought* is special. It has only one form for all the tenses and is never used with an auxiliary verb. For example, it is incorrect to say "had ought" or "should ought."

The following four sentences use *ought* correctly:

1. I *ought* to leave early.
2. *Ought* you to go without me?
3. I *ought not* to have stayed so late.
4. *Oughtn't* we to donate something?

> Never use an auxiliary verb with **ought.**

Exercise: Using ought correctly

Write five sentences using *ought* correctly and five using *ought not* or *oughtn't* correctly.

TO MEMORIZE

To See a World

To see a world in a grain of sand
And a heaven in a wild flower,
Hold Infinity in the palm of your hand
And Eternity in an hour.

WILLIAM BLAKE

Among the marks of a good poet is the ability to pack much meaning into a few words and to choose those few words with great care. William Blake is telling us how even the smallest, simplest objects in the world reflect the great plan and beauty of the larger universe.

Most of us have, at some time or other, experienced the feelings of wonder and sudden wisdom that the poet is talking about. Can you recall an experience in which you felt you were seeing the "world in a grain of sand," or "a heaven in a wild flower"?

Confusing Verb Pairs

Sometimes there are usage problems in choosing between pairs of verbs. In studying the verbs below, you must concentrate on the meanings of the verbs as well as their forms.

Rise and raise

The verb *rise* means "to go up" or "to get up."

The sun *rises* early. (present)
The farmer *rose* at six-thirty. (past)
The river *has risen* again. (past participle)

The verb *raise* means "to lift or cause something to go up."

The janitor *raises* the windows. (present)
He *raised* his hand. (past)
They *have raised* their prices. (past participle)

Borrow and lend

The verbs *borrow* and *lend* have opposite meanings. When you *borrow* something, you are accepting a loan. When you *lend* something, you are giving a loan.

The banker *lends* money.
We *borrow* money from the bank. } (present)

Joe *lent* me his bicycle.
I *borrowed* the bicycle from Joe. } (past)

He *has lent* his skates to her. } (past participle)
She *has borrowed* his skates.

Bring and take

Use *bring* when you mean an action that is *toward* the person speaking.
Use *take* when the action is *away from* the person speaking.

Bring the book to me.
Take the book to the library. } (present)

He *brought* me flowers. } (past)
He *took* flowers to Emily.

She *has brought* us candy.
What *has* she *taken* to our neighbor? } (past participle)

May and can

These verbs are always used as auxiliary verbs. Use *may* when you are referring to *permission* to do something. Use *can* when you are referring to the *ability* to do something.

May we leave now?   *Can* you play the piano?

Do not use *can* when you want to ask permission.

You have studied other confusing verb pairs in earlier grades. If you need help on *set–sit, lay–lie, learn–teach,* and *leave–let,* turn to the Review Handbook and find the ones you need to study. They are listed alphabetically in the Usage section, pages 449 and 452.

Exercises: Confusing verb pairs

1. Choose the correct word from each pair in parentheses.

1. (May, Can) I carry your books, Miss Stark?
2. He (rises, raises) this early every day.
3. I would (lend, borrow) you my book, but Jake has (lent, borrowed) it.
4. He (brought, took) my skin-diving equipment with him to Florida.
5. (May, Can) I (lend, borrow) your tools?
6. The two officers (rose, raised) the flag.
7. When I visit Marge, I (bring, take) her some cake.
8. The flood waters (rose, raised) higher and higher.
9. Mom asked, "Did you (bring, take) your report card home?"
10. We watched the rocket as it (rose, raised) from the launching pad.
11. You (may, can) play the leading role if you (may, can) find time to practice the lines.
12. He has (lent, borrowed) my paints, but he (lent, borrowed) me his guitar.
13. Did you see how the plane (rose, raised) its landing gear?
14. The prices on the menu have not (risen, raised) in two years.
15. (May, Can) I have my lawn mower, which you (lent, borrowed) last week?

2. Use each of these verbs in two sentences of your own: *rise, lend, take.* Use the verb first in the *past tense form* and second in the *past participle form.*

A Book to Read

Cold Hazard

by Richard Armstrong
Illustrated by C. Walter Hodges
Houghton Mifflin Company

You have probably never sailed aboard a tramp steamer or faced death in a lifeboat among icebergs, but by the time you have read this story of the terrifying struggle of five men against the cold fury of the North Altantic, you will feel as if you had. This exciting story ends five weeks, three days, and thirteen hours after the tramp *Drumlogan* struck the iceberg. None of the men who lived through the experience would ever be the same again.

About the author

When Richard Armstrong was sixteen, he left his home in the heart of the English mining district and went to sea. For seventeen years he sailed on colliers, tramp ships (like the *Drumlogan*), mail packets, and tankers. He began to write while he was still at sea and kept on writing books even after leaving the sea to go into newspaper work and private business. He was also an officer of the British Merchant Navy. He now lives in a cottage on a high hill in Somerset, England, in sight of the sea and passing ships.

Other books of his that you will enjoy are: *Desperate Voyage, The Big Sea, Fight for Freedom, The Secret Sea, Sea Change* (which won the Carnegie Medal, awarded by the British Library Association), and *Ship Afire.*

Test I

Next to the sentence numerals on your paper, write the correct forms of the pronouns.

1. These things belong to my sister and (we, us).
2. The shopowners were Sid and (he, him).
3. Six other girls and (I, me) made our own dresses.
4. I called Frank and (she, her) immediately.
5. Joe handed Bertha and (I, me) the oars.

Test II

Next to each sentence numeral on your paper, write the pronoun that agrees with the antecedent.

1. One person donated all of __?__ spare time.
2. Which child did not bring __?__ ticket?
3. They __?__ are to blame.
4. Each of the hikers carried __?__ own equipment.
5. Many of the girls brought __?__ own lunches.

Test III

For each sentence below, choose the verb that agrees with the subject and write it on your paper next to the sentence numeral:

1. Everyone at the party (was, were) happy at first.
2. One of the posters (has, have) fallen.
3. None of the food (was, were) wasted.
4. Both of the leaders (make, makes) decisions.
5. Either of the partners (do, does) this work.

Test IV

Choose the correct word from each pair in parentheses. Write your answers on your paper next to the appropriate numerals.

1. (This, That) eye has better vision than my left eye.
2. (Who, Whom) should we visit?
3. (Whose, Who's) performance was better?
4. (That, That there) is the best one.
5. (Whose, Who's) first on the list?
6. For (who, whom) was this purchased?

7. (Who, Whom) has the highest grade?

8. (This, This here) is my plan.

9. At (whose, who's) house shall we meet?

10. Our shutters are white. (Those, These) on the next house are black.

Test V

1. For each of these sentences, write the relative pronoun *who,* *which,* or *that* on your paper next to the sentence numeral. Be sure to use the correct forms of *who.*

1. Point out the boy __?__ is most qualified.

2. The dog __?__ has a blue ribbon belongs to my uncle.

3. The building __?__ has a clock in the tower will soon be demolished.

4. My friend, __?__ won the county spelling medal last year, has entered the state finals.

5. He is a tennis player __?__ style we should copy.

2. On your paper, copy and punctuate correctly the sentences below that need commas. Write "correct" next to the numerals of those sentences which do not need commas.

1. Joseph Banks whom you met last year is planning to visit me again.

2. Loretta is shopping with her mother who had a long list of items to buy.

3. The person who helped me most is Carl.

4. At last we have seen a movie which has a happy ending.

5. The one from whom you borrowed money has written you a note.

Test VI

On your paper, copy the italicized verbs below. Next to each one, write the tense of the verb.

1. The sailors *had feared* the captain.

2. Native women *painted* these fabrics.

3. He *will frighten* the puppy.

4. We *shall have finished* when you return.

5. I *have spoken* too quickly.

Test VII

1. Number your paper from 1 to 10. Write the correct form of the verb for each sentence. *Do not use the present tense.*

(arise)   1. There is one problem which __?__ yesterday.

(hide)   2. My sister Louise has __?__ all of the party decorations.

(hang)   3. That picture has __?__ over the fireplace for two generations.

(dive)   4. The seals at the aquarium in Florida __?__ for their food.

(hurt)   5. He has __?__ himself in the game.

(tear)   6. Stella has __?__ her best dress.

(become)   7. What has __?__ of your ambition?

(drive)   8. We had __?__ through the desert once before.

(burst)   9. The balloons had __?__ on our way home.

(wring)   10. The bathers __?__ out their bathing suits on this floor.

2. Write these headings on your paper: *Present, Past, Past Participle.* Under the correct headings, write the principal parts of these verbs:

1. beat	6. forget	11. wear
2. buy	7. forgive	12. shake
3. catch	8. get	13. swim
4. fall	9. strive	14. tell
5. find	10. swear	15. swing

Test VIII

On your paper beside the sentence numerals, write the correct word from each pair in parentheses.

1. The water in the reservoir has (risen, raised) over twice its normal depth.

2. Please (bring, take) your umbrella when you go out.

3. (May, Can) I (borrow, lend) your tent for my camping trip?

4. Everybody (rose, raised) when the judge entered.

5. (May, Can) we ask Edith to (bring, take) her cousin here for dinner?

Review and Practice

Exercise I

1. Review "Personal Pronouns" on pages 234–36.

2. Write these sentences correctly, using a personal pronoun in place of each blank:

   1. Dad divided the presents between my sister and __?__.
   2. Give Lucy and __?__ the directions.
   3. The class elected Bob and __?__.
   4. The suspects are Mr. Plot and __?__.
   5. Dan and __?__ are going to the rally with Joe and __?__.

Exercise II

1. Review the lessons on pages 236–38 and page 240.

2. Use the nouns and pronouns below in six sentences of your own. Use the nouns and pronouns on the left as antecedents of the pronouns in the list on the right.

	ANTECEDENTS		PRONOUNS
person	pianist	children	his
singers	one	each	her
			their

3. Write each sentence, using a compound personal pronoun in place of each blank.

   1. He chided __?__ silently.
   2. They divided the spoils among __?__.

Exercise III

1. Review "Indefinite Pronouns," page 239.

2. Choose the correct verb from each pair in parentheses.

   1. Each of those cows (has, have) won a prize.
   2. Neither of my parents (is, are) able to help me.
   3. One of the boys (is, are) absent today.
   4. Many of our neighbors (has, have) moved away.
   5. Another of those crows (is, are) flying overhead.
   6. Everybody (is, are) in favor of the decision.
   7. A few of the calves (has, have) strayed away.
   8. Both of them (know, knows) the answer.

Exercise IV

1. Review "Demonstrative Pronouns" and "Interrogative Pronouns," pages 242–43.

2. Choose the correct words from the pairs in parentheses. Write your answers on your paper next to the appropriate numerals.

1. With (who, whom) did he talk?
2. Are (these, these here) the most expensive?
3. (Those, These) are in your house, not here in mine.
4. (Whose, Who's) store has a sale?
5. (Whose, Who's) escorting you to the dance?
6. To (who, whom) do these belong?
7. (Who, Whom) are you inviting to the party?
8. (This, This here) is not mine.

Exercise V

1. Review "Relative Pronouns," pages 244–45.

2. Answer these questions about the use of relative pronouns:

1. Which pronoun is used only when the antecedent names a person?
2. Which pronoun is used when the antecedent names a person, animal, or thing?
3. Which form of the pronoun *who* is used when it is the subject of the clause?
4. Which form of *who* is used when it is the direct object of the clause?

3. Copy and punctuate those sentences below that need a comma or commas. Write "correct" for those sentences that do not need any commas.

1. Jonathan who loves to wear red vests is quite handsome in his new suit.
2. Is he the one with whom you often study?
3. We showed the model boat to my father who is an expert craftsman himself.
4. Show me the saleslady who took care of your order.
5. Murphy who will be here tomorrow will help us with the search.
6. Sarah who can do the job well may volunteer her services.

Exercise VI

1. Review "Tenses of Verbs," pages 247–50.
2. Name the tense of each of the following verbs:

    1. will sign   4. have seen
    2. had fired   5. repaired
    3. will have left   6. conceal

Exercise VII

1. Review "The Principal Parts of Verbs," pages 251–54.
2. Name the correct form of the verb.

(forgive)   1. Has he __?__ you for your mistake?
(forget)   2. He had quickly __?__ the address.
(shake)   3. The bear had __?__ the beehive.
(fall)   4. My hopes have __?__ again.
(buy)   5. Have you __?__ your notebook yet?
(get)   6. They have __?__ what they deserve.
(strive)   7. I __?__ to complete my project in time.
(sink)   8. His feet __?__ into the quicksand.
(swear)   9. Has the witness __?__ to tell the truth?
(wear)   10. Had your sister __?__ her heavy coat?

3. Write the three principal parts of these verbs:

    1. arise   5. hurt   9. wring
    2. hide   6. become 10. swing
    3. hang   7. drive   11. tell
    4. dive   8. burst   12. swim

4. Use *ought* and *oughtn't* in two sentences.

Exercise VIII

1. Review "Confusing Verb Pairs," pages 255–56.
2. Choose the correct verb from each pair in parentheses.

1. You (may, can) have your allowance early if you (may, can) improve your behavior.
2. The boys (rose, raised) when Mrs. Albert entered the room.
3. (Bring, Take) your report cards home so that I can see them.
4. (May, Can) I (borrow, lend) your sled tomorrow?
5. The repairman had (risen, raised) the hood of the car.

CHAPTER 10

Writing a Good Letter

You have only to hear an eager voice crying, "Any mail for me?" or to watch the shining interest on the face of a person opening a letter to know how welcome and enjoyable letters can be. Surely there is no kind of writing more important to do well than the writing of friendly and business letters.

Friendly Letters

The most important thing about a friendly letter is what it says. A friendly letter should be like a private conversation in writing, a conversation with a friend. The question to keep in mind as you write is: "What will interest and please my friend?"

There are many ways to write a friendly letter. Some people do it best by simply starting to chat informally without any careful preparation. It does them good to write about their life and feelings, and they do it entertainingly. Other people do better with some advance planning. They read over the last letter received from their friend and write down the things they want to say.

Quite a lot depends on how well you know the person to whom you are writing. If you know him well, you may not need to think much about what you are going to say before you start your letter. If you do not know him well, you will want to consider more carefully what to say. Remember, though, you will not be there to make explanations when your friend reads the letter. For this reason, avoid making vague statements that do not explain themselves. Try to put yourself in the situation of the person who will read the letter; then write as naturally as you can.

On page 266 is a letter written by Alice to a neighborhood friend who is spending a year with relatives in another state. Read it carefully and be prepared to discuss whether or not you think it is a good letter and why.

25 Healey Street
Flint, Michigan 48502
February 26, 19 —

Dear Jane,

I'm now sitting in my old chair looking out the window at the snow falling for the second day in a row.

Downstairs I can hear Mike arguing with Tom about who has to shovel the driveway. Mike is going out and has to get dressed before supper.

Sorry your aunt doesn't allow you to go to the movies very often. Our English teacher says that seeing good movies adds to our cultural education. Why not try that argument on your aunt?

Yes, I like your new hairdo very much — so does the rest of the family. Tom said, "Très chic!" when he saw the snapshot.

I wish you were with us in school this year — and I'm not the only one who does. I love getting your letters, so keep writing!

Mike asked me to send you his best. He won his argument, and I can now see Tom furiously digging his shovel into the new layers of snow. So you see, things haven't changed much.

Love,
Alice

To discuss

Answer these questions about Alice's letter on the opposite page:

1. Did Alice write the letter after careful planning, or did she write as thoughts occurred to her? How do you know?
2. How does Alice show that she has read Jane's last letter? Does Alice show interest in her friend? Explain.
3. Did Alice write about vague general things or specific people and events that would interest Jane?
4. Did Alice make excuses for untidiness or for closing the letter? Is the appearance of her letter neat?
5. Did Alice gossip in a way that will make her friend unhappy? Did she complain, show anger, and say unfriendly things?
6. How many parts are there in a friendly letter? Name them.
7. What information does Alice give in each letter part? Did she include her Zip Code? A Zip Code identifies "a delivery unit and associates that unit with a major post office through which mail is routed for delivery."

Exercise: The body of a friendly letter

Read the following excerpts from friendly letters. Number your paper from 1 to 10 and, for each excerpt, write *Yes* if it is appropriate for a friendly letter or *No* if it is not. Then, in a sentence or two, explain each answer. Compare and discuss your answers in class.

EXAMPLE: 1. No, Pooch hasn't settled down yet. He's growing fast, but he still barks at the postman, and yesterday he chewed up three pairs of shoes.

YOU WRITE: *1. Yes. The writer is answering a question in his friend's letter.*

1. Things are about the same as always here. Nothing new has happened. At school there are just as many funny things going on as usual, and we all enjoy laughing at them.
2. Guess what? I'm going to go to Camp Fields next summer. Since it's only fifteen miles from your house, maybe we can plan some visits on the weekends. The camp allows overnight guests on Saturday. Mom said that she plans to write to your mother to invite you.

3. When your letters come, they are so interesting that I read parts of them to the family at the supper table. Last night we all had a wonderful time laughing over what you wrote about your troubles with those squirrels.

4. I know this letter is a mess, but you're lucky to hear from me at all, so I hope you can read it.

5. I'm still mad when I think that it's been three weeks since you spent the weekend with us, and you've never even written to my mother to say thank you.

6. Well, I'd like to write more, but I'm pretty busy these days, so I hope you don't mind too much if I close now.

7. Do you remember that old engine Mr. Smith gave you and me last April? Well, our manual training class has repaired it and has just about finished mounting it on a ski tow at the top of Pine Knob.

8. When you get back, I advise you to stay away from Pete and Ben. They've been saying a lot of unpleasant things about you. I know they aren't true, but probably a lot of other people aren't so sure.

9. We had a wonderful junior-high canteen last Saturday. The ninth-grade boys put on a skit imitating a girls' basketball game. It was a riot, especially Fred imitating you. We all screamed with laughter.

10. Meg, would you please do me a favor? I could use pictures of some modern industrial buildings in Texas for my social studies class. I already have several from around Boston. Now don't do it if it's too much trouble. I'll pay you whatever you have to spend.

The Form for Friendly Letters

Your letters will represent you better if they are written neatly and in proper form. Read the suggestions listed below:

1. Most people prefer white stationery, with the envelope matching the letter paper. Avoid highly colored paper.

2. A friendly letter may be typed or written by hand. Some people feel that handwriting seems more personal.

3. There should be a good straight margin on the left-hand side of the paper.

4. There are two forms for arranging a friendly letter:

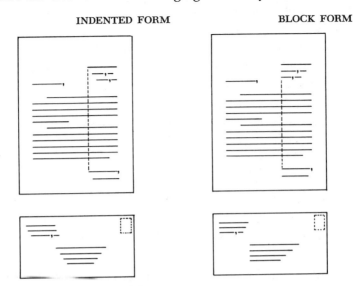

INDENTED FORM   BLOCK FORM

Use whichever form your teacher recommends. Notice the relative positions of the various parts of the letter.

5. If you are writing to a person you know well, you should sign only your first name. Otherwise, sign both your first and last names.

6. It is generally preferable not to use abbreviations in the heading and body of the letter. An exception is the fact that you *do* abbreviate titles before names: *Dr.*, *Mr.*, and *Mrs.*

Guides for capitalizing and punctuating friendly letters

1. Capitalize all proper names.
2. Place a comma between the names of the city and state but not between the Zip Code and the state.

   Portland, Oregon   97208
3. Place a comma between the day and the year.
4. Never put a comma at the end of any line in the heading.
5. Capitalize the first word of the salutation. Place a comma after the last word of the salutation.

   My dear Susan,   Dear Uncle Gerald,
6. Capitalize the first word of the closing. The other words begin with small letters. Place a comma at the end of the closing.

   Very sincerely yours,   With love,   Yours truly,

1. Write the following headings correctly:

1. 8207 wake forest drive—houston texas 77002—march 22 19—
2. 64 overwood road—akron ohio 44309—january 8 19—
3. 700 highland avenue—duluth minnesota 55801—february 17 19—
4. 2636 etna street—berkeley california 94704—april 18 19—
5. 8512 pelham road—baltimore maryland 21220—may 1 19—

2. Write the following salutations correctly:

1. my dear sue
2. dear aunt mary
3. dear dad
4. dear mr schwartz

3. Write the following closings correctly:

1. love—mary
2. sincerely yours—tom
3. your friend—frances
4. much love—ernest

Preparation for mailing

Reread and check your letter before mailing it. Make sure that it is neat and in the proper form. Also check your spelling. After you have done this, fold your letter and place it in the envelope so that it will be right side up and ready to read when it is taken out of the envelope. The sketches below show how to do this:

The envelope

Address the envelope plainly and fully. Write the return address —your address—on the upper left-hand side of the envelope. Use indented or block form, whichever you used in your letter. Use no abbreviations; they are easily misread. If you write the name of the state below the name of the city, it will make the sorting at the post office easier.

Here is the envelope for Alice's letter on page 266:

Alice Rainey
25 Healey Street
Flint, Michigan 48502

Miss Jane R. Squires
60 Exeter Street
Dallas
Texas 75201

Guides for writing friendly letters

1. Write informally, as if you were conversing with your friend. Tell what you are doing, what you are thinking, and how you are feeling. Be specific and give details.
2. Comment on the last letter you received from your friend. Answer any questions he may have asked. Be appreciative.
3. Tell some news that will interest the reader.
4. Write neatly and legibly, using the standard letter-writing form, as shown in the model letter on page 266.
5. Avoid making excuses for untidiness or for closing your letter.

Exercise: Writing letters

Think of someone who would like to hear from you, and write that person a letter. Although your letter is written as an English exercise and will be read by your teacher and perhaps by some of your classmates, try to make it sound like yourself. Write it on the type of stationery you would normally use, and prepare an envelope for it. If you prefer not to write a letter to a real person, follow one of the suggestions below, making up whatever facts you need:

1. Write to a friend who has moved away and attends another school.
2. Write to your mother, who is away for a month caring for a relative.
3. Write to a former teacher.
4. Write to your brother or sister, who is away for the summer.
5. Write to an aunt or uncle whom you know very well.
6. Write to an older cousin, now away at college.

Social Notes

It is important to be thoughtful of others, and one of the qualities of a considerate, courteous person is his awareness of this. Writing letters expressing your thanks or your sympathy and issuing and replying to invitations are some of the ways in which you can show thoughtfulness and extend courtesy.

On the following pages are examples of the principal kinds of social notes. They will suggest to you acceptable ways of writing such notes. Study them with care, but when you write your own social notes, be yourself and express your own ideas.

Thank-you note

It is always proper to thank a person for a gift or for some kindness he has shown you. Occasionally you may need to thank a person for something you really do not like. In such cases, you can certainly express your appreciation of the thoughtfulness of the donor.

452 Goundry Street
Utica, New York 13503
November 12, 19 —

Dear Uncle Fred,

The harmonica you gave me for my birthday is exactly what I wanted. Someone must have told you that I have been playing on an old mouth organ that Ray didn't want any more. Maybe you didn't know I've joined a harmonica band at school and now with this new harmonica, I'll be able to play with the best of them.

When you come to visit next spring, we ought to be good enough to put on a concert for you. Anyway, you can be sure I'm practicing every day. I'm very grateful to you, Uncle Fred. Thanks a lot!

Your appreciative nephew,
John

Bread-and-butter letter

If you have been invited to spend the night or weekend with someone, it is polite to write a note of thanks after you return home. Such a note is called a bread-and-butter letter. Your letter should do more than just say thanks. It should show the reader that you really appreciated his hospitality. Read the model on page 274.

12 Ninth Avenue South
Tulsa, Oklahoma 74111
August 30, 19—

Dear Mrs. Monks,

   I'm back home safe and sound and want to thank you for the wonderful week Peggy and I spent with your family in Boulder. How beautiful Colorado is! The trips you arranged for us were fun, especially the one in Estes Park. The sight of those snow-capped mountains in the distance is a view I'll never forget.

   I've told the family all about your house and the sleeping cabin in the woods. I'm going to try to persuade Dad to build one on our place.

   Again, thanks for everything: good food, good talk, and exciting adventures. It was one of the best weeks I've ever spent.

      Sincerely yours,

      Alberta

Note of apology

There are times when you may have done something inconsiderate or something which may have been misunderstood. Often a written note of apology is the most thoughtful way to handle such a situation.

> 77 Claremont Avenue
> Elizabeth, New Jersey 07208
> October 14, 19—
>
> Dear Mr. Faulkner,
> Mother told me about your telephone call yesterday. I certainly do understand why you object to our coming through your hedge on our way to the playground. I guess we never realized how much we were damaging it and your lawn. You can be sure we shall be more thoughtful in the future, and I apologize for having troubled you so much.
> Sincerely yours,
> Jeffrey Oakes

Letter of invitation

All letters of invitation should include information about the day, date, time, and place of the occasion, as well as what the activity will be, so that guests will know how they should dress. If the occasion is one where parents will need to pick up their boy or girl at the end, you should specify what time the party will be over.

A letter of invitation may be written on regular stationery or on a correspondence card.

Generally it is better not to issue invitations at school. It can cause embarrassment to those who are not invited.

123 East Parkway
Memphis, Tennessee 38101
May 14, 19—

Dear Barbara,

I hope you can come to lunch at my house on Saturday, May 24, at twelve o'clock, with the other girls from our section. After lunch we are going to the two o'clock showing of <u>The Weavers.</u> The show will be over at about four. Your parents can pick you up at the Aldo Theater, 56 Elm Drive, or about four-thirty at our house.

Sincerely yours,
Jean Ruff

Here is the same invitation, this time written on an informal card:

A Party!

Where? At our house, 123 East Parkway
When? 12:00, Saturday, May 24
What? For lunch and to see <u>The Weavers</u>, Aldo Theater, 56 Elm Drive

Your parents may pick you up at the theater at four or at our house at about four-thirty.

R. S. V. P. Jean Ruff
123 East Parkway
Memphis, Tennessee 38101

Notes of regret and acceptance

Invitations should be answered *promptly*. It is not polite to wait until a day or two before the occasion before replying. When you are unable to accept an invitation, it is courteous, although not necessary, to explain why.

Always reply to the address from which the invitation was issued. Do not reply at school or by telephone, unless you are specifically invited to do so. It can cause embarrassment and make it more difficult for the person giving the party to keep track of who is coming and who cannot come.

> 1318 Goodbar Street
> Memphis, Tennessee 38101
> May 16, 19—
>
> Dear Jean,
>   I'm terribly disappointed not to be able to accept your invitation to lunch and to see <u>The Weavers</u>. Unfortunately, the twenty-fourth is the day we plan to drive to the country to spend the weekend with my Aunt Frieda, and its too late to change the date.
>   Thanks very much for inviting me. I hate to miss the fun.
>   Yours sincerely,
>   Barbara Jones

1318 Goodbar Street
Memphis, Tennessee 38101
May 16, 19 —

Dear Jean,

I'll be glad to come to your house to lunch at twelve on Saturday the twenty-fourth. I've heard that <u>The Weavers</u> *is excellent.*

My mother will pick me up outside the theater at about four.

See you then, and thanks!
Sincerely yours,
Barbara Jones

Exercise: Writing social notes

Write any three of the following letters or notes:

1. An invitation for the entire class to go to a softball game, followed by supper at your house.
2. A note accepting an invitation to an afternoon movie party.
3. A note of regret for not being able to attend a birthday party.
4. A note apologizing for having knocked over and broken a lamp at your cousin's house.
5. A bread-and-butter letter thanking the mother of a classmate for a weekend you spent with them while your parents were away.
6. A thank-you note for a shirt or blouse the color and pattern of which you do not like.
7. A note congratulating a friend on having been named the most valuable player on the basketball team of a neighboring school.
8. Any social note you may need to write.

FROM *The Three Best Things.* I. WORK

Let me but do my work from day to day,
  In field or forest, at the desk or loom,
  In roaring market place or tranquil room;
Let me but find it in my heart to say,
When vagrant wishes beckon me astray,
  "This is my work; my blessing, not my doom;
  Of all who live, I am the one by whom
This work can best be done in the right way."

HENRY VAN DYKE

What does "vagrant" mean? Do "vagrant wishes" ever beckon you to stray from your homework? How does the poet look upon all honest work? Do you agree?

Memorize these lines from one of America's popular writers of both prose and poetry who lived in the late nineteenth and early twentieth centuries. Henry van Dyke was a poet, teacher, and clergyman.

Business Letters

A business letter is different from a friendly letter. Its only purpose is to arrange the business in a brief, clear, and courteous manner. If you can type well, it is preferable to type business letters. It is also wise to keep a carbon copy of your letter in case some question arises later.

The form of a business letter is the same as that of a friendly letter, with three exceptions:

1. It contains an inside address.
2. A colon (:) follows the salutation.
3. It should always be in block form.

The paragraphs may be indented or not, as you wish. On the following pages are examples of correctly written business letters.

Letter of request

A letter of request should give all the information needed in order to enable the person replying to be as helpful as possible. The following letter does a good job in this respect:

```
                                34 Avery Street
                                Topeka, Kansas  66601
                                December 13, 19--


National Council of Teachers of English
508 South Sixth Street
Champaign, Illinois  61820

Dear Sirs:

    Some of my friends and I are inter-
ested in starting a voluntary reading club.
My English teacher tells me that the Na-
tional Council of Teachers of English pub-
lishes a number of lists which are good
guides to reading for enjoyment.  Please
send me a description of the lists avail-
able and information about prices.  Our
club members range in age from thirteen
to fifteen.

    Thank you very much.

                        Very truly yours,

                        Clement Morse

                        Clement Morse
```

To discuss

Compare the form and content of Clement's business letter above with the form and content of friendly letters. Then consider these questions:

1. Which letter part is not included in a friendly letter? What information is given in this letter part?
2. What is the difference in the punctuation of the salutation between the two types of letters?
3. How do the signatures differ?
4. Are there any other differences that you notice? Discuss them.

Order letter

In an order letter, you must be sure to give exact information about numbers, sizes, prices, and method of payment. If you are not careful about this, your order may be impossible to fill correctly and will waste your time and the time of the business employee who must fill the order. If the firm provides an order blank, use that instead of writing a letter.

2311 Connecticut Avenue, N.W.
Washington, D.C.   20013
April 29, 19--

Sam's Camping Store
20 South 12th Street
Philadelphia, Pennsylvania   19104

Dear Sirs:

Please send me the following items from your new summer catalog:

No. 107-W	3 pup tents @ $4.98	$14.94
No. 109-W	6 yards of nylon netting @ $0.57 per yard	3.42
No. 72-G	1 large bottle of Mos-Go insect repellent	1.37
		$19.73

I enclose a check for $19.73. If shipment cannot be made soon enough to arrive before May 15, please let me know at once.

Very truly yours,

Selena Crosfield

Selena Crosfield

Letter of adjustment

Sometimes a mistake is made, either by you or by the firm with which you are doing business, and you need to write a letter to straighten matters out. Be sure to keep your letter polite and factual.

```
                               1230 Park Hill Road
                               Yonkers, New York  10701
                               September 13, 19--


Cedar Sport Supply Company
6024 Chew Avenue
Camden, New Jersey  08101

Gentlemen:

     On August 15, I ordered the following
items from your catalog:

          9A69312   1 "j" snorkel, 16" long
          9A7930    1 neoprene flotation device

     When I received the goods a few days
ago, and tested them, I discovered that the
flotation device had a small puncture.  Neither
could I find the CO₂ cartridge that should
come with the device.

     Therefore, I am returning the device
to you, express collect, and would appreciate
your sending me another one.  If you cannot
send me one before the end of this month,
please let me know at once so that I may
place an order elsewhere.  In this case,
please refund my money ($11.67, including
postage).

                         Yours truly,

                         Maybelle Pruitt

                         Maybelle Pruitt
```

Guides for writing business letters

1. Write your letter neatly, politely, and clearly.
2. Type your letter, if possible.
3. Include your address, city and state, Zip Code, and the date in the heading.
4. Include the inside address. Make sure that it is identical with the address on the envelope.
5. Use block form.
6. Use a colon after the salutation.
7. Give all the needed information, as, for example, prices, sizes, dates, and quantities in an order letter.
8. Be brief and to the point.
9. Close in the standard way: *Yours truly,*   *Sincerely yours,*
10. Type your name under the signature. If your letter is hand-written, print your name under the signature if it is not legible.

Exercise: Writing business letters

Write one of the following letters. When your letter has been corrected and returned by your teacher, exchange it with another member of the class for reply.

1. Order a sports uniform and a pair of socks and sneakers from a mail-order sportswear house. Make up a name for the sportswear company and a catalog number for each item. Give the quantity, size, color, and price of each article. Be sure to tell how payment is being made.

    ANSWER: There will be a three-week delay in shipment. Ask if customer wants his money back.

2. Write a letter of adjustment to Beaux-Arts Studio, 1202 Washburn Street, Scranton, Pennsylvania 18503, concerning a collection of a dozen prints you ordered. Three of the prints were torn when you opened the package.

    ANSWER: Prints cannot be replaced. Offer to refund the full price of the order or one-quarter price if the customer wants to keep the undamaged prints.

3. Write to a summer camp, requesting information about their facilities for your age group and the cost of a two-week stay.

    ANSWER: Explain that the enrollment is full until the last two weeks in August. Those wishing to spend these weeks at the camp must send in their application before May 1. Add information about the camp's facilities and rates.

Test I

1. On your paper, list the numerals from 1 to 5. Write the names of the five basic parts of a friendly letter.

2. On your paper, list the numerals from 1 to 5. Read the sentences and word groups below. Next to the appropriate numeral, write the letter of the item that would be most suitable for a friendly letter.

1. (*a*) Nothing much has happened, so I'll make this short.
   (*b*) Little has happened since I saw you last week. But knowing how Rover took to you, I thought you'd enjoy hearing about his new tricks.
   (*c*) Sorry I haven't written for two months, but I just came across your old letter.

2. (*a*) Al told me you had a great time on your trip.
   (*b*) Boy, I'm glad that Bob isn't my friend.
   (*c*) How stupid can you be?

3. (*a*) I've nothing more to say, so I'm signing off.
   (*b*) Sorry I've misspelled some words, but I'm very tired.
   (*c*) Here's wishing you the best on your new adventure.

4. (*a*) How are you? I am fine. Hope you are fine, too.
   (*b*) Why don't you write? Is your hand broken?
   (*c*) Your last letter was just wonderful. You surely haven't lost your sense of humor, Molly.

5. (*a*) Your old pal,   (*b*) Very truly yours,
       Stephen Butler   Steve Butler
                    (*c*) Your good buddy,
                            Steve

Test II

1. On your paper, list the numerals from 1 to 5. Rewrite these parts of friendly letters correctly:

1. Augusta, Ga., 30906
2. my dear aunt lizzy
3. yours most sincerely
4. 62 graham st—peoria, ill. 61607
5. march 23 19—

2. On your paper, list the numerals from 1 to 5. Read each of the statements below about friendly letters. Next to the appropriate numeral, write *T* if the statement is true and *F* if the statement is false.

1. Friendly letters must always be handwritten.
2. Letters may be written in either the indented form or the block form.
3. It is correct to abbreviate the titles *Dr.*, *Mr.*, and *Mrs.*
4. Remember to excuse yourself for untidiness.
5. Colored paper is the preferred stationery.

Test III

On your paper, answer these questions about social notes:

1. What information should be in a letter of invitation?
2. In a thank-you note, how do you thank a person for a gift you really do not like?
3. When and why is a bread-and-butter letter written?
4. Why is it better not to issue invitations at school?

Test IV

1. On your paper, list the numerals from 1 to 5. Read the statements below about business letters. Write the letter *a*, *b*, or *c* of the item which completes each statement correctly.

1. A salutation is followed by a (*a*) comma, (*b*) semicolon, (*c*) colon.
2. Unlike a friendly letter, a business letter has (*a*) an inside address, (*b*) a Zip Code, (*c*) no margins.
3. In a business letter, always use (*a*) indented form, (*b*) indented paragraphs, (*c*) block form.
4. A typed business letter should show (*a*) a handwritten and typed signature, (*b*) a printed signature, (*c*) only a handwritten signature.
5. In a letter of adjustment, (*a*) tell how upset you are, (*b*) be polite and factual, (*c*) make friendly and chatty comments.

2. Write a letter ordering from Brock's Scientific Outlet, 584 South Saginaw Street, Flint, Michigan 48502, a spectrum chart, number 57–643, that sells for $5.25 and a right-angle prism, number 57–573, that sells for $.92. Parcel post will be $.49.

Review and Practice

Exercise I

1. Review "Friendly Letters" on pages 265–71.
2. Which of the items below are appropriate for friendly letters? Write the numerals on your paper.

1. Write about vague general happenings.
2. Show interest in your friend by referring to his last letter.
3. Be sure to make excuses for closing your letter hurriedly.
4. Avoid gossip that will make your friend unhappy.
5. Write informally as if you were talking with your friend.
6. Tell news that will interest your friend.
7. Apologize for a messy letter.
8. Include the Zip Code.

3. Write a friendly letter, using your own name and address. Label the five parts of your letter.

Exercise II

1. Review page 269.
2. Write the following parts of a letter correctly:

1. 607 marshall street—boise idaho 83701—october 16, 19—
2. 1472 westview ave.—portland maine 04101—jan. 11, 19—
3. dear mr sampson
4. cordially yours

Exercise III

1. Review "Social Notes" on pages 272–79.
2. In your own words, explain the content and tone needed for each of these social notes: *thank-you note, bread-and-butter letter, note of apology, letter of invitation, note of acceptance,* and *note of regret.*

Exercise IV

1. Review "Business Letters" on pages 280–84.
2. Write an imaginary business letter to MacDonald's Athletic Goods at 108 West 6th Avenue, Topeka, Kansas 66601. Order a $6.00 megaphone, catalog number 2064A, and a $4.50 blue jersey, catalog number 5M222. Enclose a check which will also cover a postage fee of $.73. Use your own home address and include all the parts of a business letter.

CHAPTER 11

Verbals

You have already seen how difficult it is to say which part of speech a word is unless you know the work it is doing in a sentence. Which part of speech is the word *quarreling* in each sentence below?

1. Those boys are *quarreling*.   2. The *quarreling* stopped.

In sentence 1, *quarreling* is a verb, because it expresses the action of the sentence. In sentence 2, it is a noun, because it is the subject of the sentence and is signaled by the determiner *the*.

Verbs, then, can do the work of other parts of speech. In sentence 2 above, the word *quarreling* is called a **verbal** because it is a verb form that is not the verb of the sentence.

Participles

One type of verbal, which does the work of an adjective, is called a **participle.** Participles are verb forms which modify nouns or pronouns, just as adjectives do. Here are sentences in which the arrows point from the participle to the noun or pronoun modified:

1. The *crowded* bus drove ahead of the *speeding* car.
2. *Encouraged* at last, I went bravely back to work.
3. The dog, *yelping* loudly, bounded down the garden path.

It is important not to confuse a participle with a verb that is a part of a verb phrase. In a verb phrase, the *–ing* or *–ed* form of the verb goes with one or more auxiliary, or helping, verbs.

PARTICIPLE: The *drenching* rain spoiled our picnic.
VERB PHRASE: The rain *was drenching* the picnickers.

PARTICIPLE: A *watched* pot never boils.
VERB PHRASE: We *had watched* that pot for over an hour.

■ A word that is formed from a verb but does the work of another part of speech in a sentence is called a **verbal.**

■ A **participle** is a verb form that does the work of an adjective.

Exercise: Participles

For each italicized word below, tell whether it is a part of a verb phrase which makes a statement about the subject or is a participle modifying a noun. If it is a participle, name the word it modifies.

1. My dog captured the *fleeing* robber.
2. The robber was *fleeing* from my dog.
3. The lions were *growling* cheerfully in the cage.
4. A *growling* lion is probably not a cheerful lion.
5. Henry knocked over a kettle of *boiling* water.
6. The kettle had been *boiling* for five minutes when Henry knocked it over.
7. Alice, *peering* through the keyhole, was frightened by what she saw.
8. Alice had been *peering* through the keyhole.
9. Miss Smith had been *teaching* all day and needed some rest.
10. Miss Smith, *teaching* all day, needed some rest.

Participial phrases

Although participles modify nouns or pronouns as adjectives do, they retain some of the characteristics of verbs; that is, they can be modified by adverbs or adverb phrases and can have objects.

1. *Climbing quickly to the summit*, the explorer was filled with joy.
2. Suddenly I heard the train *whistling loudly*.
3. The Jones family, *missing their old community*, wrote letters to their friends.

Do you see that in each sentence the participle and italicized words related to it act as an adjective modifying a noun? In sentence 1, this modification is shown by an arrow: the word group modifies the noun *explorer*. Tell what noun is modified in sentences 2 and 3.

Such word groups are called **participial phrases.**

PUNCTUATION NOTE: If a participial phrase appears at the beginning of a sentence, always put a comma after it. If the phrase comes at the end or in the middle of a sentence, a comma is used if you feel the need to pause before and after the phrase. Otherwise no commas are needed.

■ A **participial phrase** is a group of words containing a participle and any modifiers or objects. The entire phrase modifies a noun or pronoun.

Exercises: Participial phrases

1. Pick out the participial phrases in the following sentences. Tell which word is the participle and name the noun or pronoun modified by the participial phrase.

1. Seeing the danger, John went to the rescue.
2. Our dog, running across the street, may be hit by a car.
3. The sweater, covered with burrs, was almost ruined.
4. Drinking his milk noisily, the dog frightened the cat.
5. He sat alone, playing with a torn ribbon.
6. Encouraged by the cheers, our team finally won the game.
7. The boys, cleaning the cellar, found an old car horn.
8. Puzzled by the wrong cues, the actor did not give a good performance.

2. In each participial phrase below, name the participle and then name its object or its modifiers.

EXAMPLE: 1. hurrying across the room

YOU WRITE: *1. hurrying — participle*
across the room — adverb phrase
modifying participle

1. reading an exciting new book
2. caught in the thunderstorm
3. sniffing the flowers greedily
4. finding someone there
5. lifting the heavy load gladly
6. marching bravely behind the dog pack
7. rolling across the court
8. delighted by the attention

Dangling participles

A common mistake in writing is to begin a sentence with a participial phrase that does not modify the subject of the sentence. This error is called a **dangling participle.**

Can you see what is wrong with the way the participial phrases are used in the following sentences?

1. *Having finished our picnic lunch,* the car wouldn't start.
2. *Carrying all those packages,* the door was difficult to open.

Do you see that in sentence 1, *Having finished our picnic lunch* modifies the noun *car?* However, the car obviously didn't eat the lunch, and therefore the sentence is nonsense. It would make sense if it were revised to read:

Having finished our picnic lunch, we found the car wouldn't start.

How would you revise sentence 2 so that it makes sense?

Remember: An introductory participial phrase must modify the subject of the sentence.

Exercises: Dangling participles

1. Each sentence below contains a dangling participle. Beginning with the same participial phrase, revise the rest of the sentence so that the subject is the word that the phrase modifies.

1. Eating the salted nuts, our thirst increased.
2. Having read the letter, our excitement over the plan was great.
3. Standing under the awning, the shade was refreshing to us.
4. Working quietly, the parts of the model jet were soon assembled by Jed.
5. Having started the job, no thought of resting entered Len's mind.
6. Having spent my money, there was none left for Walter's present.
7. Hiding under cover of darkness, our whereabouts was not noticed by the other fellows.
8. Looking over the ledge, a strange sight met our eyes.
9. Having read the new book, my search for another began.
10. Having missed the bus, the wait for the next one was an hour.

2. Use the phrases below to begin sentences of your own. Be sure the participial phrase modifies the noun or pronoun subject of the sentence. Since each phrase will appear at the beginning of a sentence, use a comma to set it off from the rest of the sentence.

1. having missed one of the meetings
2. needing some camp equipment
3. saddling the horse in the first stall
4. deciding on a definite plan
5. having rushed to the train station
6. having surprised everyone but me

TO MEMORIZE

Stopping by Woods on a Snowy Evening

Whose woods these are I think I know.
His house is in the village though;
He will not see me stopping here
To watch his woods fill up with snow.

My little horse must think it queer
To stop without a farmhouse near
Between the woods and frozen lake
The darkest evening of the year.

He gives his harness bells a shake
To ask if there is some mistake.
The only other sound's the sweep
Of easy wind and downy flake.

The woods are lovely, dark, and deep,
But I have promises to keep,
And miles to go before I sleep,
And miles to go before I sleep.

ROBERT FROST

The poet Robert Frost is a favorite of many Americans. A famous literary critic said that this poem is one of the most haunting lyrics ever written by an American. To explain his word "haunting" the critic said, "once in the mind of a reader, [the poem] will never leave it."

This poem lends itself to many interpretations. What meaning do you think the poet intended? Does he simply describe sitting in a sleigh by dark woods during a quiet snowfall?

Gerunds

Another type of verbal is the **gerund,** a verb form that does the work of a noun.

Here are some sentences containing gerunds. Each gerund is italicized.

1. *Skating* is great fun. (subject)
2. I like *speaking* to Jane, but I don't like *playing* games with her. (direct objects)
3. Your experience in deep-sea *diving* is a good subject for *writing*. (objects of prepositions)

Notice that all gerunds end in *–ing* and that they name an action. However, as you have seen, not all words that end in *–ing* are gerunds. Participles and parts of verb phrases may also end in *–ing*:

GERUND: *Gossiping* is a favorite sport of those girls.

PARTICIPLE: I saw two old ladies *gossiping* in the garden.

VERB PHRASE: My aunt *was gossiping* enthusiastically.

■ A **gerund** is a verb form that does the work of a noun.

Exercises: Gerunds

1. Name the gerunds in the following sentences. Tell whether each one is used as *subject, direct object,* or *object of a preposition.*

1. A good spanking is what that child needs.
2. Do you enjoy swimming so much?
3. Devouring large quantities of food is foolhardy.
4. We are tired of that yelling.
5. Laughing, joking, and whispering were the main activities at my little sister's party.

2. One or more *–ing* words are in each of the following sentences. List them in order on your paper, and after each, write *gerund, participle,* or *verb* to indicate how the word is used in the sentence. Be prepared to explain your answers.

1. Studying will help you pass your school courses.
2. My cousin was studying all weekend.
3. I saw John studying for the test.

4. Cheering loudly, the crowd urged the team forward.
5. Jacob had been teasing his sister too long.
6. There was Molly, peeking out from behind the curtains.
7. Although all nations do it, spying is not a popular occupation.
8. Creeping across the map, the spider distracted the geographer.
9. Making so much noise is not helping our class to improve its reputation.
10. Speaking frankly, I am tired of your complaining.

3. Use each of the following words in three sentences, once as a *participle*, once as a *gerund*, and once as a *part of a verb phrase*, in that order:

1. talking	5. running
2. driving	6. reading
3. lifting	7. laughing
4. disappearing	8. crying

Infinitives

The **infinitive** consists of a verb form with the word *to* before it. Here are some infinitives:

to go	to combine
to see	to sell
to believe	to refuse

The *to* before an infinitive is a part of the verbal (a kind of signal); it is not a preposition.

Infinitives can be used as different parts of speech and in different ways. They can, for example, be used in place of nouns in sentences. They can also be modifiers.

Study the infinitives in the sentences below and on the next page:

1. *To think* is very important. (*To think* is used as a noun and as the subject of the sentence.)
2. The dog wanted *to bite*. (*To bite* is used as a noun and as the direct object of *wanted*.)

3. George's early morning habit was *to walk* around the block. (*To walk* is used as a noun and as the subject complement.)
4. The boy *to ask* is Harold. (*To ask* is used as an adjective, modifying the noun *boy.*)
5. The new symphony is pleasant *to hear.* (*To hear* is used as an adverb, modifying the adjective *pleasant.*)
6. He climbed the mountain *to escape* the heat. (*To escape* is used as an adverb, modifying the verb *climbed.*)

■ An **infinitive** is a verb form that begins with *to.* It can be used as a noun, as an adjective, or as an adverb.

Exercises: Infinitives

1. Pick out the infinitives in the following sentences. Explain how each is used in the sentence. (Be careful not to choose prepositional phrases. An infinitive begins with *to* followed by a verb; if a prepositional phrase begins with *to,* it is followed by a noun or pronoun.)

1. I want to sleep.
2. George raised his voice to get attention.
3. To sign the treaty was the main reason for the conference.
4. To sit, to fish, and to dream are the ingredients of a perfect vacation.
5. This old sweater is easy to wear but difficult to wash.
6. There were too many problems to do.
7. I do not want to fail the test.
8. She baked a cake to please her brother.
9. "I don't want to return to school," said little Libby.
10. That type of note is too difficult to write.
11. He refused to admit the truth to the others.
12. To tell the truth is a joy to the teller and a relief to the hearer.

2. Use each of the following infinitives in a sentence of your own. In parentheses, write *noun, adjective,* or *adverb,* depending on how you have used it in the sentence.

1. to complain	4. to rest
2. to enjoy	5. to report
3. to harm	6. to find

Johnny Tremain

by Esther Forbes

Illustrated by Lynd Ward

Houghton Mifflin Company

At first Johnny Tremain, a fourteen-year-old orphan living in Boston, was boss of the attic of Mr. Lapham, the silversmith for whom he worked. He lorded it over the other apprentices. Then came a tragic day. A crucible broke, and molten silver streamed over Johnny's hand. His right hand was permanently maimed. Mr. Lapham was forced to break his contract with the young worker, and, feeling useless, Johnny sank into despair.

But life had not stopped for Johnny. There were exciting days ahead. He became a rider for the Committee of Public Safety, where he not only came in contact with James Otis, John Hancock, Paul Revere, and other Boston patriots, but also found himself part of the intrigue that led from the Boston Tea Party to the Battle of Lexington. In the course of these events he fell in love with Cilla, and finally regained hope and confidence in himself.

Johnny Tremain makes the reader the spectator in a difficult but glorious period in our history.

About the author

Esther Forbes is a historical novelist. It is not surprising that she is interested in early American history. One of her ancestresses died in a Massachusetts jail, accused of being a witch; another was said to be troubled by visions of the devil and by black imps biting her feet. Such family traditions served to increase Miss Forbes's interest in American history, and she has written many books about life in the American colonies.

Test I

Copy each participial phrase below and, next to it, write the noun or pronoun it modifies:

1. The natives, working with simple tools, carved these statues.
2. Plowing his land, the farmer worked until sundown.
3. Having cut the trees, the lumberjacks moved their camp.
4. We finally located Mom trying on new hats.
5. Mark, needing new supplies, drove the truck into town.

Test II

Rewrite these sentences, correcting the dangling participles:

1. Traveling on the plane, his father's advice returned to Jack's thoughts.
2. Having upset her friend, no words could console Alice.
3. Remembering Bob's request, my first task was to repair his bicycle wheel.
4. Being in no hurry, the hay wagon carried us slowly to the barn dance.

Test III

On your paper, list all the *–ing* words in these sentences. Next to each, write *participle, gerund,* or *verb,* depending on how it is used in the sentence.

1. George, seeing the danger, quickly re-entered the cabin.
2. Eating these sandwiches by the lake is pleasant.
3. Crowing loudly, the roosters annoy us on Sunday.
4. The roosters in the barnyard have been crowing for an hour.
5. We always enjoy visiting with you.

Test IV

Copy each infinitive below and next to it, write how it is used: *subject, direct object, subject complement, adjective,* or *adverb*.

1. He had no money to spare.
2. To replace one of these parts is not easy.
3. I want to see a movie.
4. My main purpose was to meet Lucas.
5. We called Marie to invite her.

Exercise I

1. Review "Participles" on pages 288–90.

2. Name the participial phrases below and the noun or pronoun each one modifies:

    1. Having reached our destination, we unpacked our suitcases.

    2. Joe Shaw, rising quickly in his political career, is now one of the candidates.

    3. Sinking deeper into the snow, the wheels of the truck spun around and around.

    4. They heard a bell tolling in the distance.

    5. The lifeguards, sitting on the beach, watched the fishing fleet return.

Exercise II

1. Review the lesson on dangling participles, page 291.

2. Rewrite the following sentences correctly:

    1. Having made some mistakes, the letter was rewritten.

    2. Hiding under the bed, I finally found the kitten.

    3. Lifting heavy boxes all day, Steven's back began to ache.

    4. Having studied the map carefully, the trip should be easy.

    5. Swimming desperately, the current carried Tom away from shore.

    6. Having written a thank-you note, my appreciation of the gift was shown.

3. Beginning with these participial phrases, write sentences of your own. Make sure that each phrase modifies the subject of the sentence. Remember the rule for punctuating introductory participial phrases.

    1. turning the corner

    2. examining the contents of the safe

    3. listening carefully

    4. having seen his face

    5. demonstrating the machine

    6. calling to his brother

    7. hiding his hands behind his back

    8. electing the club officers

Exercise III

1. Review "Gerunds," page 294.

2. Find the *–ing* words in these sentences. Tell whether each one is used as a *verb*, a *participle*, or a *gerund*.

1. My favorite sport is climbing.
2. The scouts have been climbing that hill for an hour.
3. Climbing the mountain, the explorer found a new way to the peak.
4. Wrapping all those packages is hard work.
5. We saw Carol wrapping packages in the other room.

Exercise IV

1. Review "Infinitives," pages 295–96.

2. Name the infinitives in these sentences and explain how each is used: as *subject*, *direct object*, *subject complement*, *adjective*, or *adverb*.

1. To knit these socks for the children's home has been a pleasure.
2. Joan wants to watch that television show.
3. We decorated the room to surprise Pat.
4. She has no money to spare.
5. My plan is to volunteer.

3. Use the first two infinitives below as *subjects* in sentences of your own; use the second two as *direct objects*:

1. to succeed
2. to help
3. to know
4. to leave

4. Use the first two infinitives below as *adjectives* in sentences of your own; use the second two as *adverbs*:

1. to elect
2. to win
3. to write
4. to inform

PART II

Language Study and Appreciation

CHAPTER 12

Study Skills

The ability to study efficiently and without supervision is one of the keys to success at school. Once you have become an independent learner and have mastered the tools of learning, there need be few limits to your progress. Many people with able minds regret that they never learned to study and consequently wasted time both in school and college. For those to whom school work is difficult, efficiently used study skills may spell the difference between passing and failing.

Much of the content of the earlier chapters of this book concerns the basic skills needed to do good work at school. No small body of material can be isolated as study skills. This present chapter only adds to the lessons you have already learned.

How to Study Effectively

To make the most of your study opportunities, you should try to create for yourself the best possible conditions.

Physical setting

If you can possibly arrange for ideal physical conditions of study, your task will be easier. These conditions include proper lighting, a comfortable chair, and quietude, which means that you should be safely away from all outside distractions—record player, radio, even Pal, unless he is a very well-trained dog.

Your mental attitude

The best physical conditions will not help you if you are not well motivated for study. Perhaps the first essential is determination to succeed. You must be convinced that it is important to do well.

Make sure you know the purpose of the study you are assigned. It is most difficult to stick at a piece of work if you do not know why you are doing it. If you are uncertain, ask your teacher.

Be ready to ask questions. The importance of this cannot be overemphasized. Too many students somehow fear that if they ask questions, their teacher or fellow students will think they are stupid. This is not true. Usually, the best students ask the most questions. An important study skill is to recognize what you do not know and remember it long enough to ask about it.

Do your best to *concentrate*. Do not allow yourself to dawdle and waste time.

Time for study

Most people work better if they budget their time. Find out how much time the school expects you to spend each day on independent work, and then make a schedule of study times, write it down, and follow it. If you do this, the schedule will help provide the will power. Allow time for independent reading, both for pleasure and for extra work in your courses.

First study the subject you like least, when your mind is at its best. Save the favorite subject, like dessert, for the end.

Remember: Part of planning time for study is planning time also for recreation and exercise. You should not work all the time. For most people, it is better to work hard for a period and then to take a break for refreshment.

Guides for studying effectively

1. *Have a place for study*, preferably a desk or table in a room by yourself. If this is not possible, try to claim a quiet corner for yourself away from the family.
2. *Have a firm, comfortable chair.*
3. *Have a good light*, at least 100 watts, placed so that it does not glare or cast a shadow on your paper when you write.
4. *Have essential materials*: pencils, pen, paper, ruler, eraser, dictionary, loose-leaf notebook, and homework notebook.
5. *Organize your materials.* Have a place for everything and everything in its place. Especially have a place where you routinely record your assignments and a place where you keep finished papers before they are handed in.
6. *Remove or turn your back on distractions* such as hobbies, comic books, and TV.
7. *Know the purpose* of your study and expect to succeed.
8. *Follow a daily time schedule* for studying.

Exercises: Studying effectively

1. Check your study environment against the list opposite. How do you rate? If there are things that need changing, discuss with your parents how you might achieve what you need.

2. Honestly evaluate your own attitudes toward study. If it will help you, ask your parents, a teacher, or a good friend to comment frankly.

3. Keep a record of all the time you spend in independent study during the next week. Then analyze the record and see if you think you could have used your time better. Consult with your parents and then make out a study schedule for yourself. Include recreation periods.

Your textbook

For most assignments, your textbook provides the information you need, or tells you where you may find it. Learn to use your textbook to the best advantage. Make use of all the helps it provides for understanding and learning. Many of the pages may have section or side headings that tell at a glance what the section is about and so provide a quick review. Study the pictures, the maps, the graphs and charts, and the examples. All were prepared to make your work easier. Check your knowledge of subject matter by means of the questions in your book. Here, starting from the front of the typical book, are the facts about its most important parts:

1. *The title page*

   This contains the name of the book, the author, and the publisher, as well as the place of publication.

2. *The copyright page*

   This contains the year of publication. If there are several dates, the latest of them is the copyright date; the earlier dates refer to earlier copyrights of parts of the book.

3. *The preface* or *foreword*

   This is a statement from the authors or the publisher explaining the nature and purpose of the book.

4. *Table of contents*

   This is a list of chapter titles and other parts of the book. It is most useful and should always be examined before the book is used. It will help you to put each part of the book into its context and will show you how the book is organized.

5. *Text*

This is the body of the book, its content.

6. *Glossary*

This is a handy dictionary of difficult words that the reader of the book may need to know. Not all books have a glossary, but many textbooks do.

7. *Index*

This part of a book is a detailed alphabetical listing of the contents of the book, broken down in several different ways. If you want to know whether the book deals with a specific fact or subject, the index should tell you.

To discuss

1. How does an index differ from a table of contents?

2. Which would you use, the index or the table of contents, to answer these questions about a book?

1. Does the book contain an explanation of the Dewey Decimal System?
2. Does the book contain a chapter on the history of English?
3. Does the book contain a quotation from William Shakespeare?
4. Does the book contain a lesson on when to use *good* and when to use *well*?
5. In what order are the main topics presented?
6. Is there a glossary?

3. Where would you turn to find out whether the book is recent enough to be of value?

Using the Library

You have been using the library for several years now and know how valuable it is as a source of obtaining both information and reading pleasure. A good library contains thousands of books, as well as magazines, cataloged and arranged for your convenience. Once you have mastered the system, you have at your disposal an untold wealth of material. If you need to do so, review in the next pages the essentials of using the library.

The card catalog

The center from which you can find any book in the library is the card catalog, an alphabetically arranged set of 3″ x 5″ cards. For many books there are three cards:

629.4 **Crosby, Alexander L**   Author Card
  Rockets into space, by Alexander L. Crosby and Nancy Larrick; illus. by Denny McMains. Random House 1959
  82p illus

  "Younger readers learn how rockets and satellites work, what is needed to send a man into space, how space stations are built, and what

  Rockets into space   Title Card

629.4 **Crosby, Alexander L**
  Rockets into space, by Alexander L. Crosby and Nancy Larrick; illus. by Denny McMains. Random House 1959
  82p illus

  "Younger readers learn how rockets and satellites work, what is needed to send a man into space, how space stations are built, and what will be needed for the first trip to the moon." Bk Buyer's Guide

  SPACE FLIGHT   Subject Card

629.4 **Crosby, Alexander L**
  Rockets into space, by Alexander L. Crosby and Nancy Larrick; illus. by Denny McMains. Random House 1959
  82p illus

  "Younger readers learn how rockets and satellites work, what is needed to send a man into space, how space stations are built, and what will be needed for the first trip to the moon." Bk Buyer's Guide
  About the authors of this book ₁and₁ About the illustrator of this book: p82

  1 Rockets (Aeronautics) 2 Space flight ı Jt. auth. ıı Illus.
  ııı Title   j629.4

  59W7,432   ◯   (W) The H. W. Wilson Company

If you want a book by a certain author, you will find it by looking in the card catalog under the last name of the author. If you want a specific title, you look for the title card. Sometimes you do not have a particular author or title in mind, but rather a subject. In that case you look up the subject in the catalog.

The call number

Every book in the library has a *call number*. If you need help from the librarian in finding a book, be sure to note the call number, plus the author and title. In the call number of *Rockets into Space* on the cards on page 307, the *J* stands for "juvenile collection" and means that the book is especially written for young people. The *C* is the first letter of the author's last name.

Exercises: The card catalog

1. Examine the author card on page 307 and write down on paper all the facts about the book that are given there. You should be able to make ten statements of fact.

2. This exercise will give you practice in using the card catalog of your library. Divide the class into six groups, each group to investigate one of the topics listed below. In the card catalog, find at least three books on each topic, and on a piece of paper, write the author, title, and call number of each.

1. Forestry	3. Ballet	5. Mexican History
2. Greek Mythology	4. Snakes	6. Postage Stamps

3. Here are the names of eight well-known authors. Write down the titles of all the books in your library by each author. If there is no book by an author, write *none* below his name.

1. Carl Sandburg	5. Arthur Conan Doyle
2. Elizabeth Janet Gray	6. Henry Gregor Felsen
3. John R. Tunis	7. Jack London
4. Joseph A. Altsheler	8. James A. Kjelgaard

4. Here are twelve book titles. Beside each that is available in your library, write the name of the author and the call number. If the title is not in the library, write *not available*.

1. *Up Periscope*	8. *Robin Hood and His Merry Outlaws*
2. *Mysterious Island*	
3. *When Knights Were Bold*	9. *Gold-Bug and Other Tales and Poems*
4. *Up from Slavery*	
5. *Abe Lincoln Grows Up*	10. *Captains Courageous*
6. *First Book of Jazz*	11. *Big Loop*
7. *Boy Mechanic*	12. *Famous American Negroes*

The Dewey Decimal System

Probably the most common way in which books are arranged in American libraries is the Dewey Decimal System, invented in 1876 by Melvil Dewey to classify the nonfiction books in his personal library. It is not necessary to memorize the Dewey Decimal System, but you should be familiar with it, since it will help you to find your way around the library stacks. There are ten main categories, thus:

000–099 General works (encyclopedias, periodicals, newspapers)
100–199 Philosophy (conduct, ethics, psychology, personality)
200–299 Religion (Bible stories, myths, churches)
300–399 Social sciences (economics, law, education, government, commerce)
400–499 Linguistics (dictionaries, grammars, and derivations of languages)
500–599 Pure science (mathematics, chemistry, physics, astronomy)
600–699 Applied science (engineering, radio, aeronautics, business)
700–799 Arts and recreation (art, music, games, and other recreation)
800–899 Literature (poems, plays, essays) *not* other fiction
900–999 History (travel, geography, biography)

Ask your librarian to show you the volume which gives all of the categories of the Dewey Decimal System. You will see that each of the ten main categories is divided into hundreds of lesser categories. Do you see that given nothing but a book's call number, an expert can tell at once and in some detail what the book is about and, since the books are arranged on the shelves by call number, exactly where the book is located? The Dewey Decimal System places all books on the same subject together. Remembering this will help to find the books you want.

Fiction

Books of fiction are not given a Dewey call number but are marked **F** and are arranged on separate shelves, alphabetically by the last names of the authors. If there are several books by one author, these are arranged under his name, alphabetically by title.

Exercises: The Dewey Decimal System

1. Refer to the Dewey Decimal System categories on page 309 and tell to which group each of these books would be assigned:

1. *Land of the English People*, by Alicia Street
2. *How Personalities Grow*, by Helen Shacter
3. *The Magic Circle: Stories and People in Poetry*, ed. by Louis Untermeyer
4. *All About Language*, by Mario Pei
5. *Daniel Boone*, by James Daugherty
6. *First Book of the Supreme Court*, by Harold Coy
7. *Mathematical Puzzles and Pastimes*, by Aaron Bakst
8. *Compton's Pictured Encyclopedia*
9. *Tennis for Beginners*, by B. and C. Murphy
10. *Allah: The God of Islam*, by Florence Fitch

2. On page 311 is the chart of a typical library. Visit the library you use and make a similar chart of it.

Using Reference Books

For many school assignments you will need more facts than can be found in your textbooks, and throughout your life you will want to know where to find certain facts for many different purposes. Learn, then, to use reference books, which are collections of facts designed to serve you.

Encyclopedias

Study the entry from the *Thorndike-Barnhart Advanced Junior Dictionary* reproduced below:

> **en cy clo pe di a** or **en cy clo pae di a** (en sī′klə-pē′di ə), **1.** book or series of books giving information, usually arranged alphabetically, on all branches of knowledge. **2.** book treating one subject very thoroughly, with its articles arranged alphabetically. *n.*

Copyright © 1965 by Scott, Foresman and Company, Chicago.

An encyclopedia may be general, such as *The World Book Encyclopedia, Encyclopædia Britannica,* or *Compton's Pictured Encyclopedia,* or it may be specialized like encyclopedias on science or music or art. The index in an encyclopedia may be in the back of each volume or in or at the end of the final volume.

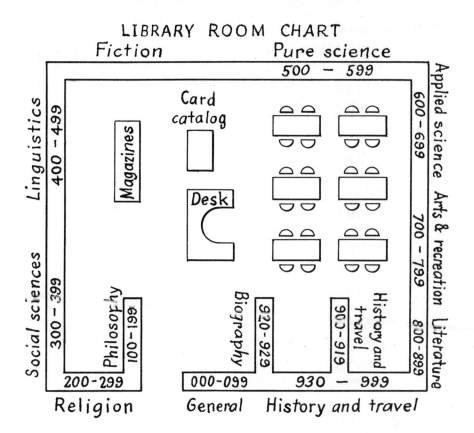

LIBRARY ROOM CHART

Fiction Pure science

Linguistics

Social sciences

400 - 499

300 - 399

Card catalog

Magazines

Desk

Philosophy

100-199

Biography

920-929

929-929

History and travel

900-919

500 - 599

600 - 699

700 - 799

800 - 899

Applied science Arts & recreation Literature

200-299
Religion

000-099
General

930 - 999
History and travel

References on biography

A most useful volume from which to get the essential facts about the lives of famous people is *Webster's Biographical Dictionary*. *Who's Who in America* gives facts about prominent *living* Americans.

Atlases

In connection with your work in history and geography, you will need a good atlas. Your school may provide a small atlas for each student, but for more detailed information, go to the larger atlases in the library, such as *Goode's World Atlas, Rand McNally's Cosmopolitan World Atlas,* or *Hammond's Ambassador World Atlas.* You will find useful the index of place names and the tables at the back of the atlas that list such items as the highest mountains, the longest rivers, the principal oceans, and so on, and the charts of information about various countries.

Almanacs

A reference almanac, such as the *World Almanac*, commonly published yearly, supplies up-to-date facts about a large number and wide variety of topics, such as tides, legislatures, resources, population, industry, farm production, trade, sports, and award winners.

Readers' Guide

If you need to find recent information or opinion on a subject, the *Readers' Guide to Periodical Literature* will serve you well. It lists by subject and author all the articles that have appeared in over a hundred magazines. The *Readers' Guide* is published every two weeks, and individual issues are later combined into larger volumes. You will use the *Guide*, of course, with the magazines to which your library subscribes. Back issues must be available.

Exercises: Reference books

1. Form a small committee to go to the library and list the titles and dates of publication of the encyclopedias and other reference works found there. Post the list on the bulletin board.

2. Choose five questions below and find the answers in the reference books in your library. On your paper, write a one- or two-sentence factual answer and tell the source of your facts.

1. How old is the earth?
2. How many plays did Shakespeare write?
3. What rivers flow into the Mississippi?
4. How are pearls formed?
5. What are the three largest deserts in the world?
6. Where and how do American bald eagles build their nests?
7. What is the cause of sleeping sickness?
8. Is cactus of any practical use?
9. What is a Venus's-flytrap?
10. What is done with worn-out money?

3. Are the names of the following persons listed in *Who's Who in America*? When you have found out, give one interesting fact you learned about each one of those listed. Write *Not listed* beside the names of those whose names do not appear.

1. Ralph Bunche
2. The author of a favorite book
3. The governor of your state
4. Walt Disney
5. Leonard Bernstein
6. Albert Einstein

Taking Notes

Whether you are taking notes on an article you are reading for a report, at an interview in connection with a talk you have to make, or in class discussion of a lesson on which you will be tested, *the purpose of your notes is to aid your memory.* Therefore, your notes must be full enough to recall to your mind the information you will need, but brief enough to serve you for a quick review. For example, in doing a report on *deserts*, you might come across a sentence like this: "Modern irrigation is making many deserts grow abundant crops where once nothing but cacti and sagebrush grew." A good note on this would be: *Mod. irrig. creates crops.*

Too brief a note would be: *irrigation.*

Too long a note would be: *Modern irrigation makes rich crops grow instead of cacti and sagebrush.*

An example of well-taken notes may help you. Below is an article on "Death Valley" taken from *The World Book Encyclopedia.* Following the article is a sample of notes taken from the first two paragraphs. Notice how the note-taker included the main facts in brief language. Notice his use of abbreviations.

Death Valley lies in east-central California, near the Nevada border. A group of pioneers named the valley after they crossed it in 1849. They called it *Death Valley* because of the desolate desert environment. It became part of the Death Valley National Monument, set up in 1933.

Death Valley is a deep trough, about 130 miles long and from 6 to 14 miles wide. The lowest elevation in the Western Hemisphere is near Badwater in Death Valley. It lies 282 feet below sea level. The Panamint Mountains stand west of the valley. Telescope Peak in the Panamint range is 11,045 feet high. The Amargosa Range, composed of the Grapevine, Funeral, and Black Mountains, rises to the east. . . .

During glacial times, the climate was moister, and a large lake occupied Death Valley. Today, rainfall averages less than 1½ inches a year. The highest temperature ever recorded in the United States (134°F.) was reported there on July 10, 1913. Summer temperatures of 125°F. are common. The valley's geological attractions and warm winter sunshine have made it a popular winter-resort area. Plants include the creosote bush, desert holly, and mesquite. Wild life includes bobcats, coyotes, foxes, rats, rabbits, reptiles, and squirrels.

Borax deposits were discovered in Death Valley in 1873. Actual mining began in the early 1880's, and famous 20-mule teams hauled the borax out of the valley. Prospectors also discovered copper, gold, lead, and silver in the nearby mountains. Mining towns sprang up around Death Valley, with such colorful names of Bullfrog, Rhyolite, and Skidoo. The towns died when the ores were exhausted.

> *Notes on Death Valley*
> *from World Book, 1968, Vol. D, pp. 53-54*
> *E.-cent. Calif.*
> *'49 pioneers disc. and named*
> *because thirst, starvation*
> *now Nat. Monument*
> *deep trough*
> *130 mi. X 6-14 mi.*
> *282' below sea lev. (lowest in U.S.)*
> *mts. to E. and W.*

Guides for taking notes

1. *Keep notes strictly on the subject.*
2. *Note only key words and figures* to jog your memory.
3. *Use your own words* to express the ideas you read or hear.
4. *Use abbreviations* to speed your note-taking.
5. *Use quotation marks when quoting directly.* (Never use other people's words without giving credit to them.)
6. *Note your sources,* giving all information available, such as author, title, publication date, publisher, and page numbers.
7. *Use 3" x 5" cards* if you are taking notes which will need to be rearranged later. It is helpful to put one idea on each card.
8. *Take notes inconspicuously* in an interview.
9. *Learn to hear and write at the same time.* This is especially important during a lecture or interview.
10. *Look over your notes* immediately after you have made them.

▶ *Twenty-mule teams were used to drag the borax out of Death Valley. Borax is used in soaps, medicine, and glass manufacturing.*

Exercise: Taking notes

Suppose you were reading the article on pages 313–14 in connection with a committee report on "Deserts of the United States."

Read the article again carefully. Copy the notes on page 314 and add notes of your own for the entire article. Decide what points from this article you will include in your notes. Write the notes on paper or cards.

Memorization

Much of your school work calls for memorization of facts or other material. The skill of memorization is a useful and pleasant one to develop. Although no single method works best for all students, many have found the following suggestions helpful when memorizing a selection of poetry or prose:

Guides for memorization

1. Read the passage through and be sure you understand it.
2. Read it three or four times aloud with full expression.
3. Close your eyes and see what snatches you can remember.
4. Now memorize a few lines at a time, reading the lines aloud and then closing your eyes and reciting them.
5. Try saying the entire passage with the book open before you to glance at if you need prompting. Even better, have a partner prompt you.
6. Long sessions tire your mind. Memorize in five- to ten-minute periods.
7. Concentrate on trouble spots. Figure out some memory device, learning a key word, perhaps, to carry you from a part that you know well through the parts that give you difficulty.
8. Repeat the passage several times just before you go to sleep.
9. After you have mastered the passage, say it over every day or so to fix it in your mind.
10. If you have a part in a play, memorize your cues (the words that come just before your lines).

Exercise: Memorization

Try the method of memorization listed in the guides on the poem "Abou Ben Adhem" on the next page.

Abou Ben Adhem

Abou Ben Adhem (may his tribe increase!)
Awoke one night from a deep dream of peace,
And saw, within the moonlight in his room,
Making it rich, and like a lily in bloom,
An angel writing in a book of gold.

Exceeding peace had made Ben Adhem bold,
And to the presence in the room he said,
"What writest thou?"—The vision raised its head,
And, with a look made of all sweet accord,
Answered, "The names of those who love the Lord."

"And is mine one?" said Abou. "Nay, not so,"
Replied the angel. Abou spoke more low,
But cheerly still; and said, "I pray thee, then,
Write me as one that loves his fellow-men."

The angel wrote, and vanished. The next night
It came again, with a great wakening light,
And showed the names whom love of God had blessed,
And lo! Ben Adhem's name led all the rest.

LEIGH HUNT

Before you memorize this well-known poem by the English poet and essayist Leigh Hunt, read it for the meaning. Why was not Abou's name recorded the first time in the angel's book? Why, on the following night, did Abou's name lead all the rest? What belief is the poet expressing in the poem?

Taking Tests

A test or examination is to give you a chance to show your teacher or yourself how much you know about a subject and how well you can do what is required in a limited period of time.

Many students do not do as well as they should in school because, despite satisfactory marks on daily work and other assignments, they do poorly on tests. There may be several reasons for this, but getting ready for taking a test is of first importance.

Before a test, you should *review* the work to be tested. Read the following suggestions:

1. Set up a schedule for review. Do not count on doing it all just before the test.
2. Assemble all the materials you have used during the unit or course: your notes, your textbook, any exercises or papers you have done and which have been returned to you.
3. Read your notes with care, and check those on which you need to reread the original materials. Reread only those parts of the text you need to review.
4. Note questions that you cannot answer yourself, and raise them in class or privately with the teacher.
5. Make a rough outline of the material covered, and on the basis of the outline, try to make up the best test you can. Do not ask yourself questions only on topics for which you know the answers.
6. Take the test you made up. If this shows up weaknesses, deal with them.
7. Get plenty of sleep the night before the test so that you can come to the test with a fresh mind.

Guides for taking a test

1. If there are several questions that require essay answers, read all of them over quickly before you answer any. This will start your mind thinking about them all.
2. Plan your time. Do not spend more time than you should on any one question.
3. Be sure you read each question carefully or understand any directions.
4. Write legibly and neatly, but not too slowly.
5. Be sure to number each item correctly if you are answering questions on a sheet of paper separate from the test questions.
6. Unless you are required to answer the questions in order, answer the easy ones first and come back to the hard ones. Never spend a long time in useless puzzling over a question you cannot answer, unless you have finished all the other questions.
7. Save a few minutes at the end to proofread your answers.
8. Make an intelligent guess, if you are not certain of an answer.

Test I

On your paper, copy the subjects listed below. After each, write the name of a reference book where you would look to find information on that subject: *encyclopedia, biographical dictionary, atlas, almanac,* or *Readers' Guide.*

> Daniel Webster
> The location of the Hebrides
> Batting averages of big-league ballplayers
> Magazine articles on deep-sea exploring
> The passenger pigeon

Test II

List the numerals 1 to 4 on your paper. For each blank space below, write a word (or words) that completes the statement correctly:

1. Notes should be __?__, but complete enough to aid memory.
2. Notes should include only the __?__ words, not details.
3. When quoting directly, use __?__, and note the __?__ of the quotation.
4. To speed note-taking, use __?__ for long words.

Test III

List the numerals 1 to 4 on your paper. Next to each, write the letter *a, b,* or *c* of the word or phrase below which makes each statement true:

1. The first step in preparing for a test is to (*a*) review the material to be tested, (*b*) talk with the teacher about what material is important, (*c*) talk with a student who took the same course last year.
2. Review the work to be tested (*a*) the hour before you will take the test, (*b*) according to a study schedule you set up, (*c*) whenever you find time the day before the test.
3. In reviewing, read (*a*) all of the text that is to be tested, (*b*) your notes only, (*c*) only those topics on which you need more study.
4. When taking a test, (*a*) begin with the first question and continue in numerical order, (*b*) answer first the questions that are easy for you, (*c*) spend all the time you need on a question you find difficult.

Review and Practice

Exercise I

1. Read "Using Reference Books," pages 310–12.

2. State briefly some types of information to be found in these reference books:

1. *Webster's Biographical Dictionary*
2. *Who's Who in America*
3. An atlas
4. *Readers' Guide to Periodical Literature*
5. An almanac

Exercise II

1. Read "Taking Notes," pages 313–14.

2. Read the following selection. Take notes for a report you are to give on the duckbill platypus.

One of the strangest animals in the world is the duckbill platypus. In the year 1799, a British scientist saw a stuffed platypus and called it a fake. His reaction was not surprising, because the platypus breaks all the rules. It combines the characteristics of several different species of animal life. For example, it has a beak like a duck, but fur like an animal. Out of its ducklike bill comes a voice that sounds like the growl of a puppy! It lays eggs like a bird, but feeds its young with mother's milk, like an animal. It has webfeet with which to swim, but also claws like a feline animal.

The platypus has still another distinction. The male is the only poisonous mammal in the world. On his hind legs are spurs which emit a deadly venom, like that of poisonous snakes.

It was not until almost a hundred years after the British scientists refused to believe the platypus was real that its eggs were found and its identity established.

The platypus is a nocturnal creature, feeding by night in the river beds of its native Australia and Tasmania. During the day it sleeps in a nest, dug into a mudbank and lined with grasses.

These rare, timid creatures are seldom seen in zoos, since they do not thrive in captivity.

Exercise III

1. Read "Taking Tests," pages 317–18.

2. Assume that you are to take a test on this chapter. List on your paper how you would review for the test.

CHAPTER 13

Using Your Dictionary

The famous dictionary maker, Samuel Johnson, once said, "Dictionaries are like watches; the worst is better than none, and the best cannot be expected to go quite true."

There are few books more misunderstood than dictionaries. Most people have the impression that when someone states, "The dictionary says . . ." he has somehow referred to the truth, absolute and unchangeable. But, in reality, dictionaries often disagree with one another, and they change as the years pass and new editions appear. They must change, because the language changes.

How to Use Your Dictionary

Though dictionaries do not always agree and do need periodic revision, for you a good dictionary is an authority, because it is based on careful study by scholars of the language and because it records the meanings, spellings, and pronunciations that educated people generally use. In your school work, you should turn to your dictionary for all sorts of information.

To use your dictionary easily and efficiently, you should master the alphabet. Know it so well that you can tell without hesitating what letter precedes or follows another. The alphabet is the key to your dictionary. Test your knowledge of alphabetical order with questions from your classmates.

Once you have mastered the alphabet, you can make better use of the **guide words** that appear at the top of each page of most dictionaries. Turn to the sample dictionary page from the *Thorndike-Barnhart Advanced Junior Dictionary* on page 331 and look at the guide words. The word at the top left, **patty,** is the first word defined on the page, and the one at the top right, **peaceable,** is the last word defined. All the *entry words* in heavy print come alphabetically between the guide words **patty** and **peaceable.**

Finding the meanings of words

Perhaps the most important use of a dictionary is to give the meanings of words. For many words, more than one meaning is given, and you must be sure to find the meaning suitable for the sentence you are reading or writing.

To discuss

In class, discuss words with which you are familiar that have more than one meaning.

Exercises: Finding words and their meanings

1. Copy the words below that would appear on the same dictionary page as the guide words **countershaft** and **court**:

countess	course	coupon	courage
counterfeit	couple	courteous	country
county	counterpart	countless	cousin
countersign	courageous	courier	couplet

2. Each of the italicized words in the sentences below has more than one meaning. Look up each word in your dictionary and write down the one definition that fits the sentence.

EXAMPLE: 1. The *lure* of the athletic field was so great that John's homework suffered.

YOU WRITE: *1. lure: attraction*

1. His *incendiary* remarks broke up the meeting.
2. The accounts showed that the company was *solvent*.
3. The reporter went to the newspaper *morgue* to find the facts he needed.
4. That violinist *executed* the phrase perfectly.
5. Yesterday the lawyer presented his *brief* in the courtroom.
6. She does not *embrace* just any idea that comes along.

3. Each of the ten words listed on page 323 has at least two meanings, one of which may be less familiar to you than the other. These less familiar meanings are listed at the right. Match each word with its meaning. You may use your dictionary.

1. digest	a. unfriendly
2. nice	b. make a profit
3. clear	c. religious ceremony
4. chilly	d. condense
5. boom	e. provide
6. air	f. melody
7. afford	g. glowing vigor
8. advance	h. supply beforehand
9. office	i. chain to keep logs from
10. flush	floating away
	j. exact

4. If any of the words in the exercises above are new to you, enter them and their meanings in your vocabulary notebook. Use each word correctly in a sentence of your own.

Usage labels

One of the facts you sometimes need to know about words and their meanings is whether their use is generally acceptable in English, that is, whether they are a part of standard English or whether they are special in some way. One way in which dictionaries show distinctions in meaning is through *usage labels*. Here are some of the most common labels: (1) *Slang* refers to words or meanings that are especially vivid and colorful but are not accepted by educated people as good English. Most slang terms are short-lived, though a few are not: it's a *cinch;* it costs one *buck*. (2) *Informal* or *colloquial* refers to words that are used in everyday speech but not in formal speech or writing: *jam-packed, nosy*. (3) *Archaic* is used to label words that are no longer in general use and are out-of-date: *methinks, doth*. (4) *Obsolete* is used to indicate words that are completely out-of-date and no longer used.

To discuss

1. Examine a page from your dictionary or the one on page 331. Discuss in class the various usage labels you find there.

2. List on the board some words that you think might be labeled *slang, informal,* or *archaic*. Then check your dictionary to see if the label there agrees with your thinking.

The Pronunciation of Words

In English, you cannot always count on the spelling of a word to tell you how it is pronounced. You will often need to use your dictionary to find the correct pronunciation. To help you, makers of dictionaries put beside each entry word a *phonetic spelling*, which means the spelling of a word as it sounds. By reading it carefully and comparing the symbols with a *pronunciation key*, you can pronounce the word correctly. A complete pronunciation key is usually found printed inside the front and back covers. Many dictionaries list the key in an abbreviated form on every other page, like the sample key on page 327 of this book.

Diacritical marks

Marks used to indicate the pronunciation of a word are called **diacritical marks**. Because there are so many of them and they vary from dictionary to dictionary, you need not memorize them all, but it will be helpful to know those that are most common.

Long vowels. One mark you should know is the **macron** (¯), which marks a *long vowel*. Each long vowel sound is identical to the sound of the vowel as you say it aloud: *a, e, i, o, u.*

EXAMPLES OF LONG VOWELS

age	(āj)
eve	(ēv)
ice	(īs)
old	(ōld)
music	(mūzik)

Exercise: Marking long vowels

Copy the words below. Put a macron over the long vowel in each. Use your dictionary only when you need to.

1. arrival	5. premium	9. patience
2. cedar	6. concrete	10. over
3. cozy	7. basis	11. executive
4. humor	8. hopeless	12. retain

Short vowels. Some dictionaries indicate a short vowel sound simply by printing the letter unmarked. Most dictionaries, however, mark short vowels with a **breve** (˘). Compare the sounds of the long and short vowels below. The long vowels are marked with a macron; and the short vowels, with a breve.

LONG VOWELS	SHORT VOWELS
rāte	răt
Pēte	pĕt
kīte	kĭt
rōbe	rŏb
cūbe	cŭb

The schwa. It is also useful to recognize the *schwa*, which looks like an inverted *e* (ə). It is used to mark most unaccented vowel sounds, whether the vowel be *a, e, i, o,* or *u.* (In some dictionaries the schwa is used also to indicate a short *u*, accented or not: *lunch—lənch.*)

EXAMPLES OF THE USE OF THE SCHWA

crystal	kristəl
lantern	lantərn
giraffe	jəraf
forbid	fərbid
helpful	helpfəl

Exercise: Using diacritical marks

Copy the words in the list below. Mark each short vowel with a breve. Use your dictionary to be sure you have marked the short vowels in these words. (Remember, dictionaries vary in the way they indicate short vowels.)

1. production
2. magnificent
3. competitive
4. original
5. presence
6. recommend
7. privilege
8. affectionate
9. beggar
10. domestic

Accent marks. Another mark that is an important key to pronunciation is the **accent mark** (ʹ) which tells which syllable is stressed. In most dictionaries the accent mark *follows* the accented syllable:

me chan ic (mə kanʹik)

Some dictionaries show the accent before the accented syllable:

me·chan·ic (miʹkan ik)

Many words in English have two accents, a heavy one (**primary accent**) and a light one (**secondary accent**). For example, in the word *concentrated* (kon´sən trāt´id) the syllable *trāt* receives the secondary accent and the syllable *kon*, the primary accent.

Sometimes a dictionary will place the accent marks before the syllables, with the primary accent at the top and the secondary accent at the bottom:

mul-ti-ply (ˈmul-tə͵ plī)

Occasionally you see more than one phonetic spelling after an entry word. The first phonetic spelling shows the pronunciation that the makers of the dictionary consider the most widely used. A second or third phonetic spelling shows an acceptable but alternate pronunciation:

ex qui site   (eks´kwi zit)   (eks kwiz´it)

To discuss

1. The ten words below have alternate pronunciations. Examine the phonetic spelling and the diacritical marks of each word and be prepared to pronounce it correctly. Discuss in class which of the two pronunciations is more widely accepted in your community. Which do you use?

1. creek	(krēk *or* krik)
2. rodeo	(rō di ō *or* rō dā´ō)
3. Nevada	(nə vad´ə *or* nə vä´də)
4. status	(stā´təs *or* stat´əs)
5. tomato	(tə mā´tō *or* tə mä´tō)
6. apparatus	(ap´ə rā´təs *or* ap´ə rat´əs)
7. was	(woz *or* wuz)
8. duke	(dük *or* dūk)
9. either	(ē´ᴛʜər *or* ī´ᴛʜər)
10. exit	(eg´zit *or* ek´sit)

2. Discuss in class other words that you have heard pronounced in different ways. Consult your dictionary to see which pronunciations are acceptable and which pronunciation is considered the most widely used.

Exercises: Pronouncing words

1. At the top of page 327 are the phonetic spellings and diacritical marks of eight words. Pronounce each word correctly and carefully. If you need a guide, refer to the pronunciation key at the bottom of

the page. Name the vowels in each word that are represented by a schwa.

1. ben′ə fit ed
2. kar′ik tər
3. kə mit′i
4. dis′ə point′ed

5. eks pēr′i əns
6. op′ər tü′ nə ti
7. tėr′bō jet′
8. ô′təm

2. On a piece of paper, write each of the words below in syllables. Then place the accent mark before or after the accented syllable. Follow the form in the dictionary that you use for this exercise.

EXAMPLE: 1. advise
YOU WRITE: *1. ad′vise′ or ad′vise*

1. pattern
2. agreeable
3. jewelry
4. physical

5. normal
6. temperature
7. religious
8. merchandise

3. Follow the instructions in the exercise above, indicating *both* the primary and secondary accents in the following words:

1. regulation
2. stationery
3. refrigerator
4. optimistic

5. recommendation
6. correspond
7. personality
8. transportation

Syllabication

A syllable is a word or part of a word that can be pronounced with a single sounding of the voice. *Back* is a one-syllable word; *backache* is a two-syllable word. The dictionary tells you how to syllabize a word. Syllabication can help you to spell a word and divide it at the end of a line. The most common ways dictionaries syllabize words are as follows: tra di tion, tra·di·tion, or tra-di-tion.

> hat, āge, cãre, fär; let, ēqual, tėrm; it, īce; hot, ōpen, ôrder; oil, out; cup, put, rüle, ūse; ch, child; ng, long; th, thin; ᴛʜ, then; zh, measure; ə represents *a* in about, *e* in taken, *i* in pencil, *o* in lemon, *u* in circus.

FROM *Pippa Passes*

The year's at the spring
And day's at the morn:
Morning's at seven;
The hillside's dew-pearled;

The lark's on the wing;
The snail's on the thorn;
God's in His Heaven—
All's right with the world!

ROBERT BROWNING

These beautiful lines are taken from a long lyrical poem, *Pippa Passes*. Pippa is a young worker in the silk mills at Asolo, Italy. On her one holiday of the year, she walks through the city singing four songs, of which the above is one. As it happens, her four songs help four important people of the city meet crises in their lives.

The Dictionary as a Study Aid

The dictionary serves other functions besides showing the pronunciation and definition of a word. As a valuable study aid, it can be used as a source of reference for several kinds of information.

There are, of course, complete dictionaries that explain words that relate only to history, biography, geography, or the like. Such dictionaries should be consulted for rather complete information. But your own dictionary can often supply you with quick reference to such terms as: *Spanish-American War, Longfellow, London.* It may even list abbreviations as well: *ed., f., geol., U.S.* Because dictionaries differ in their presentation and contents, it is always wise to read the front pages of the one you wish to use frequently. With an understanding of what is included in your dictionary, you can use it for its maximum value and with a minimum of effort.

Spelling

If a word has more than one spelling, the dictionary lists all of them, sometimes under one entry, sometimes under separate entries for each spelling.

su mac *or* su mach   bron cho *or* bron co

Read the information on page 330 about the use of a dictionary to find the correct spelling of a word.

1. **The dictionary shows the spellings for the plurals of nouns which form their plural in an irregular way:** *mouse—mice.*

   The dictionary usually does not list the plurals of nouns which form their plural in the regular way; that is, by adding *–s* or *–es.* Sometimes, however, when there is some doubt about the spelling of a plural form of a noun, it is given: *brothers-in-law.*
2. **The dictionary shows the past tense and the past and present participle forms of irregular verbs:** *go—went, gone, going.*
3. **If the spelling of a regular verb changes in any way, the spelling is listed.** For example, you will find *rob—robbing* in the dictionary because the *b* is doubled when *–ing* is added.
4. **The dictionary tells you if a word is hyphenated or written as one word or two words:** *full-grown, fullback, full blast.*

To discuss

Examine the sample dictionary page on page 331 and use it to answer the following questions:

1. What is the plural spelling of each of these nouns: *patty, paunch, pea?*
2. What is the spelling of the simple past tense and the past and present participles of these verbs: *pause, pave?*
3. Look at the words below. Should they be hyphenated or written as one word or as two words?

   pawnbroker   payoff   payday
   paydirt   paymaster   payroll

4. What word gives an informal definition for *hand*? a *slang* definition for the climax of a story?
5. For which definition of *pay* is *payed* the permissible spelling of the past tense?
6. How many verb meanings of the word *pause* are given? how many noun meanings?
7. Which word has an alternate spelling as well as an alternate pronunciation?
8. What was Pavlov's first name? Where is Pawtucket located? How long is the Peace River?
9. Can you find five words in which the schwa is used to show each of the unaccented vowels?
10. For what words do the following abbreviations stand?

    p.c.   pd.   P.D.   Pb

pat ty (pat′i), **1.** a hollow form of pastry filled with chicken, oysters, etc. **2.** a small, round, flat piece of food or candy. *n., pl.* **pat ties.**

pau ci ty (pô′sə ti), **1.** small number; fewness. **2.** a small amount; scarcity; lack. *n.*

Paul (pôl), **Saint,** died 67? A.D., Apostle who started Christian groups in many countries and wrote many of the books in the New Testament. *n.*

paunch (pônch), **1.** belly; stomach. **2.** a large, protruding belly. **3.** the first stomach of a cud-chewing animal. *n.*

paunch y (pôn′chi), having a big paunch. *adj.* —**paunch′i ness,** *n.*

pau per (pô′pər), a very poor person; person supported by charity. *n.*

pau per ism (pô′pər iz əm), being very poor; poverty. *n.*

pau per ize (pô′pər īz), make a pauper of. *v.,* **pau per ized, pau per iz ing.** —**pau′per i za′tion,** *n.*

pause (pôz), **1.** stop for a time; wait · *The dog paused when he heard me.* **2.** moment of silence; stop; rest. **3.** dwell; linger: *pause upon a word.* **4.** a brief stop in speaking or reading: *He made a short pause and then went on reading.* **5.** a punctuation mark indicating such a stop. **6.** a sign (⌣ or ⌢) above or below a musical note or rest, meaning that it is to be held for a longer time. 1,3 *v.,* **paused, paus ing;** 2,4-6 *n.*

pave (pāv), **1.** cover (a street, sidewalk, etc.) with a pavement. **2.** make smooth or easy; prepare *He paved the way for me by doing careful work. v.,* **paved, pav ing.**

pave ment (pāv′mənt), **1.** a covering or surface for streets, sidewalks, etc., made of stones, bricks, wood, asphalt, etc. **2.** a paved road, etc. *n.*

pa vil ion (pə vil′yən), **1.** a light building, usually one somewhat open, used for shelter, pleasure, etc.: *a bathing pavilion.* **2.** a large tent raised on posts; tent. **3.** part of a building higher and more decorated than the rest. **4.** one of a group of buildings forming a hospital. **5.** furnish with a pavilion; enclose or shelter in a pavilion. 1-4 *n.,* 5 *v.*

Pavilion for dancing

pav ing (pāv′ing), **1.** material for pavement. **2.** pavement. *n.*

Pav lov (päv′lôf), **Ivan,** 1849-1936, Russian physiologist famous for his studies of the digestive glands and of the modifiable capacity of the reflexes. *n.*

Pav lo va or **Pav lo wa** (päv′lō və or päv lō′və), **Anna,** 1885-1931, Russian dancer. *n.*

paw (pô), **1.** foot of an animal having claws. Cats and dogs have paws. **2.** strike or scrape with the paws or feet: *The cat pawed the mouse. The horse pawed the ground, eager to be going again.* **3.** *Informal.* hand. **4.** *Informal.* handle awkwardly, roughly, or in too familiar a manner. 1,3 *n.,* 2,4 *v.*

pawl (pôl), a pivoted bar arranged to catch in the teeth of a ratchet wheel or the like so as to prevent movement backward or to impart motion. *n.*

A, pawls; B, ratchet wheel. When the handle is raised, one pawl pushes the wheel forward; the other keeps it from slipping back.

pawn¹ (pôn), **1.** leave (something) with another person as security that borrowed money will be repaid: *He pawned his watch to buy food until he could get work.* **2.** something left as security. **3.** a pledge. 1 *v.,* 2,3 *n.*

in pawn, in another's possession as security: *His watch is in pawn.*

pawn² (pôn), **1.** in chess, one of the 16 pieces of lowest value. **2.** an unimportant person or thing used by someone for his own purposes. *n.*

pawn bro ker (pôn′brō′kər), man who lends money at interest on articles that are left with him as security for the loan. *n.*

Paw nee (pô nē′), member of an American Indian tribe that lived near the forks of the Platte River. *n.*

pawn shop (pôn′shop′), a pawnbroker's shop. *n.*

paw paw (pô′pô), papaw. *n.*

Paw tuck et (pô tuk′it), city in NE Rhode Island. 81,000. *n.*

pax vo bis cum (paks′ vō bis′kəm), *Latin.* peace be with you.

pay¹ (pā), **1.** give (a person) what is due for things, work, etc.: *He paid the doctor.* **2.** money or equivalent given for things or work: *Jim gets his pay every Saturday.* **3.** give money for: *Pay your way.* **4.** hand over (money owed); hand over the amount of: *pay a debt.* **5.** give what is due: *He owes it and must pay.* **6.** give; offer: *pay attention, pay compliments.* **7.** be profitable to; be worth while to: *It pays me to keep that stock. It wouldn't pay me to take that job.* **8.** yield as a return: *That stock pays me four per cent.* **9.** be profitable: *It pays to be polite.* **10.** source of payment. **11.** return for favors or hurts: *Dislike is the pay for being mean* (n.). *He paid them for their insults by causing them trouble* (v.). **12.** suffer; undergo: *The one who does wrong must pay the penalty.* **13.** let out (a rope, etc.). **14.** fall off to leeward. 1,3-9, 11-14 *v.,* **paid** or (*Obs. except for def.* 13) **payed, pay ing;** 2,10,11 *n.*

in the pay of, paid by and working for.

pay as you go, *U.S.* pay or discharge obligations as they are incurred.

pay back, 1. return borrowed money. **2.** give the same treatment as received.

pay off, 1. give all the money that is owed; pay in full. **2.** get even with; get revenge on.

pay up, pay; pay in full.

pay² (pā), cover (a ship's bottom, seams, rope, etc.) with tar, pitch, or another waterproof substance. *v.,* **payed, pay ing.**

pay a ble (pā′ə bəl), **1.** required to be paid; due: *He must spend $100 soon on bills payable.* **2.** that may be paid. *adj.*

pay day (pā′dā′), day on which wages are paid. *n.*

pay dirt, *U.S.* earth, ore, etc., containing enough metal to be worth mining.

pay ee (pā ē′), person to whom money is paid or is to be paid. *n.*

pay er (pā′ər), one who pays; one who is to pay. *n.*

pay mas ter (pā′mas′tər), person whose job is to pay wages. *n.*

pay ment (pā′mənt), **1.** a paying; compensation. **2.** amount paid: *a monthly payment of $10.* **3.** pay: *Baby's good health is payment enough for me.* **4.** reward or punishment. *n.*

pay-off (pā′ôf′), **1.** a paying of wages. **2.** time of such payment. **3.** returns from an enterprise, specific action, etc. **4.** *Slang.* climax (of a story, situation, etc.). *n.*

pay roll, 1. list of persons to be paid and the amounts that each one is to receive. **2.** the total amount to be paid to them.

Pb, lead.

pc., piece.

p.c., 1. per cent. **2.** post card.

Pd, palladium.

pd., paid.

P.D., Police Department.

pea (pē), **1.** the round seed in the pod of a leguminous plant, used as a vegetable. **2.** the plant itself. **3.** seed or plant like a pea. **4.** of the size of a pea: *pea coal.* 1-3 *n., pl.* **peas,** *Archaic* or *Brit. Dialect.* **pease;** 4 *adj.*

as like as two peas, exactly alike.

peace (pēs), **1.** freedom from war or strife of any kind: *work for world peace.* **2.** public quiet, order, and security. **3.** agreement between contending parties to end war: *the Peace of Paris.* **4.** quiet; calm; stillness: *peace of mind.* **5.** keep still! stay quiet! be silent! 1-4 *n.,* 5 *interj.*

hold or **keep one's peace,** be silent.

Peace (pēs), river in W Canada flowing NE through Alberta. 1050 mi. *n.*

peace a ble (pēs′ə bəl), **1.** liking peace; keeping

Exercises: Using your dictionary

1. The dots in the words below show the places where spelling errors are often made. Write the correct spelling of each word. You may use your dictionary.

1. uk . lele
2. tonsi . itis
3. z . logical
4. vol . ntary
5. i . oculate
6. ty . anny
7. s . rg . nt (military rank)
8. r . umatism
9. quar . ntine
10. picni . ing

2. Use your dictionary to find the plural spelling of the nouns below. Write the plural forms. If more than one plural spelling is acceptable, write each.

1. bus
2. quiz
3. waltz
4. patio
5. passer-by
6. motto
7. fish
8. hoof
9. buffalo
10. teaspoonful
11. dwarf
12. manservant

3. Write the simple past tense and the present participle of the verbs below. When in doubt, use your dictionary. If two forms of any tense are acceptable, write both.

EXAMPLE: 1. get
YOU WRITE: *1. got — getting*
           (past) (present participle)

1. travel
2. prefer
3. carry
4. wrap
5. occupy
6. pray
7. omit
8. notify
9. occur
10. admit
11. refer
12. quarrel

4. Refer to your dictionary to see whether the words below should be hyphenated or written as one word or as two words. Write each word correctly.

1. f l o w e r p o t
2. d o u b l e t a l k
3. f l e s h c o l o r e d
4. n i c k n a m e
5. n i g h t t i m e
6. s e a s h e l l
7. g i l t e d g e d
8. a l l r i g h t
9. i l l b r e d
10. f l a s h l i g h t
11. s u n g l a s s e s
12. a l l s t a r

Capitalization

A dictionary tells you when a word is usually capitalized. If a word is entered twice, once capitalized and once not, study each meaning to choose the correct word for your use.

Exercise: Capitalization

Use a dictionary to find whether or not to capitalize the word in parentheses in each sentence below. On your paper, write the word correctly, that is, with or without a capital letter.

EXAMPLES:
1. The New Englander traveled through the (south).
2. He was a (puritan) in his standards.

YOU WRITE:
1. *South*
2. *puritan*

1. Pour the hot soup into the (thermos) bottle.
2. That trotting horse is a (morgan).
3. To many people who do not know him, Boris is a (sphinx).
4. Four young (girl scouts) came to the door to sell cookies.
5. The airplane was housed in the (quonset) hut.
6. A (congress) was held to discuss more legislation.
7. Portland is a (northern) city.
8. I think it is a picture of a (coral) snake.
9. At this time every year (congregational) singing is held in the park.
10. The giant (panda) is native to Tibet.

GOING AHEAD

Another very valuable dictionary is a *thesaurus* (thi sô′rəs). It is a dictionary of synonyms. Professional writers use a thesaurus when they cannot think of just the right word to express their thought. The most widely used one is *Roget's Thesaurus.*

In a thesaurus, look up some synonyms for *interesting* (adj.); *successful* (adj.); *defeat* (v.); *group* (n.); and *noise* (n.). Choose five synonyms for each of the words above. For this exercise, choose synonyms that are only of the same part of speech as indicated in the parentheses. Next, turn to your dictionary, and as you must always do when you use a thesaurus, compare the slight difference in the meaning of each synonym. Then use each synonym in a sentence that will illustrate its special meaning.

A Book to Read

Tituba of Salem Village
by Ann Petry
Thomas Y. Crowell Co.

The book is based on the real-life story of a black woman who was more intelligent, more sensitive, and more capable than most of the people around her. Against her will, she was transported as a slave from the island of Barbados in the Caribbean to Salem, Massachusetts. This was at the time of the Salem witch trials of 1692, and Tituba was one of the first three "witches" condemned. The Puritans, superstitious and hysterical, believed in witches. Many white women were killed as witches, but Tituba was especially vulnerable to suspicion and attack because she was black and a slave.

In this tragic story, Ann Petry brings to life each of the participants so that we understand why they acted as they did. At the end, Tituba was pardoned and allowed to rejoin her husband.

About the author

Ann Petry, herself a Negro, has long had a special interest in slavery and believes "that the majority of textbooks used in high schools do not give an adequate or accurate picture of the history of slavery in the United States." Another book of hers, *Harriet Tubman: Conductor on the Underground Railroad,* reflects this belief.

Mrs. Petry lives in a handsome white house with green shutters in a small town in Connecticut, surrounded by wide lawns and hundred-year-old trees. Her family owns a drugstore in Old Saybrook, and Ann Petry herself graduated from the College of Pharmacy at the University of Connecticut.

Test I

1. In each list below, write the words in alphabetical order:

(1)	(2)	(3)
eternize	lighten	following
eternity	lighthouse	follower
eternal	lightness	follow
eternities	lightly	followed
eternally	lightning	follows

2. From the words that follow, copy those that will be found on a dictionary page with the guide words **glance** and **glisten**:

gleeful	glamorous	glazier	glide
glass	glimmer	glister	glaze
gleam	gladiola	glare	glimpse

3. On your paper, write the numerals from 1 to 10. Next to the appropriate numeral, write the letter of the definition that best fits the use of the word *pick* in each sentence.

a. sharp-pointed tool
b. the best or most desirable
c. steal from
d. select
e. seek and find
f. eat only a little at a time
g. put in order
h. prepare for use by removing feathers, waste parts, etc.
i. amount of a crop gathered at one time
j. dig into with something pointed

1. Please *pick* up that mess.
2. I will *pick* Josie for my partner.
3. He did not *pick* the garden before planting the seeds.
4. Those girls only *pick* at their food.
5. Loosen the rock with a *pick*.
6. Our team has the *pick* of the football players.
7. The thief tried to *pick* my pocket.
8. Cooks *pick* chickens before roasting them.
9. They *pick* flaws in my arguments.
10. The tomato *pick* this season was small.

Test II

On your paper, write the numerals from 1 to 5. Read carefully each of the statements below. Next to the appropriate numeral, write one of these usage labels to tell what kind of word (or words) each statement describes:

> slang
> informal
> archaic

1. These words are used in everyday speech but not in formal speech or writing.
2. Such words in the English language are usually short-lived.
3. Words that are out-of-date are labeled in this way.
4. This term is used sometimes to label the word *cinch*.
5. The word *methinks* would be labeled by this term.

Test III

1. Write the numerals from 1 to 5 on your paper. Look at the word below and its phonetic spelling, and next to the appropriate numeral, write the correct answers to the questions that follow:

geographical (jē′ə graf′ə kəl)

1. How many syllables are there?
2. Which syllable has the primary accent?
3. Which syllable has the secondary accent?
4. Which vowel is long?
5. Which syllable contains a short vowel?

2. Write the numerals from 1 to 5 on your paper. Match the word at the left with its meaning at the right. Then write each word and its meaning in a complete sentence.

1. breve	a. Indicates a long vowel sound
2. entry word	b. Can show an alternate pronunciation
3. phonetic spelling	
4. schwa	c. Used in some dictionaries to show a short vowel sound
5. macron	d. Looks like an inverted *e*
	e. Is placed according to an alphabetical order

Exercise I

1. Review "How to Use Your Dictionary" on pages 321–22.

2. Write ten words that might appear on an imaginary dictionary page with the guide words **plate** and **plum.**

3. Each of the words in the left column below has more than one meaning. Two of the meanings for each word are listed in the column at the right. Match the word in the left column with its two meanings at the right. You may use your dictionary.

1. brave	a. seat for one person
2. floor	b. inside bottom surface of a room
3. vault	c. having a fine appearance
4. chair	d. a story in a building
5. punch	e. to jump, leap, or spring
	f. a cellar room used for storage of valuables
	g. having courage
	h. person who presides over a meeting
	i. sweet drink flavored with fruit juices
	j. prod, poke, or strike

Exercise II

1. Review the lesson on usage labels on page 323.

2. Define each of the following terms and give a sample of each: *slang*, *informal*, and *archaic*.

Exercise III

1. Review "The Pronunciation of Words" on pages 324–27.

2. Below are four words and their phonetic spellings. Look at them closely before you answer the questions that follow.

festival (fes′tə vəl) epidemic (ep′ə dem′ik)
environment (en vī′rən mənt) reawaken (rē′ə wāk′ən)

1. Which word has a long *i* sound?
2. Which word has two *e* sounds that are short?
3. Which word contains two macrons?
4. In which word is a heavy (or primary) accent placed on the first syllable?
5. Which letters in each word are represented by schwas?
6. What is the name of the diacritical mark that follows the first syllable in the word *epidemic* and in the word *reawaken*?

337

CHAPTER 14

Poetry

Poetry must be read or listened to carefully in order to be appreciated. This is because it packs so much meaning into a few words and uses words in unusual ways. Unlike prose (ordinary writing), it does not give factual information, and, with the exception of narrative poetry and ballads, it does not tell an exciting story.

But poetry does express deep feelings; it does state important ideas in ways that are hard to forget; and it does delight the ear, tickle the funny bone, and appeal to those things inside us that are noble and fine.

Poetry or Prose?

As you read the following poem aloud, do not pause at the end of a line that has no end punctuation—keep your voice up until you come to a natural pause. Read the poem in meaningful phrases.

High Flight

Oh, I have slipped the surly bonds of earth,
And danced the skies on laughter-silvered wings;
Sunward I've climbed and joined the tumbling mirth
Of sun-split clouds—and done a hundred things
You have not dreamed of—wheeled and soared and swung
High in the sunlit silence. Hov'ring there,
I've chased the shouting wind along and flung
My eager craft through footless halls of air.
Up, up the long delirious, burning blue
I've topped the wind-swept heights with easy grace,
Where never lark, or even eagle, flew;
And, while with silent, lifting mind I've trod
The high untrespassed sanctity of space,
Put out my hand, and touched the face of God.

PILOT-OFFICER JOHN GILLESPIE MAGEE, JR., R.C.A.F.

To discuss

1. Do you like the poem? What do you think the poet is saying? Could the ideas in the poem have been expressed as well in prose?

2. Read this prose paragraph. Then answer the questions that follow it.

I have taken off from the ground and have flown in a silver-colored airplane, which made me feel glad. My plane has climbed toward the sun and flown through clouds. Sunlight shone between the clouds. In an airplane I have done all sorts of things that an earthbound person could not even imagine. I have turned and soared in the silent sky.

1. What are the differences between prose and poetry? Base your answer on the paragraph above and the first six lines of the poem "High Flight."
2. If an experienced writer were asked to present in the clearest way the technical problems connected with high-altitude flying, should he do it in prose or poetry? Why?
3. Suppose an experienced writer wanted to tell his reader in a page or less how he felt when he first viewed New York City at night from an airplane. If he wanted to express his sudden feeling that the lights of the city are even more impressive than the lights of stars in the sky and that both make him feel weak and small, should he do it in prose or poetry? Explain.

3. Are there any poems that you know and value? Share them with the class either by reciting them from memory or by bringing them in to read aloud. Be prepared to tell why you like your choice.

Exercise: Poetry or prose?

In the following pairs of brief passages one passage is prose and one is poetry. Decide which is which and be prepared to explain your choice in class. In some cases, the choice will not be easy, because the prose and poetry are rather similar.

1. (*a*) I cannot choose the best.
     The best chooses me.
   (*b*) I am not free to decide what is best for me to do. Instead, life seems to control me, and I find myself doing the best without making a choice.

2. (a) When it is sunny, I feel happy and carefree, but when it is rainy, I have a deep feeling of sadness.

   (b) The sunshine greets me with a smile.
The rain, his sad sister, talks to my heart.

3. (a) When elephants walk along a trail, the elephant behind holds with his trunk the tail of the elephant ahead of him, and he, in turn, holds with his trunk the tail of the elephant ahead of him.

   (b) Elephants walking
Along the trails

    Are holding hands
By holding tails.

4. (a) My dog's so furry I've not seen
His face for years and years:
His eyes are buried out of sight,
I only guess his ears.

   (b) My dog's hair is so long that I cannot see his face. His eyes are invisible, and it's very hard to tell where his ears are.

The Form of Poetry

An American poet once said, "Poetry is a *made* thing." He meant that a poem is very carefully fashioned; there is nothing careless or accidental about it. Good poetry is made by expert craftsmen, and their materials are words.

One of the main characteristics of most poetry is that it has *form*. In fact, it has many kinds of form. Look back at the poem "High Flight." What can you see about it that has regular form? You do not need to read the poem carefully to observe the most obvious parts of its form. For example, with one exception, alternate lines rhyme.

Read this poem by Elizabeth Madox Roberts and be prepared to discuss it:

The Branch

We stopped at the branch on the way to the hill.
We stopped at the water awhile and played.
We hid our things by the osage tree
And took off our shoes and stockings to wade.

There is sand at the bottom that bites at your feet,
And there is a rock where the waterfall goes.
You can poke your foot in the foamy part
And feel how the water runs over your toes.

The little black spiders that walk on the top
Of the water are hard and stiff and cool.
And I saw some wiggletails going around,
And some slippery minnows that live in the pool.

And where it is smooth there is moss on a stone,
And where it is shallow and almost dry,
The rocks are broken and hot in the sun,
And a rough little water goes hurrying by.

ELIZABETH MADOX ROBERTS

To discuss

1. Does the poem "The Branch" have form? Explain.
2. Turn for a moment now to the ideas expressed in "The Branch."
Which of the following adjectives are appropriate to describe the
poem? Explain your choice of each.

romantic	pleasant	factual
scientific	mysterious	ugly

Rhyme scheme of poetry

When the sounds at the end of some lines in a poem are alike,
we say that they **rhyme.** Poets spend much time and effort on the
rhyme scheme or pattern of their poetry. It sometimes helps them
as they write to mark the rhyme scheme by letters. The first end-of-
line sound is marked *a;* the next, if it is different, is marked *b.* If
the third line ends with the same rhyme sound as the first, it, too, is
marked *a.*

The ends of the lines in this poem by Robert Frost rhyme neatly. Read the poem aloud and notice the letters which label the rhyme scheme.

Lodged

The rain to the wind said,	a
"You push and I'll pelt."	b
They so smote the garden bed	a
That the flowers actually knelt	b
And lay lodged—though not dead.	a
I know how the flowers felt.	b

ROBERT FROST

Exercises: Rhyme scheme of poetry

1. On your paper, list the letters that show the rhyme scheme of "High Flight," page 339. Compare your answers in class.

2. Indicate the rhyme scheme of the poem "The Branch." Compare your answers.

3. Try to write a short four-line poem. Make the first two lines rhyme with each other, and the last two lines rhyme with each other. Your rhyme scheme would then be *a, a, b, b*. Read some of your poems aloud in class.

TO MEMORIZE

FROM *Music*

'Tis not in the high stars alone,
Nor in the cup of budding flowers,
Nor in the redbreast's mellow tone,
Nor in the bow that smiles in showers,
But in the mud and scum of things
There alway, alway something sings.

RALPH WALDO EMERSON

As you read the stanza above, notice that Emerson mentions, first, things that provide "music" in the form of beauty. Then, in the last two lines, he says that there is some music also in ugly things. What do you think he means by those two lines?

Rhythm

Another element of form in poetry is **rhythm.** The words in each line are chosen and arranged in such a way that the syllables create a beat. When you read poetry aloud, you become aware of this beat. In fact, if you emphasize the rhythm with your voice, you can clap your hands in time with it. Try it with these lines by Eleanor Farjeon:

FROM *There Isn't Time*

There isn't time, there isn't time
To do the things I want to do,
With all the mountaintops to climb,
And all the woods to wander through. . . .

ELEANOR FARJEON

A regular pattern of beats in a line of poetry is called **meter.** How many strong beats are there in each line of the poem above?

Rhythm in a line of poetry is measured in **feet.** Each foot usually contains at least one accented or stressed syllable. Observe how the feet are counted out in each of the first two lines of "High Flight":

```
      1        2      3      4      5
Oh, I have slipped the surly bonds of earth,
```

```
       1        2        3         4          5
And danced the skies on laughter-silvered wings; . . .
```

Notice that each foot in the lines above contains two syllables—the first one unstressed and the second, stressed:

Ŏh, Í | hăve slípped | thĕ súr | lў bónds | ŏf eárth, |
(foot 1)   (foot 2)   (foot 3)   (foot 4)   (foot 5)

This type of foot is called an *iamb.* The poems "There Isn't Time" and "High Flight" are in *iambic meter.* As you can see, there are five feet in the lines above from "High Flight." How many feet are there in each line of "There Isn't Time"?

The iambic meter is a very common one, but there are many others too numerous to study here. It is important to remember, however, that rhythm, like rhyme, should not be emphasized in reading a poem. If you read the poem for meaning, the rhythm will come through naturally.

Verse that is tied to a regular pattern of rhyme and meter is called **bound verse.** Verse with no regular pattern is called **free verse.** Read the following example of free verse:

As the Cat

As the cat
climbed over
the top of

the jamcloset
first the right
forefoot

carefully
then the hind
stepped down

into the pit of
the empty
flowerpot.

WILLIAM
CARLOS WILLIAMS

Limericks

An amusing form of bound verse is the **limerick.** You may enjoy writing some limericks of your own. Here is a model by the most famous limerick writer of all time, Edward Lear:

There was an old man with a beard
Who said, "It is just as I feared.
　　Two owls and a hen,
　　Four larks and a wren,
Have all made their nests in my beard."

Here is another by an unknown author:

A glamorous creature named Plunkett
Reached for a doughnut to dunk it.
　　In judgment she erred;
　　A disaster occurred;
For in trying to dunk it she sunk it.

To discuss

Read the limericks on page 346 aloud and discuss the rhyme scheme and rhythm. Find other limericks you enjoy and share them in class.

Exercises: Measuring rhythm

1. Choose any four lines from "High Flight," copy them on your paper, and mark the meter as is done on page 345.

2. Here are two lines of iambic meter. See if you can write a line in the same meter which will rhyme with each one. There are five feet in each line.

    1. We heard the striking of some distant clock.

    2. I told my story on that moonlit night.

3. Try writing a limerick of your own. Punctuate it just as you would punctuate prose.

<hr>

GOING AHEAD

Study the meter of "The Branch" on page 342. Copy on your paper the first two lines, marking out the feet. Is the meter different from the one in "High Flight"? Explain your answer to the class. Demonstrate at the board, if you wish.

Appreciating the Sound of Poetry

The sound of the words as they fit together is more important in poetry than in any other kind of writing. Full enjoyment of poetry depends on its sound, just as with music, and just as music must be performed to be fully appreciated, so poetry must be read aloud. Only a very experienced reader of poetry can appreciate rhyme and meter without hearing them read aloud.

To discuss

What two aspects of the sound of poetry have you studied thus far in this chapter? Have you discovered that the repetition of sounds that rhyme increases your enjoyment? If so, why is this true? How does the beat or meter give pleasure to the reader of poetry?

Onomatopoeia

There are two devices that poets use to get the sound effects they want. One is to use words whose pronunciations imitate the sounds they refer to, for example: *boom, crash, squeak, giggle, pop, hiss.* Can you read each of these words aloud so that its meaning is emphasized by its sound? Such words are called **onomatopoeia.** Onomatopoeia is the use of words that imitate natural sounds.

This stanza from Tennyson's poem "The Brook" uses onomatopoeia to imitate the sound of a small stream flowing down a stony hill:

I chatter over stony ways
  In little sharps and trebles,
I bubble into eddying bays,
  I babble on the pebbles.

Exercise: Onomatopoeic words

Pick out the four onomatopoeic words in the lines below and explain what they imitate.

These lines are from "Sailor's Song" by Thomas Lovell Beddoes.

1. The wanton water leaps in sport,
2. And rattles down the pebbly shore;
3. . . . the sea cows snort
4. And unseen mermaids' pearly song
   Comes bubbling up . . .
5. The anchor heaves! The ship swings free!

Find the onomatopoeic words in these lines from "The Raven" by Edgar Allan Poe:

6. As of someone gently rapping, rapping at my chamber door
7. And the silken, sad, uncertain rustling of each purple curtain
8. . . . an echo murmured back the word "Lenore"

Alliteration

Another device used by poets is **alliteration.** From the following example, can you define the word *alliteration*?

> Pop bottles pop-bottles
> In pop shops;
> The pop-bottles Pop bottles
> Poor Pop drops.
>
> MORRIS BISHOP

Alliteration is the use in a line or phrase of two or more words that begin with the same vowel or consonant sounds. Listening for alliteration in poetry will increase your pleasure in it.

To discuss

1. Alliteration is the repetition of sound at the beginnings of words. Poetry uses other kinds of repetition. Can you describe the ones you have studied so far?

2. Give your ideas as to why alliteration in poetry often makes it more humorous or more impressive.

Exercises: Alliteration

1. Find four examples of alliteration in "High Flight," page 339.

2. Explain what words make up the alliteration in lines 1, 4, 5, 6, 9, 13 of "High Flight."

3. Find other examples of alliteration in the poetry quoted in this chapter. Write the numeral of the page where each example appears. Compare your findings in class.

4. See if you can complete the following sentences. Make your words a part of the pattern of alliteration.

EXAMPLE: 1. Little ladies . . .
YOU WRITE: *1. Little ladies laugh so lightly.*

1. Pointed pencils . . .
2. Several of the sleds . . .
3. Brown books . . .
4. Daring are the devils . . .
5. Terrible teen-agers . . .

Choral Reading of Poetry

One of the best ways to enjoy the sounds of poetry is to read it in a group. Such reading encourages you to let yourself go and to use your voice freely to express the feeling of the poem. You have probably participated in choral reading of poetry in earlier grades. Look over the guides below to remind yourself how it is done:

Guides for choral reading

1. Copy the poem so that you can mark it for choral reading.
2. Familiarize yourself with the poem. Be sure you know the meaning of every part. Remember that poetry is punctuated like prose. Study the punctuation to be sure that you get the right meaning.
3. Decide which words and phrases should be emphasized, and underline them.
4. Make special note of words to be read in a certain tone of voice. You may want to emphasize long vowels and strong consonant sounds to help express the feeling of the poem.
5. Decide who will read the various parts of the poem. Mark the poem with these letters:

   BC (boys' chorus), *GC* (girls' chorus), *All* (everyone read), *Solo* (part to be read by one person).

   If the poem is to be read by different groups, mark it *Group 1*, *Group 2*, etc.
6. Remember that when several voices read together, the words tend to come out less distinctly than when only one person reads. Therefore, careful, almost exaggerated articulation is needed. There should be longer pauses between words than when one person reads.
7. Appoint a leader or conductor who gives the signal to start and who signals various pauses, stops, and starts. This person may sit inconspicuously in front of the chorus so that he will not be seen by the audience.

Exercises: Choral reading

1. Following the guides above, prepare one of the poems on the next page for choral reading.

Written in March

The cock is crowing,
The stream is flowing,
The small birds twitter,
The lake doth glitter,
The green field sleeps in the sun;
The oldest and youngest
Are at work with the strongest;
The cattle are grazing,
Their heads never raising;
There are forty feeding like one!

Like an army defeated
The snow hath retreated,
And now doth fare ill
On the top of the bare hill;
The ploughboy is whooping—anon—anon.
There's joy in the mountains;
There's life in the fountains;
Small clouds are sailing,
Blue sky prevailing;
The rain is over and gone!

WILLIAM WORDSWORTH

FROM *The Pied Piper of Hamelin*

Rats!
They fought the dogs and killed the cats,
    And bit the babies in the cradles,
And ate the cheeses out of the vats,
    And licked the soup from the cooks' own ladles,
Split open the kegs of salted sprats,
Made nests inside men's Sunday hats,
And even spoiled the women's chats,
    By drowning their speaking
    With shrieking and squeaking
In fifty different sharps and flats.

ROBERT BROWNING

2. Prepare "High Flight" or "The Branch" for choral reading.

GOING AHEAD

Select a poem that you like and think would be suitable for choral reading, choose a group of classmates, and prepare the poem for performance before the class or a larger audience.

Test I

1. Read the poem below. Then copy it on your paper and under-line the syllables that are stressed. (*Remember*, in the rhythm of a line, the stressed syllables are those which have a heavy beat.) At the end of each line, write the letters that label the rhyme scheme.

The Wilderness Is Tamed

The ax has cut the forest down, A
The laboring ox has smoothed all clear, B
Apples now grow where pine trees stood, C
And slow cows graze instead of deer. B

Where Indian fires once raised their smoke A
The chimneys of a farmhouse stand, B
And cocks crow barnyard challenges C
To dawns that once saw savage land. B

The ax, the plow, the binding wall, A
By these the wilderness is tamed, B
By these the white man's will is wrought, C
The rivers bridged, the new towns named. D

ELIZABETH COATSWORTH

2. On your paper, write the term which describes the kind of meter used in the poem above.

Test II

On your paper, copy and complete each statement below with one of the following terms: *free verse, foot, meter, alliteration, ono-matopoeia.*

1. Any kind of poetic rhythm is __?__.
2. A measurement of rhythm in a line of poetry is called a __?__.
3. Words whose pronunciations imitate the sounds they refer to are called __?__.
4. A form of poetry that has no regular pattern is __?__.
5. The term __?__ is used to describe the repetition of sound at the beginnings of words in a line or phrase of poetry.

353

Exercise I

1. Review pages 342–45.

2. On your paper, copy these stanzas from "The Rime of the Ancient Mariner." Underline the syllables that are stressed. Then, at the end of each line, write the letters that label the rhyme scheme.

> "And through the drifts the snowy clifts
> Did send a dismal sheen;
> Nor shapes of men nor beasts we ken—
> The ice was all between.
>
> "The ice was here, the ice was there,
> The ice was all around;
> It cracked and growled, and roared and howled
> Like noises in a swound!"

SAMUEL TAYLOR COLERIDGE

3. On the left of each line of the stanzas which you have copied on your paper, write the number of feet in that line.

4. What term is used to describe the type of foot used in the poem above?

Exercise II

1. Review pages 345–49.

2. Tell how many feet there are in each of these lines:

    1. What wondrous life is this I lead!
    2. And round and round it flew.
    3. The moping owl does to the moon complain.
    4. The rising morn has hid the stars.
    5. When sorrows come, they come not single spies.

3. On your paper, write the numerals from 1 to 5. After the appropriate numeral, write the word in each line that is onomatopoeic.

    1. Heard the lapping of the water . . .
    2. From the church came a murmur . . .
    3. And in the apple leaves chatters the jay . . .
    4. Heard the whispering of the pine trees . . .
    5. And he tapped with his whip . . .

4. Most of the lines below contain examples of alliteration. On your paper, copy the numeral of each line that has alliteration. Then write the words of alliteration.

1. And waves were white below.
2. The moving moon went up the sky.
3. The pointed horns of my canoe . . .
4. A silver sky is faintly etched.
5. Wanders and watches with eager ears . . .
6. A boy drove into the city, his wagon loaded down.
7. The last soft snowflake seeks the ground.
8. The slow, sad murmur of the distant seas.
9. The icicles, cracking in the cold, snapped and fell.
10. He leaps from the sea with a silken swish.
11. Blow, bugle, blow, set the wild echoes flying.
12. Horses of iron traveled across the land.

5. In your own words, explain the meaning of each of the following terms:

1. free verse	5. bound verse
2. iambic meter	6. alliteration
3. foot	7. onomatopoeia
4. meter	8. form in poetry

CHAPTER 15

Getting the Most from Your Reading

Reading gives stimulus to our youth and diversion to our old age; it adds a charm to success and offers a haven of consolation to failure. Through the night watches, on all our journeyings, and in our hours of ease, reading is our unfailing companion.

Thus wrote the Roman philosopher and statesman, Cicero, over 2,000 years ago, and men have found it to be true ever since. A good reader need never want for stimulation, amusement, consolation, or companionship.

Deciding What and How to Read

Today we have a problem that Cicero, who lived before the invention of the printing press, never had. There is such a vast quantity of reading material available to us that we can read only a small fraction of it.

Much selection of reading will be done for you. You have your school assignments, and there are many lists of recommended books, including one on page 358. Your own interests and reading ability will make a further selection for you.

The *title* of a book can be the first clue as to whether or not the book will interest you, although, of course, the title alone is insufficient grounds for making a final decision. Another basis for selecting a book is its author. If you have read and enjoyed a book written by a certain author, you are likely to want to read another of his books. Sometimes, only the familiarity of an author's name and the kind of books he writes may encourage you to read one of his books.

To discuss

1. Below are the titles of ten books recommended by the American Library Association for inclusion in junior high school libraries. Tell, from the title, in which category of the three listed under *a*, *b*, *c* you would put each book. Explain the reason for your answer.

a. probably would like to read
b. cannot tell from title
c. probably would not like to read

1. *How to Make a Home Nature Museum*
2. *Hoofbeats on the Trail*
3. *Teen-Age Diet Book*
4. *Rocket Ship* Galileo
5. *Book of Ballets and Ballet Music*
6. *Mystery of the Green Cat*
7. *White Panther*
8. *Atoms Today and Tomorrow*
9. *River of the Wolves*
10. *Life of Winston Churchill*

2. Here are the names of ten well-known authors. On the basis of what you know about each of them, tell in which category you would put a book he had written. Explain your answer.

a. probably would like to read
b. do not know the author
c. probably would not like to read

1. Stephen W. Meader
2. Ogden Nash
3. Charles Dickens
4. Louisa May Alcott
5. Howard Pease
6. Jules Verne
7. Arthur Conan Doyle
8. Robert Louis Stevenson
9. William Shakespeare
10. Charlotte Brontë

GOING AHEAD

Prepare a list of books by authors and titles that your classmates recommend highly. Arrange the list alphabetically by author's last name and underline the title, thus:

London, Jack, <u>The Call of the Wild</u>

Include the names of the students who recommend each title so that anyone can ask questions about the book.

Then post the list on the bulletin board or see if your teacher can have it duplicated so that each student may have a copy.

Types of Reading

About three hundred and fifty years ago Francis Bacon, the English statesman, wrote: "Some books are to be tasted, others to be swallowed, and some few to be chewed and digested." It can be said for all the reading you do that you must decide whether to taste it (skimming), swallow it (reading rapidly for pleasure), or chew and digest it (reading for mastery). You must, therefore, adjust your type of reading to the material.

Skimming

The title or the name of an author may not always lead you to a sound decision about whether or not to read a book or an article. A quick way to get more information is through *skimming*.

To skim is to allow your eyes to run quickly down a page of print, taking in only topic sentences and key words and phrases. *The main point of skimming is to save time.*

Skimming enables you quickly: (1) to locate a specific fact in a long passage; (2) to find a needed part of an article or chapter; (3) to discover the main idea of a selection or book; (4) to get an impression of the content of a piece of writing: for example, the subject, the level of difficulty, the style of writing.

To discuss

Go to a library and find on the shelves a book that you do not know but that you judge from its title you might enjoy reading. Write on paper the author and title. Now spend not more than five minutes skimming the book. Be prepared to explain in a class discussion the reasons why you would or would not enjoy the book. Does the subject look interesting? Are the style and level of difficulty right for you?

Exercises: Skimming

1. On the next page is an article entitled "The Beautiful Planet of Mystery." Number your paper from 1 to 4. Skim the article to find the answers to the following four questions:

1. What planet is discussed?
2. What is its diameter?
3. How hot is its surface?
4. Why is the planet a mystery?

Time yourself. An expert skimmer should be able to answer these questions in one minute, including writing time. If you can do it in a minute or two, your skill is adequate. If you take longer, you probably read too much instead of picking out key words only.

The Beautiful Planet of Mystery

Venus, the brightest and most beautiful starlike object in the heavens, is a planet of mystery. This is because it is covered with a thick layer of dense, yellow-white clouds.

When astronomers turn their biggest telescopes on Venus, they see only the outer side of these heavy clouds. The clouds are hundreds of miles deep. As a result, it is impossible to see the surface of the planet.

Sometimes Venus appears in the western sky at sunset. It grows brighter and brighter as the twilight deepens until it shines like a gorgeous jewel. At times it is one hundred times as bright as a first-magnitude star. At other times it appears in the eastern sky before sunrise. You will not see it then unless you get up very early.

Venus is the second planet in order from the Sun. First comes Mercury, then Venus, then Earth, then Mars. Venus is 67 million miles from the Sun. It takes Venus 225 of our days to go once around the Sun, traveling with a speed of 22 miles per second. When Venus is closest to the Earth, it is only 29 million miles away. No other planet comes that close to the Earth. Mars, at its closest, is 36 million miles away.

Venus has sometimes been called the Earth's twin sister because it is just about the same size as the Earth. It has a diameter of 7,700 miles, while that of the Earth is 7,920 miles. However, conditions on Venus are very different from those on Earth.

At the start of the century, some astronomers imagined that Venus was covered by great swamps with tropical vegetation and gigantic animals like the dinosaurs which once roamed the Earth. This made a romantic picture. However, astronomers are certain today that it is not so.

With the aid of spectroscopes, astronomers have studied the portion of the atmosphere of Venus which is above the clouds. Recently studies have been made with instruments carried to very high altitudes by balloons.

These studies show that there is very little water vapor in the upper atmosphere of Venus. There seems to be no oxygen at all. But there is 500 times as much carbon dioxide as in the atmosphere of the Earth.

Three conflicting theories about conditions on Venus have been advanced by astronomers to explain these findings.

According to one theory, the clouds are composed of water droplets or ice crystals, and there is so much water on Venus that the whole planet is covered by a universal ocean.

The second theory is just the opposite. According to it, the surface of Venus is a great rocky desert with no water at all. The clouds are clouds of dust.

The third theory is the strangest of all. It holds that there are oceans of oil instead of water on Venus, and that the clouds are composed of droplets of oil.

The astronomers all agree, however, that the surface of Venus must be very hot. They are certain that the thick clouds hold in the heat of the Sun just as the glass roof and walls of a greenhouse do. Estimates of the temperature on the surface of Venus range from that of boiling water, 212 degrees Fahrenheit, to as high as 600 degrees.

Astronomers are also certain that the surface of Venus is lost in eternal darkness because of the thickness of the clouds.

from *Highlights for Children,* by DAVID DIETZ

2. Skim Chapter 2 of this book to find three phrases you should avoid in introducing a person. Jot down on a scrap of paper the number of the pages and lines where this information is given. Be sure to use the topic headings to accelerate your skimming.

3. Using the daily newspaper as your source of information, find some of the main causes of automobile accidents in your community during the past week. Choose a copy of a recent local newspaper and skim the paper, circling any articles that appear to be on the subject. Then skim each marked article and jot down on a sheet of paper the cause of the accident, if given.

Remember, you need here both speed and accuracy. You are not *reading* the newspaper. You are skimming to find certain information and reading only the part that gives that information.

Reading for mastery

If you have mastered the material in a chapter or article, you should be able to:

1. State the main ideas
2. Remember important supporting details
3. Draw conclusions from the material

Follow the guides listed below to master your next assignment for science or social studies:

Guides for reading for mastery

1. *Know the purpose of the assignment.* Find out the purpose of an assignment before doing it.
2. *See how the content of the assignment relates to its context.* Examine the book it is in, especially the chapters preceding and following it. Recall previous assignments.
3. *Skim the material.* Note especially the title, the subheadings, the first and last sentences of each paragraph, the captions, and any study questions at the end.
4. *Read the material closely.* Mentally summarize each paragraph and each section after you have read it; read with special care all headings, italics, boldfaced words, and numbered items. Look up unfamiliar words. If there is a glossary, use it.
5. *Recall the material* when you have finished step 4. If you find there are sections you cannot recall, reread them.
6. *Think about the significance of the assignment.* Did it change your thinking at all? Can you draw any conclusions from the material? How does the material fit into your school work?

While you are reading an assignment for mastery, write down on paper all questions that puzzle you or that you think would make interesting material for discussion in class. Raise these questions in class as soon as opportunity arises. Then take notes on any explanations given and any points especially emphasized by your teacher.

To discuss

1. Think back over recent assignments for which you have been required to master material. How have you gone about it? Did you omit any of the steps suggested above? What changes should you make in order to improve your technique of mastery? Exchange ideas in class discussion.

2. If you are not already using the plan for mastery outlined above, do so the next time you are assigned a chapter. Follow every step exactly. Discuss your success or lack of it in class.

Exercises: Reading for mastery

1. Suppose you are taking a general science course on a unit called "The Planets of Our Sun." You have been assigned several articles to read for the purpose of learning the main characteristics and importance of each planet. One of the articles is the one you have skimmed on pages 360–61. Read this article again for mastery.

2. Test your mastery of "The Beautiful Planet of Mystery" by completing the statements below. Number your paper from 1 to 5 and, after each numeral, write *a*, *b*, *c*, or *d*, depending upon which group of words correctly completes the statement. *Do not refer to the article while doing this exercise.*

To test knowledge of main ideas:

1. On Venus, probably life as we know it is impossible because . . .
   a. it is too close to the sun.   c. it is too hot and dark.
   b. it is too dry and windy.   d. it is too cold and wet.

2. Compared to Earth, Venus is . . .
   a. about the same size.   c. much farther from the sun.
   b. considerably smaller.   d. more beautiful.

To test memory for important details:

3. When Venus is closest to Earth, it is . . .
   a. 6 million miles away.   c. 29 million miles away.
   b. 67 million miles away.   d. 36 million miles away.

4. Seen in the sky at night, Venus is . . .
   a. bright and beautiful.   c. dim and hazy.
   b. a dull red.   d. rapidly moving.

To test your ability to draw conclusions:

5. To get accurate information about conditions on Venus . . .
   a. is very difficult because of the distance and heavy cloud layers.
   b. would be easy if scientists were granted sufficient funds.
   c. will be impossible, because Venus is too distant from Earth ever to be explored by spacemen.
   d. would be easy if only a method could be devised to blow away the cloud layers.

Word-for-word reading

A special type of reading is required for mathematics and science problems and for directions. Since, in all such writing, there are usually no words wasted, each word must be read carefully.

To discuss

In class, share experiences you have had, such as: misunderstanding directions, finding explanations unclear, failing to solve a mathematics or science problem. Was your failure a result of careless reading or unclear directions? Be prepared to read a short problem or directions to the class. Are they easily followed if read carefully?

Guides for reading directions and problems

1. Read each word slowly.
2. Say the words aloud, or whisper them, so that each will make an impression.
3. Read the problem again, deciding how you will go about solving it. When you have worked the problem, read the words again to be sure you have done exactly what was called for and have given your answer in proper terms.
4. Do not jump to conclusions when you read directions. Read them through; then perform them, step by step.

Exercise: Word-for-word reading

Ask yourself these three questions about the problem below:

1. What facts to work from are given in the problem?
2. What problem or problems are to be solved?
3. What helpful suggestions are given in the directions?

PROBLEM: The difference between what a merchant pays for his merchandise and what he receives for it is called the *margin*. With what he receives as margin, the merchant pays his business expenses. Any amount that is left over is his profit.

A used-car dealer bought a car for $800. After making repairs on the car, he sold it for $1,200. What was the margin?

The dealer figured that his expenses were 25 per cent of the selling price of the car. What was his profit on the car? The profit was what per cent of the selling price?

Reading for pleasure

There is no more useful pleasure than reading, for through reading you broaden your experience, deepen your understanding of people, increase your store of information, and enrich your vocabulary. Form the habit of reading for pleasure. Always carry a book with you to read for enjoyment when no other activity is required.

A good way to discover books you will enjoy reading is to ask your friends what they have enjoyed. And if you yourself are enjoying a book, tell others about it, for you will be doing them a favor.

One good way for a class to share information about books is for each member to maintain a reading record, which is kept available for classmates to study. These reading records may be filed in the classroom, so that anyone may look at them when he needs a suggestion for a good book.

Exercise: A reading record

Prepare a list of books you read for pleasure, according to the following or similar form:

Title	Author	Date started and completed	Rating E=excel G=good F=fair P=poor	Difficulty H=hard A=average E=easy	Comment
Born Free	Joy Adamson	Sept. 20 – Oct. 2	E	a	Exciting true story of bringing up lion in Africa
Captains Courageous	Rudyard Kipling	Oct. 4 – Oct. 21	G	H	Realistic sea story; spoiled boy becomes a man; some parts too long
The Adventures of Sherlock Holmes	A. Conan Doyle	Oct. 21 – Nov. 2	E	H	Clever, realistic detective stories; hard vocabulary and sentences

Keep the list up to date for the remainder of the school year and work out with your classmates a plan for sharing reading records.

A book report

Another way of sharing information about books is through written book reports. A good report, like a good review in a magazine or newspaper, gives the information and opinion that a prospective reader of the book will want in order to decide whether or not to read the book. It will be organized in paragraphs and tell the reader the title and author; what the book is about (setting, main characters, plot); important characteristics of the book (style, illustrations); whether or not it is recommended, and for whom.

Here is a good book report written by an eighth-grader:

The Pearl

The Pearl (102 pp.), by John Steinbeck, is set in the vicinity of a primitive Mexican village on the Gulf of Mexico. The writing is simple and poetic, and the story is simple, too. However, the book deals with an important idea: the effect of greed on the lives of men.

Kino, a poor but happy fisherman, finds a precious pearl. This event affects him, his family, and the whole village where he lives. The sad, exciting story involves theft, murder, escape, and a search for criminals. It shows the worst side of different kinds of people —the merchants, a doctor, the simple village folk. The climax of the story, in which Kino and his wife Juana decide what to do with the pearl, is tragic.

I found this book easy to read and hard to stop reading. I recommend it to everyone, boy or girl, except those who don't like to think or who insist upon happy endings. I shall never forget the book or what it taught me.

Exercise: A book report

Choose a book you have enjoyed and would recommend to classmates. Write a report on it. If there is time, read your report to the class. While others are reading their reports, write down the authors and titles of any of the books you think you might enjoy.

GOING AHEAD

Join a small committee to prepare a list of twenty-five books, fiction and nonfiction, the committee recommends for eighth-grade reading. Check your library and see how many of the books listed are available. Post a list on the bulletin board. The librarian may be willing to put the books on a reserved shelf for a few days.

Increasing Your Enjoyment of Reading

The more you know about writing, the more you will enjoy reading. For example, what you have learned on pages 215–17 about how a story is constructed should help you appreciate more the stories you read. Observing how the characters in a story are described and how they develop will increase your reading pleasure. Awareness of the author's style, how he selects words and puts them together, is another source of interest. Is the style smooth, quick, relaxed, eager? Does it change as the story enters different phases? Does the author use long words and long sentences, or are they plain and short?

Figurative language: similes and metaphors

Some readers miss important ideas because they fail to recognize that there is more to the words than what they plainly say. For instance, Benjamin Franklin once wrote: "Where liberty dwells, there is my country." Franklin's words mean more than first meets the eye. He is *comparing* liberty to a dweller, a person who remains in a place, and he is saying that wherever liberty lives or stays, there he (Franklin) would feel at home, as if he were in his own country. He suggests, further, that wherever there is liberty, whether in America, or in another country, he feels the same sort of loyalty and affection for that place that a person normally feels for his own country. But he manages to say all this in just seven words: "Where liberty dwells, there is my country."

This sort of language, where one thing is compared to another, is called **figurative language.** When you use such language, you are using **figures of speech.**

When you use an expression such as "He ran away as fast as a greyhound," you are making your language more colorful through the use of **similes.** A simile is a figure of speech that makes a comparison of one thing with another, using the words *like* or *as.*

A **metaphor** also makes a comparison, but without the use of *like* or *as,* as in this sentence, in which raindrops are compared to bullets:

Bullets of rain pounded on the roof.

Notice in the two sentences below how the comparison is *expressed* in the simile, and merely *implied* in the metaphor:

SIMILE: He was as strong as an ox.
METAPHOR: He was an ox for strength.

To discuss

1. Tell whether the comparisons listed below are *similes* or *metaphors*. Give reasons for your answers.

1. Thin as a rail
2. Bright as a dollar
3. The ship plowed through the water.
4. The daisies danced in the sun.
5. Still as a mouse
6. Clouds of whipped cream

2. Tell what two things are being compared in 3, 4, and 6 above.

Exercises: Similes and metaphors

1. Here are four examples of figurative language. In each, tell what is being compared to what.

EXAMPLE: 1. His fat cheeks were like little round balloons.
YOU WRITE: *1. Cheeks are compared to balloons.*

1. He dove down into the cellar like a rat into its hole.
                                              —A. CONAN DOYLE
2. They drove with such speed that the horses were extended like rubber bands.—SELMA LAGERLÖF
3. Estella's light came along the dark passage like a star.
                                              —CHARLES DICKENS
4. He gazed at me as if I were a slot machine into which he had, without results, dropped a nickel.—JAMES THURBER

2. Here are four more figures of speech. The comparisons are made without *as* or *like*. Tell what is being compared to what.

EXAMPLE: 1. Mother groaned, "This house is a real pigsty."
YOU WRITE: *1. House is compared to pigsty.*

1. Slowly, silently, now the moon
   Walks the night in her silver shoon.
       —WALTER DE LA MARE
2. The dog boasted an immense mouth formed of black rubber.
                                              —MAC KINLAY KANTOR
3. I caught that boy and shook him until his freckles rattled.
                                              —O. HENRY
4. Emotion is the spark plug that gets action.—ROGER BABSON

1. Find examples of figurative language and bring them to class. You will find many in the sports pages and in advertisements.

2. Try your hand at writing a descriptive paragraph in which you use figurative language. Do not overdo it. Comparisons should add clarity and interest to your writing.

Literal language

The opposite of figurative language is **literal language,** the kind of language most of us use most of the time, in which we simply say what we mean directly, without comparisons.

FIGURATIVE: The sun of liberty is set.—BENJAMIN FRANKLIN

LITERAL: There is no more liberty.

FIGURATIVE: Alice is timid as a mouse.

LITERAL: Alice is very timid.

When you are reading, try to recognize figurative language when you come across it. That is, be aware of the fact that the writer is trying to tell you something special by making a comparison. He is not stating his idea directly. Only by distinguishing figurative from literal language can you get full meaning and enjoyment from a piece of writing. "Alice is timid as a mouse" means more than "Alice is very timid," and is more colorful as well.

Exercise: Literal and figurative language

Read the following five passages carefully and be prepared to point out and explain any figurative language. They are excerpts from literary writing and the figurative language is more mature than in your previous exercises. Tell what is compared to what in each selection. One of the passages contains a long metaphor of several sentences. Two of the passages are entirely literal. Can you identify them?

1. My first most vivid and broad impression of the identity of things seems to me to have been gained on a memorable raw afternoon towards evening. At such a time I found out for certain that this bleak place overgrown with nettles was the churchyard . . . and that the dark flat wilderness beyond the churchyard . . . was the marshes; and that the low leaden line beyond was the river; and that the distant savage lair from which the wind was rushing was the sea; and that the small bundle of shivers growing afraid of it all and beginning to cry was Pip.

from *Great Expectations,* by Charles Dickens

2. "Look it up in the dictionary" has become a popular slogan in both home and school. Growing knowledge of science encourages the quest for accurate information. World activities presented by the press and on the screen stimulate an expanding interest in human affairs. The speed with which modern life is changing is reflected in our marvelously flexible language. New words are constantly being added. . . . Almost hourly, use of a good, up-to-date dictionary is essential to clear understanding.

Preface, *Winston Dictionary for Schools*

3. Witness the extraordinary powers of the human ear—the most elaborate sound-receiving mechanism ever designed. On a still day, it can hear clearly the feeble buzzings of a quarter inch fly at a distance of six feet. The fly's wings send out sound waves in all directions, but the ear receives only a tiny portion of them—roughly 1/300,000th of all the sound emitted by the tiny fly.

from "The Marvel of Hearing," by Peter Farb

4. Moon-green and amber, a strip of fading sky glowed across the trail of the vanished sun. Far below, the opal sea paled to mother-of-pearl. Then, over sea and sky, strode the sudden dark of the tropics and in an instant the southern stars flamed and flared through the violet night.

from "The Reef," by Samuel Scoville, Jr.

5. Ten years pass with that cabin on Little Pigeon Creek for a home, and that farm and neighborhood the soil for growth. There the boy Abe grows to be the young man, Abraham Lincoln.

Ten years pass and the roots of a tree spread out, finding water to carry up to branches and leaves that are in the sun; the trunk thickens, the forked limbs shine wider in the sun, they pray with their leaves in the rain and the whining wind; the tree arrives, the mystery of its coming, spreading, growing, a secret not even known to the tree itself; it stands with its arms stretched to the corners the four winds come from, with its murmured testimony, "We are here, we arrived, our roots are in the earth of these years."

from *Abe Lincoln Grows Up*, by Carl Sandburg

The tone of writing

"It wasn't *what* he said; it was the *way* he said it." You know how a person's tone of voice can affect the meaning of what he says. He can speak with a friendly tone, a harsh tone, a cold tone, a serious tone, a humorous tone.

It is easy to recognize the tone of spoken language, because there is a voice to speak it, and voices have tones. *But written language can also have a tone.* Its tone must be conveyed entirely by the words.

You will enjoy your reading more and understand it better if you train yourself to be aware of the tone of the writing. Is the author being serious with you, or is he being humorous? Does he feel deeply about his subject, or is he light-hearted?

Exercises: The tone of writing

1. Below and on page 374 are six versions of a newspaper notice that the members of a school baseball team might write, urging students to come out to a championship game. Number your paper from 1 to 6 and, beside each numeral, write the pair of adjectives from this list that best describes the tone of each notice:

serious, enthusiastic	sarcastic,* sullen	friendly, humorous
bitter, humorous	serious, neutral	angry, excited

1. The Central High baseball team would greatly appreciate a large crowd at its game next Tuesday, when they will play for the city championship.
2. If we don't get a large crowd of you fans out to our baseball game next Tuesday, people are going to think teachers have started giving homework in the afternoon. Come on, everyone, drop your books and help us win that championship!
3. Come on, everybody, out to the game next Tuesday! See your baseball team win the city championship. We've done well without crowds up till now. With the whole school out there in the stands when we face Northern, we'll slaughter them and make you proud of Central.

---

* *sarcastic*: bitter, meaning the opposite of what the words say, as saying, "What a lovely day!" when it is cold and rainy and you were hoping to go on a picnic.

4. If the members of the Central High baseball team don't get a better crowd out next Tuesday for their championship game, the school will well deserve the defeat it will probably suffer. It is not fair for the team to work so hard for the school and then to be ignored. Come on, students, show you have *some* appreciation!

5. The Central High baseball team has deeply appreciated the absence of fans at its recent games. The profound quiet in the stands has enabled them to concentrate on their hitting and fielding. So please keep up the good old Central High tradition and stay away next Tuesday. The team will probably do better without you.

6. Here lies the Central High baseball team, dead of discouragement because only twenty-five students showed up at their championship game on Tuesday, April 17. Please omit flowers.

2. Read the four beginnings to short stories printed below. Choose from the list of adjectives those which describe the tone of each selection. In most cases you will probably want to use more than one adjective. The adjectives in the list are only suggestions. Use others if you wish. If you need to write some sentences to describe the tone accurately and fully, do so. Compare and discuss your answers in class.

cold	sarcastic	dry	natural
harsh	conversational	casual	sincere
friendly	sympathetic	angry	insincere
formal	frightened	happy	mocking
bitter	matter-of-fact	nervous	frantic
humorous	sad	excited	confused
weary	tough	slangy	forbidding

1. The day had been one of the unbearable ones, when every sound had set her teeth on edge like chalk creaking on a blackboard, when every word her father or mother said to her or did not say to her seemed an intentional injustice. And of course it would happen, as the end to such a day, that just as the sun went down back of the mountain and the long twilight began, she noticed that Rollie was not around.

from "The Apprentice," by Dorothy Canfield

2. I had called upon my friend Mr. Sherlock Holmes one day in the autumn of last year and found him in deep conversation with a very stout, florid-faced elderly gentleman with fiery red hair. With an apology for my intrusion, I was about to withdraw when Holmes pulled me abruptly into the room and closed the door behind me.

"You could not possibly have come at a better time, my dear Watson," he said cordially.

from "The Redheaded League," by Sir Arthur Conan Doyle

3. Personally, I do not care for coppers, but I believe in being courteous to them at all times, so when Johnny Brannigan comes into Mindy's restaurant one Friday and sits down in the same booth with me, because there are no other vacant seats in the joint, I give him a huge hello.

from "Earthquake," by Damon Runyon

4. In a forest of mixed growth somewhere on the eastern spurs of the Carpathians, a man stood one winter night watching and listening, as though he waited for some beast of the woods to come within the range of his vision, and later, of his rifle. But the game for whose presence he kept so keen an outlook was none that figured in the sportsman's calendar as lawful and proper for the chase; Ulrich von Gradwitz patrolled the dark forest in quest of a human enemy.

from "The Interlopers," by Saki (H. H. Munro)

TO MEMORIZE

FROM *The Declaration of Independence*

We hold these truths to be self-evident: that all men are created equal, that they are endowed by their Creator with certain unalienable Rights, that among these are Life, Liberty, and the pursuit of Happiness. That to secure these Rights, Governments are instituted among Men, deriving their just powers from the consent of the governed.

Thomas Jefferson was the member of a committee of five who wrote the Declaration of Independence. Discuss the last sentence in the above selection. How do governments secure the rights of the people they govern? How do they derive their powers from the consent of those people? Now memorize this famous statement, which reflects some of the noblest beliefs of free people.

Speeding Up Your Reading

A fast reader has a great advantage over a slow one. He gets through his work more readily, he can read more and learn more, and in many cases he understands and appreciates more of what he reads.

Some people are slow readers because they just get into the habit of reading slowly. If you are one of these, *use your will power* for a while and *make yourself read faster*. This alone may increase your speed, and after you get used to it, you will not have to force yourself.

Remember, though, that speed is not the most important thing in reading. Comprehension and appreciation are. It will only be harmful to speed up your reading if the result is failure to understand and enjoy. Also, there are many kinds of reading that should never be done fast: good poetry, mathematics problems, legal documents, directions, and works of literature to which the author has devoted love and skill in his choice of words and style.

It is the casual reading which you should learn to do rapidly: the newspaper, the detective story, and many novels.

Many good readers enjoy reading on the floor, slouched in an easy chair, in bed, or even in the bathtub. If you enjoy these things, do them; but remember that you will read with maximum efficiency if you follow certain guides.

Guides for efficient reading

1. Read in a good light; have another lamp on in the same room; avoid glare from the page.
2. Sit in a firm, upright chair if you tend to get sleepy.
3. Try to hold your book so that the top and bottom of the page are about the same distance from your eyes. (Otherwise the constant change of focus will tire them.)
4. Rest your eyes every fifteen minutes or so. Close them for a few seconds or look at a distant object.
5. Concentrate completely. Remove or learn to ignore distractions. If possible, before you read, settle any pressing problem that may occupy your mind. Read in a quiet place, if possible. Know your purpose.

A Book to Read

War Beneath the Sea

by Frank Bonham
Thomas Y. Crowell Co.

The *Mako* was a brand new submarine, cold, efficient, dangerous and beautiful, and a shiver of excitement ran through Keith Stocker when he first saw her. The story of Keith's life aboard her during World War II makes the thrill and hardship of modern submarine warfare come alive for you. Perhaps the most difficult thing that Keith has to face is the fact that a submarine is a hunter, and that a hunter kills. Here is the world of deep water, where the enemy is identified by the echo of a single sound, and where the destruction, whether given or received, is real and horrible.

About the author

Frank Bonham has written over 500 short stories and 20 novels. He enjoys writing novels best because, he says, "I don't like to say good-by to a set of characters just as I have gotten to know them." Before finishing *War Beneath the Sea*, Mr. Bonham read over 30 books on the subject, took a submarine trip, rode a subtender, and talked at length with "old submariners."

Other books of his that you will enjoy are *Burma Rifles, Deepwater Challenge, The Loud, Resounding Sea, Honor Bound, Speedway Contender, Durango Street*, and *The Mystery of the Red Tide*.

Test I

Decide which of the four types of reading you should choose for each of the assignments listed below: *skimming*; *reading for mastery*; *word-for-word reading*; *reading for pleasure*. Write the type of reading next to the appropriate numeral on your paper.

1. Section of a newspaper to find the time a movie begins
2. Tomorrow's history lesson
3. A story in your favorite magazine
4. An article in an encyclopedia to check on two dates
5. A mathematics problem you find difficult

Test II

1. Next to the appropriate numerals on your paper, write *simile* or *metaphor* to describe each comparison below:

1. They are not words at all, but the wind rising.
2. The plane disappeared in the red waves of the sunset.
3. Foam floated on top of the shallow pool, like soapsuds left standing in a dishpan.
4. The long, red tongues of flame lapped at the house.
5. The rainbow was as colorful as the face of a circus clown.

2. For each statement above, write what two things are being compared.

Test III

Read the list of subjects below. From the adjectives at the end of each subject, select the one that *best* describes the tone of writing which will help to make each story lifelike and interesting to read.

1. A young man tries to teach his aunt to drive (humorous, sad, bitter)
2. A girl has an unhappy time at a party, but makes a good friend at the end (sympathetic, sarcastic, formal)
3. A mountain climber has an accident and is rescued (angry, thrilling, sad)
4. A ghost story (serious, mocking, spooky)

378

Review and Practice

Exercise I

1. Review "Types of Reading" on pages 359–65.

2. Complete the following statements with words or groups of words that will make the statements true:

    1. To run down a page, reading only the headings and key words, is to __?__.

    2. To prepare for a test in one of your school subjects is to __?__.

    3. A humorous book usually calls for __?__ reading.

    4. The directions on a complicated kit to be assembled should have __?__ reading.

Exercise II

1. Review the lesson on figurative language on pages 368–69.

2. Complete each of the following statements with a word or words that will make a true and vivid comparison:

    1. At the end of the hot day, the setting sun hung in the sky like a __?__.

    2. The scared pup looked like a __?__ as he dashed down the road.

    3. The embarrassed girls walked off the stage, drooping like __?__.

    4. In the dark, silent old house, every squeak of a board sounded as loud as a __?__.

3. Make each of the italicized expressions below stronger by adding a comparison:

    1. Suddenly our dog *began to howl.*

    2. The snow *covered the bushes.*

    3. Billy got up that day *very much out of sorts.*

    4. That is a *very dull story.*

    5. The wind blew *at the windows.*

Exercise III

1. Review the lesson on the tone of writing on page 373.

2. Write these four headings across your paper: *Sympathetic, Quiet, Weird, Thrilling.* Under each, write six words a writer could use to set the proper tone for a story.

CHAPTER 16

Making Sentence Diagrams (Optional)

To understand how a house is built, a radio is wired, or an engine is put together, it is usually helpful to study a diagram, a drawing that explains how the parts fit together. Likewise, a sentence diagram is a line picture that shows the relationship of words and word groups in a sentence. Sentence diagrams can help you to increase your understanding of grammar and sentence structure.

The Simple Subject and Verb   (See page 130.)

To diagram a sentence, first pick out the verb in the sentence and write it on the right-hand half of a base line.

Alice's dog <u>barked</u> all night.

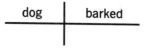

Then decide what the simple subject is by asking *who* or *what* performed the action of the verb. Write the simple subject on the left-hand half of the line. Separate the simple subject from the verb with a short vertical line that crosses the base line.

dog	barked

Remember that a verb may contain more than one word, as in the verb phrase *has fallen*.

That old <u>sign</u> <u>has fallen</u>.

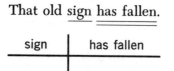

Exercise: Diagraming simple subjects and verbs

Find the simple subjects and the verbs (or verb phrases) in the sentences below. Place them correctly on diagrams.

1. We strive for excellence.
2. My favorite goldfish died.
3. Those noisy boys are shouting at my friend.
4. This automobile travels much too fast.
5. The old house was sold to a new family.
6. Our packages have been damaged rather severely.
7. A dark, heavy tan appeared on the faces of the skiers.
8. In fear, Mr. Bradshaw tiptoed into the dark room.
9. Last Friday our team defeated Salem Junior High.
10. He may have lost his wallet in the station.

The Four Types of Sentences (See pages 135–37.)

Below are listed the four types of sentences. Notice how the simple subject and verb in each one are placed on a diagram.

DECLARATIVE: His watch stopped.

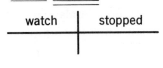

| watch | stopped |

INTERROGATIVE: Did his watch stop?

| watch | Did stop |

IMPERATIVE: Sit quietly.

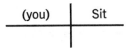

| (you) | Sit |

EXCLAMATORY: How suddenly Max jumped!

| Max | jumped |

In the interrogative sentence, the subject often comes between the two parts of a verb phrase. In the imperative sentence, there is no expressed subject. Rather, the subject is *you* understood.

Sentences in inverted order

Sentences which do not follow the usual order of subject first and predicate second are in inverted order. Although the predicate in these sentences appears before the subject, this does not show on a diagram.

A diagram shows grammatical relationship between words, not the order, or sequence, of words. In a diagram, the placement of the simple subject first and the verb second does not change.

Into the room walked the boys.

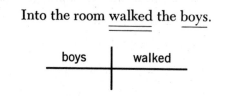

Exercise: Diagraming simple subjects and verbs

On your paper, write the numerals from 1 to 15. In each of the sentences below, diagram only the simple subject and the verb. Some of the sentences are in inverted order.

1. George behaved rather well.
2. Down the steps rolled our vase.
3. When did Oscar enlist in the army?
4. Relax for a minute.
5. How fast the fire is spreading!
6. Above the din was heard the crash.
7. Why do porpoises learn tricks so easily?
8. Look at me very carefully.
9. How creamy those desserts are!
10. Around the corral roamed the two stallions.
11. Did you call your employer?
12. In the vestibule stood two firemen.
13. Along the highway raced the large, modern trucks.
14. How quickly the sun sets!
15. Walk quietly through the hospital corridors.

Modifiers: Adjectives and Adverbs (See pages 76 and 82.)

Adjectives and adverbs are placed on a diagram to show their close relationship to the words they modify.

Adjectives modify nouns and pronouns.

Strange things are happening.

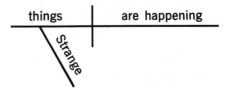

Noun adjectives, possessives, and articles are diagramed in an identical manner.

My guppies are multiplying in *a* small tank.

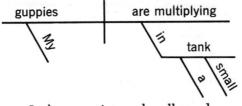

Joe's magazine rack collapsed.

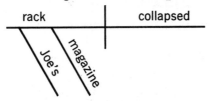

Adverbs, also, are connected to the words they modify. Most of them, as you have seen, modify verbs.

Today we may be defeated.

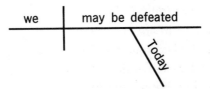

Remember, the order of words in a sentence is not always shown on a diagram. Therefore the adverb *Today* is hinged to the verb it modifies. As the first word in the sentence, it remains capitalized.

383

A few adverbs modify adjectives and other adverbs. They answer the questions *how much?* or *to what extent?* The adverb *not* or *n't* is shown in the same way as any other adverb. Here are some examples:

That *very* nervous girl does *not* talk *too* often.

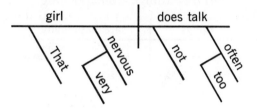

Notice that the adverb *very* modifies the adjective *nervous*, and the adverb *too* modifies another adverb, *often*.

Exercises: Diagraming sentences

1. Diagram all of the words in these sentences:

1. Sharp steel blades glittered brightly.
2. Many firemen fought bravely.
3. The man's luggage has suddenly opened.
4. Has the priceless diamond been sold?
5. Our oldest boy is working busily.
6. The small wooden bridge suddenly snapped.
7. Ruth's pet horse is limping slightly.
8. Have Mother's mahogany bookcases been polished?

2. Diagram all of the words in the sentences below. Pay special attention to the adverbs and the words they modify.

1. The big box fell heavily.
2. Suddenly we were quietly yawning.
3. Drive very carefully.
4. Doesn't that little engine begin quickly?
5. We haven't looked there.
6. The very yellow bird disappeared quite quickly.
7. Today she may be promoted.
8. Father's rather efficient electric heaters are glowing so warmly.

The Prepositional Phrase   (See pages 94–97.)

In a diagram, prepositional phrases are connected to the words they modify. A prepositional phrase that modifies a noun or pronoun is called an *adjective phrase.* One that modifies a verb is called an *adverb phrase.*

Acres *of wheat* have been planted *in the fields along that river.*

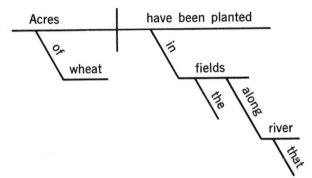

The adverb phrase *in the fields* modifies the verb *have been planted.* Notice that the adjective phrase *along that river* modifies the noun *fields*; *fields* is the object in the phrase *in the fields.* The adjective phrase *of wheat* modifies the noun *Acres.*

Exercise: Diagraming sentences

Diagram all of the words in the following sentences, but pay close attention to the prepositional phrases:

1. A ton of coal was dumped into the bin.
2. The glass of soda fell on the floor.
3. The wet umbrella in your hand is dripping.
4. Those seats near the back are never taken before the show.
5. Is the bottle of ink inside the desk?
6. The policeman on the corner is standing in the cold.
7. The man with the deep voice can be heard in this room.
8. The actress on the stage cried into a handkerchief of soft silk.
9. Under the bridge sped the last express from Chicago.
10. Recently some divers without aqualungs have gone beneath that body of water.

The Direct Object (See page 183.)

Direct objects are shown on a diagram in this way:

Dogs gnaw *bones.*

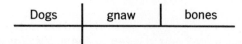

Here is the same sentence with the addition of modifiers:

The dogs gnaw *the steak* bones *from dinner.*

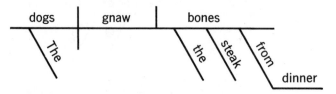

Notice that the vertical line which separates the subject from the verb crosses the base line. The vertical line which separates the verb from the direct object stops at the base line.

Exercise: Diagraming direct objects

Diagram all of the words in the sentences below:

1. The fleecy snow covered the ground.
2. Those pupils in the office are praising our principal.
3. Have you noticed the signs in the window of the shop?
4. Those heavy tank trucks are carrying milk to the next town.
5. Submit your suggestions for the theme of the spring dance.

The Subject Complement (See pages 185–86.)

A noun or pronoun used as a subject complement is diagramed in this way:

Dad became an *engineer.*

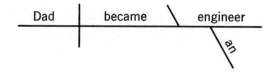

My aunt is *she*.

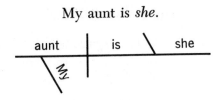

Notice that the line between the verb and the subject complement slants toward the subject to show that the complement refers to the subject.

Most adjectives precede the words they modify. Sometimes, however, an adjective appears after a linking verb and modifies the subject. These adjectives are also subject complements and are diagramed as such.

My pet is very *sick*.

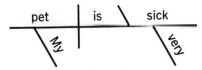

Exercises: Diagraming direct objects and subject complements

1. Diagram all of the words in these sentences, which contain subject complements:

1. Wintry weather is fun.
2. Edith's ideas were good.
3. Mark has become a member.
4. The Parkers are our closest neighbors.
5. The talkative woman is she.
6. Is Joan my partner in this game?

2. Diagram all of the words in these sentences, each of which contains a subject complement or direct object:

1. They did not find the exit.
2. His ideas are surprisingly good.
3. The policeman on our street caught the thief in the drugstore.
4. The package on the truck is a bundle of straw.
5. Freddie is a person with a lively imagination.
6. We removed the toys from our driveway.

The Indirect Object   (See pages 187–88.)

The indirect object has a close relationship with the prepositions *to* and *for*, since the indirect object tells *to whom* or *to what* or *for whom* or *for what* the action of the verb was performed.

John sent *us* flowers.

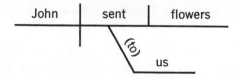

Notice that the indirect object *us* is diagramed as the object of the preposition *to,* but that *to* is enclosed in parentheses because it is not expressed—only understood.

Exercise: Diagraming sentences

Diagram all of the words in the following sentences:

1. Vicky sent me some tiny yellow roses.
2. Offer him a choice.
3. Mr. Simmons earned himself a very long vacation.
4. I mailed the winner my letter of congratulations.
5. Many people gave the political candidate loud cheers.
6. Are you baking us a chocolate cake?

Compound Sentence Elements
(See pages 140–41, 183, 191–92, and 234–35.)

The conjunctions *and, but, or, either–or,* and *neither–nor* connect various elements in a sentence. They are diagramed like this:

Compound subjects and predicates

Those *ponies* and that *horse* eat oats.

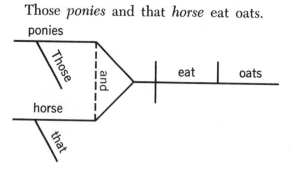

He *buys* and *sells* antiques.

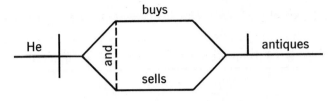

The boy *caught* the bird and *tamed* it.

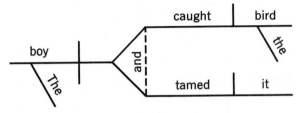

Exercise: Diagraming sentences

Diagram all of the words in these sentences:

1. Chlorine and helium are elements.
2. Those girls cut and strung the decorations.
3. My brother caught the mackerel and fried it.
4. Will Helen or Dot make a good score?
5. Within the capsule sat the astronaut and his partner.
6. Our club led at first but was defeated in the end.
7. Haven't you and your friend in Tokyo been corresponding?
8. Rise from your seats quickly and walk into the auditorium.
9. We pushed the car and pulled it.
10. A small bobcat and a large wildcat were seen in this area.

Compound objects

The diagram below shows a compound direct object:

We collect *coins* and *stamps*.

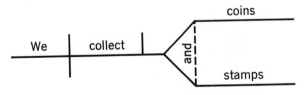

The following diagram shows a compound indirect object:

Mr. Brew offered *Charles* and *me* some interesting reproductions.

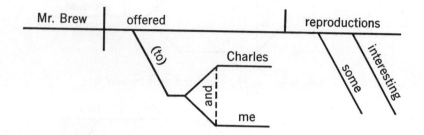

This sentence contains a compound object of a preposition:

We brought our box of *coins* and *stamps* for Mr. Brew's examination.

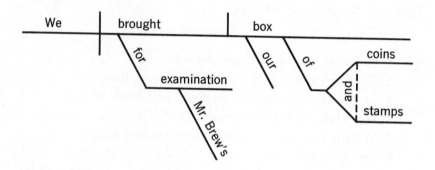

Exercise: Diagraming sentences

Diagram these sentences, each of which may contain a compound direct object, a compound object of a preposition, or a compound indirect object.

1. She added salt and pepper.
2. That musician performed with grace and beauty.
3. My sister stitched the skirts and blouses.
4. My old aunt gave Ned and me an invitation.
5. Have you hidden my orange socks and purple necktie?
6. Save your ticket stubs and the program.
7. The concert was sponsored by that group and our club.
8. Don't tell Ted or George the names of the winners.
9. Where do you always spend your time and your money?
10. Mr. Pipps didn't give Doris and Janet the grocery bill.

Compound subject complement

The subject complements in the first sentence below are nouns; in the second sentence, they are adjectives.

Hank became an *assistant* and a very good *friend*.

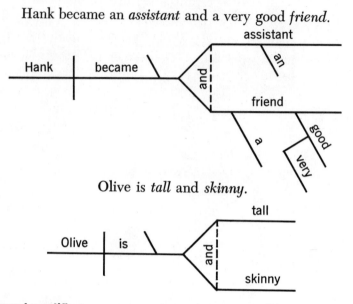

Olive is *tall* and *skinny*.

Compound modifiers

Notice how these adjectives and adverbs are diagramed:

The *short* and *husky* robber escaped *quickly* but *quietly*.

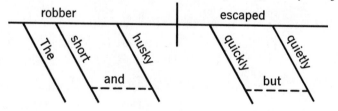

Compound sentence

There are two base lines in the diagram of a compound sentence.

Gently the sun rose, and the dew disappeared.

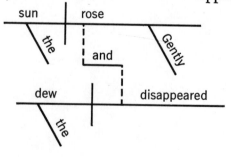

Exercise: Diagraming sentences

Diagram all of the words in these sentences:

1. The tall and rugged mountains soared into the sky.
2. Rodney has become weary and sullen.
3. Slowly but gradually the snail advanced along the edge.
4. Mark Sterling is a clever mechanic and a smart seaman.
5. He heard the noise of a light switch, and suddenly the room was thrown into darkness.
6. The puppy yelped, and the cat departed.
7. Babe Ruth slammed the ball over the fence, but his team did not win the game.
8. Separate the red particles from the tiny but important black particles.
9. Will Mr. Lennon become the president of the company and the chairman of the board?
10. Sleet has pounded the tin roof mercilessly, but no water has leaked into our house.
11. Joan quickly washed the dinner dishes and served dessert.
12. The storekeeper and his clerk were washing the display windows.

Special Sentence Elements

Sentences that contain nouns of direct address, the word *there* as an introductory word, or interjections are all diagramed similarly. They are placed on a line above the base line of the diagram.

Noun of direct address

A noun of direct address is never the subject of the sentence. It should be placed on a separate line above the diagram.

Children, listen carefully.

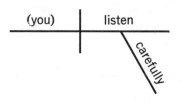

There as an introductory word

There often begins a sentence that is in inverted order.

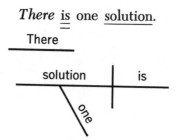

There is one solution.

Remember, the subject and predicate in a diagram are always arranged subject first, then predicate. With sentences in inverted order, rearrange the words, putting them in natural order: *One solution is there.* *There* is sometimes used as an adverb, but in this sentence it is an introductory word independent of the rest of the sentence.

Interjection

Interjections are also placed on a separate line above the diagram. (If you do not know what an interjection is, turn to page 419.)

Hooray! We won the game.   *Well,* we found him.

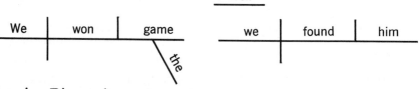

Exercise: Diagraming sentences

Diagram the following sentences. One sentence is a compound sentence.

1. Ugh! Those apples in the bowl are sour.
2. Boys, put your tools into the big box under the shelf.
3. Larry, I designed that boat and built it.
4. There are many entrances to the museum on Liberty Street.
5. Well, we didn't mind the mellow sound of the violins, but we did react to the somber beat of the drum.
6. Oh! I lost my wallet and my keys.
7. Jay, give the milkman the empty bottles and this note.
8. There are too many shoppers and children in the aisle.

The Complex Sentence   (See pages 198–205.)

A complex sentence is composed of one main clause and one or more subordinate clauses. The relationship between the clauses can be shown clearly on a diagram. When you diagram a complex sentence, diagram each clause as though it were a simple sentence. Then connect the clauses in the various ways shown in the diagrams on the following pages.

Adverb clause

If a subordinate clause modifies a verb, it is called an *adverb clause*.

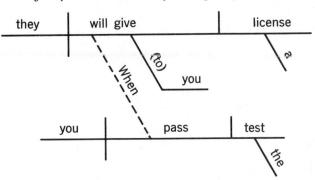

When you pass the test, they will give you a license.

Notice that the main clause appears first in the diagram and that a dotted line connects the *verbs* in the clauses.

Exercise: Diagraming complex sentences

Diagram all of the words in the following sentences:

1. The girls started after the rain had ceased.
2. While the orchestra played, the winners were announced.
3. As we passed the drugstore, we saw Oscar inside at the counter.
4. Paul, we shall start when the noise stops.
5. Kirk ran down the street until he panted for breath.
6. Members of the team do not drink sodas before they play a game.
7. After you adjusted the television, we got a better picture.
8. There has been a leak in the ceiling since that last storm hit the town and flooded the streets.

395

Adjective clause

If a subordinate clause modifies a noun or pronoun, it is called an *adjective clause.* Notice, in the examples below, how the dotted line shows which word each clause modifies:

The man *who greeted you* is my father.

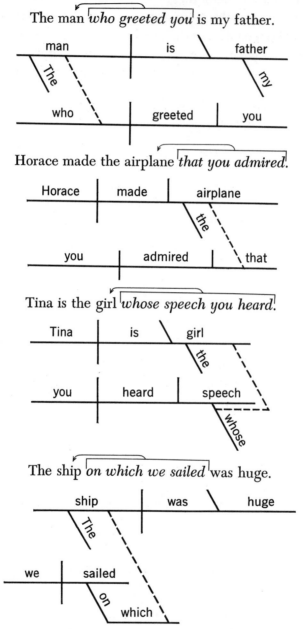

Horace made the airplane *that you admired.*

Tina is the girl *whose speech you heard.*

The ship *on which we sailed* was huge.

Remember, the relative pronoun *who* (*whom, whose*), *which,* or *that* is a sentence element in its own clause. It may be the subject, object, or modifier.

Exercise: Diagraming complex sentences

Diagram the following sentences:

1. New Yorkers planned a canal that would connect Lake Erie with the Hudson River.
2. The United States Government, to which the people looked for help, would not build a canal.
3. Governor Clinton was a governor whom people trusted.
4. He was the man whose farsightedness and determination will long be remembered.
5. The canal, which encouraged trade with the West, aided in the settlement of the West.

Noun clause

A noun clause is connected by a vertical line to the base line of a diagram where a single noun could appear. In the first sentence, the noun clause rests on the base line where a subject belongs.

Where I have been is a secret. (subject)

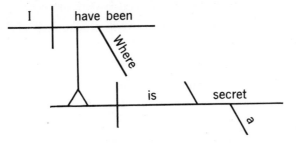

The fact is *that he was not ready*. (subject complement)

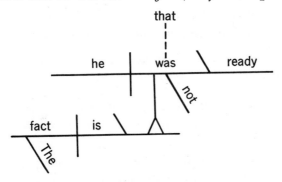

The conjunction *that* is placed on a separate line in the sentence above, since it is not a basic sentence part in the main or in the subordinate clause.

397

Notice that the conjunction *what* in the second example below is a basic sentence part in the noun clause.

I heard *that Jim was coming.*   (direct object)

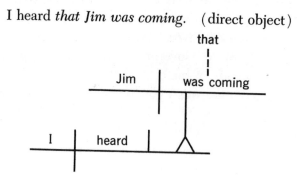

We were surprised by *what he did.*   (object of preposition)

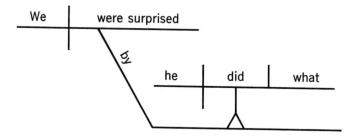

Exercises: Diagraming complex sentences

1. Diagram the following sentences:

1. I know that you can play the piano.
2. That he was sincere cannot be doubted.
3. The trouble was that the committee had not made complete arrangements.
4. We were encouraged by what he had said.
5. No one could imagine where he had gone.

2. The sentences below contain adverb, adjective, and noun clauses. Diagram all of the words in the sentences.

1. Although the job is hard, Adam will surely succeed in it.
2. Norman, I noticed a light that shone through a crack in the door.
3. What the council decides will govern our plans.
4. We searched for the book where he had lost it.
5. The candidate for whom we voted won the election by a large majority.

398

Appositives

The relationship between an appositive expression and the noun or pronoun with which it is in apposition can be shown clearly on a diagram. The appositive nouns are placed in parentheses.

Mr. Bobkins, my snoopy *neighbor*, saw us *boys*.

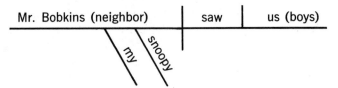

Exercise: Diagraming sentences

Diagram all of the words in the following sentences. Two of the sentences are complex sentences.

1. We boys sailed on the *Emperor*, a luxury liner.
2. Becky, our star player, could not play in the final game of the season.
3. Rex's tail, a shaggy mop, was tangled with burs.
4. The author of the story that we have just read is Hans Christian Andersen, a Danish writer.
5. Did you know that my favorite relative, Aunt Clara, is visiting us?

The Participle (See pages 288–90.)

Since the participle does the work of an adjective, it modifies a noun or a pronoun. The participle or participial phrase is diagramed as follows:

Fighting valiantly to the end, Duke won the game.

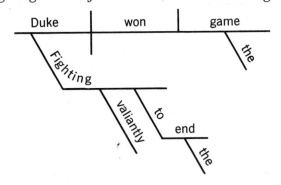

We saw a picture of them *wearing their new suits.*

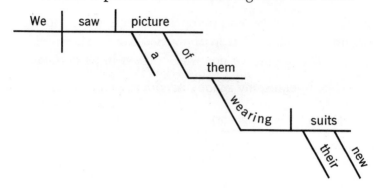

Exercise: Diagraming participles

Diagram the sentences below. Pay special attention to the participles and participial phrases.

1. Stepping carefully, I crossed the rickety bridge.
2. The property surrounding the firehouse has been sold.
3. Gladys, making some fudge in the kitchen, was too busy.
4. Our committee didn't see any houses needing repairs.
5. Kevin was the player scoring the most points.
6. Parched for hours, we finally found a spring trickling under the rocks.

The Gerund   (See pages 294–95.)

Gerunds and gerund phrases do the work of nouns in sentences. They are also diagramed according to the function they perform.

They practiced their *skiing.*   (direct object)

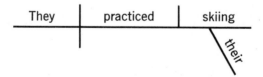

The scout earned his badge in *boating.*   (object of a preposition)

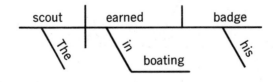

Baking a cake is not too easy.   (subject)

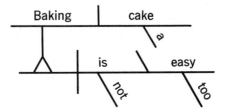

Exercise: Diagraming gerunds

Diagram the sentences below.   There is one complex sentence.

1. Now you must stop interrupting.
2. Thinking is an important factor in discussion.
3. Modern farm machinery reduces the labor of reaping the crops.
4. Her loud squealing became the center of attraction.
5. Remembering the details is a difficult part of his job.
6. Reducing her weight was the challenge that Molly faced.

The Infinitive   (See pages 295–96.)

An infinitive or an infinitive phrase can act as a noun, as an adjective, or as an adverb.

To win at chess is his ambition.   We intend *to leave early.*
(subject)   (direct object)

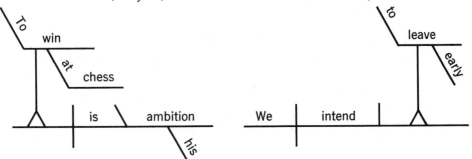

Her chief desire was *to help Harry.*   (subject complement)

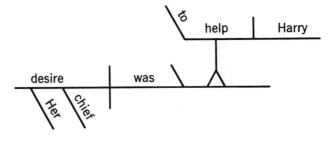

401

I have money *to spend*. (adjective)   We read *to learn*. (adverb)

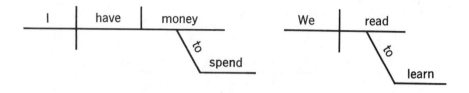

Exercise: Diagraming infinitives

Diagram the sentences below. Pay special attention to the infinitives and infinitive phrases.

1. I do not expect to sell many magazines.
2. Wanda quickly rose to ask a question.
3. To converse well is an art.
4. The time to depart has arrived.
5. The plan was to begin at the corner.
6. We have agreed to work more quickly.

GOING AHEAD

The sentences below contain many of the elements you have diagramed throughout this chapter. Diagram each sentence correctly.

1. A large map, showing the route, is in the front of the book which I gave you yesterday.
2. Because she wants to save her eyesight, Pamela, my sister, wears her glasses continually.
3. Roy, do you like playing in the school orchestra?
4. To master that skill is my idea of working too hard.
5. There was no gasoline to run the engine.
6. Recognizing defeat, we boys finally saw that we weren't the best runners.
7. Puffing heavily, Mr. Boylston gave Quincy and me suggestions for ways to help him.
8. Sowing the seeds was an easy and quick task, but harvesting the crops lasted for a week.
9. Well, the time to start school is not always my favorite time of year.
10. I think that pupils should start planning their careers early.

Test I

Diagram all of the words in the following sentences:

1. Their goat has ruined our lawn.
2. The energetic members of our team are lanky.
3. Will Kelly Stokes become a good swimmer?
4. The speaker on the shallow platform has answered quite sharply the question about the new policy.
5. Give me Ned's notebook for a moment.

Test II

The sentences below have compound elements. Two of them are compound sentences. Diagram all of the words in each sentence.

1. That road and this path are equally bumpy.
2. The mechanic greased and oiled my car.
3. Place the cup and the saucer on the table.
4. My brother bought this plastic airplane and repainted it.
5. Quickly and dangerously, the strong and fearless acrobats performed that feat.
6. There are my cat and your dog under the walnut chair in the very long hallway.
7. My uncle became an explorer of old cemeteries and a hunter of rare teacups.
8. Has the mysterious man in the lobby just given Malcolm or Hubert a package?
9. The brilliant red sun sank in the western skies, and the majestic cactus cast its shadow into the still water.
10. The old woman threaded her needle with long and shaky fingers, and then she mended the socks.

Test III

Diagram all of the words in each sentence below:

1. Hurrah! Earl, our champion, has scored another point.
2. When the store closed, everyone started rushing.
3. Leonard has not located the gyroscope which you mailed to him.
4. Vera, we wondered where you were going.
5. Giggling loudly, the girls wanted to tell a joke.

Review and Practice

Exercise I

1. Review pages 380–88.
2. Diagram all of the words in the following sentences:

    1. Our large raft has recently sprung a leak.
    2. Those kittens certainly are very cute.
    3. Send me the address of Pat's office in the city.
    4. Was Roger a skin diver once?
    5. Along the side of the mountain chugged a locomotive with several cars.

Exercise II

1. Review pages 388–94.
2. Diagram all of the words in the following sentences:

    1. The varnish and this paint are quite sticky.
    2. My father plowed and planted our garden.
    3. Give your name and your address to the clerk.
    4. That actor will slowly but surely show his vocal skills.
    5. Yesterday Jack bought the book and is now reading it.
    6. Did the comedian show the cast and audience his funny hats?
    7. Bob became president of his class and a trumpeter in the orchestra.
    8. There are several tubes and other pieces of apparatus in the closet.
    9. The violent wind blew from the north, and the thin and lonely sapling surrendered easily to its force.
    10. The jaguar lay quietly in the trap, but he schemed and found a way to escape.

Exercise III

1. Review pages 393–402.
2. Diagram all of the words in the following sentences:

    1. Oh, we already asked Mr. Kingsley, the principal.
    2. This room was really quiet until Mr. Johns made an announcement about talking in class.
    3. The lunch which we ate yesterday consisted of various fruits.
    4. Walking quickly, the man returned to his cottage.
    5. Jill, tell us what you want to sing.

PART III

Review Handbook

CONTENTS

Composition

The Parts of Speech

Mechanics

Usage

Composition

The Sentence

A **sentence** is a group of words, including a subject and predicate, that expresses a thought which, when read aloud, sounds complete. In writing, the beginning of a sentence is marked by a capital letter, and the end is marked by a period, a question mark, or an exclamation point. In speaking, the end of a sentence is usually shown by a short pause and a drop in voice pitch.

A **fragment** is a piece of a sentence punctuated as a sentence.

Exercises

1. Read aloud the word groups below. Tell which ones are sentences and which are fragments. On your paper, revise each fragment to make it a sentence.

1. We stopped for a soda at the drugstore.
2. When it began to rain this morning.
3. That record near the phonograph.
4. Has the airplane landed yet?
5. Sit down.
6. Beside the bubbling fountain in the park.

2. Take turns reading paragraphs aloud in class. As each one is read, listen carefully and count the number of sentences in the paragraph.

Subject and predicate

The two main parts of a sentence are the subject and predicate. The **complete subject** names what the sentence is about. The **complete predicate** tells something about the subject.

COMPLETE SUBJECTS	COMPLETE PREDICATES
Six jet airliners	are now on the runway.
The girls in my family	like caramel candy.

The **simple subject** is the key word in the complete subject; it is usually a *noun* or a *pronoun*. The nouns *airliners* and *girls* are the simple subjects in the two sentences above.

The **simple predicate** is the key word (or words) in the complete predicate; it is always a *verb*. The verbs in the two sentences above are *are* and *like*.

Inverted order

The natural order of a sentence is subject first and predicate second. Some sentences are in inverted order. Study these examples:

PREDICATES	SUBJECTS
In the sky appeared	signs of a storm.
There sat	ten idle men.

Types of sentences

Each of the four kinds of sentences is classified by the purpose it serves. Examine the end punctuation of each.

Declarative sentence—makes a statement:

My father is an electrician.

Interrogative sentence—asks a question:

Is your father an electrician?

Imperative sentence—gives a command or makes a request:

Obey all traffic rules.

Exclamatory sentence—makes an exclamation:

What a wonderful time we had!   How foolish that was!

In an interrogative sentence, the subject often comes between two parts of a verb:

Has he telephoned you?   Are they coming on Tuesday?

In an imperative sentence, the subject *you* is understood:

(You) Close the door gently.   (You) Rest for a minute.

Exercise

Copy each sentence below on your paper, punctuating it correctly. Draw a single line under each simple subject (except in an imperative sentence) and a double line under each verb.

1. Terri has a monogram on her stationery
2. Open the porch door
3. Within the scientist's mind lay the formula
4. There was a large watermelon in the garden
5. Does Owen play with the varsity squad
6. What an unusual rose this is
7. The trout in this stream have disappeared
8. Did you visit New York City

Direct object

Subjects and verbs sometimes need another word (or words) to complete the thought of the sentence.

1. Ross drew a *cartoon*.
2. Lois invited *Patty* and *me*.

The nouns *cartoon* and *Patty* and the pronoun *me* receive the action of the verbs in the sentences above. They are called **direct objects,** or *objects of the verb.*

A **direct object** is a word that names the receiver of an action.

Indirect object

In the following sentences the italicized words tell *to whom* or *for whom* the action of the verb is performed:

1. I gave *him* the keys.
2. We bought *Polly* a bracelet.
3. They sent *Joe* and *me* a pamphlet.

The pronouns *him* and *me* and the nouns *Polly* and *Joe* are called **indirect objects.**

An **indirect object** is a word that precedes a direct object and usually tells *to whom* or *to what* or *for whom* or *for what* the action of the verb is performed.

Notice that the words *to* and *for* are not stated; they are implied.

Subject complement

Sometimes, a word may follow a linking verb and describe or refer to the subject. In sentence 1 below, *Ray* and the *treasurer* are the same person. In sentence 2, *one* and *it* are the same thing. In sentence 3, *sweet* and *kind* describe the subject.

1. Ray is *treasurer*. (predicate noun)
2. That one is *it*. (predicate pronoun)
3. She is *sweet* and *kind*. (predicate adjectives)

Linking verbs do not express action; they connect subjects to a *predicate noun,* a *predicate pronoun,* or a *predicate adjective.* All three are also called **subject complements.**

A **subject complement** is a word in the predicate of a sentence that refers to or describes the subject. It appears after a linking verb in a sentence.

408

Exercise

Find and write down the direct objects, indirect objects, or subject complements that follow the verbs in the sentences below. Label each word.

1. This chapter tells us many interesting facts.
2. Clouds have different formations.
3. Mrs. Bart showed me the differences.
4. Three types are common.
5. Cirrus clouds are thin and wispy.
6. They contain countless little ice crystals.
7. The cottonlike cumulus cloud fascinates me.
8. This type of cloud is a sign of fair weather.
9. Stratus clouds form low, uniform layers.
10. Usually they are dark and ominous.

Avoiding sentence fragments and run-on sentences

Fragments are only pieces of sentences. Combine a fragment with a sentence to make the idea complete:

FRAGMENT: Because it was getting late
SENTENCE: I left because it was getting late.

FRAGMENT: After you called Joe
SENTENCE: After you called Joe, he left the house.

Break up a run-on sentence by punctuating each part separately:

RUN-ON: There is Bill he's the captain.
RUN-ON: There is Bill, he's the captain.
RIGHT: There is Bill. He's the captain.

Exercise

Rewrite the following paragraph correctly:

Although Robert Fulton is known mainly for the invention of the steamboat. He was actually a man of many talents. As a young boy, Fulton designed household utensils and painted miniature portraits and landscapes he worked for jewelers and gunsmiths in later life. One of his many inventions was the diving boat called the *Nautilus*. Which could descend twenty-five feet and remain submerged for nearly five hours. The invention, in fact, interested Napoleon. Who investigated it for possible use as a military weapon.

The Paragraph

A sentence is the basic unit we use to express ideas in writing. The **paragraph** is the next larger unit—it is a series of sentences which develop one topic or idea.

A **topic sentence,** which often appears at the beginning of a paragraph, states the topic or subject of the paragraph. For paragraph unity, the other sentences in the paragraph must *develop* the topic.

Here are a few guides for writing a good paragraph:

1. Indent the first word.
2. State the main idea in a topic sentence.
3. Keep to the topic.
4. Develop the topic logically, using facts or examples, incidents or anecdotes, reasons or explanations.

Three typical kinds of paragraphs are:

Narrative—tells a story.
Descriptive—describes persons, places, objects, or feelings.
Explanatory—explains a subject or opinion.

Exercises

1. Read the following paragraph and then answer the questions below it:

Today scientists are developing a process of dehydration by which fruits and vegetables can be fired from a low-pressure puffing gun, yet still retain their texture, taste, and shape. When the fruits and vegetables are shot from a closed, heated cylinder, the water in them vaporizes immediately. Fruits and vegetables are important to health because they contain many vitamins. Later during the cooking process, the tiny pores which are formed by the explosion can be refilled rapidly with water. My mother prefers to peel her own potatoes.

1. What is the topic sentence?
2. Which two sentences detract from the paragraph and should be dropped?
3. How is the paragraph developed—by anecdotes, facts, or reasons?
4. Is it a narrative, descriptive, or explanatory paragraph?

2. Write a paragraph on any subject. Begin with a topic sentence and develop the topic with at least five sentences.

The Letter

Friendly letters and business letters have these five parts: the *heading*, the *salutation* (or the *greeting*), the *body*, the *closing*, and the *signature*. The business letter, however, has one additional part called the *inside address*. In a friendly letter or social note, a comma is used after the salutation; in a business letter, a colon is used.

Business Letter

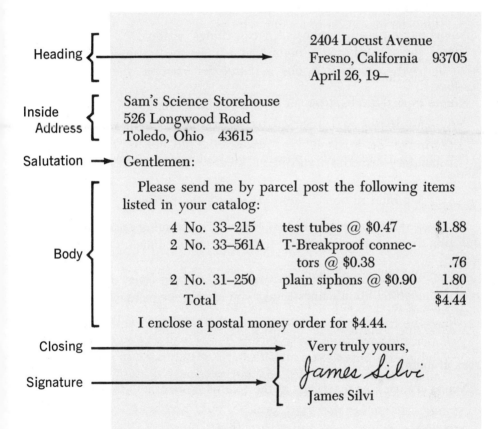

Heading

2404 Locust Avenue
Fresno, California   93705
April 26, 19—

Inside Address

Sam's Science Storehouse
526 Longwood Road
Toledo, Ohio   43615

Salutation

Gentlemen:

Body

Please send me by parcel post the following items listed in your catalog:

4 No. 33–215	test tubes @ $0.47		$1.88
2 No. 33–561A	T-Breakproof connec-tors @ $0.38		.76
2 No. 31–250	plain siphons @ $0.90		1.80
	Total		$4.44

I enclose a postal money order for $4.44.

Closing

Very truly yours,

Signature

James Silvi

James Silvi

Exercises

1. Study the six parts of the business letter above. Notice carefully the capitalization, punctuation, and spacing of the parts. Then, with the book closed, write a business letter of your own.

2. Write a friendly letter, using less formal phrases for the salutation and closing. Do not include an inside address or a typed signature.

411

The Parts of Speech

Words name things, describe things, tell what happens, and connect parts of sentences. They can be classified into **eight parts of speech.** The part of speech that a word is often depends on its function in a sentence.

The Noun

Nouns name persons, animals, places, things, or ideas.

Nouns show **number.** A noun that names one is *singular.* A noun that names more than one is *plural;* for example, *boy—boys; fly—flies.*

Nouns show **possession** or ownership: *a bear's den.*

Nouns are frequently preceded by **determiners** (noun signals). The words *a, an, the, my, their, your, its,* and *our* are determiners. When one of these words appears in a sentence, a noun always follows:

a blue ribbon   *an* octopus   *the* bottle

(See page 424 and pages 433–34 for rules on forming possessives and plurals, and pages 420–21 for rules on capitalizing proper nouns.)

A *concrete* noun names things you can see: *boy, river, automobile.* An *abstract* noun names things you cannot see or touch: *fear, love.*

A *collective* noun names a group: *flock, team.*

Uses of nouns

Nouns are used in sentences in the following ways:

AS SUBJECT

This *poem* is about the beginning of the American Revolution.

AS DIRECT OBJECT

Henry Wadsworth Longfellow wrote this *poem.*

AS INDIRECT OBJECT

It gave *Longfellow* a place in literary history.

AS OBJECT OF A PREPOSITION

It has immortalized the tower of an old Boston *church.*

AS SUBJECT COMPLEMENT

The warnings from the church belfry were *lamps*.

AS APPOSITIVE NOUN

Minutemen, a *group* of colonists, soon learned of the alarm.

AS NOUN OF DIRECT ADDRESS

"Listen, my *children,* and you shall hear
Of the midnight ride of Paul Revere."

Exercises

1. Write five *concrete* nouns, five *abstract* nouns, and five *collective* nouns.

2. Find and list the nouns in these sentences. Explain why you think each word you have chosen is a noun.

1. Our new friend has written a play.
2. Main parts have been assigned to Janet's classmates.
3. Sir Walter Raleigh was a prisoner in the Tower of London.

3. Copy each italicized noun below. Then tell how it is used in the sentence.

1. *Paul Revere* was the *hero* in Longfellow's *poem*.
2. He gave the *colonists* the *alarm*.
3. *Revere* heard *sheep* in *Concord*, a *town* near *Boston*.
4. Have you read the *poem, Alex?*

The Verb

Every sentence contains a *verb*. Verbs express *action* or *being*.

Verbs of action can tell what the subject does. They are verbs such as *scamper, twist, lunge, dive*, which express physical action; or such as *suppose, wonder, acknowledge*, which express mental action.

Transitive verbs

The action in some verbs is carried over to a receiver. These verbs are called **transitive verbs.**

When the action of the verb is carried to the direct object, it is a transitive verb, **active voice.** When the action is carried back to the subject, it is a transitive verb, **passive voice.**

Joe *plays* chess.   (active voice)
Chess *was played* all evening.   (passive voice)

413

Intransitive verbs

When there is no receiver of the action, the verb is **intransitive**.

Joe *plays* well.   Joe *is playing* in the yard.

Another type of intransitive verb is the **linking verb,** which tells what the subject *is* or what it *is like*. The most common verb used as a linking verb is *be*. Some of its forms are: *am, is, are, was, were*. Other verbs used in this way are *become, remain, look, seem, feel, taste, smell, sound*, and *appear*.

Raisins *are* dried grapes.   Folk music *became* popular.

Exercises

1. Tell whether each italicized verb is transitive or intransitive.

1. He *whispers* constantly in the library.
2. I *whispered* the message to Joan.
3. Rumors *were carried* from person to person.
4. She *admired* my new dress.
5. We *were* partners.

2. Choose three action verbs and use each in two sentences. First, use the verb as a transitive verb, active voice. In the second sentence, use the verb as a transitive verb, passive voice.

3. Write five sentences using a different form of *be* as a linking verb.

Auxiliary verbs

A verb may include more than one word, as in this verb phrase:

Sarah | could have been nominated.

Nominated is the **main verb;** *could have been* are the **auxiliary verbs.** Another term for auxiliary verb is *helping verb*.

Verbs and tense

Verbs express *time* (or *tense*) in two ways: by changing form, by adding auxiliary verbs, or both.

Almost all verbs have three forms through which they express the *present, past*, and *future* tenses. These are called **principal parts.** Here are the principal parts of two *regular verbs*:

PRESENT	PAST	PAST PARTICIPLE
amuse, amuses	amused	(have, has, had) amused
print, prints	printed	(have, has, had) printed

Regular verbs form the past and the past participle by adding *d* or *ed* to the present form.

(For a listing of the principal parts of irregular verbs, see page 447 in the "Usage" section of this Review Handbook.)

Exercises

1. Copy the verb phrases in the sentences below. Circle the main verb and underline the auxiliary verbs once.

1. The pipe has burst.
2. He has practiced on the parallel bars.
3. Will you mail the letter, please?
4. Jack has very seldom lost his temper.
5. Could I have done better?

2. Explain two ways in which a verb can express time (or tense).

3. How do regular verbs form the past and the past participle?

The Pronoun

A **pronoun** is a word used in place of a noun. This table will help you remember the different forms of *personal pronouns*:

Subject Pronouns		Object Pronouns	
SINGULAR	PLURAL	SINGULAR	PLURAL
I	we	me	us
you	you	you	you
he, she, it	they	him, her, it	them

Possessive Pronouns	
SINGULAR	PLURAL
my, mine	our, ours
your, yours	your, yours
his, her, hers, its	their, theirs

The noun for which a pronoun stands is called the **antecedent.**

Ned was given a guitar and a case for *it*.

Here is a list of other kinds of pronouns:

1. Indefinite pronouns such as *everyone*, *someone*, and *anyone* make general references to people.

Everyone was planning to bring his parents.

415

2. Demonstrative pronouns point out; they are *this*, *that*, *these*, and *those*.

This is my favorite color.

3. Interrogative pronouns ask questions; they are *who* (*whom*, *whose*), *which*, and *what*.

Whom shall I ask?   *Who* called?

4. Relative pronouns connect adjective clauses to the main clause in a sentence.

The man *who called Sally* was a detective.

See page 451 in the "Usage" section to find the pages you need for study and practice on using pronouns correctly. Individual items are listed alphabetically throughout pages 437–57.

Exercises

1. Write in the same order in which they appear the twelve pronouns in the paragraphs below. After each pronoun, write its antecedent in parentheses.

Dave made his campaign speech to his classmates last week. They were very impressed with his sincerity.

In fact, a friend remarked, "I have never met a more sincere person. The class could have its most productive year under Dave's leadership. I am casting my vote for him, and Sue said that she is joining me with her ballot."

2. Write a sentence to illustrate each of these types of pronouns: *indefinite, demonstrative, interrogative, relative.*

The Adjective

An **adjective** is a word used to modify a noun or pronoun. *Descriptive* adjectives tell *what kind*:

We ate the *creamy* éclairs.
They were very *busy*.

Limiting adjectives tell *how many* or *which one*:

That marlin was caught in Florida.
I saw *several* people laugh.

Limiting adjectives, including the articles *a, an,* and *the,* are called determiners. They **signal** that a noun will soon follow.

Exercise

Copy each sentence below. Underline each adjective and draw an arrow from it to the word it modifies. Above each adjective, write *D* if it is a descriptive adjective, and *L* if it is limiting. Ignore the articles.

1. This knot is too tight.
2. Several members of that stamp club won prizes.
3. Giant redwoods cast shadows onto the dusty roadway.
4. Those hardy pioneers pushed across the hot desert.

The Adverb

Most **adverbs** modify verbs and answer the questions *how? when?* or *where?*

$$\text{We searched} \begin{cases} \textit{frantically.} & (\textit{how?}) \\ \textit{yesterday.} & (\textit{when?}) \\ \textit{everywhere.} & (\textit{where?}) \end{cases}$$

A special adverb which makes verbs negative is the word *not.* Its contraction, *n't,* is also considered an adverb, separate from the verb with which it appears: *wasn't.*

A small group of adverbs called **intensifiers** modify adjectives and other adverbs. They answer the questions *to what extent?* or *how much?*

The team was *very* jubilant.   You are working *too* slowly.

Exercises

1. In the order in which they appear, list the adverbs in the paragraph below. In parentheses after each one, write the word it modifies and what part of speech that word is: *verb, adjective,* or *adverb.*

Part of the earth moves gradually into the direct rays of the sun. During this period, the days are very long and rather hot. When June 21, the longest day of the year, finally occurs, the days after that become progressively shorter. In midwinter the days end too quickly.

2. Use each of these adverbs to modify a verb in a sentence of your own: *gradually, impatiently, soon,* and *quickly.*

3. Use each of these adverbs to modify an adjective or another adverb in a sentence of your own: *too, really, quite,* and *very.*

The Preposition

Prepositions are words such as *on, up, across, in, from,* and *over.* A preposition is always followed by a noun or a pronoun called the **object of the preposition.** Together with any modifiers of the object, these form a **prepositional phrase.**

Prepositional Phrases

PREPOSITION	MODIFIERS OF OBJECT	OBJECT OF PREPOSITION
in	the small	shop
above		him
over	a shallow, rocky	stream

A prepositional phrase always begins with a preposition and ends with a noun or pronoun.

Exercise

List the prepositional phrases in the sentences below. Underline the preposition in each phrase.

1. Jill ran around the corner and into the park.
2. The sunglasses fell near the edge of the window sill.
3. The book for you is on the shelf in my locker at school.
4. Iced tea with lemon is a good drink for hot summer days.

The Conjunction

A **co-ordinating conjunction** is a word used to join equal elements in sentences—words, phrases, or clauses. The most common of these are *and, but, or, neither . . . nor, either . . . or,* and *both . . . and.*

When these conjunctions join subjects, objects, predicates, and clauses, they form compound subjects, compound objects, compound predicates, and compound sentences.

COMPOUND SUBJECT: *Rose* and *Liz* play the piano.

COMPOUND OBJECT: We plant *corn* or *wheat.*

He sat near *Henry, Oscar,* and *us.*

COMPOUND PREDICATE: The bronco *kicked suddenly* and *threw the cowboy to the ground.*

COMPOUND SENTENCE: *The bronco kicked suddenly,* and *the cowboy was thrown to the ground.*

A **subordinating conjunction** makes a group of words dependent.

The game was over.   (sentence)
When the game was over   (subordinate clause)

A subordinate clause cannot stand alone; it needs to be connected to a main clause.

When the game was over, we met at my house.

The words *when, after, if, because, until,* and *unless* are examples of subordinating conjunctions.

Exercise

Pick out the conjunctions in the sentences below.   Tell which ones are *co-ordinating conjunctions* and which ones are *subordinating conjunctions.*   Explain your answers.

1. Draw either a chameleon or an iguana on the poster.
2. He is packing, and I am helping him.
3. If you don't hurry, you will be late.
4. I'll use water colors unless you prefer oil paints.
5. The bookcase and desk are made of either pine or oak.
6. We have the tools but do not have the directions.

The Interjection

An **interjection** is a brief expression, not a sentence, used to express strong feeling.   It is punctuated by an exclamation point, unless it is a mild interjection.   In that case, a comma is used.

Phew!   Ouch!   Hurrah!   Oh!
My, the weather is warm.

Exercise

Name the part of speech of each word in the following sentences:

1. Paul, call your mother immediately.
2. When Horace wrote the letter, he seemed happy.
3. The girls themselves actually designed their skirts.
4. Wow!   This part of the mountain is surely steep.
5. The actor was young and famous.
6. Oh, I forgot my notebook.

Mechanics

Capitalization

Main Rule: **Capitalize all proper nouns and proper adjectives.**

A **proper noun** is the name of a particular person, place, thing, or group:

> Hank   Mercer High School   April   House of Representatives

A **common noun** does not name any particular person, place, thing, or group:

> child   country   book   club

A **proper adjective** is an adjective formed from a proper noun:

> Swedish   French   European

Note: If a proper noun has more than one word, capitalize the first letter in the first word and in all the important words.

Main categories of proper nouns

1. Calendar items: months, days, holidays, and special days

> February   Thursday   Fourth of July   Christmas
> Hanukkah

2. Organizations, institutions, businesses, government departments

> Chrysler Corporation   Clinton Junior High School
> the Department of Agriculture

3. Brands or trade names of products

> Lita soap   Moray trucks

4. Historical and special events, documents, and periods

> the Industrial Revolution   the Gadsden Purchase
> the Mayflower Compact   the Dark Ages

5. Races, nationalities, and languages

> Caucasians   Negroes   Italian   Hindustani

6. Geographical names

Mason Street	Belgium	Lake Maracaibo
Seattle	Ohio	Spadina Parkway

7. Names of persons, including initials and titles

Ambassador Tey   Stephen P. Staples   Captain Angelo

8. Names of relationships when used as a proper name

Hello, Dad, I'm here.   There is Aunt Ella.

(These names are not capitalized when used merely to show relationship: *My dad criticizes me. I love my aunt.*)

9. Names of ships, trains, planes, satellites

the *Leonardo da Vinci*   the *Silver Streak*   Telstar
Ranger 7

10. Names of buildings, monuments, and natural wonders

the Pentagon   Jefferson Memorial   Niagara Falls

11. Names of political parties and members

the Democratic Party   the Republicans   a Whig

12. The Deity, sacred documents, and religions

God   the Bible   the Torah   Christianity

13. Abbreviations of proper names

Calif.   Mr. Crow   Dr. Wm. Farrell   Y.W.C.A.

Nouns that are not capitalized

1. Names of seasons

spring   fall

2. Names of breeds of animals and birds, unless they contain a proper adjective or noun

terrier   Doberman pinscher   peacock

3. Compass directions (north, east), unless referring to a region

Ted traveled west.
Ted traveled around the West.

4. Names of diseases, flowers, trees, games, foods, and musical instruments, unless they contain a proper adjective or noun

measles   checkers
German measles   Chinese checkers

5. Names of subjects in school, unless they contain a proper adjective or name a particular course

biology   French history   Biology I

Exercises

1. Write each of the following items correctly:

1. studies english on friday
2. waiting at the corner of lincoln avenue and troy boulevard
3. the department of commerce
4. signing the atlantic charter
5. luxury hotels in the south
6. over at trabold junior high school
7. on top of the empire state building
8. the range of temperature in the summer and winter
9. wounded in the korean war
10. the youmakeit toy company
11. on a hot june day our class in geometry II
12. the dance on columbus day
13. temper of a kilkenny cat
14. during the middle ages
15. crossing the golden gate bridge

2. Copy the following sentences on your paper, inserting capital letters where they are needed:

1. At union theological seminary my mother heard lectures about hinduism.
2. "Oh, dad, can we take a trip to washington to see the lincoln memorial?" asked my younger sister.
3. The ambassador honored representatives of the negro, the mongolian, and the caucasian races.
4. We had some chinese food at the swedish buffet; and then later we saw a greek drama, which starred a brilliant irish actress.
5. On saturday, rev. l. c. thompson visited mr. and mrs. dorman.
6. The republican representative and the democratic leader held a conference.

Other uses of capitals

1. Capitalize the first word:

   (a) In a sentence
   (b) In a quotation

   *T*he clerk asked, "*M*ay I help you?"

   (c) In the greeting or closing of a letter

   *M*y dear Tim,   *Y*ours sincerely,

   (d) In a line of poetry   (There are exceptions to this rule.)

   *T*he world stands out on either side
   *N*o wider than the heart is wide.
   —EDNA ST. VINCENT MILLAY

   (e) In a topic in an outline

   I. *T*ypes of horses
      A. *D*raft
      B. *S*addle
   II. *C*are of horses

2. Capitalize the words *I* and *O*, but do not capitalize *oh* unless it begins a sentence.

   "He is oh so rich!" *I* murmured.
   "Send us rain, *O* Jupiter," she said.

3. Capitalize all words in a title except *a*, *an*, and *the*, short prepositions, and conjunctions, unless one of these appears as the first or last word in the title.

   Have you read the book *A Tale of Two Cities*?
   "*T*he *C*ity in the *S*ea" is a poem by Edgar Allan Poe.

Exercise

Copy and capitalize correctly the following items:

1. the teacher asked, "what is the correct formula?"
2. dear Mr. Wick,   cordially yours,   my dear Ronald,
3. II. sources of energy
      A. the sun
         1. fission
         2. fusion
      B. the wind
4. I am reading the book *the stars by clock and fist.*

Punctuation

Apostrophe

1. Use an apostrophe in a contraction to show where letters have been omitted.

doesn't   I'll   o'clock (of the clock)

2. Use an apostrophe to show possession in nouns.
(a) If the noun does not end in *s*, add an apostrophe and *s*:

Bill's idea   women's club   children's games

(b) If the noun ends in *s*, add only an apostrophe (unless it is a singular noun that ends in *s*):

girls' shoes   spies' plans   James's hat

3. Use an apostrophe to form the plural of letters, figures, or words used out of context.

There are four *8*'s, three *a*'s, and entirely too many *and*'s in your paragraph.

Exercises

1. Show the possessive form of each of the nouns below. After each one, write a noun to show what is possessed.

1. Beth   3. fireman   5. people   7. actresses
2. man   4. babies   6. singer   8. ships

2. Revise the following phrases by using the possessive form instead of a prepositional phrase:

1. the aroma of the steak   3. sounds of engines
2. pastel shirts for girls   4. the schedule for today

3. Copy the following sentences, using apostrophes correctly:

1. Cant you see what youre doing?
2. Its the last issue of the newspaper that we cant get.
3. Lets meet at two oclock.
4. You begin your sentences with too many *thes*.

Colon

1. Place a colon after the greeting in a business letter.

Dear Sir: Gentlemen: Dear Mr. Iversen:

2. **Place a colon between the numeral that represents the hour and the numeral that represents the minutes.**

6:05 A.M.   9:30 P.M.

Comma

1. **Place a comma between the parts of dates.**

January 16, 1924   Thursday, March 4, 1926

If the date is in a sentence, use a comma after the year.

On April 6, 1962, I made my first plane trip.

2. **Place a comma between the city and state and between the city and country in an address.**

Lansing, Michigan   Rome, Italy

If the address is in a sentence, separate the parts of the address in this way:

His address is 416 Hope Valley Road, Durham, North Carolina.

3. **Place a comma after the closing in a letter and after the greeting in a friendly letter.**

Very truly yours,   Your friend,   Dear Jill,

4. **Use a comma between last and first names when listing last names first.**

Hawthorne, Nathaniel   Irving, Washington

5. **Use commas to set off nouns in direct address.** The noun of direct address is the person or group spoken to.

Horace, add more oregano to the pizza.
Do you have anything to say, Bill, before we leave?

6. **Use a comma to set off the introductory words *yes*, *no*, and the mild interjections *oh* and *well* at the beginning of a sentence.**

Yes, I made the map.   Well, who is he?

7. **Use a comma to set off interrupting expressions, such as *however*, *for example*, and *in fact*; and, in formal writing, *therefore* and *of course*.**

In fact, my parents prefer a convertible top.
Woolens, however, are not practical in this climate.

425

8. **Use a comma to set off *also*, and *too* when it means "also," in formal writing.**

I, too, cheered loudly.   He likes jazz, also.

9. **Use a comma to set off appositives.** An appositive appears after a noun to rename or explain it. *Note*: Usually, an appositive of one word is not set off.

Joe Barnes, my former roommate, went to another school.
We visited Larry Adams, a neighbor of mine.
My sister Karen likes licorice sticks.

10. **Use a comma to separate words, phrases, or clauses in a series.**

We ate hot dogs, hamburgers, and French fries.
Down the hill, across the meadow, and into the river rippled the little stream.

11. **In a direct quotation, use a comma to set off the quoted words from the rest of the sentence.**

Cory said, "I play the guitar."
"That's just a fad," Bertha commented.
"I wonder," said Lenny, "if I can beat my record of last year?"

12. **Use a comma before a conjunction in a compound sentence, unless the sentence is very short.**

Farmers in that country could grow wheat, but they need years of agricultural assistance.
Martha sang and Jane danced.   (very short)

13. **Use a comma if you need one to make your meaning clear.**

After sewing, Grace went to bed.
Near the telephone, books were piled high.

14. **Use a comma to set off an introductory adverb clause.**

When your turn comes, Jerry will give you a card.

15. **Use a comma (or commas) to set off a nonrestrictive adjective clause.** If the adjective clause is necessary to the meaning of the sentence, no commas are needed.

Ruth, who is quite a traveler, will show some slides tonight.
The boy who started the fight left.

16. **Use a comma to set off an introductory participial phrase.**

Having lost the battle, the Indians moved on to another state.

Exercises: Colon and comma (rules 1–3)

1. Copy the following parts of friendly letters, and the business letter, adding commas and colons where they are needed:

1. *Friendly letter*
   Dear Loren
   With love

2. *Business letter*

   > 42 Madison Avenue
   > Austin Texas   78757
   > June 4 19–

   Fir Tree Haven
   22 Avon Court
   Milwaukee Wisconsin   53208

   Dear Mr. Anthony

   Thank you for confirming our reservations.   We will arrive at 3 15 P.M. on Friday July 3.

   > Yours truly
   > Stephen Kenyon

Tues

2. Copy and punctuate the following:

1. Gary was born on July 16 1943 in Paris France.
2. She lives at 124 Bayberrie Drive Stamford Connecticut.
3. Rose's pen pal lives in Madras India.
4. On Friday October 16 1964 we opened our store at 732 West Laurel Street Phoenix Arizona.

Exercise: Comma (rules 4–9)

Copy and punctuate each of the following sentences.   One sentence is correct as it stands.

1. Agnes did you lose your purse also?
2. That sapling in fact has withstood six storms this year.
3. No I've never been on water skis.
4. However we gradually became adjusted to the new climate.
5. Is this the way we should list the author's last name first: Kipling Rudyard?
6. My brother Josh told us some whaling tales.
7. The two hobbies fishing and skin diving are Maggie's favorites.
8. Mr. Kelly our coach helped us to improve our defense.

WeD

Exercise: Comma (rules 10–13)

Copy the sentences below, punctuating each one correctly. One of the sentences does not need a comma.

1. For the experiment Isabel needed sugar starch and litmus paper.
2. Myna birds talk but pelicans do not.
3. "Take the first turn to the left" the policeman directed.
4. Beside the track meet me at four o'clock.
5. The explorers made their way through the forest across the river and onto the dusty plains.
6. "I will try" said Melba "if I am able."
7. The river looks inviting but it is infested with alligators.
8. With the green paint brush in an upward stroke.

Exercise: Comma (rules 14–16)

Copy and punctuate these sentences. One sentence is correct as it stands.

1. Holding his letter of introduction Johnny bravely rang the doorbell.
2. Although our funds were low we met and planned a party.
3. Sitting near the window I suddenly felt the first flutter of a breeze.
4. They visited Amsterdam which is famous for diamond cutting.
5. The girl whom you just invited is my cousin.

Exclamation point

1. **Place an exclamation point at the end of an exclamatory sentence.**

   What a magnificent scholar he is!   Look out!

2. **Place an exclamation point after an exclamatory word or phrase and after a strong interjection at the beginning of a sentence.**

   How amazing!   "What luck!" he shouted.
   Phew!   That was a narrow escape.

   Note: Do not overuse the exclamation point. Never use more than one after a word.

Hyphen

1. **Use a hyphen to divide words between syllables at the end of a line.**

   Those judges are particular.

2. **Use a hyphen in writing certain numbers and compound words.**

   eighty-eight   daughter-in-law

   Compound words beginning with *self-* and *ex-* followed by a noun usually need a hyphen.

   ex-champion   ex-ambassador   self-control

3. **Use a hyphen when two very closely related words are used as a modifier.**

   a three-way tie   one-third full

Italics

See "Underlining."

Period

1. **Use a period to end declarative (statement) and imperative (request, command) sentences or direct quotations.**

   The thruway leads to the Catskill Mountains.
   Please be seated.
   Larry said, "Dad just called."

2. **Use a period after initials or other abbreviations.**

   Mrs. R. S. Lofft   George Roberg, M.D.   Y.W.C.A.
   A.D. 100

3. **Use a period after numerals and letters in an outline.**

   III. Authors of mystery stories
       A. Edgar Allan Poe
         1. Stories of the grotesque
         2. Stories of puzzlement
       B. Arthur Conan Doyle

Question mark

Place a question mark after an interrogative sentence.

Who won the pennant that year?
"Did you visit the White House?" he asked.

Exercises

1. Copy and punctuate the following items correctly:

    1. IV Hardships of pioneers
          A Travel
             1 Few roads
             2 Few maps
          B Dangers

    2. Is Mr R B Granson his father in law
    3. "Is he an ex millionaire" she asked
    4. The S P C A, the Society for the Prevention of Cruelty to Animals, had its beginning in England in A D 1824
    5. My goodness   I've lost my way
    6. This is a two way street

2. Look up the following words in your dictionary and divide each one into syllables:

    1. probably   2. grandiose   3. phosphorous

Quotation marks

1. Use quotation marks to enclose words quoted.

"The corn has already been harvested," Ned replied.
Ralph says "You know" too often.

(a) If a sentence is divided into two parts by words such as *he said* or *Tom answered*, use two sets of quotation marks.

    "By Wednesday," Mary added, "we must make a final decision."

(b) If several sentences are quoted in a row, do not close the quote until the speaker has finished.

    "Suddenly it grew dark. I could see the tornado coming our way," George recalled.

(c) When you write conversation or dialogue, begin a new paragraph whenever the speaker changes.

2. Use quotation marks to indicate the title of a story, poem, article, essay, or chapter of a book, when these titles appear in a sentence.

The magazine article is called "Your Leisure Time."
We read the chapter "Pushing Beyond the Mississippi."

Exercise

Copy and punctuate the following, inserting commas and quotation marks where they are needed:

1. Answer each question before you go on to the next our teacher advised.
2. Answer each question our teacher advised before you go on to the next.
3. Try again. It isn't so difficult the coach said encouragingly.
4. Nancy asked do you know what time you will be there?
5. Don't say Golly all the time.
6. Her favorite poem is The Road Not Taken.

Underlining (italics)

Underlining is the way you indicate italics when you write by hand or typewrite.

1. Underline the titles of books, plays, movies, magazines, and newspapers.

We presented a scene from the book <u>The Adventures of Tom Sawyer</u>.

2. Underline the names of ships, planes, trains, and works of art when used in a sentence.

Leonardo da Vinci painted the <u>Mona Lisa</u>.

3. Underline a word, numeral, or letter used out of context.

There is only one <u>m</u> in the word <u>tomorrow</u>.

Exercise

Copy and punctuate the following items correctly, using underlining where necessary:

1. The name of the ship the Merrimack is spelled with two r's.
2. Have you read the book Invincible Louisa?
3. My Fair Lady, a musical that ran for years on Broadway, was based on a play entitled Pygmalion.

Spelling

A good visual memory is helpful in learning to be a good speller. However, even without one, you can improve your spelling by following the suggestions listed below:

1. Never risk misspelling a word. Look it up in a dictionary; learn it; then use it.
2. Learn words by this system:

    STEP 1: Pronounce the word.
    STEP 2: Divide the word into syllables by underlining each syllable.
    STEP 3: Finger the word, pronouncing each syllable as it becomes visible.
    STEP 4: Write the word.
    STEP 5: Compare; if wrong, start over.
    STEP 6: Write the word three more times.

3. Master five spelling rules:

    RULE 1: **One-syllable words and words accented on the last syllable, if they end in a single consonant after a single vowel, double the final consonant when you add a suffix beginning with a vowel.**

    tap—tapped   compel—compelling

    RULE 2: **When sound is ee,
    Put i before e
    Except after c.**   shield, receive

    **When sound is not ee,
    Put e before i.**   height

As always, there are a few exceptions, but they are not hard to remember. There are five common words spelled *ei* and yet sounded as *ee.* They are all contained in this nonsense sentence:

He seized neither (either) weird leisure.

Also, there are three common *ie* words that are not pronounced *ee.* They are contained in this nonsense sentence:

His friend sieved the mischief.

Memorize the two nonsense sentences above.

RULE 3: **Words that end in silent *e* drop the final *e* before a suffix beginning with a vowel but keep the final *e* before a suffix beginning with a consonant.**

> rate—rating   love—lovely

Four common exceptions are *argument, judgment, ninth,* and *truly.*

RULE 4: **Words that end in *y* with a consonant before it change the *y* to *i* before any suffix except a suffix which begins with *i*.**

> cry—cries   study—studying   baby—babyish

RULE 5: **Prefixes are added to the root word without changing the spelling of the root word.**

> mis + step = misstep
> dis + appoint = disappoint

Spelling plural nouns

1. Most nouns form their plurals by adding *s* to the singular: *word—words*
2. Nouns ending in *s, ss, ch, sh,* or *x* add *es*: *gas—gases, glass—glasses, patch—patches, box—boxes, wish—wishes.*
3. Nouns ending in *y,* preceded by a consonant, change *y* to *i* and add *es.* If the *y* is preceded by a vowel, add *s* only: *sky—skies, boy—boys.*
4. Some nouns ending in *o* add *s*; others add *es*: *studio—studios, piano—pianos, hero—heroes, potato—potatoes, Negro—Negroes.*
5. Many nouns ending in *f* or *fe* change *f* to *v* and add *s* or *es*: *wife—wives, loaf—loaves, calf—calves.*
   Here are some exceptions: *safe—safes, reef—reefs, chief—chiefs, waif—waifs, chef—chefs, roof—roofs.*
6. Some nouns do not follow any rule; you must learn their plural forms individually: *woman—women, foot—feet, mouse—mice, tooth—teeth, goose—geese, man—men, ox—oxen, child—children.*
7. Some nouns have the same form for singular and plural: *trout, moose, sheep, salmon, deer.*
8. In a compound word the important word takes the plural ending: *sisters-in-law*

9. In a compound word that is not separated, the *s* is added at the end: *cupfuls, handfuls, spoonfuls.*

10. A few nouns have a plural form only: *news, scissors, measles, physics, trousers, shears.*

Some of these nouns require a plural verb.

These scissors are too small.

Others are singular in meaning and require a singular verb.

Physics is my favorite subject.

Series is used in a singular as well as a plural sense.

This series of books is popular.

These series of lectures are free.

Use the dictionary when you are not sure.

Exercise

Write the plurals of the following nouns:

1. lunch	5. thief	9. potato
2. fox	6. life	10. brother-in-law
3. ox	7. liberty	11. attorney
4. child	8. radish	12. deer

One hundred spelling demons

There are a few words which cause more than their rightful share of trouble. *These few you should master!* They have been chosen by experienced teachers who have carefully studied thousands of student papers to see what the trouble-words are.

Included in the list below are **homonyms,** words that sound the same but are spelled differently and have different meanings. Learn these homonyms in meaningful phrases or sentences.

100 SPELLING DEMONS

(You will note that the syllables are underlined to help you learn these words according to the system explained on page 432.)

1. absence	7. again
2. accept	8. amateur
accept the job	9. appearance
3. ache	10. beautiful
4. acknowledge	11. believe
5. across	12. benefited
6. affect	13. bicycle
Will it affect his work?	14. built

15. capital
    a capital letter
16. capitol
    the state capitol
17. cemetery
18. certain
19. choose
    I choose you.
20. chose
    Yesterday I chose you.
21. conscience
22. cough
23. country
24. deceive
25. discipline
26. doctor
27. education
28. effect
    to effect change; means:
    bring about; a beautiful
    effect (noun)
29. except
    Everyone went except Pat
    and me.
30. exercise
31. existence
32. experience
33. February
34. friend
35. fundamental
36. governor
37. guess
38. having
39. hear
    hear with your ear
40. here
    here and there
41. hoping
    hoping for good luck
42. instead
43. its
    on its wings

44. it's
    It's here. Means: *it is*
45. judgment
46. knew
    He knew the answer.
47. know
    I know him.
48. language
49. library
50. literature
51. loose
    a loose bolt
52. losing
    losing his way
53. making
54. niece
55. occurred
56. opportunity
57. parallel
58. peculiar
59. precede
    One precedes two.
60. principal
    principal of a school
    the principal idea;
    means: *main*
61. principle
    Telling the truth is my
    principle. Means: *rule*
62. privilege
63. proceed
    proceed rapidly
64. quiet
    a quiet place
65. realize
66. receipt
67. receive
68. recommend
69. repetition
70. resistance
71. restaurant
72. schedule

73. secretary
74. seize
75. similar
76. sophomore
77. stationary
    A stationary object does not move.
78. stationery
    Stationery is letter paper and envelopes.
79. surprise
80. telephone
81. than
    poorer than that
82. their
    their house
83. there
    here and there
    There are two.
84. they're
    They're gone. Means: *they are*
85. though
    strong though small

86. threw
    He threw the ball.
87. through
    through the door
88. tongue
89. too
    too much; I went, too.
90. tragedy
91. twelfth
92. two
    two girls
93. vegetable
94. visitor
95. weather
    stormy weather
96. whether
    whether or not
97. who's
    Who's there? Means: *who is*
98. whose
    Whose idea is it?
99. writing
100. written

Exercise: Spelling demons

This exercise will take you several days, or possibly a week or two.

1. Take a pretest on the first 25 words. That is, have the words dictated to you and write down only the words you are absolutely sure of. Leave the others blank. (Be sure to number each word with the same numeral used in the list of demons.) If homonyms are involved, write each word in a meaningful phrase.

2. Have the pretest marked.

3. Learn the words you misspelled and the ones for which you left blank spaces. Use the system suggested on page 432.

4. Take a pretest on the next 25 words . . . and so on until you have learned all 100 demons.

5. Take a final test on all 100 demons.

6. If you missed any words on the final test, learn them. Have someone test you until you know all the demons perfectly.

Usage

A and an

Use *a* before a word that begins with a consonant sound or a long *u* sound. Use *an* before a word that begins with a vowel sound other than a long *u* sound.

Exercise

Choose the correct word in each pair in parentheses.

1. (A, An) unicorn is (a, an) mythical animal.
2. Place (a, an) *i* before (a, an) *e* in the word *field*.
3. (A, An) honorable person wouldn't give (a, an) excuse.

Adjectives and adverbs   (See also pages 85–87 and 90–91.)

Use an adverb—not an adjective—to modify a verb, adjective, or adverb.

The weather was *really* cold.   He performed it *easily*.
(adv.) (adj.)   (verb)   (adv.)

Real and *easy* are adjectives and must modify nouns or pronouns.

Exercise

Choose the correct word.

1. She sews (neat, neatly).
2. He found his way (easy, easily).
3. Oscar is (real, really) clever.
4. Marie was (real, really) happy about winning.

Adjectives and adverbs have three degrees of comparison: the *positive, comparative,* and *superlative degrees.* Most of them use the endings *–er* and *–est* or the words **more, most, less,** or **least** to make comparisons. A few are irregular, for example:

POSITIVE	COMPARATIVE	SUPERLATIVE
good well	better	best
many much	more	most
bad	worse	worst
little	less	least

437

When comparing *two* things, use the comparative degree. When comparing *three* or more, use the superlative degree.

Of the two craters, Copernicus is *wider.*
That inlet is the *roughest* of them all.

Use only one method of comparison. Never use both the ending and the word *more* or *most.*

Exercises

1. Use each of these words in two sentences, using the word first in the *comparative degree* and second in the *superlative degree*:

1. good   2. many   3. bad   4. little

2. Choose the correct word.

1. Which is (darker, darkest), aqua or purple?
2. Of the four contestants, Mr. Revson is (brighter, brightest).
3. Calypso is the (more, most) rhythmical of these three types of music.
4. Of the two books, the one (nearer, nearest) you is the (lighter, lightest).
5. The drum is (easier, more easier) to play.

Agreement of subject and verb   (See also pages 143–45.)

A verb must agree with its subject in number and person.

1. A singular subject takes a singular form of the verb. A plural subject takes a plural form of the verb:

Doris types rapidly.   (singular)

The others type slowly.   (plural)

The pronouns *I* and *you* are exceptions to these rules:

I type.   You type.

2. A compound subject takes a plural form of the verb except when singular words are joined by *or, either . . . or,* or *neither . . . nor.* When one part of a compound subject that is joined by these conjunctions is singular and the other part is plural, the verb agrees with the part that is nearer.

The butcher *and* the baker know the candlestick maker.
Neither the butcher *nor* the baker knows the candlestick maker.
Either Lois *or* my sisters are using the glue.
Either my sisters *or* Lois is using the glue.

3. **Collective nouns** name groups. A singular verb is used when the noun acts as a unit. A plural verb is used when there is individual action.

The <u>group</u> <u>has won</u> a trophy.
The <u>group</u> <u>have been arguing</u> for an hour.

4. Always use the singular form of a verb after a singular pronoun as subject. These indefinite pronouns are always singular:

each	neither	everyone	anybody
either	one	someone	somebody

<u>Each</u> of the boys <u>wants</u> a turn.
<u>Somebody</u> in the room <u>has</u> a loud voice.

Exercise

Choose the correct verb.

1. Both he and she (is, are) guilty.
2. The teachers or the principal (know, knows) the winner.
3. Either cornstarch or flour (make, makes) gravy thicker.
4. Our club (need, needs) a new name.
5. Each of the players (try, tries) for a score.
6. One of them (own, owns) a high-powered microscope.

<u>Almost</u> and <u>most</u>   (See also page 91.)

Almost is always an adverb, has two syllables, and answers the question *to what extent?*

She *almost* fainted.   That is *almost* rude.

Do not use the word *most* in place of *almost*. In these sentences, *most* is used correctly:

Most cats purr.   *Most* of the parents laughed.
(adj.)   (noun)

Exercise

Choose the correct word.

1. We (almost, most) lost the trophy.
2. Jack (almost, most) spilled the milk.
3. He reads (almost, most) magazines, but not this one.
4. I enjoy (almost, most) any kind of sport.

Among and between

Use the preposition *among* in referring to three or more people or things. Use the preposition *between* in referring to two people or two things only.

> *Among* my classmates there is a friendly feeling.
> The secret shall be *between* you and me.

Remember to use an object pronoun after a preposition.

> Put the desk between Clara and *me*.

Exercise

Choose the correct word.

1. (Among, Between) the jurors there was one woman.
2. (Among, Between) two candles stood an ivory statue.
3. Victor stood (among, between) Ralph and (I, me).
4. Divide the pie (among, between) all those children.

Antecedents of pronouns   (See also pages 24–26, 236–37, and 239–40.)

A pronoun must agree with its antecedent in gender (masculine—*he*, feminine—*she*, neuter—*it*) and number (singular or plural).

> *Neither* of the girls has *her* answer.   (Think: Neither *one* has . . .)
> (anteced.)   (pron.)

> *Both* of the men have *their* umbrellas.
> (anteced.)   (pron.)

To make the meaning clear, avoid using a pronoun whose antecedent is unclear.

> UNCLEAR: Take the vase off the counter and then polish it.
> CLEAR: Before you polish the *vase*, take *it* off the counter.
>   (anteced.) (pron.)

Exercises

1. Choose the correct pronoun.

   1. Will everyone please open (his, their) book?
   2. Neither of the men wore (his, their) hat.
   3. Each candidate has (his, their) own viewpoint.
   4. Many ordered (his, their) samples yesterday.
   5. Both of the boys carried (his, their) tents.

2. Revise the following sentences to make the meaning clear:

1. The bike struck the building and it was damaged.
2. As I poured juice from the pitcher into the cup, it dropped and broke.
3. The boys saw the policemen and they started to run.

Any and no

See "Double negative," page 445.

Are and our

Are and *our* should be pronounced as they are spelled. Do not confuse them. *Are* is the verb; *our* is the possessive pronoun.

Our neighbors *are* planning to move next month.

Exercises

1. Choose the correct word.

1. Vermilion is (are, our) favorite color.
2. Where (are, our) (are, our) books stored?

2. Use *our* and *are* in two sentences of your own.

At and to

Use *at* to show that "someone or something is in a certain place." Use *to* to show "movement toward someone or something."

WRONG:	My sister is ~~to~~ home.	He is ~~to~~ the beach.
RIGHT:	My sister is *at* home.	He stayed *at* the beach.
RIGHT:	He ran *to* the corral.	Send the message *to* me.

Do not use *at* or *to* needlessly with *where*. See why they are unnecessary in the sentences below:

WRONG:	Where did he send it ~~to~~?	Where did he put it ~~at~~?
RIGHT:	Where did he send it?	Where did he put it?

Exercises

1. Choose the correct word.

1. Mark went (at, to) the sports shop.
2. He made a stop (at, to) the corner.
3. Sam is (at, to) the movies.
4. Is she (at, to) the market?

2. Read aloud all the "right" sentences above several times.

Bad and badly   (See also pages 92–93.)

Bad is always an adjective. *Badly* is always an adverb.

It was a *bad* speech.   Malcolm sings *badly*.

The climate is *bad*.   She accepts praise *badly*.

Always say: "He feels *bad*," and "Kim looks *bad*." The verbs *feels* and *looks* in these sentences are linking verbs; therefore, the adjective *bad* modifies *He* and *Kim*.

Exercises

1. Read aloud the sentences below several times:

1. Bob looks *well*.   3. Bob looks *bad* (unwell).
2. She feels *well*.   4. She feels *bad* (unwell).

2. Choose *bad* or *badly* in place of each blank below:

1. One of the guests behaved __?__.
2. Does Jill look __?__ after her illness?
3. He felt __?__ after your critical remarks.

Be   (See also page 31.)

Learn the frequently used forms of the verb *be*, as they are used with pronoun subjects:

SINGULAR PRONOUNS	PRESENT	PAST	PLURAL PRONOUNS	PRESENT	PAST
I	am	was	we	are	were
you	are	were	you	are	were
he, she, it	is	was	they	are	were

Notice that the singular pronoun *you* must use the plural forms of the verb *be*: *are* and *were*.

Exercise

Choose the correct form of the verb *be* for each blank in the sentences below:

1. Last year you __?__ listless, but this year you __?__ energetic.
2. __?__ you on the TV panel last night?
3. We __?__ luckier in last month's game than they __?__.
4. Ken, now they __?__ only teasing you.
5. Last night he __?__ planning a big surprise.

Beside and besides   (See also page 95.)

Beside means "at the side of." *Besides* means "in addition to."

The dog lay *beside* the hearth.
Besides her, we invited three other girls.

Exercise

Choose the correct word.

1. The man stood (beside, besides) the lamppost.
2. We are buying cake and pie (beside, besides) cookies.
3. (Beside, Besides) the lake there rose a dense forest.

Between and among

See "*Among* and *between*," page 440.

Borrow and lend   (See also pages 255–56.)

Use *borrow* when you mean "to accept a loan." Use *lend* when you mean "to give a loan."

PRESENT	PAST	PAST PARTICIPLE
borrow	borrowed	(have, has, had) borrowed
lend	lent	(have, has, had) lent

My sister *lent* me money for the movies.
I *borrowed* it from her last night.

Exercise

Use the correct form of *borrow* or *lend* in place of each blank.

1. We would like to __?__ your camera for our trip.
2. I __?__ our lawnmower to Mr. Jones yesterday.
3. Jerry __?__ my microscope; he __?__ me his paints.

Break—broke—(have, has, had) broken

To *break* something means "to make it come apart." When you want to say that something has already come apart, you mean *it broke* or *has broken.* Never use *bust* or *busted.*

WRONG: He ~~busted~~ the piccolo.   His piccolo has ~~busted~~.
RIGHT: He *broke* the piccolo.   His piccolo *has broken.*

Exercise

Use *broke* and (have, has, or had) *broken* each in a sentence of your own.

Bring and take   (See also pages 255–56.)

Bring indicates action *toward* the person who is speaking. Note that its principal parts are *bring, brought, bringing,* (have, has, had) *brought.*

Use *take* when the action is *away from* the person speaking. Its principal parts are *take, took, taking,* (have, has, had) *taken.*

Please *bring* me some lemonade.	Please *take* this glass into the kitchen.
He *brought* me my horse.	I *took* your book to the library.

Exercise

Choose the correct word.

1. Sam (brings, takes) joy to his family.
2. (Bring, Take) this letter to the post office.
3. We will (bring, take) fruit baskets to the hospital patients.
4. I am (bringing, taking) my rock collection to the museum.

Can and may

See "*May* and *can*," page 450.

Comparison of adjectives and adverbs

See "Adjectives and adverbs," pages 437–38.

Could have and should have

The word *of* is a preposition and may not be used as an auxiliary verb. Use the auxiliary verb *have* with the verbs *could* and *should.* Often they are pronounced "could've" and "should've."

Could I *have* done as good a job?	He *should have* listened.
The aerialist *could*n't *have* fallen.	

Exercise

Read aloud the sentences above, emphasizing *have* in each.

Doesn't and don't   (See also pages 143–44.)

When the subject is a singular noun or one of the pronouns *he, she,* or *it,* use the verb *doesn't.* When the subject is plural, or *I* or *you,* use *don't.*

Vicky *doesn't* want cantaloupe.	He *doesn't* do his chores.
She *doesn't* want cantaloupe.	It *doesn't* matter.

When a compound subject is joined by *and,* use *don't.* When it is joined by *or* and each part is singular, use *doesn't.*

> *Don't* Mary and Lee sing?   *Doesn't* Joe or he care?

Exercise

Choose the correct word for each of the following sentences:

1. She (doesn't, don't) mind her own business.
2. The phonograph (doesn't, don't) work.
3. (Doesn't, Don't) the nut and the bolt hold the axle in place?
4. (Doesn't, Don't) Louise or Ted know the way?

Double negative   (See also page 99.)

The contraction *n't* and the words *not, no one, hardly, no, never, none, nothing, nobody, nowhere* are **negatives.** Do not use two of them in a sentence where one negative is sufficient.

> WRONG: Tom has*n't no* money.
> RIGHT: Tom has *no* money.   Tom has*n't* any money.

Exercise

Choose the correct word.

1. They don't have (any, no) excuse.
2. None of us has (ever, never) tasted avocados.
3. We will never find (any, no) way to escape.
4. Haven't you (nowhere, anywhere) to go?

Easy and easily

See "Adjectives and adverbs," pages 437–38.

Good and well   (See also pages 92–93.)

Good is an adjective; do not use *good* to tell how an action is performed. *Well* is mainly an adverb, but it can be used as an adjective when stating that someone is not ill.

> Can you play the banjo *well?*   (not *good*)
> My cousin is not very *well.*

Exercise

Choose the correct word.

1. The tempo was (good, well).
2. Are you (good, well) enough to leave the hospital?
3. Jo dances rather (good, well).
4. She always speaks (good, well).

445

Hear and here

The words *hear* and *here* differ in meaning and spelling.
Hear is a verb which means "to receive sounds."
Here is an adverb which means "this place."

Did you *hear* the overture?   *Here* they are.

Exercises

1. Write the correct word for each sentence.

   1. (Hear, Here) is the wallet I found.
   2. I can hardly (hear, here) you.
   3. When did you come (hear, here)?

2. Use *hear* and *here* each in a sentence of your own.

Himself, themselves, myself   (See also page 238.)

Pronounce the following words carefully, with special emphasis on
the *m*:   *himself, themselves.*

Everyone must work by *himself.*   They surprised *themselves.*

Do not use *myself* as part of a compound subject in a sentence
such as, "My brother and myself will go." You should say, "My
brother and I will go," or "I myself will go."

Exercises

1. Write two sentences using *himself* and two using *themselves.*
2. Write a sentence using *myself.*

In and into

In means "within or inside." *Into* shows movement from outside
to inside.

The letter is *in* the mailbox.
Earlier, Pete put the letter *into* the mailbox.

Exercise

Choose the correct word.

   1. Narcissus stared (in, into) the pool.
   2. The detectives dashed (in, into) the room.
   3. Pterodactyls lived (in, into) prehistoric times.
   4. We walked from one aisle (in, into) another.

Indefinite pronoun subjects

See "Agreement of subject and verb," pages 438–39. and "Antecedents of pronouns," page 440.

Irregular verbs   (See also pages 251–54.)

Many common verbs do not form their past tense in the regular way, that is, by adding *d* or *ed* to the present tense. They are called **irregular verbs.** Here is a list of the principal parts of the irregular verbs you have studied this year and in earlier grades.

PRESENT	PAST	PAST PARTICIPLE (have, has, had)	PRESENT	PAST	PAST PARTICIPLE (have, has, had)
arise	arose	arisen	know	knew	known
beat	beat	beaten	lay	laid	laid
become	became	become	leave	left	left
begin	began	begun	let	let	let
blow	blew	blown	lie	lay	lain
break	broke	broken	ride	rode	ridden
bring	brought	brought	ring	rang	rung
burst	burst	burst	run	ran	run
buy	bought	bought	say	said	said
catch	caught	caught	see	saw	seen
choose	chose	chosen	set	set	set
come	came	come	shake	shook	shaken
do	did	done	shrink	shrank	shrunk
draw	drew	drawn	sing	sang	sung
drink	drank	drunk	sink	sank	sunk
drive	drove	driven	sit	sat	sat
eat	ate	eaten	speak	spoke	spoken
fall	fell	fallen	spring	sprang	sprung
find	found	found	steal	stole	stolen
fly	flew	flown	strive	strove	striven
forget	forgot	forgotten	swear	swore	sworn
forgive	forgave	forgiven	swim	swam	swum
freeze	froze	frozen	swing	swung	swung
get	got	got	take	took	taken
give	gave	given	teach	taught	taught
go	went	gone	tear	tore	torn
grow	grew	grown	tell	told	told
hang	hung	hung	throw	threw	thrown
hide	hid	hidden	wear	wore	worn
hit	hit	hit	wring	wrung	wrung
hurt	hurt	hurt	write	wrote	written

Exercises

1. List the irregular verbs that cause you trouble, and learn them. Practice using them in sentences of your own.

2. Tell the correct form of the verb. *Do not use the present tense.*

(arise)   1. When the sun has __?__, we will leave.
(become)   2. It had suddenly __?__ cloudy.
(buy)   3. Has he __?__ new equipment?
(catch)   4. The referee __?__ the ball and blew the whistle.
(drive)   5. Last month I __?__ through the Ozarks.
(fall)   6. The egg whites have __?__ on the floor.
(find)   7. Shari __?__ a perfect solution to her problem.
(forget)   8. They __?__ to repair the water pipe.
(forgive) 9. This morning we were __?__ for our rudeness.
(get)   10. The cowboy __?__ his pistol from the bunkhouse.
(hang)   11. Oscar __?__ the picture on this wall.
(hide)   12. Have you ever __?__ an elephant?
(hit)   13. The locusts have __?__ the crops already.
(hurt)   14. Had he ever __?__ your feelings before?
(strive)   15. We __?__ to make them understand.
(swing)   16. Young boys __?__ on these birches.
(tear)   17. They have __?__ their clothes on the barbed wire.
(tell)   18. We haven't __?__ anyone of our fears.
(wear)   19. Has the ballerina __?__ her new costume?
(wring)   20. After our swim, we __?__ out our suits in the bath-
           house.

3. Use each of the following verbs in two sentences each. First, use the past tense form of the verb and, second, use the past participle form.

1. bring	4. ride	7. spring	10. speak	13. take
2. freeze	5. shrink	8. sink	11. swear	14. swim
3. shake	6. burst	9. steal	12. beat	15. teach

Its and it's   (See also pages 26–28.)

Its is a possessive pronoun. *It's* always means "it is."

The camel took *its* time to drink.   *It's* a fascinating century.

Exercise

Choose the correct word.

1. (It's, Its) not our responsibility.
2. The tiger made (it's, its) way through the jungle.
3. (It's, Its) easy to do.
4. Our parrot learned (it's, its) vocabulary quickly.

Lay and lie

Lay means "to put or place something."

Today they *lay* the cornerstone.   (present)
Yesterday they *laid* the cornerstone.   (past)
They *have laid* the cornerstone.   (past participle)

Lie means "to rest or recline."

Please *lie* down.   (present)
Yesterday I *lay* down for a nap.   (past)
The dog *has lain* there for hours.   (past participle)

Exercise

Choose the correct verb.

1. (Lie, Lay) the pencil on the pad.
2. Oil has (lain, laid) on the surface for days.
3. She (lay, laid) her purse on the desk.
4. Heavy dew (lay, laid) on the foliage.

Learn and teach

Learn means "to gain knowledge or skill."   *Teach* means "to give instruction."

He *learned* to use the aqualung.
The aquatic star *taught* a large group.

Exercise

Choose the correct verb.

1. That incident (learned, taught) my brother a lesson.
2. Dad (learned, taught) me to cast the anchor.
3. He is (learning, teaching) his horse to canter.
4. (Learn, Teach) me to use the trampoline.

Leave and let

Leave means "to go away (from)."   *Let* means "to allow or permit."

I *let* Bob *leave* the exhibition.   *Let's* go along with you.

Exercise

Choose the correct verb.

1. (Leave, Let) us climb Pike's Peak.
2. I will (leave, let) you do as you please.
3. My uncle will (leave, let) us use some of his tools.
4. (Leave, Let) me try once more.

Lend and borrow

See "*Borrow* and *lend*," page 443.

May and can   (See also page 256.)

Use *may* in referring to *permission* to do something. Use *can* in referring to the *ability* to do something.

> *May* I go with you?   *Can* you lift this weight?

Exercise

Choose the correct word.

1. (May, Can) I go to the dance?
2. You (may, can) go if you (may, can) finish your work early.
3. (May, Can) you memorize this poem?

Most

See "*Almost* and *most*," page 439.

Naming yourself last

When you speak of someone else and yourself, put the other person's name first:

> Beryl and I enjoy botany.   The aviary is for George and me.

Exercise

Write three sentences in which you talk about someone else and yourself.

Object pronouns

See "Subject and object pronouns," pages 452–53.

Ought   (See also page 254.)

Ought has only one form in all tenses. Never use *ought* with a helping verb. *Ought* is almost always followed by an infinitive: "*ought* to say," "*ought*n't to leave."

> WRONG: She ~~had~~ ought to sing.   RIGHT: She *ought* to sing.

Exercise

Use *ought*, *ought not*, and *oughtn't* twice each in sentences of your own.

Our and are

See "*Are* and *our*," page 441.

Pronouns

See "Agreement of subject and verb," pages 438–39; "Antecedents of pronouns," pages 440–41; "*Himself, themselves, myself,*" page 446; "Naming yourself last," page 450; "Subject and object pronouns," pages 452–53; "Unnecessary pronouns," page 455; "*We* or *us* with nouns," page 456; "*Who, which, that,*" page 456; "*Who, whom, whose,*" page 457; "*Your* and *you're,*" page 457.

Real and really

See "Adjectives and adverbs," pages 437–38.

Rise and raise   (See also pages 255–56.)

Use *rise* when you mean "to go up." Use *raise* when you mean "to lift or cause something to go up."

	rise	**raise**
PRESENT:	We *rise* early.	He *raises* the flag.
PAST:	I *rose* at dawn.	He *raised* my wages.
PAST PARTI- CIPLE:	The water *has risen* to the top.	He *has raised* the latch.

Exercise

Choose the correct word.

1. The bird (rose, raised) its wings.
2. The jet had (risen, raised) and disappeared in a flash.
3. The water in the streets has (risen, raised) to the curb.
4. Mr. Sel (rose, raised) his eyebrows in wonderment.

Say and said

Do not use *say* or *says* when you are talking about something that has happened in the past. *Say* or *says* is present tense. Use *said* to show the past tense.

WRONG: Yesterday I ~~says~~ that to her.
RIGHT: Yesterday I *said* that to her.

Exercise

Use each of the following in a sentence: *say, says, said, have said.*

Set and sit

Set means "to place or put in order." *Sit* means "to rest, as in a chair."

Set the steak on the platter.   He *sat* on the sofa.

Exercise

Choose the correct verb.

1. Don (sat, set) at his desk for hours.
2. Bill (sat, set) the cabinet on wheels.
3. Nancy and Lois were (sitting, setting) on the lawn.
4. Please (sit, set) your packages on the table.

Somewhere, anywhere, nowhere   (See also page 99.)

Do not add an *s* at the end of the words *somewhere, anywhere,* and *nowhere* in writing or pronouncing them.

Exercise

Practice writing these short sentences and saying them aloud:

1. He is somewhere in the house.
2. I will not go anywhere.
3. I will go nowhere.

Subject and object pronouns   (See also pages 234–36.)

Most personal pronouns have a subject form and an object form:

SUBJECT PRONOUNS: I, we, he, she, they
OBJECT PRONOUNS: me, us, him, her, them

Note: You and *it* can be either subject or object pronouns.

Use the subject pronoun as the subject of a sentence or as the subject complement after a linking verb:

Bud and *he* came to dinner.   (subject)
The visitors were my aunt and *I.*   (subject complement)

Use the object pronoun as the direct object (object of a verb), indirect object, or the object of a preposition:

Mrs. Tripps praised Carl and *me.*   (direct object)
The postman gave Paul and *him* the letter.   (indirect object)
Divide it between Sue and *her.*   (object of preposition)

Note: To make sure, use your ear. Use the pronoun alone in the sentence. For example, your ear would never let you say "Mrs. Tripps praised I." You would naturally say *me*.

Exercise

Choose the correct pronouns.

1. Our principal pointed to Frank and (he, him).
2. Between you and (I, me) there is a mutual admiration.
3. I'm sure the queen will be (she, her).
4. My neighbor and (I, me) are amateur astronomers.
5. The beekeeper gave Gordon and (I, me) a tour.

Subject and verb agreement

See "Agreement of subject and verb," pages 438–39.

Take and bring

See "*Bring* and *take*," page 444.

Teach and learn

See "*Learn* and *teach*," page 449.

Their, there, they're

Their is a possessive pronoun.

Their petunias are grown without soil.

There is an adverb telling where. It is also a way of starting a sentence.

Our friends are *there*. *There* are many parts to an atom.

They're is a contraction of "They are."

They're a new team of astronauts.

Exercise

Write these sentences, choosing the correct homonym *their*, *there*, or *they're* in place of each blank space:

1. I think that __?__ the musicians.
2. __?__ is no place to swim __?__.
3. __?__ planting __?__ vegetables over __?__.

Themselves

See "*Himself, themselves, myself*," page 446.

453

There with forms of is

There is never the subject of a sentence. It is often used as a way to get a sentence started. In such a sentence, the subject follows the verb:

> There are Grace and Paul on the corner.
> There is no backbone in an invertebrate.

The verb must agree with the subject: Grace and Paul *are*; backbone *is*.

With a singular subject you may say *there's*: "There's a raccoon here."

Exercise

Choose the correct verb.

1. There (was, were) two mechanics on duty.
2. There (is, are) strange sounds in the attic.
3. (There's, There are) the designs I like best.
4. There (is, are) Tod and his brother pitching hay.

This, that; these, those   (See also page 242.)

Do not use the words *here* and *there* after *this, that, these,* and *those.*

> WRONG: This h~~ere~~ bread is moldy.
> RIGHT: *This* bread is moldy.

> WRONG: That t~~here~~ is mine.
> RIGHT: *That* is mine.

Use *this* and *that* with *kind*; use *these* and *those* with *kinds.*

> WRONG: Those ~~kind~~ of birds are nearly extinct.
> RIGHT: *Those kinds* of birds are nearly extinct.

Exercise

Read all of the "right" sentences above aloud three times. Then choose the correct word from each pair in parentheses below:

1. (This, This here) comic strip is hilarious.
2. These (kind, kinds) of berries are poisonous.
3. (That, That there) leather is chamois.
4. Those (kind, kinds) of tools are useful.
5. (This, This here) is the one you want.

454

Those and them

Them is an object pronoun. It is *never* an adjective.

WRONG: The captain called ~~them~~ orders in a loud voice.
RIGHT: The captain called *those* orders in a loud voice.

Exercise

Read the following sentences aloud several times:

1. *Those* poems were written by Carl Sandburg.
2. We can't remember *those* names.

To, too, two

To means "in the direction of" or is used before a verb.
Too means "also" or "excessively."
Two means 2.

She meandered *to* the library.   He wants *to* finish it.
She likes strawberries, *too*.   (also)
The sculpture is *too* ornate.   (excessively)
There are *two* armadillos in that cage.

Exercise

Copy these sentences; write *to*, *too*, or *two* for each blank:

1. They like __?__ please me.
2. The __?__ of them wore the same costume __?__ the party, __?__.
3. Those __?__ boys want __?__ ask a question, __?__.

Unnecessary prepositions

See "*At* and *to*," page 441.

Unnecessary pronouns

Do not use an unnecessary pronoun after a noun subject.

WRONG: The mastodon ~~it~~ stood about nine feet tall.
RIGHT: The mastodon stood about nine feet tall.

Exercise

Choose the correct subject.

1. (Sara, Sara she) collects all kinds of buttons.
2. (Men, Men they) are usually stronger than women.
3. (That parrot, That parrot it) seems to talk endlessly.

455

We or us with nouns

Use expressions like "we boys" and "we girls" when they are subjects or when they are subject complements after a verb of being.

WRONG: ~~Us~~ boys are building a radio.
RIGHT: *We* boys are building a radio.

Use "us boys" and "us girls" when they are direct objects, indirect objects, or objects of a preposition:

WRONG: Wendy spoke to ~~we~~ girls.
RIGHT: Wendy spoke to *us* girls.

Exercise

Choose the correct word.

1. The scientist and (we, us) boys studied the spectrum.
2. Snakes do not appeal to (we, us) girls.
3. The Talltown Tankers defeated (we, us) boys.
4. The silly ones are (we, us) girls.
5. Give (we, us) boys the tools.

Well

See "*Good* and *well*," page 445.

Who, which, that   (See also pages 244–45.)

As a relative pronoun, *who* is used to refer to antecedents that name persons.

Which is used when the antecedent names a thing.

That is used when the antecedent names a person, animal, or thing.

The person *who* knows best is Mom.

The picnic table *which* I always use has collapsed.

Here is a dog *that* can protect your home.

Exercise

Choose *who, which,* or *that* for each blank.

1. This is a cat __?__ ignores mice.
2. You have heard the story __?__ I like best.
3. The friend __?__ writes most often lives in Alaska.
4. Here is a museum __?__ charges admission.

Who, whom, whose   (See also pages 242–43.)

Do not confuse *whose* with the contraction for "who is" or "who has"—*who's*. *Whose* is a possessive pronoun.

> *Whose* gym suit is this?
> The teacher wonders *who's* talking.   (*who is* talking)

Use *who* when it is the subject of a sentence or clause.

> *Who* heard the noise?
> This is the man *who* heard the noise.

Use *whom* when it is a direct object or object of a preposition in a sentence or clause.

> To *whom* did you pay attention?
> *Whom* did you see?
> This is the man *whom* we saw.

Exercise

Choose the correct word.

1. (Who's, Whose) turn is it at bat?
2. (Who, Whom) did you choose?
3. (Who's, Whose) taking insect repellent on the hike?
4. For (who, whom) did you cheer?
5. I'd like to know (who's, whose) the guilty party.
6. She is the first person (who, whom) we invited.

Your and you're

Your is a possessive pronoun. *You're* is a contraction of "you are."

> *Your* big zinnia has won first prize.   *You're* a good farmer.

Exercise

Choose the correct word.

1. Have you selected (your, you're) topic?
2. (Your, You're) losing weight!
3. When is (your, you're) recital being held?
4. (Your, You're) too funny for words.

MAKING SURE

Use these exercises after Chapter One.

I. Proper Nouns and Common Nouns

1. Review pages 17–19.

2. Under the headings *Common Nouns* and *Proper Nouns* on your paper, list the nouns in the sentences below:

1. One of the early American writers, Washington Irving, was born in New York in 1783.
2. In his boyhood, he spent much of his time hiking in the Catskill Mountains, which were mentioned on many occasions in his writing.
3. *The Sketch Book*, one of his better known works, is enjoyed by many people.
4. Ichabod Crane, a schoolmaster in the book, is chased by a headless horseman and is never seen again.

II. Nouns

1. Review pages 20–24.

2. Determine whether or not each of the words listed below can be used as a noun. Copy only the words that can be used as a noun.

1. cud	5. excellent	9. exhaustion
2. harmless	6. belief	10. resign
3. recite	7. precept	11. winner
4. luggage	8. harmonize	12. precaution

III. Personal Pronouns

1. Review pages 26–28.

2. List all the personal pronouns in the passage below:

When I was about seven, my parents decided that they would buy me my first bicycle. It was shiny and blue and all mine. My brother, however, not having a bicycle of his own, decided that he liked it too. Very soon it was broken—but then he got his bicycle!

460

3. Copy each sentence below, choosing the correct word from each pair in parentheses.

1. (It's, Its) a mistake.
2. I don't think (it's, its) really that way at all.
3. There should be water in (it's, its) cage.
4. (It's, Its) lid is very small.
5. Whether (it's, its) green or blue is not important.

IV. Pronouns and Their Antecedents

1. Review page 28.

2. Change the following sentences to make sure that the antecedents of the pronouns are not confusing.

1. Fred accidentally hit Paul with his new golf club.
2. Sidney loves to take his dog Rip on walks, but he always insists on going past the butcher shop.
3. Mrs. Jones taught Mary all she knows.

V. Action Verbs and Linking Verbs

1. Review pages 30–32.

2. Copy the sentences below. Underline the complete verb; label it *action* or *linking*.

1. Which man is the one?
2. The wind whistled through the trees.
3. The man became the President.
4. Pedro is going to the beach.
5. The boy climbed over the fence.

VI. Words That Can Be Nouns or Verbs

1. Review pages 36–37.

2. Number your paper from 1 to 5. Write *noun* or *verb* for each italicized word below.

1. Did you *water* the flowers?
2. I drank a glass of *water* after supper.
3. The *guide* insisted that we follow him.
4. *Guide* me to the water fountain.
5. It took a strong *force* to push the door open.

461

Use these exercises after Chapter Two.

I. Making Announcements

1. Review pages 47–49.
2. On your paper next to the appropriate numeral, tell what important information is missing from each announcement below:

1. Dirty tennis shoes and lots of feet will be needed by all on Saturday, May 12, when our businessmen will again sponsor the United Nations' project "Walking for Hunger." Ten cents a mile will be given to the project for any walker who first comes to Central School to be signed in. The walk will end at Dr. Sander's farm where the walkers will be served refreshments.

2. Noble and virtuous thoughts should follow everyone on Friday, September 21, as they go to vote for Student Council officers. VOTE!

II. Giving Explanations

1. Review page 57.
2. Read the statements below. Each is a beginning for an explanation. Copy the numerals on your paper and write *good* next to the good beginnings. Rewrite the poor beginnings.

1. Have you ever watched lawyers on T.V.? They rush out to find the missing witness. Or, at the last minute, they bring in some secret bit of evidence that wins the case. Well, actually lawyers are much different in real life.

2. There are many different kinds of glue. I shall tell you about them.

3. Interior decorating is a fascinating field. There are many aspects to the profession.

III. Making and Acknowledging Introductions

1. Review page 57.

2. On your paper, list the numerals 1 to 4. Read each group of statements given on page 463. If the statements are suitable for making or acknowledging introductions, write *Yes* next to the appropriate numeral. If they are not suitable, write *No* and explain *why*.

1. Mother, I'd like you to meet my new friend Edna. Edna, this is my mother.
2. Mr. Simon, shake hands with Nathan. Nathan, this is Mr. Simon.
3. Estelle, I'd like you to meet William Baxter. William, this is Estelle Lucas.
4. Hi, Reverend Dyson.

IV. Group Discussions

1. Review pages 58–62.

2. On your paper, list the numerals 1 and 2. Choose the letter which corresponds to the correct completion of the sentences below:

1. The most informal discussion is the (a) round-table discussion (b) panel discussion (c) parliamentary discussion.
2. *Robert's Rules of Order* might help you learn about the (a) round-table discussion (b) panel discussion (c) parliamentary discussion.

V. Articulation and Voice Control

1. Review pages 66–67.

2. Copy the following words on your paper. Draw a line between the syllables and underline the syllable that receives the stress.

Example: ar/tic/u/late

1. example   2. election   3. gallant

Use these exercises after Chapter Three.

I. Adjectives

1. Review pages 75–81.
2. On your paper, list the adjectives in the following sentences. Include articles, possessive pronouns, and noun adjectives. Next to each one, write in parentheses the word it modifies.

1. The Ceglios have an unusual flower garden behind their garage.
2. The garden is quite bountiful and contains numerous varieties of prize-winning flowers.
3. My favorite one is a yellow English rose which has delicate petals although it is apparently very hearty.
4. Mrs. Ceglio, who is very kind, said that she would give me a small shoot of her yellow rosebush.

II. Proper Adjectives

1. Review page 81.
2. On your paper, write these sentences correctly.

1. Van Gogh was a famous dutch painter.
2. He was influenced by japanese artists.
3. He was so impressed with one french artist that he painted several pictures in his style.
4. His pictures are appreciated all over the world and can be seen in many european art galleries.

III. Adverbs

1. Review pages 82–84.
2. On your paper, list the adverbs in these sentences. In parentheses, write the word each one modifies.

1. Morris slipped quietly down the quite narrow steps.
2. Having reached the kitchen safely, he carefully prepared everything.
3. He chuckled happily as he reached his mother's door with an extremely rare birthday breakfast.

IV. Comparisons of Adjectives and Adverbs

1. Review pages 85–87.

2. On your paper, list the numerals from 1 to 6. Write the correct form of the adjective or adverb in parentheses.

1. He plays the violin (well) than his friend.
2. The car is (fast) than the horse.
3. Paul studies (intensely) than Francine.
4. Angela gets the (good) grades in the class because she studies (hard).
5. Because of the ice on the road, Bernard had to drive (slowly).
6. Jean was (hesitant) than her sister, who responds to things immediately.

V. Using Adjectives and Adverbs

1. Review page 87.

2. On your paper, list numerals from 1 to 4. Write the correct word from each pair in parentheses.

1. That was a (real, really) exciting game.
2. He swims very (good, well).
3. Bert is the (least, littlest) qualified candidate.
4. The meat tasted (badly, bad).

VI. Prepositional Phrases as Modifiers

1. Review pages 94–98.

2. List each prepositional phrase on your paper. Then write *adjective phrase* or *adverb phrase* next to it. In parentheses, write the word it modifies.

1. The book on the oaken desk is by Salinger.
2. Under the bed rests Felix our cat.
3. The man got wet because he had left his umbrella at home.

Use these exercises after Chapter Four.

I. Narrative, Descriptive, and Explanatory Paragraphs

1. Read pages 109–10.

2. Tell what kind of paragraph would best develop each topic or idea listed below—*narrative, descriptive,* or *explanatory.* Write your answer next to the sentence numeral on your paper.

1. My messy room
2. The most embarrassing minute of my life
3. How to hit a golf ball

II. Analyzing Paragraphs

1. Review pages 111–13 and 118–121.

2. Copy from the following two paragraphs both the *topic sentence* and the sentence that does not belong.

1. Today's farmers in the Midwest are quite sophisticated. Many have gone to college to learn about plants and soil. Farmers must be investors too, because they must buy very complex equipment, and they hope to be able to pay for it eventually with their profits. Many people buy their houses in much the same way by getting a mortgage from the bank. They are also careful organizers. They will contact people who have land and need someone to farm it.

2. Textbooks like this one have gone through many steps before being sold. First, an author writes a manuscript which an editor must look through and adjust to the company's style. Then the manuscript is typed, marked, and retyped until it is in the form which goes to the printer. The secretaries get tired of typing things over and over again. The book is then printed, and the cover is put on. After a final check for correctness, the book is sent out to the salesmen and customers.

Use these exercises after Chapter Five.

I. Simple Subject and Verb

1. Review page 130.
2. Pick out only the simple subject and the verb from each of these sentences and write them on your paper. Underline the simple subject once and the verb twice.

    1. The bee's hive under the roof was causing much alarm.
    2. There is the first robin of the year!
    3. The cat played on the couch.

II. Transitive and Intransitive Verbs

1. Review page 133.
2. Number your paper from 1 to 5. After each number write the verb in that sentence and after it write *transitive* or *intransitive* in parentheses.

    1. Toni ate the apple.
    2. Ritchie reached into the closet for his coat.
    3. He has been sleeping since nine o'clock last night.
    4. The teacher instructed the class in multiplication and division.
    5. The man wandered aimlessly through the desert for almost ten years.

III. Active and Passive Verbs

1. Review pages 133–34.
2. Number your paper from 1 to 5. After each number write the verb in that sentence and after it write *active* or *passive* in parentheses.

    1. The dish was broken by me.
    2. My mother cried during *Gone with the Wind*.
    3. The small child was sitting by the window.
    4. The puzzle had been assembled without his help.
    5. Alice threw the ball to the first baseman.

IV. Four Types of Sentences

1. Review pages 135–38.
2. Copy the following sentences on your paper and insert the correct end punctuation. In parentheses, write *declarative, interrogative, imperative,* or *exclamatory.* Underline each simple subject once and each verb twice.

   1. Tornadoes often occur in the spring
   2. What causes them
   3. Please make a report on the tornado

V. Compound Subjects and Compound Verbs

1. Review pages 140–41.
2. Copy the compound subjects and compound verbs from the sentences below. Underline each coordinating conjunction. Write *S* over each subject and *V* over each verb.

   1. Cotton and wool are both used in making sweaters
      but are obtained through very different methods.
   2. They both must be cleaned and processed.

VI. Making Subject and Verb Agree

1. Review pages 143–45.
2. Choose the correct verb from each pair in parentheses. Write it on your paper next to the sentence numeral.

   1. Chess (is, are) a very challenging game.
   2. A box of apples (was, were) on the table.
   3. Neither Elissa nor Vicki (enter, enters) the house with wet feet.

VII. Fragment and Run-On Sentences

1. Review pages 146–48.
2. On your paper, correct the paragraph below.
   Jody sat in her room and cut out a large red heart. she liked Valentine's Day. Using only a scissors, some red paper, and glue. She had created a beautiful valentine for her best friend Natalia.

Use these exercises after Chapter Six.

I. Learning New Words from Context

1. Review pages 159–60.
2. Determine the meaning of each italicized word below by examining its context. Write the meaning next to the appropriate numeral on your paper.

1. He was so *penurious* that he would not give to any charity.
2. The baby threw the plastic toy around the room repeatedly, but it remained *infrangible*.
3. The sailor placed a *quid* on the counter to pay for his room.
4. He lifted the glass to his lips and began to *imbibe* the clear liquid.

II. Prefixes, Roots, and Suffixes

1. Review pages 163–66.
2. Copy the following words and circle any prefixes or suffixes. Underline roots. Write the meaning of the word after it in parentheses.

1. postwar
2. trumpeter
3. foreseer
4. contestant
5. autograph
6. misuse

III. Choosing the Right Word.

1. Review pages 170–75.
2. Number your paper from 1 to 6. Next to each numeral, write the letter of the word (*a*, *b*, or *c*) which best expresses in one word what all the italicized words say. You may use the dictionary.

1. Rena wrote a *humorous verse of five lines, of which the first, second, and fifth have three accents and rhyme with each other.* (a) sonnet, (b) limerick, (c) hendecasyllable

2. At first the doctor thought he had *a generally fatal disease of the blood which shows a marked increase in the number of white blood cells.* (a) leukemia, (b) bursitis, (c) multiple sclerosis
3. The zoo received *a fierce hoglike animal from Central or South America.* (a) anemone, (b) scincoid, (c) peccary
4. The biologist was studying *a genus of microorganisms typically parasitic in the bodies of certain ticks and lice, but transmissible to other animals and to man.* (a) flabellum, (b) rickettsia, (c) ridotto
5. The boat finally set out on a voyage only to suddenly hit *a rocky obstruction lying beneath the surface of a river or other stream.* (a) riffle, (b) estivation, (c) carillon
6. Clara had a scarf made from *a strong, horizontally corded silk fabric.* (a) dasheen, (b) filament, (c) grosgrain

3. After each italicized word below are five other words. *Two* of the five are synonyms for the italicized word. Copy the italicized word and then write its two synonyms next to it.

1. *frivolous:* (a) silly, (b) peculiar, (c) serious, (d) lacking seriousness, (e) careful
2. *vanquish:* (a) misbehave, (b) conquer, (c) become ill, (d) disappear, (e) defeat
3. *omnipotent:* (a) not capable of holding water, (b) unpopular, (c) red in color, (d) having unlimited power, (e) having overwhelming influence
4. *succumb:* (a) give up, (b) eat rapidly, (c) yield, (d) become emotional, (e) make peace
5. *rejuvenate:* (a) to grow worse, (b) to make young, (c) to intensify, (d) to renew (e) to increase

Use these exercises after Chapter Seven.

I. Sentence Patterns 1 through 5

1. Review pages 181–89 and the summary on page 208.

2. On your paper, copy the sentences below. In the left-hand margin, write the sentence pattern number. Over the *subject* write S, over the *verb* write V, over the *direct object* write *DO*, over the *indirect object* write *IO*, and over the subject complement write *SC*.

1. Anita is an adventurous girl.
2. She loves traveling.
3. She went to Spain last year.
4. Spain was very exciting with its cafes and bull fights.
5. When she returned, she brought her mother a necklace.
6. Next year she will travel again.
7. Perhaps France will be the spot that she will visit.
8. Maybe she will go to Hawaii.
9. Maria, her friend, visited Egypt.
10. Her main problem is the expense.

II. Compound Sentences

1. Review pages 191–92.

2. Copy these compound sentences. Underline the simple subject once and the verb twice in each clause.

1. Carol is fat, but Edna is quite thin.
2. The lawyer cautioned his client, and then he told him the facts.
3. I love Thanksgiving dinner, but it always causes me to gain weight.
4. Aryah won a blue ribbon, and his brother won a red one.
5. Komondors are attractive, but I prefer rough-coated collies.

III. Punctuating Compound Sentences

1. Review pages 194–96.
2. There are simple sentences and compound sentences listed below. On your paper, copy only the compound sentences and punctuate them correctly.

    1. The pioneers raised crops and domesticated animals.
    2. Rusty could not reach the top branch of the tree and he started back down.
    3. The lady told the salesman no but he sold her some soap anyway.
    4. The men of the forests and the natives of the village tried to put out the fire.

IV. Simple, Compound, and Complex Sentences

1. Review pages 191–205.
2. List the numerals from 1 to 4 on your paper. Identify each sentence as *simple, compound,* or *complex.*

    1. The sun was shining, and there was no breeze at all.
    2. Hoppy Rabbit was sitting under a tree and sipping lemonade.
    3. After he had sat for a while, Blinkley Bear came down the road.
    4. For a while they both just stood there because they were too hot to talk.

V. Adjective, Adverb, and Noun Clauses

1. Review pages 198–206.
2. Find and list the clauses in the sentences. Next to each one, write *adjective clause, adverb clause,* or *noun clause.*

    1. Blinkley Bear said that he wanted to go swimming, but Hoppy Rabbit did not want to go.
    2. Although he hadn't bothered anyone recently, Bothersome Wolf had been known to irritate those who were at the swimming hole.

Use these exercises after Chapter Eight.

I. Writing a Story

1. Review pages 213–19.
2. Number your paper 1 to 3. Read the following statements and write *true* or *false* next to the corresponding numbers.

    1. You can write best about things you know little about.
    2. You can make an exciting story by writing about something that happened to you and changing small details to make things more interesting.
    3. The plan of the story is called the plot.

3. Number your paper from 1 to 5. Next to the number write the one word answer to the following questions.

    1. Which part of the story should set the stage?
    2. Which part of the story tells how the story comes out?
    3. Which part of the story is the high point?
    4. Which part of the story arouses interest?
    5. Which part presents a series of events and actions?

II. Using Dialogue

1. Review pages 219–21.
2. Copy the following conversation. Insert capital letters and punctuation in the proper places.

    I'd love to go shopping this weekend said Kenzi
    I'd love to go too, but I have two papers to write replied Georgia
    Well, what about next Monday night Kenzi asked
    That's a bad night too Georgia sighed. I have to go to choir practice
    But Crayton's has a big sale; and if you don't go at least by Monday night, you'll miss it Kenzi complained
    Somebody please tell that to my English teacher and my choir director grumbled Georgia

III. Planning a Report

1. Review pages 222–29.
2. Number your paper from 1 to 8. Read the statements below and answer them *true* or *false* after the appropriate number.

1. When writing a report, the purpose is to be as witty as possible.
2. You should be very careful not to choose too broad a topic.
3. If you have a current topic, you should probably check the *Readers' Guide* to find recent magazine articles.
4. One source is sufficient for a short report.
5. An outline is to be used by some people in preparing a report, but it is not necessary for everyone.
6. Exposition is a type of writing which clearly and interestingly presents information, but it is seldom used in a report.
7. Your initial outline should change in form to adapt itself to the new information you have found.
8. A topic like "A Look at All the States in the United States" would make an interesting topic for a report.

IV. Making an Outline

1. Review pages 223–28.
2. Arrange the list of headings below in correct outline order and form. First decide on the main headings. Then group the subheadings under them.

how to study

quiet place
proper techniques
memorizing
straight-backed chair
proper conditions
organizing your time
adequate writing surface
proper lighting
notetaking skills

Use these exercises after Chapter Nine.

I. Using Personal Pronouns

1. Review pages 234–36.
2. Next to the sentence numerals on your paper, write the correct forms of the pronouns.

1. (We, Us) were not at home when they called.
2. They tried to reach (we, us) for several hours.
3. It was (I, me) who answered the phone.
4. With (he, him) was his mother.
5. We decided to go with Alex and (she, her).
6. Beside my father and (I, me) sat Mrs. Epstein.

II. Pronoun Agreement

1. Review pages 236–37.
2. Next to each sentence numeral on your paper, write the pronoun that agrees with the antecedent.

1. My mother left _____ gloves on the chair in the conference room.
2. We wanted to take _____ umbrellas, but we forgot them.
3. The sailors painted _____ new ship.
4. The bird spilled the seeds all over _____ cage.
5. The man brought _____ chair right in front of the door.

III. Pronoun and Verb Agreement

1. Review pages 239–40.
2. For each sentence below, choose the verb that agrees with the subject and write it on your paper next to the sentence numeral:

1. Some of the students in our class (has, have) been ill.
2. Each (was, were) absent about three days.
3. Another of the students (was, were) gone today.
4. Everybody (misses, miss) Walter because he is our group leader.
5. Everything that we planned for our group reports (is, are) being changed because of the illnesses.

IV. Choosing the Correct Pronoun

1. Review pages 242–45.

2. Choose the correct word from those in parentheses. Write your answers on your paper next to the appropriate numerals.

1. (Who, Whom) is responsible for the damage?
2. (That there, That) was not a very nice thing to do.
3. (Whose, Who's) sweater was left on the table?
4. With (who, whom) is she going to the dance?
5. The car (which, what) was left in the parking lot received a ticket.
6. (This here, This) typewriter was broken four times this week.
7. (Whose, Who's) going to fix it this time?
8. The man (who, which) fixed it last time is not here.

V. Restrictive and Nonrestrictive Clauses

1. Review pages 245–47.

2. On your paper, copy and punctuate correctly the sentences below that need commas.

1. Peggy, who frequently forgets what she is told tried to tell us what happened to her friend Ann.
2. The story that she revealed was quite confusing.
3. Ann's mother, whom you have met, arrived at the school rehearsal last night at 8:00 P.M.
4. Ann who was nowhere in sight was at her own home.

VI. Principal Parts of the Verb

1. Review pages 247–54.

2. On your paper, copy the italicized verbs below. Next to each one, write the tense of the verb.

1. My dog Blinky *learns* very easily.
2. I *had found* him on the kitchen table eating pot roast.
3. I really *yelled* at him for doing that.
4. I *shall* never again *find* him on the table.
5. I *have taught* him many other things too, but I *shall have eaten* many pot roasts before I forget that lesson.

476

Use these exercises after Chapter Ten.

I. Parts of a Friendly Letter

1. Review page 266.

2. Number your paper from 1 to 5. Next to the numeral put the word that belongs in each blank in the following sentences.

1. "Sincerely" is an example of a _____.
2. A signed name is called the _____.
3. The main part of a letter is the _____.
4. The address and the date is the _____.
5. The name of the person to whom you are sending the letter appears in the _____.

3. Number your paper from 1 to 3. Below are parts of letters. If they are suitable for a friendly letter, write *yes* next to the numeral. If they are not suitable, write *no.*

1. How are you? I'm fine. I was sick last week, but I'm better now.
2. Guess what! Clermont Jr. High just got a trampoline. It is really fantastic. I learned to do flips on it, but I was cautioned to be very careful.
3. I really hate to write letters. I never know what to say. Nothing ever happens to me, and everything around our town is really boring.

II. Capitalizing and Punctuating Friendly Letters

1. Review page 269.

2. On your paper, list the numerals from 1 to 5. Rewrite these parts of friendly letters correctly:

1. october 24 19 __

2. dear fred

3. love

4. 330 third street dekalb illinois 60115

5. sincerely yours

III. More About Friendly Letters

1. Review the lesson on pages 268–69.
2. On your paper, list the numerals from 1 to 3. Read each of the statements below. Write *T* if the statement is true and *F* if the statement is false.

1. Some people feel that handwriting seems more personal than typewriting in a friendly letter.
2. Even though you know a person well, always sign your full name.
3. Letters may be written in indented style or block style.

IV. Social Notes

1. Review pages 272–80.
2. On your paper, answer these questions.

1. What information should an invitation contain?
2. What does R.S.V.P. mean at the bottom of an invitation?

3. Number your paper from 1 to 3. Read the statements below. Next to the appropriate numeral write *T* if the statement is true and *F* if the statement is false.

1. You should only write a thank you note for something you received that you really like.
2. If you stay overnight at a friend's house, you should write his mother a bread-and-butter letter.
3. Sending a note of apology is often the best way to handle a situation in which you have done something inconsiderate.

V. Business Letters

1. Review pages 280–84.
2. Number your paper from 1 to 3. Read the statements below. Next to the appropriate numeral write *T* if the statement is true and *F* if the statement is false.

1. It is preferred that business letters be handwritten.
2. A colon follows the salutation in a business letter.
3. In a business letter, indented form can be used.

478

Use these exercises after Chapter Eleven.

I. Participial Phrases

1. Review pages 288–90.
2. Copy each participial phrase below and, next to it, write the noun or pronoun it modifies in parentheses.

1. The apples hanging on the tree were big and juicy.
2. Having noticed them, Madeline eagerly climbed the tree.
3. The branch, swaying back and forth, held its prizes away from Madeline's reach.
4. From a lower branch, Madeline reached her apples by pulling on the limb hanging above her.
5. Finally, Madeline, carrying two large apples, dropped to the ground with a heavy thud.
6. Sitting on the ground in a dazed condition, Madeline decided that next time she was hungry for fruit, she would snack on grapes.
7. Being very low to the ground, grapes seemed much better for her health.

II. Dangling Participles

1. Review page 291.
2. Rewrite these sentences, correcting the dangling participles.

1. Having run down the stairs, only one door was found unlocked by Tom.
2. Watching a horror movie, monsters are outside every window, in Tom's imagination.
3. Wagging his tail, Tom is comforted by Snuggles, his terrier.

479

III. ing-Words

1. Review pages 288–94.

2. On your paper, list all the -ing words in these sentences. Next to each, write *participle, gerund,* or *verb,* depending on how it is used in the sentence.

1. Shiela saw a bug crawling across the floor.
2. The little girl with the blue coat had been crying all afternoon.
3. Rena's favorite winter pastime is skiing.
4. The vine growing on the tree is poison ivy.
5. In the summer, mowing the lawn is what I like to do least.
6. Jeannette is going to Hawaii next week.
7. Having finished his breakfast, he felt much better.

IV. Infinitives

1. Review pages 295–96.

2. Copy each infinitive below and next to it, write how it is used: *subject, direct object, subject complement, adjective,* or *adverb.*

1. Don't forget to go shopping this afternoon.
2. To have Evelyn for dinner was the plan for tonight.
3. Evelyn must rush to arrive here by eight o'clock.
4. The object of the dinner was to present a gift.
5. The package to be opened was for Evelyn.
6. The package contained two very special tickets to be used on Friday night.
7. To see an opera had always been a secret wish for Evelyn.
8. She was very excited to get them.

Use these exercises after Chapter Twelve.

I. Using Reference Books

1. Review pages 310–12.
2. On your paper, copy the subjects listed below. After each, write the name of a reference book where you would look to find information on that subject: *encyclopedia, biographical dictionary, atlas, almanac,* or *Readers' Guide.*

    1. Who hit the most home runs in 1955?

    2. You need information on the activities of the governor of Wisconsin.

    3. Tropical birds

    4. Where was golf originally played?

    5. The name of the fattest person in the world

    6. Charles Chaplin

    7. You would like to find a magazine article by Elwood Todd.

II. Taking Notes, Studying Effectively, and Memorizing

1. Review pages 303–06.
2. On your paper, list the numerals from 1 to 5. Read each of the statements below. Next to the appropriate numeral, write *T* if the statement is true and *F* if the statement is false.

    1. Knowing why you are learning something is often necessary for motivation.

    2. You can always tell a stupid student by all the questions he asks.

    3. Always start to study with the subject you like the most.

    4. Never take a break while studying, it wastes time and only makes you more tired.

    5. The first step in memorizing something is to read the selection through carefully and be very sure you understand it.

3. Number your paper from 1 to 4. After the appropriate number, write the answer that goes in the blank.

1. The _____ of a book is a statement of the nature or purpose of the book.
2. The _____ is a dictionary of difficult words; it is usually found in the back of a text.
3. _____ is an alphabetical listing of the contents of the book. It usually tells the page numbers to which one can refer.
4. The _____ contains the date of publication.

III. Using the Library

1. Review pages 306–12.

2. List the numerals from 1 to 4 on your paper. For each blank space below, write a word (or words) that completes the statement correctly.

1. Most library books have three types of cards in the card catalogue. They are _____, _____, and _____.
2. The number on the book that helps you to find it on the shelf is called the _____.
3. The system that most libraries use to organize their books is called the _____.
4. _____ books are marked with an *F* and arranged alphabetically by the last names of the authors.

IV. Taking Tests

1. Review pages 317–18.

2. On your paper, list the numerals from 1 to 3. Read each of the statements below. Next to the appropriate numeral, write *T* if the statement is true and *F* if the statement is false.

1. The best time to review the materials on which you are to be tested is early the night before the test.
2. The first step in preparing for the test is to review the material to be tested.
3. Answer the easiest questions on the test first.

Use these exercises after Chapter Thirteen.

I. Alphabetical Order

1. Review pages 321–22.
2. In each list below, write the words in alphabetical order:

1.	2.	3.
pentose	combustion	bestow
people	comb	bestir
peon	coma	bestead
peony	colza	bestiary
pepper	combination	bestrew
pepo	combine	bet

3. From the words that follow, copy those that will be found on a dictionary page with the guide words *luminous* and *lurch:*

luminary	lunar	lummox
lump	luncheon	lure

II. Meanings of Words

1. Review pages 321–23.
2. On your paper, write the numerals from 1 to 4. Next to the appropriate numeral, write the letter of the definition that best fits the use of the word *bowl* in each sentence:

    a. an amphitheater or stadium
    b. to move smoothly and swiftly
    c. something shaped like a bowl
    d. to roll a ball or rounded object

1. The bowl of his pipe cracked when it hit the cement walk.
2. The bus will bowl down the highway once we get out of the city limits.
3. The bowl was completely filled and the excitement was intense; this was the big game of the year.
4. Emerson was the next person to bowl, and he could not even knock one pin down.

III. Pronunciation

1. Review pages 324–27.

2. Write the numerals from 1 to 5 on your paper. Look at the word below and its phonetic spelling, and next to the appropriate numeral, write the correct answers to the questions that follow:

circumnavigate (sûr′kəm·nav′ə·gāt)

1. How many syllables are there?
2. Which syllable has the primary accent?
3. Which syllable has the secondary accent?
4. Which syllable has a long vowel?
5. Is there a syllable with a schwa? Which?

IV. Using the Dictionary

1. Review pages 321–36.

2. Number your paper from 1 to 8. Next to the appropriate number put the word that belongs in the blank in each statement below.

1. The _____ words in a dictionary are the words at the top of the page.

2. _____ words have meanings that are often colorful but are not accepted as good English by educated people.

3. _____ words are used in daily speech but not in formal speech or writing.

4. _____ marks are used to indicate the pronunciation of a word.

5. _____ marks are used to show which syllables are stressed.

6. A _____ is a part of a word that can be pronounced with a single sounding of the voice.

7. A _____ is a dictionary of synonyms.

8. A _____ is used to mark short vowels.

9. A _____ is used to mark long vowels.

Use these exercises after Chapter Fourteen.

I. Looking at Poetry

1. Review pages 339–49.
2. Number your paper from 1 to 6. Next to the numeral, put the word that belongs in each blank in the following sentences.

1. The accented and unaccented syllables of a poem create a beat which is called _____.

2. Verse that is tied to a regular pattern of rhyme and meter is called _____.

3. Verse with no regular pattern is called _____.

4. One foot of poetry containing first an unstressed beat and second a stressed beat is called _____.

5. A humorous bound verse with five lines is a _____.

6. Repetition of the same sound at the beginning of several words is _____.

II. Words That Rhyme

1. Review pages 342–44.
2. Number your paper from 1 to 10. After the number, write the letter and the word from column 2 that *rhymes* with the word in column 1. Remember that words that rhyme need not be spelled the same way.

1.	2.
1. late	a. lest
2. choir	b. toad
3. moat	c. should
4. busy	d. higher
5. guessed	e. dizzy
6. good	f. rough
7. wear	g. wrote
8. drew	h. wait
9. puff	i. air
10. mode	j. through

III. Onomatopoeia

1. Review pages 348–49.
2. Number your paper from 1 to 5. Next to the numeral, write the word from each statement that illustrates *onomatopoeia*.

    1. Ellen's voice squeaked as she tried to hit a very high note.
    2. The snake hissed as Arthur passed its resting place.
    3. The brick dropped to the ground with a thud.
    4. The buzz of the insects kept him awake throughout the long night.
    5. Ada splashed into the cold water and promptly decided to run for her towel.

3. In the following sentences, try to be creative in your choice of words that show onomatopoeia. Number your paper from 1 to 5 and, after the numeral, write the word you think should go in the blank.

    1. The wild animal _____.
    2. Mamie dropped the milk pitcher and it _____ on the floor.
    3. The stream _____ past the silent bank.
    4. The boy _____ in horror.
    5. All we could hear that night was the faint _____ of the wind.

IV. Alliteration

1. Review the lesson on page 349.
2. Number your paper from 1 to 3. After the appropriate number, list the words in each sentence that illustrate alliteration.

    1. Pam gave Patty a pink pocket pen.
    2. Our fat fellow Benny fixes fish in February.
    3. Watch the wonderful Wanda Durkin wander through the wilderness.

486

Use these exercises after Chapter Fifteen.

I. Types of Reading

1. Review pages 359–66.

2. Decide which of the four types of reading you should choose for each of the assignments listed below: *skimming, reading for mastery, word-for-word reading, reading for pleasure.* Write the type of reading next to the appropriate numeral on your paper.

1. You are reading a poem to find the examples of alliteration and onomatopoeia.
2. You have an article on Tom Edison and must find the year that he invented the electric light.
3. You are reading a play over Christmas vacation because your friend recommended it.
4. You are in a doctor's office and you are reading an article on football.
5. You are baking a cake, and you have a good recipe.
6. Your teacher has given you an article entitled "A Closer Look at Our Four-Footed Friend," and she wants you to write a paragraph answering the question "What is the author's attitude toward dogs?"
7. You have been given a book, and you must tell what it is generally about in class tomorrow.
8. For a history assignment, you must look through a booklet about countries in Europe. Your teacher would like you to write a paragraph comparing the exports of those countries.
9. You have received an article on English authors, and you are asked to list five books by Charles Dickens.
10. Your friend has given you directions on how to get to his house.
11. You are alone in the house at night, and you are reading Mary Wollstonecraft Shelley's *Frankenstein.*
12. You are looking in your dictionary for the word "fey."
13. You must read the editorial column in today's paper to find out if the editor is for the new state tax.

II. Similes and Metaphors

1. Review pages 368–72.
2. Next to the appropriate numerals on your paper, write *simile* or *metaphor* to describe each comparison below:

> 1. Her anger was a violent tornado twisting everything in its path.
> 2. The tears streamed endlessly down her cheeks like waves slapping on the tired sand.
> 3. Her dress was yellow as a fresh banana.
> 4. She was the world to him.
> 5. Beyond the door of success lies happiness.

3. For each statement above, write what two things are being compared.
4. Complete each of the following statements with words that will make a true and vivid comparison:

> 1. Having been caught in the midst of a thunderstorm, the girls came in looking like _____.
> 2. Carlos was so tired from helping his father, that he felt like _____.
> 3. Gwen had just decorated her room with purple, olive, and red paint. When her mother saw it, she said it looked like _____.
> 4. Alex, while putting a math problem on the board, scratched the chalk across the board making a sound like _____.

III. The Tone of Writing

1. Review pages 373–75.
2. Read the following paragraph carefully. Then decide what you think is the author's tone. Write either a, b, or c on your paper after the numeral. (a) angry, (b) sympathetic, (c) thrilling

> Jeff's hand was shaking. Why him — why then, after all those years. Hurriedly, he ran into the study and sifted through all his father's papers and books. Nothing — nothing. Suddenly, he felt the answer coming to him.

488

INDEX

INDEX

Numerals in heavy black type indicate the teaching pages.

Directions, giving, **51, 53, 72**
Discussion:
  group, **58–61, 73**
  panel, **61,** 62, 73
  parliamentary, **61,** 73
  round-table, **59,** 73
Double negatives, 99, 102, 104, **445**

Encyclopedias, using, **310,** 312, 319
English language:
  basic, **8–9**
  changes in, **10–11,** 12–13
  French and, **2,** 4–6, 8, 163
  from Indo-European family of languages, **2, 3**
  German and, **2, 4, 5, 8**
  Greek and, **163, 164**
  Latin and, **2, 5, 6, 8, 163–65**
  levels of usage in the, **168,** 323, 337
  new words in, **11**
  Old, **4**
  origin of, **2, 4**
  use in the world today, **14**
  vocabulary of, **8–9**
Exclamation points, **137, 138,** 151, 153, 168, **407, 428**
  in dialogue, **220,** 231, 232
Exclamatory sentences, **137,** 138, 151, 153, **407**
  diagraming, **381,** 403–04
Explanations, giving, **50–51,** 53, 72
Explanatory paragraph (exposition), **109–10,** 111, 125–26, **213, 222, 229, 410**
Expository paragraph. *See* Explanatory paragraph

Figurative language, **368–69,** 370, 372, 378, 379
Fragments, sentence, **146, 147,** 149, 152, 154, **406, 409**
Friendly letters. *See* Letters, friendly

Gerunds, **294,** 295, 298, 300
  diagraming, **400,** 401, 404
Going Ahead:
  choral reading, 351
  common and proper nouns, 19
  diagraming, 402
  figurative language, 370
  making announcements, 49
  meter in poetry, 347
  paragraphs, 111, 115, 117

prepositional phrases, **98**
reading lists, 358, 366
sentence patterns, **29, 38, 80, 88, 132, 139,** 192, **197, 206, 240–41**
symbols for parts of speech, **80, 88,** 197, 240–41
synonyms (the thesaurus), **333**
topic development, 117
vocabulary, 159, **168,** 175
word form, **38**
word origins, 6, 9, 14
writing stories, 221
Guides:
  for building good paragraphs, **123, 410**
  for capitalizing and punctuating friendly letters, **269**
  for choral reading of poetry, **350**
  for conversation, **55**
  for efficient reading, **376**
  for making announcements, **49**
  for making speeches, **69**
  for memorization, **316**
  for punctuating dialogue, **220**
  for reading directions and problems, **364**
  for reading for mastery, **362**
  for remembering words, **162**
  for studying effectively, **304**
  for taking notes, **314**
  for taking a test, **318**
  for writing business letters, **284**
  for writing friendly letters, **271**

Helping verbs. *See* Auxiliary verbs
Homework. *See* Studying
Homonyms, **434–36**
Hyphens, **11,** 168, **330,** 332, **429**

Imperative sentences, **136,** 138, 151, 153, **407**
  diagraming, **381–82,** 403, 404
Indefinite pronouns, **239–40,** 258, 261, **415, 439–40**
Independent clauses, **191,** 192, **198,** 208
Indirect objects:
  compound, 235, 236, **390, 452, 453**
  defined, **188, 408**
  diagraming, **388, 390,** 404
  nouns as, **187–88,** 208, 210, **408, 412**

using words to convey feelings, **167**, 177, 179

word order, **29**, 38, **76, 82, 135–37**

words as symbols, **1**

See also English language; Sentences, patterns of; Words

Linking verbs, **31**, 32, 42, 44, 45, **80**, 90, **185–86, 408, 414**
  symbol for, 197, 240–41

Listening:
  in conversation, **53**, 55, 56
  to improve vocabulary, **162**
  to improve your voice and speech, **63–65**, 66, 67
  in an interview, **314**
  to poetry, **339–49**
  to sentences, **127**, 128, **146–48**
  to speeches, 69

Main clauses, **198–99**

Mastery Tests, 41–42, 70–71, 101–02, 125, 151–52, 176–77, 208–09, 231, 258–60, 285–86, 298, 319, 335–36, 353, 378, 403

Memorization:
  from Abraham Lincoln's "Second Inaugural Address," 187
  aids for, **316**, 317
  from The Declaration of Independence, 375
  in making announcements, **48**
  of poetry:
    "Abou Ben Adhem" by Leigh Hunt, 317
    from "The Arsenal at Springfield" by Henry Wadsworth Longfellow, 117
    from "Endymion" by John Keats, 56
    "I Never Saw a Moor" by Emily Dickinson, 36
    from "Music" by Ralph Waldo Emerson, 344
    from *Othello* by William Shakespeare, 228
    from "Pippa Passes" by Robert Browning, 328
    from "Prayer" by Louis Untermeyer, 166
    "Preparedness" by Edwin Markham, 145
    from "Stanzas on Freedom" by James Russell Lowell, 87

"Stopping by Woods on a Snowy Evening" by Robert Frost, 292
    from "The Three Best Things" by Henry van Dyke, 280
    "To See a World" by William Blake, 254

Metaphors, **368–69**, 378, 379

Models:
  bread-and-butter letter, **274**
  envelope, **271**
  final outline, **226**
  friendly letter, **266**
  letter of adjustment, **283**
  letter of invitation, **277**
  letter of request, **281**
  note of acceptance, **279**
  note of apology, **276**
  note of regret, **278**
  notes (for outlines and reports), **314**
  order letter, **282**
  preliminary outline, **223**
  thank-you note, **273**
  vocabulary notebook page, **162**

Modifiers:
  adjectives as, **76**, 77, 81, **88**, 101, 103
  adverbs as, **82–84**, 101, 104
  clauses as, **201–04**, 209, 211
  defined, **75**
  infinitives as, **295–96**, 298, 300
  nouns as, **78**
  participles and participial phrases as, **288–90**, 298, 299–300
  prepositional phrases as, **94–95**, 97, 98, 102, 105
  sentence patterns and, **88, 132, 182, 183, 185**

Narrative paragraphs, **109–10**, 111, 125, 126, **213–18, 410**

Nonrestrictive clauses, **245**, 247, 259, 262, **426**, 428

Notes:
  social, *see* Social notes
  taking, **313–14**, 316, 319, 320

Noun clauses, **205**, 209, 211
  diagraming, **397–98**, 403, 404

Nouns:
  abstract, **412, 413**
  appositive, **399, 413, 426**
  characteristics of, **20–22**, 23, 41, 43, **412**
  collective, **144**, 145, **412, 439**

495

Nouns (*cont.*)

common and proper, **17, 19**, 41,
43, **412**

concrete, **412, 413**

defined, **17, 19, 412**

determiners of, **22**, 23, **36**, 37, 80,
412

of direct address, **393, 394, 413,
425**

as direct objects, **183**, 208, 210,
408, 412

as indirect objects, **187–88**, 208,
210, **408, 412**

as objects of prepositions, **94–95,
205, 412**

possessive of, **21**, 43, 168, **412,
424**

predicate, **185–86, 408, 413**

proper, **17, 19**, 81, 103, **420–21**

signals of, *see* determiners of

singular and plural, **20, 21, 144,**
145, **412**

as subject complements, **185–86,
408, 413**

as subjects, **30, 130, 412–13**

symbol for, **80**, 197, **240–41**

used as adjectives, **78**, 101, 103,
383

verbals used as, **294–96**, 298,
300

Object of a preposition, **94–95, 205,
234–35**, 236, 238, **294, 412,
418, 452–53**

compound, **235**, 236, **390, 418**

Old English. *See* English language,
Old

Outlining, **222–24, 225–28**, 231, 233

Paragraphs, **107–23, 125–26, 213,
220, 221, 229, 230, 232,
410**

defined, **108, 410**

descriptive, **109–10**, 111, **125–26,
410**

developing the topic, **113–16,**
117, **410**

in dialogue, **220, 221**, 232

explanatory (exposition), **109–10,**
111, **125–26, 213, 229, 410**

indentation of, **107**

narrative, **109–10**, 111, 125, 126,
213–18, 410

staying on the topic, **118**, 120–
21, **125–26**

topic sentence in, **111**, 112, **113,
125–26, 410**

transitional words and phrases in,
121–22, 123

types of details used in, **113–16,**
117

Parlimentary discussion. *See* Discussion, parliamentary

Participial phrases, **289–90**, 298,
299

defined, **290**

punctuation, **290**, 299, **426, 428**

Participles, **288**, 289, 295, **298–**
300

dangling, **291**, 292, 298, 299

defined, **288, 289**

diagraming, **399–400**, 403, 404

past, **251–52**, 253, 260

Passive voice, **134**, 151, 153, **250,
413**

Periods:

after abbreviations, **269**, 270, **429,**
430

after declarative sentences, **135,**
138, 151, 153, **429**, 430

after imperative sentences, **136,**
138, 151, 153, **429**, 430

in an outline, **225–26, 429**, 430

Personal pronouns, **25–28**, 41, 44,
234–35, 236, **238**, 258, 261,
415, 452–53

Phrases:

adjective, **95, 97, 98**, 102

adverb, **97, 98**, 102

participial, **289–90**, 298, 299,
426, 428

prepositional, **94–95, 97–98**, 102,
105, **143, 385, 418**

transitional, **121–22**, 123

verb, **35, 288**, 295

Poetry:

alliteration in, **349**, 353, 355

appreciating the sound of, **347–**
49

bound verse, **346**, 355

choral reading of, **350**, 351

feet in, **345**, 353, 354, 355

the form of, **341**, 355

free verse, **346**, 353, 355

limericks, **346**, 347

memorization of, *see* Memorization, of poetry

meter in, **345**, 347, 353, 355

onomatopoeia in, **348**, 349, 353,
354, 355

Pronouns (*cont.*)
  as subject complements, **185–86,**
    234–35, 236, **408, 452–53**
  subject forms of, **234–35, 415,**
    452–53
  as substitutes for nouns, 27, 44
  symbol for, **80,** 197, 240–41
  unnecessary, **455**
Pronunciation, **65–66,** 67, 73, **324–**
    27, 337
  accent marks, **325–26,** 336, 337
  defined, **66**
  diacritical marks, **324,** 325–26
  phonetic spelling, **324–26,** 336,
    337
  spelling and, **66**
  syllabication, **327,** 336, 337
Proofreading class papers, **230**
Proper adjectives, **81,** 103, **420**
Proper nouns. *See* Nouns, common
    and proper
Prose:
  difference from poetry, **339,** 340–
    41
  See also Articles (literary); Books;
    Stories
Punctuation, rules for, **424–31**
  Check Test, 168
  See also Apostrophes; Colons;
    Commas; Exclamation
    points; Hyphens; Periods;
    Question marks; Quotation
    marks; Underlining (Italics)

Question marks, **136,** 138, 151, 153,
    430
  in dialogue, **220,** 231, 232
Quotation marks, 168, **430–31**
  in dialogue, **220–21,** 231, 232
Quotations:
  direct, **220,** 221
  indirect, **220,** 221

Readers' Guide to Periodical Litera-
    ture, using, **312,** 319, 320
Reading:
  choral, *see* Poetry, choral reading
    of
  figurative language, **368–69,** 370,
    372, 378, 379
  guides for efficient, **376**
  literal language, **370,** 372
  poetry, *see* Poetry, reading
  a record of, **365**
  selecting books, **357–58**

speeding up, **376**
the tone of writing, **373,** 374–75,
    378, 379
types of, **359–66,** 378, 379
  for book reports, **366**
  for mastery, **361–62,** 363, 378,
    379
  for pleasure, **365,** 378, 379
  skimming, **359,** 360–61, 378,
    379
  word-for-word, **364,** 378, 379
Reference books, using, **310–12,**
    319, 320
Reflexive pronouns. *See* Compound
    personal pronouns
Relative pronouns, **202–03,** 204,
    244, 245, 259, 262, **416,**
    456
Reports:
  exposition in, **222**
  the final outline, **225,** 228
  getting the facts for, **224–25**
  making a bibliography for, **229**
  planning, **222–25,** 228, 232
  preliminary outline for, **222–24,**
    231, 233
  proofreading and revising, **230**
  selecting a topic, **222,** 231, 232
  writing, **222–30,** 231–33
Restrictive clauses, **245,** 247, 259,
    262
Review and Practice Exercises, 43–
    45, 72–73, 103–05, 126,
    153–55, 178–79, 210–11,
    232–33, 261–63, 287, 299–
    300, 320, 337, 354–55, 379,
    404
Rhymes, **342,** 344, 353, 354
Rhythm, **345–46,** 347, 353
Roots of words, **164,** 165, 176, 178
Run-on sentences, **146,** 147, 152,
    154, **409**

Schwa, the, **325,** 337
Sentences:
  complex, **198–205,** 206, 208, 209,
    211
  compound, **191–96,** 197, 209,
    211, **392,** 393, **418**
    punctuating, **194–95,** 209, 210–
    11, **426**
  declarative, **135,** 136–38, **139,**
    151, 153, **381,** 403–04, **407**
  defined, **406**
  diagrams, *see* Diagrams, sentence

exclamatory, **137, 138, 151, 153, 381,** 403–04, **407**

fragments, 146, **147,** 149, 152, 154, **406, 409**

imperative, **136,** 138, **151, 153, 381–82,** 403–04, **407**

interrogative, **136,** 137–38, **139,** 151, 153, **381–82,** 403–04, **407**

inverted order in, **135,** 136, **382,** 403

patterns of, **29, 38, 80, 88, 132, 139,** 181–83, 184, **185–88,** 189, 190, 191, 192, **197, 206,** 208, 210, **240–41**

revising, **141,** 142, 196, 204, **230**

run-on, 146, 147, 149, 152, 154, **409**

simple, **181–90, 194–95,** 209, 210–11

the sound of, **127,** 128, **146–47,** 154–55

topic, 111, 112, 113, 125, 126, **410**

transitional words and phrases in, **121–22,** 123

two main parts of, **128–29,** 146, 153, **406**

word order in, **29, 38, 76, 82,** 135–37

Similes, **368–69,** 378, 379

Simple predicates, **130,** 151, 153, **406**

Simple sentences, **181–90, 194–95,** 209, 210–11

Simple subjects, **130,** 151, 153, **406**

Slang words, **168, 323,** 336, 337

Social notes, **272–78,** 279, 286–87. *See also* Letters

Speaking:
  in conversation, **53–54,** 55–56
  in giving explanations and directions, **50–51,** 53, 72
  in group discussions, **58–59, 61,** 73
  making announcements, **47, 49,** 72
  making introductions, **57,** 72–73

Specific words, **173,** 174

Speech:
  articulation in, **65–66,** 67, 73
  chart of organs, 65
  colloquial (informal), **12, 323,** 336, 337
  making a prepared, **68–69**

pronunciation in, **65–66,** 67, 73
voice characteristics, **63,** 64

Spelling:
  adding a prefix to a root word, **165, 433**
  compound personal pronouns, **238**
  dictionary as an aid to, **328, 330,** 332, **432**
  homonyms, **434–36**
  method of learning, **432**
  one hundred demons, **434–36**
  phonetic, **324–26,** 336, 337
  plurals of nouns, **20, 330,** 332, **433–34**
  pronunciation and, **66**
  rules for, **432–33**

Story(ies):
  choosing the subject, **213–14**
  climax of, **215, 231,** 232
  closing of, **215, 231,** 232
  development of, **215, 231,** 232
  excerpts from
    "The Apprentice" by Dorothy Canfield, 374
    "Earthquake" by Damon Runyon, 375
    "The Interlopers" by Saki (H. H. Munro), 375
    "The Marvel of Hearing" by Peter Farb, 372
    "The Redheaded League" by Sir Arthur Conan Doyle, 375
    "The Reef" by Samuel Scoville, Jr., 372
    "Talk and Talkers" by Robert Louis Stevenson, 47
    "Titania of the Airways" by Archibald Rutledge, 110, **114**
    See also Articles (literary); Books
  opening of, **215, 231,** 232
  planning a, **213–14**
  plot of, **215**
  selection and development in, **217,** 218–19
  telling, 214
  using dialogue in, **219–20,** 232
  writing, **213–21,** 231

Studying, **303–18,** 319
  dictionary as an aid to, **328, 330,** 332, **432**
  guides for, **304**
  library use, **306–09,** 310

D   5
E   6
F   7
G   8
H   9
I   0
J   1
    2

502